EUROPEAN
MARKET
AND THE
IRISH
ECONOMY

THE SINGLE EUROPEAN MARKET AND THE IRISH ECONOMY

Edited by

ANTHONY FOLEY
AND MICHAEL MULREANY

Institute of Public Administration

First published 1990 by the
Institute of Public Administration
57–61 Lansdowne Road
Dublin, Ireland.
Tel: (01) 686233
Fax: (01) 698644

ISBN 1 872002 05 6 hbk
ISBN 1 872002 10 2 pbk

Cover and title pages designed by Gerard Butler Design

Typeset in 11/12 Bembo by Computertype Ltd., Dublin
Printed by Betaprint Ltd., Dublin

To my parents, and Irene
and Brian, Niall, Conor and Eoin

To my parents, and Thérèse

A.F.

M.M.

Contents

List of Figures

List of Tables

List of Contributors

Bernadette Andreosso is Lecturer in Economics, University of Limerick

Peter Bacon is Director of the Fixed Interest Department, Goodbody Stockbrokers

Mary Bateman is Lecturer in Economics, Waterford Regional College and was formerly Economist with Goodbody Stockbrokers

John Blackwell is Principal Administrator, Social Affairs and Industrial Relations Department at the Organisation for Economic Cooperation and Development, Paris

Sean Cromien is Secretary, Department of Finance

Michael Cuddy is Professor of Economics, University College, Galway

Joe Durkan is Lecturer in Economics, University College, Dublin

Tom Ferris is Head of Planning, Department of Tourism and Transport

Anthony Foley is Lecturer in Economics, Dublin Business School, Dublin City University

Richard Harrison is Senior Lecturer in Economics, Ulster Business School, University of Ulster, Jordanstown

George Hennessy is an economist with the Construction Industry Federation

David Jacobson is Senior Lecturer in Economics, Dublin Business School, Dublin City University

Michael Keane is Lecturer in Food Economics, University College, Cork

Michael J. Keane is Lecturer in Economics, University College, Galway

Owen Keegan is an economist with Davy Kelleher McCarthy, Economic Consultants

Denis Lucey is Professor of Food Economics, University College, Cork and deputy chairman of the Higher Education Authority

Fergal Lynch is a civil servant in the Department of Health

Michael Mulreany is Lecturer in Economics, Institute of Public Administration

Ewing Paterson is Director of Standards, Eolas, the Irish Science and Technology Agency

Geert Sanders is Scientific Collaborator, West Flanders Economic Study Office, Bruges

Jerry Sexton is Research Professor, Economic and Social Research Institute

Rodney Thom is Lecturer in Economics, University College, Dublin

Norbert Vanhove is professor at the College of Europe in Bruges and general manager of the Regional Development Authority of West Flanders

Foreword

CHARLES J. HAUGHEY, TD
An Taoiseach
President of the European Council

Recently we have seen a dramatic change in the political map of Europe which creates prospects for a new era of peaceful prosperity and stability over the whole continent once transitional problems are resolved. The drive towards economic, monetary and political union within the European Community has been intensified, in part motivated by consciousness of its responsibilities to the wider Europe at this historic turning-point. But the more dramatic developments should not distract attention from the most fundamental change which will have a major impact on the whole European economy.

Completion of the Single European Market will be an achievement that is revolutionary in scale and effect. The Single Market will affect the lives of the people of Europe for the foreseeable future.

What we are talking about when we speak of the Single Market is a new economic area, where the freedom of movement of persons, goods, services and capital is complemented by other factors on which cohesion is built: a reduction in regional disparities, implementation of the Social Charter, strong and effective cooperation on the fiscal front for greater stability and increased growth, joint research and development endeavours, and the establishment of a more balanced relationship with the environment.

A Community of 340 million people with no barriers or restrictions to trade and with a combined purchasing power of over £3,000 billion will be the largest economic entity in the world, and is likely to be the most dynamic. As part of it, Ireland can be a successful and profitable location for industry and services, selling into the wider European market.

The Government's National Development Plan, which provides for an investment programme of £10 billion over five years, with Community support from the structural funds amounting to some £3 billion, represents the investment strategy designed to help maximise the benefit that Ireland can achieve from the Single Market.

The special European Council of April 1990, held in Dublin under the Irish Presidency, confirmed that not only will all the key decisions on the Single Market be taken by the end of 1992, but that the arrangements for economic and monetary union will be in place, together with agreement on the shape of political union.

Progress to date in completing the Single Market is on schedule. Over 60 per cent of the 279 Directives necessary to give effect to the Single Market have now been agreed. Inevitably, agreement remains to be reached on the most difficult questions, such as harmonisation of VAT and custom duties, but the political commitment to the achievement of the Single Market will ensure that consensus is reached even on the more intractable issues. Progress during the Irish Presidency has included the adoption of several important Directives, such as public procurement in key utilities, and environmental information. By the end of the Presidency, we will also have made progress on agreeing the European Company Statute, on the second phase of air transport liberalisation, and in many other sectors.

The Government's Information and Awareness Campaign on the Single Market, EUROPEN is aimed to bring home the implications of the Market to the general public and to Irish business and manufacturing industry. A key element of the EUROPEN campaign has been to provide targeted information on the opportunities and threats posed by completion of the Single Market so that senior managers can take informed decisions on how their firms will respond to the challenge of 1992.

I greatly welcome the appearance of this detailed comprehensive and opportune study on *The Single European Market and the Irish Economy* edited by Anthony Foley and Michael Mulreany with articles by many distinguished contributors. This textbook survey will be an important and essential companion to other authoritative publications on the subject, such as the EUROPEN Sectoral reports and the NESC study, *Ireland in the European Community*.

There are two themes, in particular, in this study which go to the heart of the challenge facing us. The first is the necessity to translate potential into performance, and the second, closely related, concern is the need for us to remain competitive as an economy. There is a particular challenge facing indigenous industry to increase exports. In realising these objectives, it is absolutely vital that Government and the social partners continue to work together in following a coherent and integrated strategy in order to secure the optimal benefit from the opportunities presented by the Single Market.

Anthony Foley and Michael Mulreany have produced a very detailed and timely study, which identifies the principal issues involved.

June 1990

Preface

The Single Market through the reduction of physical, technical and fiscal barriers to trade will have wide-ranging effects on the Irish economy. This book has been written to provide a comprehensive assessment of these effects.

We strongly believe that the European Community and the Single Market are so important for Irish economic development that they should be thoroughly treated in business and economic courses. In our roles as teachers we have found that this objective was difficult to achieve because published material was both limited and fragmented.

This book draws together the research of leading economists and experts on the impact of the Single Market. We intend the book to be of use to undergraduate students in economics and in business studies, to students of professional bodies and to students of public policy who take courses on the Single Market, international trade, the Irish economy and industrial development. It will also be of value to post-graduate students taking courses in international economics, international business and international marketing. The book will be of interest to the many institutions and organisations concerned with the impact of the Single Market on the Irish economy and it should also be accessible to the general reader.

The book is organised to reflect our objectives and our views of what are the important issues. Chapter one introduces the concept of the Single European Market and reviews Ireland's socio-economic position and performance within the European Community. Chapter two provides an overview of the Single Market and places particular emphasis on its impact on less developed regions in the European Community. Chapter three presents a review of the theories of international trade, economic integration and outward-looking policies, all of which assist the understanding of how the Single Market operates and how it affects Ireland. The performance of the EC economy affects Ireland; chapter four assesses the effects of the Single Market on the EC economy.

The Single Market with its increased harmonisation of policies may affect the independence of Irish economic management; this issue is dealt with in Chapter five. Chapter six reviews the experience of monetary integration in the EC and assesses proposals for further integration. The exchequer effects of indirect tax harmonisation are examined in chapter seven. Chapter eight deals with one of the key aspects of the Single Market — the removal of technical barriers. Because of Ireland's location and its dependence on exports, transport is an important issue. The Single Market proposals on transport and their implications for Ireland are discussed in chapter nine.

Chapters 10 to 14 deal with the effects of the Single Market on the production of goods and services. Because of the nature and development experience of the Irish economy, we have distinguished between the Single Market effects on the indigenous and direct foreign investment components of Irish industry in chapters 10 and 14 respectively. The Single Market will facilitate labour mobility and will have other effects on the labour market. Chapters 15 and 16 deal with the effects of the Single Market and of the Social Charter on the labour market in Ireland. Chapters 17 and 18 deal with Ireland and Northern Ireland as peripheral regions within the European Community. Overall conclusions and synthesis are presented in chapter 19.

Two appendices dealing with Single Market documentary sources and with the development of the EC are provided to ease the teaching and learning processes.

Such are the wide-ranging effects of the Single Market on the Irish economy that but for space limitations other issues such as effects on tourism could be included. However, given these limitations we believe that this book is the most comprehensive treatment available on the effects of the Single Market on the Irish economy.

The contents of the book for the most part reflect developments up to early 1990. Interested readers may wish to update their knowledge for instance by using some of the regularly appearing sources referred to in appendix A.

Acknowledgements

We are grateful to the contributors for agreeing to write, for meeting deadlines and for tolerating our editorial intrusions. We are also grateful to the EC Commission and to the Europen Bureau for permission to use materials in chapter 13 and appendix B. Thanks are due to Martin Mansergh and Pat Nolan of the Department of the Taoiseach for their assistance. We are indebted to the IPAs Publications Committee, to editorial support staff, to academic referees and to numerous colleagues for their comments and advice. The assistance of Mary Mason and Anne Marie Winick at DCU is gratefully acknowledged. At the IPA, Pat Hall was an ever present source of support and encouragement and Jim O'Donnell provided assured guidance. Patricia Ryan transcended her normal duties to provide constant assistance with cheerful efficiency; to her we are deeply grateful. The IPA Library provided invaluable help. The support and forbearance of our families was an essential input, the importance of which we cannot overstate. A special acknowledgement is due the IPA's Publications Division without whose assistance the book would not have appeared. Finally we are grateful to an Taoiseach and President of the European Council Charles Haughey for agreeing to write the foreword.

As editors and contributors we have tried to match the high quality of the above mentioned assistance. Where we have failed so to do, we alone are culpable.

List of Abbreviations

BSI	British Standards Institute
CEN	European Committee for Standardization
Cenelec	European Committee for Electrotechnical Standardization
CII	Confederation of Irish Industry
Comett	Community programme in education and training for technology
CTT	Córas Tráchtála (Irish Export Board)
EAGGF	European Agricultural Guidance and Guarantee Fund
Ecu	European currency unit
EFTA	European Free Trade Association
EMS	European Monetary System
Erasmus	European Community action scheme for the mobility of university students
ERDF	European Regional Development Fund
ESF	European Social Fund
ETSI	European Telecommunications Standards Institute
ETCI	Electrotechnical Council of Ireland
GATT	General Agreement on Tariffs and Trade
G7	Group of seven — the word's most industrialised nation
IDA	Industrial Development Authority
ILO	International Labour Office
MCA	Monetary compensatory amount
OECD	Organization for Economic Cooperation and Development
Sprint	Strategic programme for innovation and technology transfer
YES	'Youth for Europe' programme (youth exchange scheme)

1

Introduction

MICHAEL MULREANY and ANTHONY FOLEY

This chapter is in three parts. The first introduces the concept of the Single European Market. It explains the need for the new impetus that arose in the 1980s to complete the Single Market and outlines the proposals for economic integration set down by the European Commission. The Single Market has significant implications for the Irish economy and an assessment of these forms the substance of this book. In the course of outlining the content of the Single Market programme, we shall introduce subsequent chapters of the book that deal with the detailed implications for the Irish economy. A useful background to a consideration of the implications of the Single Market is to examine the position and performance of the Irish economy since it joined the European Community. A brief examination of these issues is presented in the second part of this chapter.

The final part of the chapter presents an outline of the book as a whole.

The Single European Market

The concept of a Single European Market is not new. It was present in the Treaty of Rome in 1958 and indeed was seen as the foundation for the economic and political unification of the member states.

The ambition behind the Single Market is to remove all trade barriers, but the EC has only partly achieved this. Although tariffs and quantitative restrictions to trade were mostly eliminated for the original members in 1968, non-tariff barriers to trade in goods and services remained.

Non-tariff barriers

Non-tariff barriers discriminate in favour of a domestic economy's goods and services. These barriers are many and varied, but they take three genera¹ forms: physical, technical and fiscal.

Physical barriers are caused by delays at frontiers and are the most visible of the barriers. Technical barriers are the result of national product standards and technical regulations. These regulations and standards come about because of advances in technology or because of concern for health safety and consumer protection. They may exceed 100,000 in number (Emerson, 1988, p. 39). Variations in standards impose costs on businesses that serve different member states; industrialists regard them as one of the most important types of trade barrier (Nerb, 1988, pp. 5–11, p. 64). Finally, fiscal distortions to trade result from variations in the rates of indirect tax imposed in different member states. The distortions to trade occur when countries with lower rates of indirect taxes attract trade from neighbouring countries with higher rates. A fuller treatment of physical, technical and fiscal barriers is given in Chapter 2.

The above-mentioned non-tariff barriers can be as effective (and in some cases more effective) as tariffs in protecting domestic markets from foreign competition. Tariff barriers may be countered by reducing the price of goods, but a non-tariff barrier (with which foreign suppliers cannot comply) affords absolute protection.

The effects of trade barriers

The division into physical, technical and fiscal barriers is one form of classification used in examining the fragmentation of markets. Another perspective on trade barriers can be obtained by means of an alternative classification into tariffs, quantitative restrictions, cost-increasing barriers, market-entry restrictions, and market-distorting subsidies and practices.

Tariffs are present in the EC in the form of monetary compensatory amounts (i.e. border taxes and subsidies on agricultural products that offset currency differences between member states and thereby provide common prices across the Community). Spain and Portugal are permitted to apply tariffs during their transition period to full EC membership. Both forms of tariff will be eliminated as monetary compensatory amounts are phased out, by agreement of the member states, and as Spain and Portugal complete the transition period.

Tariff reductions were the major focus of developments in the EC up to 1968. The cost of tariffs falls mostly on consumers, either in the form of increased costs of imports or as extra profits earned by protected producers in the domestic economy. On the other hand, tariffs have the budgetary advantage of raising revenue. Nevertheless, they have been almost eliminated from intra-Community trade. The effects of tariffs and their elimination are examined in more detail in Chapter 3.

Quantitative restrictions (quotas) are also largely absent from intra-Community trade, but some persist. Production quotas exist for agricultural products and have similar effects as trade quotas. In services there are quotas in road and air transport in the form of licensing and regulatory systems. Furthermore, there persist some national quotas on imports from non-EC countries. These national quotas apply particularly to imports of cars and textiles and are enforced at intra-Community borders. Unlike tariffs, quantitative restrictions do not raise revenue. However, by limiting competition, they impose costs on consumers through higher prices.

Cost-increasing barriers arise out of either border delays or out of the costs of complying with technical regulations. Once again, costs are imposed on consumers through higher prices as competition is reduced. These barriers also impose costs on suppliers from other member states. Furthermore, there is no tariff revenue to counter the adverse effects on consumers.

Market-entry restrictions take several forms: restrictions in public procurement; restrictions in the right of establishment for some professions and services; restrictions that prevent or limit direct trading across borders of some services, such as insurance and electricity; and restrictions on entry to some regulated markets, such as civil aviation. Market-entry restrictions are sometimes hard to distinguish from cost-increasing barriers. The essential difference is that market-entry restrictions prevent competition, whereas cost-increasing barriers reduce competition but still admit it. Despite these differences, the effects of market-entry restrictions are similar to those of quantitative restrictions and of cost-increasing barriers, namely that the higher costs are borne by consumers through higher prices and that no tariff revenue is raised.

Market-distorting subsidies and practices exist in the form of state aid to industry or of abuse of market power by enterprises that exercise a monopoly. These barriers deter suppliers from other member states and allow inefficiency on domestic markets. Once again the consumer pays, but in this case not in higher prices; instead, through higher taxes.

The existence of the various types of trade barriers clearly limits competition in the EC and facilitates inefficiency. It follows that the removal of these barriers should create a growing market that would direct labour, capital and materials more efficiently to sectors of greatest economic advantage and promote competitive activity and innovation. This, in a nutshell, is the objective of the Single Market. The above-mentioned non-tariff barriers had fragmented the EC economy, had obstructed economic growth, and, as we shall see in Chapter 4, had contributed to the Community's performance in competitiveness and economic growth lagging behind that of the US and Japan.

The White Paper and the Single European Act

Concerns about the intra-Community non-tariff barriers led the European Commission to publish a White Paper entitled *Completing the Internal Market* in 1985. It contained 300 draft directives (since reduced to 279) intended to bring about a Single Market over a seven-year period. Between 1986 and 1987 the twelve member states agreed (although referenda were required in Denmark and Ireland) to amend the Treaty of Rome in order to include a commitment to the Single Market.

The 279 directives apply to the following: veterinary and phytosanitary regulations, technical harmonisation, financial services, indirect tax, transport, free movement of people, company law, intellectual property, labour and the professions, environmental policy, improvements in the control of goods, public procurement, telecommunications, consumer protection, and competition policy.

The Single European Act contained two departures that facilitate the achievement of the Single Market. First there was a change in the decision-making process because of the introduction of qualified majority voting to the Council of Ministers. The votes allotted to member states on the basis of size are 10 each to West Germany, France, Italy and the UK; 8 to Spain; 5 each to the Netherlands, Belgium, Greece and Portugal; three each to Denmark and Ireland; and 2 to Luxembourg. Under the qualified majority voting system, a directive is passed if it receives at least 54 votes out of the total of 76. This system, which replaces the requirement of unanimity for certain cases but particularly for Single Market directives, speeds up the acceptance of directives.

The second departure in the Single European Act is the replacement of harmonisation with mutual recognition. Up to the end of the 1970s, harmonisation was seen as the route to integration. The turning-point can be traced to 1978 when a West German company that was unable to import Crème de Cassis, also known as Cassis de Dijon, brought a challenge to the European Court of Justice. A West German regulation, which held that Crème de Cassis did not contain enough alcohol to qualify as a liqueur, was the barrier to importation. The European Court of Justice found that West Germany could not show justification for exclusion by reason of health, of fiscal supervision, of consumer protection or of fair trading. The Court ruled that West Germany could not impose barriers to the importation of a drink that was on sale in France. The Cassis de Dijon case presented a fresh perspective on industrial standards by allowing for mutual recognition. The Single European Act adopts mutual recognition as a means of abolishing trade barriers.

The effects of the Single Market

The Single Market has significant and wide-ranging effects. Some of these were evaluated by a research project on the 'cost of non-Europe' conducted by a number of research teams under the chairmanship of Paolo Cecchini (Commission of the EC, 1988).

Below, we briefly introduce some of the major effects expected to result from the Single Market. A fuller treatment of the effects will be given in Chapter 2.

The total direct costs of customs procedures were estimated at between ECU 8.4 billion and 9.3 billion, or between 1.7 and 1.9 per cent of intra-Community trade. Within this figure, the costs, to firms, of administration related to customs formalities were estimated at ECU 7.5 billion, the costs of delays at borders at between ECU 400 million and 800 million, and administration costs to public authorities were estimated at between ECU 500 million and 1 billion.

However, detailed quantification of the costs of technical barriers was not possible, because of the large number of regulations and their continuous growth. Still, the fact that the research project's survey of industrialists found these barriers to be among the most important, indicates that the benefits of a Single Market are considerable.

Research on the liberalisation of public procurement estimated that there would be savings of ECU 17.5 billion, or ECU 21.5 billion if defence is included. These savings represented between 0.5% and 0.6% of Community GDP in 1986. The implications for Ireland of the Single Market proposals on technical barriers and public procurement issues are examined in particular in Chapters 8 and 13 and also in Chapters 9 and 10.

Substantial gains are expected to flow from the freeing of capital movements, from the freedom of financial services to be sold across borders, and from the right of establishment for financial firms across EC member states. Research on the effects of liberalisation of financial services in eight member states (Denmark, Greece, Ireland and Portugal were not included) estimated that gains could amount to ECU 22 billion. Gains in efficiency in the financial services sector, however, have important implications for competition in smaller markets such as Ireland, an issue that is treated in Chapter 12.

The Commission's proposals on fiscal barriers revealed different reactions in the member states. VAT rates and excise duties vary considerably across the Community and it was feared that high taxing countries would not remove their border controls because of fears of revenue losses to their exchequers through cross-border shopping, fears of business losses in border areas and fears of fraudulent sales in high tax countries. To minimise these dangers, the Commission drew on American experience of the acceptable tax differentials between states, and proposed that VAT rates should differ by no more than 6 per cent. The Commission originally proposed that the reduced rate of VAT in the Community should fall in the range 4–9 per cent and that the standard rate should fall within the range 14–20 per cent. The Commission also proposed to harmonise excise duties for beer, wine, pure alcohol, cigarettes and petrol.

These proposals gave rise to difficulties because they entailed revenue losses for Denmark, France and Ireland. Chapter 7 presents an estimation of the revenue losses for Ireland. The UK resisted the proposals because they would necessitate the introduction of VAT on food and on children's clothes. Fears were also expressed about loss of tax sovereignty, about the effectiveness of a 6 per cent differential in curtailing tax evasion, and about the requirement for some countries to reduce excise duties on unhealthy products such as cigarettes.

These objections have led to alterations in the original proposals which, although not finalised at time of writing, are likely to incorporate such changes as the inclusion of zero-rating in the reduced rate of VAT. Moreover, the Commission dropped its proposals for the harmonisation of excise duties in favour of minimum rates. Nevertheless, the question of fiscal barriers seems likely to remain a sensitive one.

'Wider context' issues in EC economic integration

Apart from the specific proposals dealing with the physical, technical and fiscal barriers to trade, a number of other policy questions are important to economic integration in the EC. These include regional, social and monetary policies.

The significant regional disparities within the EC have been acknowledged since the foundation of the Community. The Single Market programme has increased the emphasis on measures to narrow regional disparities. To promote economic and social cohesion in the EC, the Community's structural funds (i.e. the European Regional Development Fund, the European Social Fund, and the Guidance Section of the European Agricultural Guidance and Guarantee Fund) were doubled for the period up to 1993.

The issues concerning EC regional disparities, EC regional policies and EC structural funds are examined in Chapters 2, 17 and 18.

Conditions for workers vary across the Community and this gives rise to a number of worries both for richer and for poorer member states. Workers in rich member states are concerned that moves toward a Community-wide labour market might lead to a levelling down of pay and conditions. Another fear is that the Single Market will lead to unemployment in certain countries. There is also concern that social protection standards should not be reduced when workers move from one member state to another.

To deal with these and other concerns, the Commission of the EC prepared a Social Charter. It makes provision for freedom of movement for workers; fair remuneration; adequate social security benefits; vocational training; equality; health, protection and safety; and information, consultation and participation. The content of the Social Charter and an assessment of its implications for Ireland are presented in Chapter 16.

We have noted above that freedom of capital movement is part of the Single Market programme. An inevitable concomitant of this is that member states will lose some discretion over monetary and other macroeconomic policies. This loss of autonomy provides the basis for suggestions that responsibilities for monetary policy be pooled. In 1989 a commission of central bankers and monetary experts chaired by Jacques Delors envisaged progress to an EC system of central banks and locked exchange rates (Delors, 1989). The realisation of these goals would entail not only a loss of autonomy by member states over monetary policy but also, through the establishment of EC guidelines for macroeconomic policy, the loss of autonomy over other instruments of macroeconomic policy. The implications of these developments for Ireland are considered in Chapters 5 and 6.

The foregoing discussion of the Single Market has signalled some of the implications for the Irish economy. Before turning to the detailed implications in succeeding chapters, we first review the position and performance of Ireland in the European Community.

Economic experience since 1973

This section outlines Ireland's economic position in the European Community and the country's economic experience since joining the Community in 1973. Ireland's position is compared with the other eleven member states and we also refer to Ireland's position relative to the regions of the Community. We do not examine the increase in public borrowing and public debt which assisted economic growth in the early period of membership but which was a constraint on economic growth throughout most of the 1980s. Nor do we examine the causes for the improvement in Ireland's economy since 1987.

The analysis concentrates on three groups of socio-economic indicators — income, employment and demography[1] — and there is some analysis of Ireland's trade dependence. Later chapters in the book refer to aspects of economic performance, including Chapter 10 (indigenous manufacturing), Chapter 14 (direct foreign investment), Chapters 15 and 16 (employment) and Chapters 17 and 18 (regional comparisons).

Income

Details of income, as measured by GDP per head of population in purchasing power parities, are presented in Table 1.1. GDP (or GNP) per head is generally recognised as being one of the most important, if not the most important, indicator of economic welfare.

Table 1.1: **Gross Domestic Product per head of population (purchasing power parities)**

	1973	*1988*	*1990 (forecast)*
EC Average*	100	100	100
Ireland	59.9	64.6	67.3
Highest	(Lux.)	(Lux.)	(Lux.)
	123.9	128.0	128.7
Lowest	(Portugal)	(Portugal)	(Greece)
	54.2	53.8	53.6
Ireland's ranking (of 12)	10	10	10

Source: Derived from *European Economy*, No. 42 (1989), Table 9.
*EC refers to the current 12 member states, although only 9 of these were members in 1973.

As Table 1.1 illustrates, Ireland has improved its income position relative to the EC average over its period of membership. The Irish GDP per head was 59.9% of the EC average in 1973. This had increased to 64.6% in 1988 and, at time of writing, was forecast to rise to 67.3% in 1990. Most of this improvement has occurred either in the early years of membership or since 1986. Between 1973 and 1978 the measure increased from 59.9% to 64.6%, i.e. the same level as in 1988. Between 1978 and 1988 the measure fluctuated slightly, reaching a maximum of 66.3% in 1982 and a minimum of 63.4% in 1986. Since 1986 it has risen each year to the forecast level of 67.3% in 1990.

Table 1.1 also shows that the improvement in GDP per head relative to the average EC figure, has not been sufficient to alter Ireland's ranking among the twelve member states. Ireland was ranked tenth in 1973 and was in this position in each year up to 1990.

The degree of convergence is much less if one uses different starting and ending years. For example, in 1975 Ireland's GDP per head was 62.7% of the EC average. In 1986 it was 63.4%. Thus, over the 1975–86 period there is only a negligible narrowing of the gap. However, Ireland's position relative to the EC average has improved since 1986.

Table 1.2 outlines Ireland's position relative to the other EC countries.

Ireland has improved its position relative to all other EC countries over its period of membership, but the income disparities remain very large. In 1988, eight of the member states had levels of GDP per head that were more than 50 per cent greater than Ireland's level. Spain's GDP per head was 15.8 per cent more than Ireland's in 1988. Ireland's GDP per head was greater than those of Greece and Portugal.

Ireland is, therefore, among the poorest of the EC economies. The income gap has improved slightly over the period of membership, but still remains very wide relative to both the EC average and the individual member states.[2]

Changes in GDP per head are influenced by both the growth of GDP and the growth of population. An above-average GDP growth performance, relative to the EC, coupled with a relatively high population growth, could result in a worsening of the GDP per head position. Moreover, for a given level of GDP per worker,

Table 1.2: **GDP per head (purchasing power parities) in Ireland relative to other EC countries**

	1973	1988
Ireland	100	100
Belgium	167.9	156.6
Denmark	188.8	169.5
France	182.5	168.3
Germany	183.8	175.2
Greece	94.0	84.2
Italy	164.9	162.2
Luxembourg	206.8	197.2
Netherlands	187.0	159.8
Portugal	90.5	83.3
Spain	129.2	115.8
UK	179.0	163.6
EC Average	166.9	154.8

Source: Derived from *European Economy*, No. 42 (1989), Table 9.

Table 1.3: **Annual average percentage change in GDP (volume)**

	Bel	Den	Fr	Ger	Gr	Irl	It	Lux	Neth	Port	Sp	UK	EC12
1961/ 1970	4.9	4.5	5.6	4.5	7.6	4.3	5.7	3.7	5.1	6.4	7.3	2.8	4.8
1971/ 1980	3.2	2.2	3.3	2.7	4.7	4.5	3.1	2.7	2.9	4.9	3.5	2.0	2.9
1981/ 1990	1.9	1.9	2.1	2.1	1.6	2.8	2.5	3.3	1.8	2.7	2.9	2.4	2.3

Source: Derived from *European Economy* No. 42 (1989), Table 10.

the higher the labour force dependency ratio (i.e. the number of non-workers relative to each worker), the lower will be the GDP per head of population. As will be shown below, Ireland has a high labour force dependency ratio and has experienced rapid population growth. These factors will tend to worsen the GDP per head position for a given overall economic performance. Details of the growth of GDP are presented in Table 1.3.

Ireland has a reasonable GDP growth record relative to the EC average performance. In the 1960s, Irish GDP grew by an average 4.3% per year, compared with 4.8% for the EC as a whole. Ireland was the only one of the twelve to experience a higher growth performance in the 1970s than in the 1960s. The Irish average growth rate was 4.5%, compared with 2.9% for the EC as a whole. In the 1980s, the Irish growth rate was 2.8%, compared with an EC figure of 2.3%. The 1980's Irish performance can be divided between 1981 to 1986 and 1986 to 1990. In the first six years, GDP grew by 11%, and by 19% in the four years from 1987 to 1990. Ireland exceeded the EC growth rate in 1987 and 1989 and is forecast to do so again in 1990. The 1988 growth rate was 3.8% for the EC and 3.7% in Ireland. Ireland also exceeded the EC growth rate in 1981, 1982 and 1984.

Employment

Ireland has a relatively high proportion of employment in agriculture (15.7% in 1986) compared to most EC countries. However, Portugal (23.9%) and Greece (28.5%) have substantially higher shares. Spain's figure of 16.1% is similar to the Irish share. Of the other eight member states, only Italy has a figure in excess of 10%, with the UK being the lowest (2.5%) (see Table 1.4).

Generally, as economic development proceeds, agriculture declines as a share of total employment. It would be expected, too, that the services sector share would grow with higher levels of economic development. The industrial share of total employment is not as clear-cut an indicator of stage of development. Economic development can be characterised by a growing industrial share during the early stages, but at high income levels the industrial sector's share can decline as the services or tertiary sector becomes more important (Foley and Walbridge, 1981). Ireland's industrial and services shares are below the average EC figure.

The Irish unemployment rate is very high by EC standards. The average unemployment rate of 15.9% in the 1980s was exceeded only by Spain, which had an unemployment rate of 18.6%. The 1989 unemployment rate was 16.7% in Ireland and 17.6% in Spain. The Irish employment rate increased throughout the period of EC membership (with the exceptions of the 1977–1980 period, when it declined, and the period since 1986 when it has also declined). By and large, the EC experienced

Table 1.4: **Employment by main sector of economic activity,
1986**

	Agriculture	Industry	Services
Ireland	15.7	28.7	55.5
Germany	5.3	40.9	53.7
France	7.3	31.3	61.3
Italy	10.9	33.1	56.0
Netherlands	4.9	25.5	69.6
Belgium	2.8	29.1	68.1
Luxembourg	4.0	33.0	63.1
United Kingdom	2.5	30.9	66.6
Denmark	5.9	28.2	65.9
Greece*	28.5	28.1	43.4
Spain	16.1	32.0	51.8
Portugal	23.9	33.9	42.2
EUR 12	8.2	33.2	58.6

*1985 figure *Eurostat Review 1976–1985*.
Source: OECD Labour Force Statistics 1966–1986, Paris, 1988. (Reproduced from NESC No. 88)

the same broad pattern of an increasing unemployment rate from 1973 to the mid-1980s since when it has declined (Table 1.5).

Details of the change in total employment are presented in Table 1.6.

Total employment increased in Ireland from EC entry to 1986. The performance was better than the EC average, but was substantially worse than the better performing EC countries. Over the period since 1973, Irish employment grew by 1.5%, but Portugal had the highest increase of 22.5%. Ireland's performance was ranked seventh of the twelve countries.

The Irish employment performance since 1973 can be divided into two very different sub-periods (as is done in NESC No. 88). In the early years of EC membership, Ireland had the second best performance (behind Portugal). Employment grew by 7.9%, compared with 1.3% for the EC as a whole. This contrasts greatly with the later period of membership from 1980–86. In this period Ireland had the worst employment performance, with a decline

Table 1.5: **Unemployment rate (percentage of civilian labour force)**

	Bel	Den	Fr	Ger	Gr	Irl	It	Lux	Neth	Port	Sp	UK	EUR12
1973	2.4	0.9	2.8	1.0	2.0	5.7	6.4	0.0	2.3	2.7	2.6	2.2	2.8
1976	5.9	6.4	4.5	4.1	1.9	9.1	6.8	0.3	5.6	6.4	4.9	4.9	5.1
1977	6.7	7.4	5.1	4.0	1.7	9.0	7.2	0.5	5.5	7.5	5.3	5.2	5.4
1978	7.3	8.4	5.3	3.8	1.8	8.3	7.3	0.7	5.4	8.1	7.1	5.2	5.6
1979	7.5	6.0	6.0	3.3	1.9	7.2	7.8	0.7	5.5	8.2	8.8	4.7	5.8
1980	7.9	6.6	6.4	3.3	2.8	7.4	7.7	0.7	6.2	7.8	11.6	5.7	6.4
1981	10.2	10.4	7.6	4.7	4.0	10.0	8.0	1.0	8.6	7.6	14.4	9.1	8.1
1982	11.9	11.1	8.3	6.8	5.8	11.6	8.7	1.3	11.6	7.5	16.3	10.5	9.5
1983	12.6	9.5	8.2	6.9	9.0	15.2	9.0	3.6	12.5	7.7	17.8	11.2	10.0
1984	12.6	9.1	9.9	7.1	9.3	17.0	9.5	3.0	12.5	8.4	20.6	11.4	10.8
1985	11.7	7.6	10.3	7.3	8.7	18.4	9.4	3.0	10.4	8.5	21.9	11.5	10.9
1986	11.9	5.8	10.4	6.5	8.2	18.3	10.6	2.7	10.3	8.3	21.2	11.5	10.8
1987	11.5	5.8	10.5	6.4	8.0	18.0	10.1	2.7	10.2	6.8	20.5	10.6	10.4
1988	10.4	6.4	10.2	6.4	8.5	17.8	10.6	2.2	10.3	5.6	19.6	8.7	10.0
1989	9.4	7.4	9.5	5.6	8.5	16.7	10.5	1.8	9.9	5.2	17.6	6.8	9.0
1990	8.8	7.6	9.1	5.4	8.5	16.2	10.6	1.7	9.6	5.2	16.5	6.5	8.7
Average (forecast) 1981/90	11.1	8.1	9.4	6.3	7.9	15.9	9.7	2.3	10.6	7.1	18.6	9.8	9.8

Source: Reproduced from *European Economy* No. 42 (1989), Table 3.

of 6.4% relative to the EC decline of 1.2%, and was ranked last of the twelve countries. Since 1986, however, the employment performance has improved and was similar to the overall EC performance in 1989 (Ireland had a 1.2% increase, compared to 1.5% for the EC as a whole).

All member states experienced declines in agricultural employment. The Irish decline since 1973 was slightly above the decline for the Community as a whole.

Table 1.6: **Total employment changes 1973–86 (percentages)**

	1973–80	*1980–86*	*1973–86*
Ireland	+7.9	−6.4	+1.5
EC 12	+1.3	−1.2	+0.1
Best performance	+19.9 (Port)	+7.3 (Gr)	+22.5 (Port)
Worst performance	−8.8 (Sp.)	−6.4 (Irl)	−14.7 (Sp.)
Ireland's ranking (of 12)	2	12	7

Source: Derived from data in NESC No. 88 and OECD Labour Force Statistics, Paris, 1988.

Table 1.7: **Employment performance, industry, services 1973–86; Ireland and EC**

		Industry	*Services*
1973–86	Ireland	−7.6	+22.5
	EC	−19.8	+21.2
	Ireland's ranking	3	7
1973–80	Ireland	+9.7	+16.8
	EC	−6.4	+11.2
	Ireland's ranking	3	4
1980–86	Ireland	−17.3	+5.7
	EC	−13.3	+10.0
	Ireland's ranking	11	10

Source: Derived from data in NESC No. 88, Tables 5.19 and 5.20 and ILO Statistics. The NESC data do not include Portugal. Portugal's position was derived from ILO Annual Labour Statistics (various years). There are data comparability problems with Portugal's data. Even allowing for these, however, the data suggest that Portugal performed better in both industry and services in each period. The EC 12 totals as given in NESC No. 88 are used in the table.

A summary of the trends in industrial and services employment is presented in Table 1.7. Over the full period of EC membership, Ireland's employment performance was ranked third in industry and seventh in services. Industrial employment declined in the EC as a whole, but the Irish decline was substantially less than the EC decline. The two sub-periods had very different employment experiences. In the first sub-period, Ireland performed very well in industrial employment, but had a very poor performance in the second sub-period. In the 1980–86 sub-period, no EC country increased its industrial employment. However, Ireland had the second worst performance of the 12 member states. Only the UK had a worse performance in industrial employment between 1980 and 1986.

Services employment grew throughout the Community. Once again,the early Irish performance was better than the later one. Between 1973 and 1980, Ireland had the fourth largest increase, and exceeded the EC increase. Between 1980 and 1986, the Irish services increase was just over half the EC increase and Ireland's increase was ranked tenth of the twelve countries. Germany and Belgium had smaller increases than Ireland in this sub-period.

Demography

In this section we outline the positions on population, population growth, age structure, labour force dependency rate, and migration. Table 1.8 deals with population.

Table 1.8: **Population level and growth 1973–90**

Bel	Den	Fr	Ger	Gr	Irl	It	Lux	Neth	Port	Sp	UK	EC
Level 1990 (millions)												
9.9	5.1	56.2	62.4	10.1	3.5	57.7	0.4	14.9	9.8	39.3	57.4	326.8
% Increase 1973/90 (forecast)												
1.4	2.3	8.1	0.6	13.0	14.7	5.3	6.3	11.1	15.8	12.9	2.1	5.8

Source: Table 1 *European Economy* (November 1989).
Note: 1990 figures are a forecast.

Ireland has the second lowest population, after Luxembourg, of the twelve member states. Irish population growth over the 1973–90 period was the second highest of the EC countries, behind Portugal. The Irish population growth rate was almost three times the growth rate for the total EC. Greece, Spain and the Netherlands each had population increases in excess of 11%.

The age structure of the population and the labour force dependency rate have important economic implications. The dependent age-groups are defined as under 15 years and 65 and over. These two groups tend to have above-average demand for public services such as education, health care and pensions. Consequently, a high proportion of the population in these age-groups leads to relatively high demand for public services. This, in turn, leads to higher tax rates to finance these services. As Table 1.9 indicates, the Irish age dependency rate (defined as dependent age share as a percentage of other age share) is the highest of the EC countries. In 1986, it was 0.66 or 66 age-dependent persons per 100 non age-dependant persons. The next highest was Portugal at 0.54. Portugal, France, UK, Denmark,

Table 1.9: **Population by age (percentage of total) and age dependency rates 1986**

	Under 15 %	15–64 %	65+ %	Age Dependency Rate
Ireland	28.9	60.2	10.8	0.66
Germany*	15.1	70.0	14.8	0.43
France	20.9	65.9	13.2	0.52
Italy	16.8	69.6	13.4	0.45
Netherlands	19.0	68.7	12.3	0.45
Belgium	18.5	67.4	14.1	0.48
Luxembourg	16.9	69.8	13.3	0.44
United Kingdom	19.0	65.7	15.3	0.52
Denmark	18.1	66.6	15.3	0.50
Greece*	20.9	65.7	13.4	0.52
Spain	22.6	65.2	12.2	0.53
Portugal	22.5	65.2	12.3	0.54
EUR 12	19.1	67.2	13.7	0.49

*1985 figures
Source: *Eurostat Review 1976–1985*, European Commission. (Reproduced from NESC No. 88).

Greece and Spain were all between 0.50 and 0.54. The other five countries were all at or below 0.48, with West Germany having the lowest figure of 0.43.

Consequently, there are 66 age-dependent persons per 100 others in Ireland, compared with, for example, 43 in West Germany. It can readily be seen that, for a given quality and level of public service, the relative public financial burden would be substantially greater in Ireland and hence taxation also would be greater.

The labour force dependency rate is defined as the ratio of the population that is not in the labour force to those in the labour force. A ratio of 1.71 indicates that, on average, 1.71 persons must be supported by each member of the labour force i.e. GDP per worker must be divided between 2.71 persons to get GDP per head. The labour force dependency rate is itself determined by, *inter alia*, the age structure of the population, labour force participation rates and the availability of jobs. The labour force dependency rate has a significant impact on the income or GDP per head of population indicator. This is illustrated in Table 1.10.

Table 1.10: **Illustration of effect of labour force dependency rate**

	GDP per worker	*Labour force dependency rate*	*GDP per head of population*
Country A	£10,000	1.75	£3,636
Country B	£10,000	1.25	£4,444

The two countries, A and B, have the same income or GDP per worker. Because of the different labour force dependency rates, the incomes per head of population are substantially different. Country B's income per head is 22% greater than Country A's. If the aim was to have equal incomes or GDP per head, Country A would have to have a GDP per worker of £12,221, which, when associated with the labour force dependency rate of 1.75, would give a GDP per head of £4,444 (12,221 divided by 2.75), i.e. the same as Country B.

The impact of labour force dependency rates on GDP per

head should be borne in mind when considering regional cohesion and convergence. While the aim might be to narrow disparities in GDP per head, it is unrealistic to expect that the narrowing process should attempt to compensate for the impact of high labour force dependency rates which widen income-per-head disparities. Of course, high labour force dependency rates could be due to low levels of economic activity, as well as to the preferences of people.

The labour force dependency rates for the twelve EC member states are presented in Table 1.11.

Ireland is ranked second in the table behind Spain. The Irish and Spanish figures, at 1.71 and 1.73 respectively, are almost identical. The lowest labour force dependency rates are found in Denmark and the UK. The UK rate of 1.04, compared with the Irish rate of 1.71, means that if both countries were to have the same GDP per head of population, Ireland's level of GDP

Table 1.11: **Labour force dependency rates, 1986**

	Labour force dependency ratio
Ireland	1.71
Germany	1.18
France	1.31
Italy	1.37
Netherlands	1.49
Belgium	1.34
Luxembourg	1.21
United Kingdom	1.04
Denmark	0.82
Greece	1.56
Spain	1.73
Portugal	1.16
EUR 12	1.29

Source: OECD Labour Force Statistics 1966–1986, Paris, 1988 (reproduced from NESC No. 88).

per worker would have to be 33 per cent higher than in the UK, i.e. average GDP per worker is spread over 2.04 persons in the UK and 2.71 in Ireland. Therefore, the demographic structure accounts for part of the income per head disparity between Ireland and the EC average. Even if Ireland had the same level of output per worker as the EC average (in fact, the Irish output per worker is lower than the EC average), the EC average income or GDP per head would be 18 per cent higher than Ireland's.

Ireland had net emigration for every intercensal period from 1926 to 1971. In this period, total net emigration exceeded one million people. In the period 1971 to 1979, there was net immigration of 108,934 persons. Net emigration resumed after 1979 at relatively small levels, but rose from 9,000 in 1983/84 (April 1983 to April 1984) to 20,000 in 1984/85, 28,000 in 1985/86, 32,000 in 1987/88, and 46,000 in 1988/89.

Ireland's emigration level is high by EC standards. In the first half of the 1980s, most EC countries had net immigration. The two exceptions were Ireland and Belgium.

Trade dependence

The Single Market is intended, *inter alia*, to facilitate and ease trade flows between the member states. This is of considerable importance to economies that depend on international trade. Ireland has one of the highest levels of international trade of the EC countries. As can be seen in Table 1.12, the role of trade has increased greatly since Ireland joined the Community in 1973.[3]

Table 1.12: **Significance of trade, Ireland and EC 12**

	Exports of goods & services as a % of GDP			Imports of goods and services as % of GDP		
	Ireland	EC12	Ireland's ranking	Ireland	EC12	Ireland's ranking
1973	38.0	22.5	4	44.8	20.5	3
1988	64.1	27.1	3	54.8	26.4	3

Source: European Economy No. 42 (1989), Table 35.

Ireland's export to GDP ratio was 38% in 1973.[4] This was the fourth highest export ratio of the 12 member states, behind Belgium, the Netherlands and Luxembourg. In 1988, this ratio was 64.1%, compared with 27.1% for the EC as a whole; Ireland had the third highest ratio, behind Belgium and Luxembourg. Ireland ranked third on the import ratio in both 1973 and 1988. The role of international trade is of great importance in the Irish economy. Ireland is also heavily dependent on the EC countries for export markets. In 1988, 72% of Irish exports of goods went to EC countries. For the EC as a whole, 60% of exports of goods went to countries within the Community.

Ireland had a deficit on the current account of the balance of payments in each year from 1973 to 1986. Since 1987, however, there have been surpluses on the current account.

Irish exports of goods and services grew, in volume terms, by an average 8.6% per year between 1981 and 1990. This was the best performance in the Community and was almost double the overall EC increase. Portugal's average annual growth rate of 8.0% was close to the Irish figure and was the second best performance within the Community.

Ireland relative to the regions of the Community

An understanding of Ireland's economic position and performance within the European Community is improved by regional level comparisons. In the brief summary that follows, we confine the analysis to 'level I' regions, except in the case of Denmark, where we include its three 'level II' regions.[5] For EC regional policy purposes, Ireland is treated as one region. The number of regions is 66: Belgium (3 regions), Denmark (3 regions), Germany (11 regions), Greece (3 regions), Spain (7 regions), France (8 regions), Italy (11 regions), Luxembourg (1 region), Netherlands (4 regions), Portugal (3 regions), UK (11 regions) and Ireland (1 region). The indicators used in the examination are GDP per inhabitant, GDP per employed person, and unemployment. The presentation format is as used in Foley and Walbridge (1981).

Ireland's ranking in GDP per inhabitant is 57th of 65 regions, as shown in Table 1.13. The eight regions below Ireland are the three Greek regions, three Spanish regions, and two regions in Portugal. The region with the highest level of GDP per head is Hamburg. Its level of 188 is almost three times the Irish level. The lowest regional incomes in each of the countries (excluding Luxembourg and Ireland, which are each classified as single

Table 1.13: **Regional indicators, level I regions, mid-1980s**

	GDP per inhabitant 1984 EC Avg = 100	GDP per employed person 1984 EC Avg = 100	Unemployment rate % of labour force 1987 EC Avg = 10.6
Maximum	188	213	29.9
Minimum	43	43	2.7
Ireland's indicator	66	81	18.1
Ireland's† ranking	57	Joint 58	58
Total number of regions	65*	65*	66

†In columns one and two, the higher the indicator, the higher the ranking. The highest indicator for GDP per inhabitant, 188, is ranked first. In column three, the higher the indicator, the lower the ranking. The highest unemployment rate, 29.9 per cent, is ranked 66th and last.
*No date for the ILHAS region in Portugal.
Source: 1988 Regions Statistics Yearbook, EC, 1989. The data in this refer to the mid-1980s.

regions) are: Belgium, 85% of the EC average; Denmark, 98%; France, 93%; Germany, 97%; Greece, 52%; Italy, 71%; Netherlands, 88%; Portugal, 43%; Spain 56%; and UK, 79%. Southern Italy is often considered to be a relatively poor area, but none of its regions are below the Irish level of GDP per head. Its three poorest regions have GDP levels of 71%, 72% and 73% of the EC average, respectively, compared with the Irish figure of 66%.

It should be realised that the eight regions that are below the Irish GDP per head level are in the three most recent entrants to the EC. If we compare Ireland with the regions in the nine countries that were members in 1973, the Irish position worsens since it is the poorest region of the 1973 member states. It ranks last of the 53 'level I' regions in these nine countries. This represents a disimprovement in Ireland's position since 1973 when the five southern Italian regions were below Ireland's income level.[6] All other regions, however, had income levels greater than Ireland's in 1973.

Overall, it is clear that Ireland's income level is very low compared with the other EC regions. Of 65 regions, 57 regions, or 88 per cent of the total, have higher income levels than Ireland. Of the 53 regions in the nine member states in 1973, Ireland is ranked last in terms of GDP per head. This is a worsening of the 1973 situation when Ireland was ranked sixth last.

The regional data refer to the mid-1980s. Since Irish GDP per head improved relative to the EC average between 1986 and 1990, there could also be some improvement in Ireland's regional position. However, this would not fundamentally alter Ireland's low ranking relative to other EC regions[7].

Ireland's GDP per employed person is 81% of the EC average, i.e. much closer to the average than is the GDP per head of population measure. This would be expected because Ireland's high labour force dependency rate brings down its GDP per head of population for a given GDP per worker.

Paradoxically, however, Ireland's ranking on this indicator is slightly worse. The ranking is joint 58th, with only six regions below the Irish level of 81. These six regions are the three Greek regions, two in Portugal and one in Spain. The Spanish region is not one of the three that were below Ireland's income level. All three of these Spanish regions had higher GDP per employed person than Ireland.

The maximum value of 213 on this indicator is due to the Dutch region of Noord-Nederland. Its value is due to one of its 'level II' regions, i.e. Groningen, with an indicator of 332, which when included with the other two sub-regions of Noord-Nederland becomes 213. After Noord-Nederland, the region with the next highest value on this indicator is Hamburg at 138. Despite the extreme value of 213 and the wider range than on the income indicator, there is generally less variation between the regions on the output per worker indicator than on the output per head indicator.

On employment, Ireland is ranked 58th of the 66 regions. The higher the level of unemployment, the lower is the ranking. Eight regions have higher unemployment rates: five regions in Spain, two in Italy, and Northern Ireland.

The EC Commission has devised a summary indicator, or 'Synthetic index', to rank regions. This index includes output and labour market indicators, which are aggregated on a weighted basis. As would be expected from its ranking on individual components of the index, Ireland also ranks poorly on this index. This is discussed in Chapter 2 and Chapter 18.

Summary

The broad summary of Ireland's position and performance in the European Community is quite bleak. Ireland has low income per head. The gap has narrowed slightly, but the income disparities are still large. At the national level, only Portugal and Greece have lower GDP per head of population. Eight of the twelve member states have incomes per head that are more than 50 per cent greater than Ireland's income.

At the regional level, only eight (of 65 regions) have lower income per head than Ireland. In terms of output per worker, only six (of 66 regions) have lower levels than in Ireland. Of the 53 regions in the nine member states in 1973, Ireland is ranked last in income per head. This is a slight worsening of the situation as existed at the time of entry. Irish output per worker is closer to the EC average than income per head of population.

Over the full period of membership, growth in Irish GDP is reasonable relative to the EC average. However, as NESC No. 88 noted, this '. . . has coincided with the build-up of very large public debt . . .' (p. 144). Since 1987, however, the growth rate has been good compared to the EC performance, while at the same time improvements have been made in the public finances. Ireland has a relatively high proportion of employment in agriculture and has performed poorly, particularly in the later period of membership, in employment creation. The county has a very high unemployment rate, exceeded only by Spain.

Ireland has experienced rapid population growth and has the highest age dependency rate in the EC. It has the second highest labour force dependency rate in the EC and the highest emigration levels. The Irish economy is heavily dependent on trade and has the best export growth performance of the twelve member states.

An overview of the book

It is clear that the Single Market will have wide-ranging effects on the Irish economy. This chapter and the three that follow give an overview of the Single Market. In this chapter we have given a general introduction to the Single Market and have reviewed the performance of Ireland in the EC. Chapter 2 provides a more detailed examination of the Single Market and analyses a number of regional issues in the Community. The various elements of economic theory used in analysing economic integration are presented in Chapter 3. Chapter 4 examines the performance of and the prospects for the overall EC economy.

The Single Market has important implications for macro-economic policy. Chapter 5 analyses the implications of the Single Market for national economic management. The implications of monetary integration are examined in Chapter 6. Chapter 7 evaluates the costs for Ireland of proposals for indirect tax harmonisation.

Chapter 8 examines technical barriers affecting Irish industry and assesses the implications of Single Market proposals. Chapter 9 examines the Single Market proposals on transport and their implications for Ireland.

Chapters 10 to 14 analyse the implications of the Single Market in the various sectors of the Irish economy. Specifically, these chapters cover indigenous manufacturing, agriculture, services, building and construction, and foreign direct investment.

The effects of the Single Market and of the Social Charter on the labour market in Ireland are considered in Chapters 15 and 16 respectively.

The next two chapters deal with the Republic of Ireland and Northern Ireland as peripheral regions in the European Community.

The effects of the Single Market on the Irish economy are brought together in Chapter 19, where general conclusions are presented.

Notes

1. See Foley and Walbridge and NESC No. 58 for a discussion of socio-economic indicators. We use GDP statistics, although GNP statistics are important for Ireland because of the rate of factor payment outflows. The GDP variable, however, is used by the Commission.
2. As was shown earlier, this comment is sensitive to the choice of beginning and end years, but because we wish to comment on changes since joining

the Community, we have looked at changes since 1973. There are some differences between the data used for Tables 1.1 and 1.2 and data presented in NESC No. 88 on the same indicator. The data we used are as published in *European Economy*.

3. Certain features of Ireland's industrial structure, in particular the large role of foreign firms, can result in somewhat 'artificially' high export ratios and export levels. See Foley (1988) and O'Leary (1984).

4. Because of their more specialised patterns of production, one expects small economies to have higher trade ratios than large economies, other things become equal.

5. 'Level I' regions are the largest territorial units taken into consideration for each member state. 'Level II' consists of the regional units next largest in size to 'level I'. Each 'level I' region generally consists of a number of 'level II' regions. Sometimes a 'level I' region is also a single 'level II' region e.g. Ireland. Denmark is just one 'level I' region and has three 'level II' regions.

6. One would get different results if one looked at 'level II' regions in that a 'level I' region which is above Ireland may include one or some 'level II' regions that are below.

7. It does not necessarily mean that Ireland's recent improvement relative to the EC average would improve its regional ranking because some other regions that are close to Ireland's level could also be improving their positions.

2

The Single European Market: an Overview

NORBERT VANHOVE and GEERT SANDERS

In 1985 the European Commission published a White Paper, *Completing the Internal Market*. Its main objective was to eliminate all barriers to the free flow of goods, services, capital and labour within the Community before 31 December 1992.

This chapter analyses the White Paper and the broad effects of the economic integration it proposes, and highlights some important topics touching on the relationship between the creation of an internal market and the EC's peripheral regions. The possible impact on Ireland as a peripheral region will be discussed in Chapters 17 and 18.

Europe: a success story?

The Treaty of Rome, which established the European Economic Community on 25 March 1957, envisaged the creation of a common market based on four essential freedoms: free movement of goods, services, capital and people.

A first success was the creation of a customs union, with the abolition of internal tariffs and quotas and the establishment of common tariffs for third countries. The customs union was achieved on 1 July 1968, eighteen months before the established deadline. A second success was the enlargement of the Community's original six member states — Belgium, France, the Federal Republic of Germany, Italy, Luxembourg and the Netherlands — to include Denmark, Ireland, and the United Kingdom in 1973, Greece in 1981, and Portugal and Spain in 1986. With the enlargement of the Community, however, progress towards a common market began to slow down.

The integration process was given new impetus when the European Commission published *Completing the Internal Market* in 1985. This White Paper sets out a detailed programme and a timetable for the removal of the remaining barriers to trade in the Community by the end of 1992. The heads of state and government of the member states gave the programme their formal backing at the European Council in Milan in June 1985.

On 1 July 1987 the Single European Act came into force, giving the integration process another boost. The act writes the commitment and deadline for the completion of the internal market into the Treaty of Rome itself: a commitment to create a region without frontiers, in which the free movement of goods, services, capital and labour is ensured by the end of 1992. The act also revolutionised the way in which the Community makes legislation, by introducing qualified majority voting in many areas in place of unanimity.

The White Paper

The White Paper comprised some 300 separate proposals to complete the internal market. Some of these have been withdrawn because they became outdated or were overtaken by alternative strategies. Others have been added to prevent the formation of new barriers to trade or to reinforce safeguards. As a result, the programme now comprises 279 measures. The White Paper has identified three categories of barriers — physical, technical and fiscal — to trade in the Community and has set out a detailed programme for their removal.

The removal of physical barriers

The intra-Community trade in goods amounts to some 500 billion ECU. This represents a little over half the Community's total trade and about 14 per cent of the Community's GDP. Physical barriers to intra-Community trade are the controls that member states currently impose at internal Community borders on goods and persons entering and leaving their respective national territories. The total direct costs of frontier formalities and associated administrative costs for the private and public sector amount to 8 to 9 billion ECU a year. This is equivalent to 1.8 per cent of the total value of the goods traded within the Community.

The declared goal of the Single European Act is to create a Community without internal frontiers and border controls. The removal of the border controls is to be the symbol of an internal market and is to be the psychological trigger for commercial activity. The Commission has adopted a two-stage approach: first, the dismantling of existing controls and, second, the removal of the underlying obstacles to trade in the form of technical barriers.

Existing border controls have been reduced by simplifying the present formalities. The most important one until now was the introduction on 1 January 1988 of the Single Administrative Document for the control of imports, exports and goods in transit within the Community. The Commission also tries to provide for cooperation between customs authorities concerning the carrying out of those formalities, in particular by the introduction of common border posts.

Border controls are maintained for a number of reasons. Various Community policies require or permit controls on the flow of goods at internal frontiers, such as the application of monetary compensatory amounts in the intra-Community trade of certain agricultural products in accordance with the Common Agricultural Policy. Transport-related border checks are necessary for the application of Community and national transport quotas, as well as for fiscal and for safety and regulatory checks. Internal customs posts are often used for making veterinary and phytosanitary checks. The Commission plans to reduce the need for such investigations by harmonising essential national animal and plant health requirements. It has also proposed to replace veterinary border checks by examinations at the place of dispatch, supported by spot checks at the place of destination. Frontier formalities are also carried out for statistical purposes relating to the trading of goods between member states, for fiscal verification (differences in Value Added Tax rates and excise duties) and for police and other checks on individuals to do with drugs control, arms legislation, immigration, right of asylum, status of refugees, national visa policies and extradition. In each of these matters, the Commission plans to eliminate frontier controls by removing the underlying causes and/or by finding means other than frontier control to attain comparable levels of information and protection.

The removal of technical barriers

The removal of border controls will not in itself create a genuine common market. If technical barriers are allowed to remain, the obstacles to trade will be met within the other member states instead of at the borders. These technical regulations are complex and multiplying because of technological developments and the increasing concern for health, safety and consumer protection.

The free movement of goods

All member states have their own rules on the production and marketing of goods; these apply for reasons of health, safety, and environmental and consumer protection. Yet the rules often act as substantial barriers to trade, by preventing goods produced in one member state from being marketed in another.

The principle of the Commission's policy for removing technical barriers is that, if a product is lawfully manufactured and marketed in one member state, it should be available throughout the Community. This principle was established in 1978 by the European Court of Justice in the 'Cassis de Dijon' ruling and has been substantiated by further judgments. It is in fact an application of the mutual recognition principle towards national regulations; it reduces the need for harmonisation. However, member states can still restrict the free movement of goods because of certain public policies or interests, in the absence of specific Community legislation (Article 36 of the Treaty). So other policy instruments are required.

In the past the Commission sought to remove technical obstructions by harmonising national technical regulations. But this process was relatively slow because of the difficulty of agreeing on the detailed technical specifications set out in various directives. The new strategy of the Commission is for member states to recognise differences in non-essential standards and regulations which should not legitimately restrict free movement. On the other hand, differences in essential standards and regulations still have to be removed and this is done through the Commission's new approach to harmonisation.

The White Paper's new approach is that Community legislation should be limited to indicating essential safety requirements, or other requirements in the general interest, with which products put on the market must conform. Thus, the only essential requirements are those for health, safety and environmental and consumer protection. Once agreement has been reached on the essential requirements, the task of writing the detailed specifications and actual standards is entrusted to the relevant European standardisation bodies, usually CEN (European Committee for Standardisation) and CENELEC (European Committee for Electrotechnical Standardisation). These European bodies also have to help to provide technical specifications needed by public authorities for new industrial technologies like telecommunications and informatics. A similar approach to the removal of technical barriers exists in the following sectors: motor vehicles, tractors and agricultural machines, food law, pharmaceuticals and high-technology medicines, chemical products, construction and construction products.

Since 1983 the Commission has had at its disposal the mutual information directive concerning new regulations and standards. This directive restrains the creation of new trade barriers and aims to encourage the reconciliation of national demands at an early stage.

The technical barriers commit companies to considerable expenditures: duplication in the costs of research and development; loss of manufacturing efficiency; increased inventory and distribution costs; and competitive weaknesses. For public authorities, there is a duplication in the costs of testing and certification, and technical barriers cause higher prices for consumers and taxpayers. Since the cost of technical barriers differs considerably by product, it is practically impossible to estimate an aggregate for this type of barrier.

Public procurement

In 1986 public purchasing represented approximately 530 billion ECU in the European Community, or 15 per cent of GDP. It includes all purchases of goods and services by government at all levels and by public enterprises, i.e. enterprises that benefit from a monopoly, franchise or special status in the provision of public services. Only part of public purchasing is put out to tender or is governed by formal contracts. This part is called public procurement. In 1986 it represented between 240 and 340 billion ECU in the Community, or between 6.8 per cent and 9.8 per cent of Community GDP. Public procurement is one matter where governments continue to favour their national champions, or in other words, favour domestic producers, whenever possible. This market effectively is closed to intra-Community competition. Community rules exist but they are frequently broken.

The 1992 programme aims to tighten up the existing directives and to provide for better enforcement of the rules, to ensure that firms from other member states have an equal chance. The Commission also wishes to extend the rules to the now excluded sectors of water, energy, transport and telecommunications. The Commission's philosophy on public procurement policy is to ensure that major public sector purchasing bodies, which usually are constrained to buy at home, are protected from such intervention and are allowed to use their commercial judgment. The Commission also intends to ensure reciprocal access in all sectors of public procurement.

The opening of public procurement markets will create many benefits for the Community's economy. It will reduce costs to major public utilities, transport and telecommunications. Public administration will also save costs, which can be passed on either through tax reductions or through infrastructure investment. Companies supplying public markets will have to become more competitive when their relationship with the sponsoring procurers has been eliminated. Those firms that can reduce costs will have the competitive propensity to expand their markets beyond their traditional customers. The total savings associated with the liberalisation of public procurement are considerable. They were approximately 18 billion ECU in 1984, or 0.6 per cent of the

THE SEM AND THE IRISH ECONOMY   33

Community's GDP. The economic effects of liberalisation can be broken down into: a static effect of 4.4 billion ECU, arising from public authorities buying from the cheapest supplier; a competitive effect of 2.3 billion ECU, arising from an alignment of the prices of domestic suppliers to the price of the most competitive foreign suppliers; and, most important, a restructuring effect of 7.2 billion ECU, arising from the economies of scale as industry reorganises under the pressure of new competitive conditions. Finally, we have still to include an additional saving of 4 billion ECU in the defence sector.

Free movement of employees, the self-employed and professionals

A crucial part of the Commission's programme is the removal of the remaining obstacles to the free movement of workers, the freedom of establishment and the freedom to provide services. Comparability of vocational training qualifications is a high priority here. The intention is that a vocational training card will serve as proof that the holder has been awarded a specific qualification.

Rather than providing individual directives covering each professional activity, the Council has adopted a general system for the recognition of higher education diplomas. This is designed to help those individuals who have acquired their higher education in a member state other than the one in which they wish to engage in professional activity. The holder of the diploma has to prove that he has successfully completed a post-secondary course of at least three years' duration.

The Council has also adopted several programmes to stimulate student mobility and cooperation between universities (ERASMUS), youth exchanges (YES) and cooperation between universities and industry training in the field of new technologies (COMETT).

Services

The objective of the internal market in the service sector is to assure adequate prudential and safety standards and market openness. The former is in most countries assured, but market openness, competition and low-cost efficiency are often not guaranteed.

The establishment of a common market in financial services (banking, insurance and securities transactions) is closely linked to and dependent upon the liberalisation of capital movements. The 1992 programme calls for the introduction of a single licensing system for financial institutions, permitting both the establishment of branches and the provision of services throughout the Community. Financial institutions already can set up business in any member state, but strictly according to the requirements of that state. The Commission wishes to allow enterprises to provide cross-frontier services without the need to set up offices in another member state. The regulation of the activities would be according to the requirements of the state where the institution's head offices are situated, rather than those of the states where the services are provided. This is the principle of home country control. There will be a degree of harmonisation of national regulatory systems in order to ensure common basic requirements for probity and security. Member states also will be required to recognise the regulatory systems of other member states. The liberalisation in financial services will stimulate greater competition and efficiency in the provision of these services. As a result, the consumer will benefit through greater choice, lower prices, and better service. If this liberalisation accompanies macroeconomic cooperation or monetary integration, it will probably lead to further economic gains.

The 1985 White Paper pointed out that transport represents more than 7 per cent of the Community's GDP. This means that the development of a free transport market would have a considerable economic influence on industry and trade. The Commission wishes to eliminate distortions of competition in international and national transport. Completing the internal market in transport means that any carrier in a member state should be allowed to provide transport services in another member state without having to be established there under the same conditions as national carriers. Important measures have to be taken in international carriage within the Community, national carriage by road, inland waterway and sea (cabotage), air transport and maritime transport.

The Commission plans to introduce changes in new technologies and services: broadcasting, information services, new payment cards and telecommunications. In the field of audiovisual services, the objective is a single Community-wide broadcasting area. All those who provide and receive broadcast services should be able to do so regardless of national borders. The creation of a common information market is of prime importance to commerce and industry. It would stimulate the competitive capability of European suppliers and promote the use of advanced information services within the Community. The Commission aims to use the same payment card throughout the Community to purchase goods and obtain cash. The telecommunications authorities have been asked to implement the detailed requirements concerning the coordinated introduction of certain types of cellular digital land-based mobile communications in the Community. An internal market without technical barriers will have to be established if Community firms wish to catch up with their international competitors.

Capital movements

The abolition of restrictions and discriminations concerning the free movement of capital is closely linked to the freedom to provide financial services. There is little point in being able to provide cross-frontier services if one cannot receive cross-frontier payments in return. Liberalisation, helping member states adapt to liberalisation, and the prevention of tax distortions and abuses are all reflected in the 1985 White Paper.

Creation of suitable conditions for industrial cooperation

The 1992 programme aims to facilitate cross-border activities by harmonising member states' company laws to secure the freedom of establishment and by permitting the institution of single entities, such as a European Economic Interest Grouping, which already exists, and a European Company.

The White Paper proposes the coordination or approximation of existing member states' intellectual property laws and the creation of supranational Community-wide intellectual property rights and rules. So the introduction of a Community trademark will make it possible for undertakings to obtain, on a single application, one trademark covering all member states.

Double taxation, differences in corporation tax regimes, and the high cost of repatriating profits earned abroad discourage cross-border investment and other forms of cooperation between enterprises, and also give rise to substantial distortions of competition. The Commission has drawn up a series of directives to eliminate these problems, but very little progress has been made on implementing them.

The removal of fiscal barriers

By the removal of fiscal barriers, the Commission means the approximation of indirect taxation, in particular VAT and excise duties. The Commission has put forward proposals on the approximation of the rates and harmonisation of the structures of VAT and on the harmonisation of excise duties.

The Commission originally proposed an approximation of the VAT rates within two bands: a standard rate of 14–20 per cent and a reduced rate of 4–9 per cent that would apply to foodstuffs, energy products for heating and lighting, supplies of water, pharmaceutical products, books, newspapers, periodicals and passenger transport. A clearing house mechanism would ensure that VAT collected in an exporting state accrues to the revenue authorities of the member state where consumption takes place. VAT controls at the border will be abolished since cross-border sales would be treated in the same way as domestic sales.

The ultimate aim is to make it possible to abolish frontiers. Yet there is still a long way to go and the Commission will encounter many political difficulties. Up to the time of writing, there have been considerable revisions to the original proposals. A treatment of the effects on the Irish exchequer of the Commission's proposals is contained in Chapter 7.

The physical and the fiscal barriers are closely related. As long as the VAT and excise duties are not harmonised, member states will not remove border controls and this will lead to a failure to complete the internal market. The benefits of removing fiscal barriers are very difficult to separate from the benefits of eliminating other barriers to the internal market. The various barriers reinforce each other.

Once fiscal barriers have been removed, there will be an immediate cost-saving for enterprises as customs formalities and related administrative costs are eliminated. The increased competition will lead to price and cost reductions. The approximation of indirect taxation would tend to reduce distortions in prices of goods and services which now exist because of different rates of tax. The investment choices of individuals and enterprises will be less affected by uncertainty about the evolution of indirect taxes.

The effects of market integration

The main economic effects of completing the internal market stem from an integration process that will promote the efficiency and competitiveness of companies through economies of scale and increased competition. These economic effects can be divided primarily into: cost reductions resulting from economies of scale through larger markets and restructuring processes, and from economies of learning through managers and workers becoming more knowledgeable about production techniques as their experience increases with longer production runs; the effect of competition which should lead to a reduction in price-cost margins and to incentives for firms to reduce their margins to the level imposed by competition and to cut their costs; increased competition which also should have non-price effects as firms are encouraged to improve their organisation and the quality and range of their products, and to engage in innovation at both the process and product levels.

The Commission's estimate of the potential consequences of completing the internal market for the Community in the medium term and long term is found in Table 2.1. Two types of approach have been used: the microeconomic and the macroeconomic. These estimates must be treated cautiously and a margin of error of around 30 per cent must be allowed for.

The assessment of the consequences of the internal market at the microeconomic level suggests that the welfare gains for the Community could amount to between 4.25 per cent and 6.5 per cent of GDP in the medium to long term. This is an assessment for all sectors and all types of cost-saving and potential price reductions.

Table 2.1: **Potential consequences of completion of the internal market for the EC in the medium term and in the long term**

Microeconomic approach	Welfare gains as % of GDP 4.25–6.50		
Macroeconomic approach	GDP as per cent	Prices as per cent	Employment in millions
Without accompanying economic measures	4.50	–6	1.75
With accompanying economic measures	7	–4.50	5

Sources: Commission of the European Communities, 'The Economics of 1992', *European Economy*, Luxembourg, Office for Official Publications of the European Communities, March 1988, p. 167.

A macroeconomic evaluation of completing the internal market presents the gains to be expected in terms of growth in GDP, employment and inflation. Without accompanying economic measures, the additional GDP could amount to 4.5 per cent after five or six years; the prices would decrease by 6 per cent, and the number of jobs created in the medium term would be around 1.75 million. If a more active macroeconomic policy were to be pursued, one that recognised the potential for faster growth, the GDP gains for the Community would be about 7 per cent in the medium term; 5 million additional jobs would be created and prices would decrease by 4.5 per cent.

The results of both the microeconomic and the macroeconomic methods are mutually supporting. However, it remains difficult to predict when those effects will materialise.

The Single European Market and the peripheral regions

A properly functioning single internal market is not feasible while there are important disparities between the regions of the EC. How important are these disparities? What are the major regional policy issues at national and at EC levels? What is the possible impact of the internal market on the peripheral regions? What does the European Commission think about the possible negative effects of integration? The answers to these questions are discussed in this last section.

The regional disparities within the EC

The Community's regional disparities are expressed in many forms: population density, age structure, participation rates, production and income level; or we can consider employment balance, migration balance, economic structure, the consumption pattern, unemployment, and so forth (see Chapters 17 and 18). All these indicators, except for the employment balance, emphasise one aspect of regional disparity, but are not necessarily an indicator of an unequal welfare system.

If we are analysing the regional disparities in welfare, two aspects are very important. The first concerns the production and/or income level; the second concerns the labour market. For the latter, the employment balance — at present and in the medium term — expresses the job opportunities in a particular region. In principle, an employment balance should combine all aspects of the labour market: population of working age, participation rates, migration, unemployment, and the demand for labour.

Unfortunately the necessary data are not available to prepare employment balances for all regions of the Community. So the Commission applied a 'second best' indicator. In fact, in the Commission's Third Periodic Report (1987) on the social and economic situation and the development of the regions, four variables were employed to calculate the synthetic index of the intensity of regional problems in the Community. For each item the weights attached are:

- GDP per head (in Purchasing Power Parities) : 25 per cent
- GDP per person employed in ECU : 25 per cent
- unemployment adjusted for underemployment : 40 per cent
- prospective labour force change until 1990 : 10 per cent

From this it follows that the two criteria of a region's economic strength and its labour market are given equal weight.

The extreme values of the synthetic index vary from:

- Basilicata (Italy)   :   36.9
- Calabria (Italy)   :   38.0
- Andalusia (Spain)   :   38.8
- Extremadura (Spain)   :   39.2
- Canary Islands (Spain)   :   46.1
- Ireland   :   47.6
  ⋮
- EC   : 100.0
  ⋮
- Stuttgart (Germany)   : 160.5
- Oberbayern (Germany)   : 165.7
- Darmstadt (Germany)   : 171.8

The regions that have the highest problem intensity as measured by the synthetic index are:

- Greece
- Ireland
- the Mezzogiorno in Italy (except the Abruzzi)
- Portugal
- Spain
- Northern Ireland

It is clear that many of these are peripheral regions within the European Community.

A common characteristic of all problem regions is the low labour productivity. This is a central theme of the Third Periodic Report (1987):

> In order to reduce this competitive disadvantage, which is also impeding regional convergence, it is necessary both to increase labour productivity and to ensure that wage determination is flexible enough to adapt to regional economic differences, as the Commission has already emphasised in its Annual Economic Report 1986–87. In order to strengthen competitiveness and economic development through a higher level of productivity, not only is there a need for a sufficient level of infrastructure directly linked to economic activity, but also a higher level of capital equipment in firms. For the lagging regions to be sufficiently attractive to investors, the profitability of investment there must be at least as high as in regions in a more favourable position. Appropriate

regional differentiation in wage rises would permanently enhance the prospects of achieving the sort of production, employment and real wage trends necessary to promote convergence. Given the relatively long periods required to make tangible progress towards convergence through increased productivity, and in view of the obstacles presented by above-average unit labour costs in problem regions, this dual approach is an essential precondition for a successful regional policy. These considerations are also of relevance to achieving the single internal market and dealing with its regional impact.[1]

The regional disparities within the Community are very high and much higher than in the United States. We refer to an interesting contribution by G. Clausse, J. Girard and J.M. Rion (1986).[2] The Theil-index, a very good measure of regional disparities, amounts to 1.14 in the EC (54 regions) and 0.32 for the USA.

Regional policy issues in the EC

Regional policy issues can be viewed from a national and from a European Community perspective. The national issues, which also apply to the Community as a whole, can be divided into their economic, social, environmental and political aspects. The social arguments prevailed in the 1950s. The full employment argument, regional income distribution and welfare considerations were often used to justify an intervention in favour of a number of regions. It was in the late 1950s and the beginning of the 1960s that economic motives for a regional economic policy dominated the debate. These issues can be summarised thus:

- the full use of all factors of production
- the economic growth argument
- the optimum location of firms
- the cost of congestion
- the impact on inflation of regional disparities

The environmental issue was put forward in the 1970s. Locational preferences of households tend to encourage dispersion by maintaining a higher level of population in lagging regions than would be expected on the basis of income differentials. Locational preferences of firms, on the other hand, tend to encourage and perpetuate concentration and agglomerations.

Finally there are the important political issues. These are not only a matter of the self-interest of a government or a political party, or of the cohesion of the state: they are above all human and moral issues.

Besides the motives at the national level, there are a number of specifically EC issues. The first is to be found in the Treaty: the need for 'a continuous and balanced expansion'. Continuous expansion has been achieved; balanced expansion has been lacking. The Thomson Report (Commission, 1973) indicated this target as a human and moral requirement of the first importance. It emphasised that no Community can survive while some of its citizens have much poorer standards of living and have cause to doubt the shared will to help each member state to better the conditions of its people.

The EC summit meeting of December 1988 in Luxembourg agreed to bring regional policy within the scope of the Single European Act. In Title V of this act, 'Economic and Social Cohesion', a number of articles are significant, in particular:

Article 130A
In order to promote its overall harmonious development, the Community shall develop and pursue its actions leading to the strengthening of its economic and social cohesion.

In particular the Community shall aim at reducing disparities between the various regions and the backwardness of the least-favoured regions.

Article 130B
Member States shall conduct their economic policies, and shall coordinate them, in such a way as, in addition, to attain the objectives of Article 130A. The implementation of the common policies and of the internal market shall take into account the objectives of Article 130A and of Article 130C and shall contribute to their achievement. The Community shall support the achievement of these objectives by the action it takes through the structural funds (Guidance Section of the European Agricultural Guidance and Guarantee Fund [EAGGF], European Social Fund [ESF], European Regional

Development Fund [ERDF]), the European Investment Bank and the other existing financial instruments.

Article 130C
The ERDF is intended to help redress the principal regional imbalances in the Community through participating in the development and structural adjustment of regions whose development is lagging and in the conversion of declining industrial regions.

The strengthening of the Community's economic and social cohesion and, in particular, the reduction of the gaps between the different regions and the economic improvement of the least favoured regions, are cardinal provisions of the Single European Act.

The risk of member states bidding up the incentives to industry is a second argument in favour of intervention. Free competition is a leading principle of integration. The Commission has to promote the coordination and consistency of regional incentives.

Since the creation of the EC, regional policies have remained largely in national hands. In each member state, the national incentive systems have been extended for two reasons: first, with the elimination of tariffs and export subsidies, governments increasingly have applied measures of regional assistance; secondly, with greater incentives, these measures have become instruments of competition among national firms and also a means of attracting foreign investments.

A third argument is to be found in the relationship between regional disparities and inflationary pressure in the member states. Therefore a weakening of the disparities is a precondition for the realisation of an internal market and monetary and economic union.

The governing idea of the Treaty of Rome is that there should be a single internal market: an area organised according to the principles of a market economy, with free movement of factors of production and the abolition of discrimination in the interest of free competition. Competition policy and the aim of a single internal market form the general infrastructure for all economic, social and political considerations. In his address to the European Parliament, H. von der Groeben, a former member of the Commission, stressed that competition is not a target in itself and that competition regulations are not sufficient to solve all problems. It is necessary to have a common economic and monetary policy. He went even further in suggesting that good regulation of competition and coordination of general economic and monetary policy are not sufficient to guarantee the development of the common market. The structural differences in the individual member states are not only detrimental to the inhabitants and to the general economy, but such inequalities are a danger to the development of the common market. The unequal evolution of costs and prices is due not only to differences in economic policy. Unequal inflationary pressures are also the result of structural disparities. It is necessary to eliminate regional and structural differences before a common economic policy can be achieved. Regional economic policy is a precondition for the achievement of a monetary and economic union, and a number of other common policies could be realised more easily and much faster if they were sufficiently linked to a regional policy programme.

A further motive for a regional economic policy at the EC level is to be found in the unequal impact of the integration process in the different regions of the Community. 'To meet the impact of the integration process' was a new aim for a Community regional policy. In the early 1980s, it became a major argument. The regional policy guidelines laid down in the Council resolution of 6 February 1979 and reiterated in a Commission communication, *New Regional Policy Guidelines and Priorities* of July 1981, emphasised the need to knit together regional policy and other Community policies by making regional impact assessments of Community policies. By systematically assessing the regional impact of its major policies, the Community is pursuing two objectives: (a) to ensure that when other Community policies are framed and implemented, greater account is taken of their regional dimensions, and (b) when necessary, to prepare specific Community measures to mitigate any harmful effects that other policies may have on the regions.

The regional impact of the integration process

The last-mentioned motive brings us to the question: What is the regional impact of the integration process? A fuller analysis of the possible impact of the integration process is contained in *Regional Policy: A European Approach* (Vanhove and Klaassen, 1987).[3]

In the late 1950s and the beginning of the 1960s certain analysts and politicians expressed their anxiety about the impact of economic integration on the disadvantaged regions within the Community. The ideas of these prominent figures led to one conclusion: there was in the EC a general feeling that integration would alter Europe's regional economic map. There were five underlying factors for this:

1. Increased competition would be harmful to firms with relatively low competitive power, especially in the peripheral regions.
2. Integration would necessitate the reconversion of a number of one-sided regions that rely too heavily on stagnating activities.
3. The influence of external economies on the location of new firms would increase the attractiveness of the existing industrial centre. In other words, an intensification of agglomerative tendencies could be expected.
4. The geo-economic position of certain regions on both sides of a border would change — a phenomenon that, as we shall see, need not be detrimental to the regions concerned.
5. The evolution of agricultural structures.

A more detailed theoretical analysis of the spatial impact of a customs union (on existing activities and on the location of new activities), and of monetary union, reinforces the belief that it would be negative. In 'The All-Saints' Day Manifesto for European Monetary Union' (1979) nine prominent European economists recognised that the tendency for labour and capital to move from the peripheral regions to the central developed regions may be accentuated by a monetary union. They attribute this to the fact that wages in the peripheral low productivity areas may be increased to the level of those in the high productivity areas, while differences in productivity remain unchanged:

> Consequently, unit labour costs in the peripheral areas may become so high that firms which previously were viable may

no longer be able to pay their way and the prospect of a satisfactory return on new investment may disappear. Should that happen, capital would tend to move to the high productivity areas and thereby attract labour to move from the peripheral to the central areas. In Europe regional diversity is highly, and in our view rightly, valued. We consider, therefore, that monetary union should not be permitted to encourage the movement of labour and capital to the central developed areas at the expense of the peripheral and less developed regions. For this reason we look upon a vigorous regional policy as an integral part of monetary unification in the European Community. We regard it as essential that such a policy should concentrate on eliminating the causes of regional imbalance by raising productivity levels in the poorer areas and that income transfers to alleviate the consequences of low productivity should be used as an interim measure only.[4]

However, it would be incorrect to deny any positive effect of integration on less developed regions. For one thing, it makes for more economic growth (economies of scale), a *conditio sine qua non* for a successful regional policy. In a period of full employment, the availability of labour becomes one of the most important location factors. For another, integration improves the geo-economic position. Moreover, certain specialisation effects can be expected because of the reallocation of outputs. Specialisation effects stem from differences in natural factor endowments; land and climate may be important in this respect.

The cohesion of the EC and the structural funds

Article 130D of the Single European Act is the basis for the reform of the structural funds. These funds are the main instrument for solving the economic problems of many poorer regions and the EC peripheral regions in particular. Article 130D calls for reform of the structural funds, particularly through regulating the tasks and effectiveness of the funds and by coordinating their activities with the operations of the European Investment Bank and the other financial instruments.

The reform took definite shape with the Council Regulation (EC) No 2052/88 of 24 June 1988 on the tasks of structural funds.

This comprehensive regulation was followed by four implementing regulations, published in December 1988. These concern the coordination of the activities of the different structural funds: the ERDF, the ESF and the EAGGF Guidance Section. The reforms have been in operation since 1 January 1989.

What are the key concepts underlying the reform of the structural funds?

1. Concentrating the activities of the Funds on specific objectives:

- Objective 1 : Promoting the development and structural adjustment of the regions whose development is lagging behind.
- Objective 2 : Converting the regions, frontier regions or parts of regions seriously affected by industrial decline.
- Objective 3 : Combating long-term unemployment.
- Objective 4 : Facilitating the occupational integration of young people.
- Objective 5a: Speeding up the adjustment of agricultural structures.
- Objective 5b: Promoting the development of rural areas.

The structural funds: the EAGGF Guidance Section, the ESF and the ERDF, shall contribute, each according to the specific provisions governing its operations, to the attainment of objectives 1 to 5 on the basis of the breakdown given below:

- Objective 1 : ERDF, ESF, EAGGF Guidance Section
- Objective 2 : ERDF, ESF
- Objective 3 : ESF
- Objective 4 : ESF
- Objective 5a: EAGGF Guidance Section
- Objective 5b: EAGGF Guidance Section, ESF, ERDF

Meanwhile, the regions affected by objectives 1, 2 and 5b have been specified. The regions concerned by objective 1 are:

- France: French overseas departments, Corsica
- Greece: the entire country
- Ireland: the entire country
- Italy: Abruzzi, Apulia, Basilicata, Calabria, Campania, Molise, Sardinia, Sicily

- Portugal: the entire country
- Spain: Andalusia, Asturias, Canary Islands, Castilla y Léon, Castilla-La Mancha, Ceuta-Melilla, Extremadura, Galicia, Murcia, Valencia
- United Kingdom: Northern Ireland.

2. Complementarity

The Commission takes the view that, in accordance with the subsidiarity principle, one major feature of Community action through the structural instruments must be that it should seek to complement national measures. It should be a response to suggestions put forward by the member states, backed up by appropriate analysis and evidence. In the light of the Community's set priorities and the limited budgetary resources it can mobilise, the Commission must be able to consult closely with the member states to arrive at a division of tasks between the Community and the national governments.

3. Partnership

Partnership is the key principle underlying the reform of the structural funds since it determines the implementation of the other principles. The framework regulation defines it as 'close consultation between the Commission, the member states concerned and the competent authorities designated by the latter at national, regional, local or other level, with each party acting as a partner in pursuit of a common goal.' According to the same regulation, partnership also covers 'the preparation, financing, monitoring and assessment of operations.'

Partnership reflects the principle of subsidiarity. In accordance with that principle, the Commission believes that its structural action should seek to complement measures in the field.

Practical applications of partnership are:

(i)   preparation of the plans for which maximum consultation is required

(ii) negotiation of the Community support frameworks

(iii) implementation of the operational programmes at a highly decentralised level and the award of global grants

(iv) the monitoring and assessment of the adopted measures.

4. Programming

Programming should make it possible to give Community action the necessary depth and width, while at the same time allowing greater flexibility. Community operations spread over a number of years, with joint action by the structural funds, the European Investment Bank and the other financial instruments, will be better able to respond to changing economic and social realities. From management's point of view, the recourse to programming and the gradual disappearance of Community assistance to small projects will make it possible to take a coherent medium-term view of the operations to be mounted in pursuit of each priority objective, and to establish a framework for the coordination of these operations.

5. Geographical and functional concentration

There are demanding eligibility criteria for Community structural action. These are sometimes geographical (objectives 1, 2 and 5b) and sometimes functional (objectives 3, 4, and 5a).

The regions selected for objective 1 represent 21.5 per cent of the EC's population; for objective 2 the corresponding percentage amounts to 15 per cent and for objective 5b it amounts to 5.1 per cent. Although geographical concentration is a key characteristic of the reform, the regions selected for objectives 1, 2 and 5b represent a high proportion, 41.6 per cent, of the EC's population. However, 80 per cent of the appropriations are devoted to objective 1 regions.

6. Adequate financial resources

The resources allocated to the structural funds will be doubled in real terms up to 1993, increasing from approximately 7 billion ECU to 14 billion ECU (at 1988 prices). The regions covered by objective 1 should benefit significantly from this increase in resources through the operation of the three structural funds.

The reform of the structural funds and the resources available can be a real support for the peripheral regions. According to calculations of J. Van Ginderachter (1989), the appropriations of the structural funds for 1992 would represent 3.6 per cent of GNP in Portugal, 2.7 per cent in Ireland and 2.6 per cent in Greece.[5]

Conclusion

The internal market will affect the Community's peripheral regions. However, its realisation is not possible without convergence. Convergence is necessary if cohesion is to be attained. In this respect, two aspects need to be properly differentiated:

- nominal convergence, which is concerned with improved control over monetary developments and nominal incomes and with moves to secure and maintain price stability in public finance and the balance of payments
- real convergence between regions and member states, which involves bringing living standards and the generation of income more closely into line at the highest possible level while evening out disparities in unemployment at the lowest possible level.

Nominal convergence is a necessary, but not a sufficient, condition for real convergence. It is necessary in order to ensure that growth is not impaired by macroeconomic imbalances. The improvement in the conditions necessary for growth in income and employment in the problem regions, without which a greater measure of real convergence will prove elusive, is conditional on the existence of a sound macroeconomic environment.

Notes

1. Commission of the European Communities, *Third Periodic Report from the Commission on the Social and Economic Situation and Development of the Regions of the Community,* Brussels, 1987, p. 28.
2. G. Clausse, J. Girard and J.M. Rion, 'Evolution des disparités régionales dans la Communauté', 1970-82, EIB Papers, September 1986, p. 21.
3. See also W. Molle and R. Cappellin, 'Regional Impact of Community Policies in Europe', Aldershot, 1988.
4. 'The All-Saints' Day Manifesto for European Monetary Union', *The Economist,* 1-7 November 1975.
5. J. Van Ginderachter, 'La réforme des Fonds Structurels', *Revue du Marché Commun,* May 1989, p. 272.

3

Economic Theory and the Single Market

ANTHONY FOLEY and MICHAEL MULREANY

Many branches of economic theory contribute to an understanding of how the Single Market will affect Ireland. Since Ireland is a peripheral and relatively disadvantaged region of the Community, core-periphery and regional development theories are valuable in examining the impact of the Single Market. These aspects are discussed in Chapters 17 and 18. Because the Single Market is intended to stimulate growth, the theory of economic growth is discussed in Chapter 4. The present chapter deals with three matters: international trade theory, the theory of economic integration, and industrial development under outward-looking strategies. The chapter's purpose is to provide readers with the main elements of these three branches of economic theory so as to better understand and interpret the Single Market process and its impact on the Irish economy.[1]

International trade theory explains why trade takes place and identifies which products will be imported and which will be exported. Several elements in the theory concern us here: absolute and comparative advantage, as developed by Smith and Ricardo; the factor endowments approach of the Heckscher-Ohlin theory, and the theories dealing with trade between countries with similar factor endowments and involving broadly similar products. We also illustrate the effect of removing barriers to trade (Figure 3.1).

The theory of economic integration examines the impact of different degrees of integration between economies. The range of possible integration goes from complete self-sufficiency, or autarky, to full economic integration — with the participating economies operating as a single economy, as do regions within an economy at present. The assessment of economic integration is strongly based on the findings of trade theory. Increasingly, however, it has involved recourse to other aspects of economic theory, such as core-periphery relations and a greater emphasis on dynamic factors.

Outward-looking strategies link industrialisation and trade liberalisation. They relate in particular to the impact of free (or freer) trade on the development prospects of economies that are attempting to reach advanced country levels of economic development. Given Ireland's relatively underdeveloped economic and industrial position within the EC (see, for example, Chapters 1 and 10), the theory dealing with the effect of trade liberalisation, and criticisms of this theory, are important in understanding Ireland's position and potential.

International trade theory

The effects of removing cost increasing barriers are illustrated in Figure 3.1.

S_i and D_i respectively represent home country supply and demand curves. The price in the rest of the customs union is P_r'. The barrier to exporting encountered by the rest of the customs union is represented by t, which is equal to $(P_r-P_r')/P_r'$. In other words, t represents a 'mark-up which consumers or importers in the home country face due to the extra costs imposed by the barriers' (Cawley and Davenport, 1988). P_r therefore represents the import supply curve (or the rest of the customs union export supply curve).

With free trade, the home country imports $Q_1'Q_2'$ and domestic suppliers produce $0Q_1'$. Quantity demanded by domestic consumers is $0Q_2'$. Because of the barrier, which pushes prices up to $0P_r$, imports are reduced to Q_1Q_2 and consumption declines to $0Q_2$. However, there is a positive production effect on the home country, with domestic supply increasing to $0Q_1$. It can be seen,

Figure 3.1: **Effects of removing cost increasing barriers**

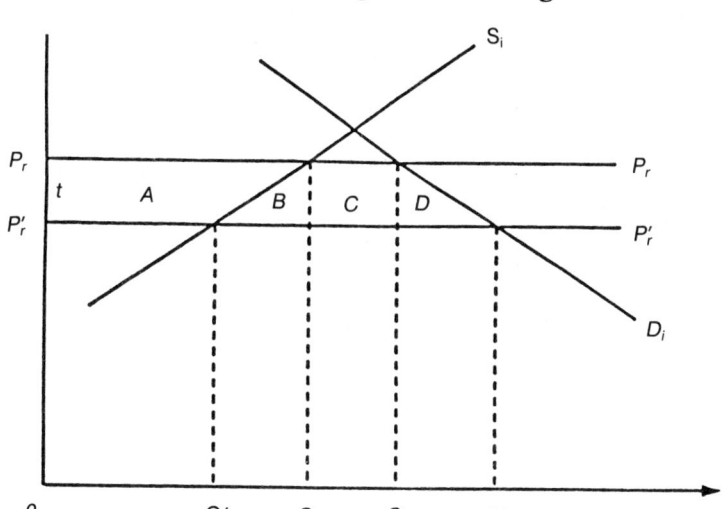

Source: Diagram reproduced from Cawley and Davenport (1988)

therefore, that the barrier has a trade or import effect, a production effect and a consumption effect. Where the barrier is a tariff, there would also be a government revenue effect of t multiplied by Q_1Q_2. This is represented by area C in the diagram.

When the non-tariff barrier is removed, price drops to P_r' and consumer surplus increases by areas (A+B+C+D). Producer surplus declines by A. The net welfare or surplus gain is therefore area (B+C+D). If the barrier had been a tariff, the net gain would be area (B+D), due to the revenue loss, which is area C.

We now turn to the determinants of trade.

Adam Smith argued that two countries could gain from trade if each had an absolute advantage in the manufacture of a product. If country I was more efficient in the manufacture of product A and country II was more efficient in the manufacture of product B, economic welfare would be improved by country I specialising in the manufacture of product A and country II specialising in the manufacture of product B. Each country would satisfy its needs for the other product through international trade.

Although much trade is based on absolute differences in efficiency, this is not a very profound explanation of trade (Sodersten, 1985). The theory of comparative advantage shows that trade can be beneficial even where one country is more efficient in the manufacture of all products. It rests on the principle of opportunity cost. To illustrate his argument, Ricardo used the case of England and Portugal producing wine and cloth. In his model, Portugal was assumed to be more efficient (measured in labour hours) in the production of both wine and cloth. However, England's relative inefficiency was not the same for both products. The efficiency (or productivity) gap was less in cloth than in wine. Gains could arise through Portugal concentrating on the manufacture of the product in which its productivity gap over England was greatest, and through England manufacturing the product in which its productivity gap over Portugal was least. Thus, while Portugal had an absolute advantage in both products, it had a comparative advantage in only one (i.e. its absolute advantage was relatively greatest). England had an absolute disadvantage in both products but a comparative advantage in one (i.e. its absolute disadvantage was relatively lowest). The gains arose because Portugal could use its factors of production in the sector where they were most efficient. The gains from this compensated for the 'sourcing' of the other product from the less efficient trading partner.

The original comparative advantage principle was based on one factor of production, labour. Trade arose because of different labour productivities between countries. The Heckscher-Ohlin trade model extended this analysis into two factors of production, capital and labour. This model argues that trade arises because countries have different resource endowments. The principle of comparative advantage still applies, but it is expressed in terms of factor abundance and factor intensity of production. The model uses two countries, two products and two factors of production to show that gains can arise from trade.

In the model, one product is described as labour intensive, i.e. relatively more labour than capital is used in its manufacture. The second product uses more capital and hence is described as capital intensive. The model assumes that the resource endowments, or quantities of capital and labour, are different for each country. Consequently, one country is described as labour abundant and the other as capital abundant. The model broadly predicts that the labour abundant country will export the product that is labour intensive in its production technique and will import the capital intensive product. The capital abundant country will export the capital intensive product and will import the labour intensive product.

As with the Ricardian model, the gains in the Heckscher-Ohlin model arise because of comparative advantage. Absolute advantage is not necessary. Even if one country can manufacture both products more efficiently, it will concentrate on producing the one in which it has a comparative advantage, which, in turn, is based on resource or factor endowments.

International trade results in specialisation in each country. Resources are expected to flow to the sector(s) or products in which the comparative advantage lies. Resources will leave the sector(s) whose products are imported. If specialisation is complete, each country will make only the product(s) in which it has a comparative advantage and will import the others. This is the fundamental gain from, and objective of, free trade — i.e. that resources flow to the area of greatest efficiency, thereby enabling total output to increase.

However, if the situation was as clear-cut and unambiguous as the basic trade models say that it is, there would be relatively little objection to free trade and the removal of protection. Why then is the movement to free (or freer) trade so slow and, indeed, why has it taken the EC so long to tackle purposefully the barriers to trade within the Community?

Before attempting to answer this question, it is necessary to identify another implication of the trade models; namely that competitiveness seems not to be an issue. If specialisation occurs in the two-country model, each country will *either* import *or* export a product, but will not both import *and* export the product. Each country (but not firms within each country) would be a monopoly or sole supplier of a product. Therefore, competition from suppliers in other countries does not arise. The competitive position of each country effectively is embodied in its production pattern, which, in turn, is determined by comparative advantage. In other words, a country's competitive capacity is reflected in the internal resource allocation. It does not manufacture those goods where it would have competitive difficulties.

Krugman (1987, p. 18) argues as follows:

> ... the first misconception is that integration is only beneficial
> to a country if that country is able to achieve productivity
> comparable to that of its trading partners. That is, the popular
> concern is that a country will be hurt by enlarged trade
> if it is too inefficient to be 'competitive'. What the concept
> of comparative advantage makes clear is that absolute
> productivity advantage in some areas is not necessary for
> a country to gain from integration. Even a country that is
> less productive than its trading partners across the board can
> gain by specializing in those sectors in which its productivity
> disadvantage is smallest. 'Competitiveness' is not a long-run,
> microeconomic issue. To the extent that international
> competitiveness is a legitimate concern, it is a short-run
> macroeconomic issue ....

This argument suggests that the principle of comparative
advantage and opportunity cost always will enable an 'inefficient'
producer to 'find something' to produce. Of course, there would
be income consequences as productivity declined. This is the
relatively benign conclusion from the trade models. They
effectively suggest that the principle of comparative advantage
ensures that there will be no long-term losers, whatever about
short-term adjustment problems.

The trade models assume perfect factor mobility internally
and immobility of factors externally. The first assumption does
away with any geographic, skill or other barrier to the flow
of resources from the sector that had produced the goods that
now are imported to the export production sector. In the long
term, barriers to mobility will be eliminated as new resources
flow to the export product, and thus the comparative advantage
predictions eventually will apply. However, the longer the long
term, the less attractive are the gains from trade. Furthermore,
the greater the barriers to factor mobility, the higher will be
the costs of adjustment to free trade in, for example, increased
unemployment of factors hitherto employed in the manufacture
of the imported product. It must be recognised also that
comparative advantage can change, so that adjustment to new
patterns of production would be a continuing process rather than

a once-off adjustment. This should not be seen as an argument against free trade and for protection, because there are welfare gains from trade based on comparative advantage. Rather, it should help focus on the need to promote and facilitate flexibility and mobility of factors of production in response to, and ideally, concurrent with, changes in the international division of labour. However, the economic, social and political difficulties of achieving this flexibility should not be underestimated.

A more fundamental problem arises if factors are mobile internationally. As the EC moves towards a Single Market where factors of production are mobile between the member states, part of the Irish adjustment to the freer trade environment might be through emigration and capital outflows. Even without the Single Market measures that facilitate labour mobility, Irish labour is already very mobile internationally, and high levels of emigration have been a feature of Ireland's economy throughout most of its modern history.

The greater the degree of integration between economies, the less relevant is the assumption on international factor immobility, which is part of the comparative advantage model and on which some of its conclusions depend.

A country may wish to change its comparative advantage. For example, many developing countries have a comparative advantage in agricultural products. Trade theory indicates that these countries should concentrate on such products. However, for various reasons — productivity potential, income levels, fluctuations of income, and output and demand prospects — developing countries generally try to develop their manufacturing sectors and to reduce their trade dependence on agriculture. The link between trade policy and industrial development will be discussed later in the chapter.

Trade theory informs us of the gains from trade and the pattern of trade, but it tells us little about the determinants of relative export performance. If the trade models are extended from the two-country assumption into a many-country assumption, then, for the comparative advantage principle to hold true, an extended comparative advantage chain is needed, whereby each country specialises in certain products that no other country exports. If, however, some countries have the same broad pattern of resource endowments, they will be competing producers of the same product or range of products. For example, if exports from the Far Eastern newly industrialising economies are based on broad Heckscher-Ohlin factor endowments principles, what determines the relative export performance of these countries? It may be changes in the factors of production or changes in competitiveness.

Baldwin (1986, p. 13) makes the point that 'modern international economics is quite weak in explaining how the structure of trade changes over time', and that our knowledge of what determines the growth of factor supplies, such as physical and human capital, entrepreneurial vigour and technological knowledge — which in turn influence trade patterns, is very weak.

EC trade with the developing world is reasonably consistent with the Heckscher-Ohlin factor endowments model. The Community exports capital- and human-capital-intensive products and imports agricultural products and labour-intensive, low-skill manufactured products. The relative trade performance of individual EC economies is not explained by the theory.

The trade models do not explain that many countries may be engaged in the manufacture of a particular product or range of products and that trade performance (as indicated by growth and market share) differs between countries. They explain what will be exported and imported, but not the export performance of individual countries. The latter is probably the more important issue. It is of less interest to know the determinants of the commodity composition of the EC's and Japan's trade than to know the determinants of their relative export performance.

Nonetheless, despite these caveats, the comparative advantage principle remains important as a basis for understanding the gains from trade and the potential benefits that can arise from freer trade; it is also useful for explaining part of world trade. So far we have concentrated on trade based on comparative advantage and factor endowments, which involve a country in either importing or exporting a product, but not both. Such trade commonly is described as inter-industry. However, there are certain features of world and EC trade for which comparative advantage is not an adequate explanation (see Williamson, 1983).

Much intra-Community trade and world trade occurs between economies with broadly similar resource endowments — West

Germany, France, Italy and the UK. Consequently, this trade cannot be due to different comparative advantages based on different resource endowments. There is substantial 'intra-industry' trade. This is a two-way trade in similar products. For example, West Germany imports and exports cars. This would not be predicted by the comparative advantage theory, where a product would not be both imported and exported by the same country.

In addition, the new approaches to trade recognise that economies of scale are a significant feature of industrial activity and play an important role in explaining trade, that markets are generally oligopolistic and do not approach the perfectly competitive assumption of the trade models discussed above, that product differentiation is an important feature of international trade, and that technological competition and innovation are significant determinants of trade (Helpman and Krugman, 1985).

The new theories of trade that draw together these issues are less deterministic in their predictions than the Ricardo and Heckscher-Ohlin models. Factors such as technology, oligopoly and economies of scale introduce a degree of uncertainty about the effects of trade liberalisation. They also raise the possibility that losses may arise because of trade, and that gains may be unevenly distributed. They indicate that difficulties will be faced by economies that are attempting to develop an industrial base in free trade conditions. These models also reintroduce the notion of competitiveness in determining export performance. Technological capacity, scale of enterprise, marketing efficiency, cost factors and management capacity all have a role to play in determining export performance. These concepts are not compatible with the perfect competition, identical production functions and constant returns assumptions of the early trade models. In addition, intra-industry trade implies competition between firms producing close substitutes. One can say about the new trade theories that they are more relevant, more in tune with actual trade patterns and with business and economic life, but less precise in their predictions.

Baldwin (1986, p. 12) has commented:

In some ways trade models with imperfect competition are even more deficient in their dynamic implications than the

Heckscher & Ohlin model. In models where differentiated products are introduced, for example, the question of which country produces a particular variety of a product is indeterminate.

These new theories of trade incorporate many of the economic features in which peripheral economies, including Ireland, are weak. As NESC (1989, p. 348) noted:

> ... the new theory of trade takes account of those features of the modern economy — increasing returns, external economies, the advantages of experience, monopoly power and the barriers to entry created by high capital and R&D requirements — which were originally used to explain regional inequality and divergence.

It can readily be seen that the new trade theories suggest a somewhat more pessimistic view of the effect of freer trade than the traditional comparative advantage model. We must remember, however, that the Irish economy is not moving from autarky to free trade, but from a relatively high degree of free trade to a greater degree of free trade. Consequently, many of the adverse implications of trade based on imperfect competition and increasing returns to scale are already a feature of industrial life.

Nevertheless, it must be noted that the more important are economies of scale, the greater is the need for a small economy to have access to international markets. Export markets allow firms in small economies to escape the constraint of a small domestic market. In fact, it may be the only way for small economy firms to reach minimum efficient scale. If economies of scale are significant, then small economies need international trade more than do their larger counterparts.

The terminology of 'comparative advantage' can be reconciled with the new theories of trade, albeit on a relatively broad level. Large economies will have a comparative advantage in the manufacture of products with substantial scale economies. Industrially advanced economies will have a comparative advantage in technology-intensive products. Ireland, given its market size and industrial competence, does not have a comparative advantage in such products. However, the objective of industrial policy is to raise Ireland's industrial capacity to the same standard as advanced countries. The section on outward-looking policies (below) examines this issue. Krugman (1987) argued that trade which is based on economies of scale 'probably involves less conflict of interest within countries and more conflict of interest between countries'. If trade is based on Heckscher-Ohlin principles, trade liberalisation will change the distribution of income between capital and labour — in favour of the abundant factor and against the scarce factor. On the other hand, trade based on scale economies — intra-industry trade — takes place between economies with similar factor endowments, and the theory concludes, in this case, that trade liberalisation will not greatly affect income distribution between the two factors. Hence, it is argued, there will be less conflict within countries.

The possibility of increased conflict between countries arises from the desire of countries to capture as large a share as possible of the rent that can be earned by factors of production '... because of imperfect and oligopolistic market structures and the role of technology' (Krugman, 1986). In addition, 'some sectors [high technology sectors] have strategic importance relative to other sectors in that substantial external economies may be generated' (Foley, 1989). Consequently, countries may have a preference in terms of specialisation between sectors. Economies that gain a disproportionately high share of high return (rent-generating) industries are in a more advantageous position than economies that do not. The conflict between countries arises because of their attempts to acquire 'a larger share of world rent for the domestic economy' (Foley, 1989).

In the early trade models, which assumed perfect competition, rent would not be earned and perfect competition would equate returns to factors of production. In such a situation, countries would be less concerned about the pattern of specialisation.

Theory of economic integration

The seven different degrees of economic integration between countries are outlined in Figure 3.2. At point A there is complete non-integration or self-sufficiency (autarky). The other extreme is point G, which is full or complete economic integration (see Viner, 1953 and Balassa, 1961).

When there is complete economic integration, the participating countries operate economically as regions of the now larger
economy and not as separate national economies.

It will be recognised from the above that the EC is already
at an advanced stage of integration. The economic integration
theory tends to focus, at least in textbook presentations, on the
customs union stage of integration. The individual stages, especially

Figure 3.2: **Stages of economic integration**

A	B	C	D
Autarky Complete self-sufficiency	*Trade occurs* but tariffs and other restrictions are imposed on products	*Free trade area* Participating economies eliminate tariffs and quotas on imports from each other, but maintain their own restrictions on non-participants	*Customs union* As with C, plus the agreement on a common tariff against non-participants

E	F	G
Common market As with D, plus the free movement of factors of production	*Economic and monetary union* As with E, plus monetary integration and harmonisation of national policies	*Economic integration* Unification of national economic policies and a single supra-national economic authority

the last three, tend to merge and overlap in the EC. For example,
agriculture has a common EC policy, a common structure and
EC administrative authority and has gone well beyond stages
D and E. In the EC there is a degree of coordination and supranational authority with regard to grants and assistance to industry,
which again takes the EC beyond stage E. On the other hand,
there is not yet complete mobility of factors and right of
establishment, which are expected to be features of stage E.
Thus, some sectors and policies have gone beyond the common
market stage, while in other respects the EC has not yet reached
the common market stage of integration.

It is worth noting that Ireland has already experienced a

degree of economic integration which surpasses that of many of its EC partners. In effect, Ireland has long had a common labour market with the UK; up to 1979, Ireland had a fixed exchange rate with the UK; there is a substantial degree of harmonisation of technical standards (i.e. Ireland adopting UK standards) and there is relatively widespread recognition of qualifications between Ireland and the UK. These features of integration are in addition to free trade, which was initiated by the Anglo-Irish Free Trade Agreement in the 1960s. High degrees of economic integration are not new to the Irish economy.

The Single Market programme aims to complete the common market stage for the EC and to move to a greater extent towards stage F. The technical, administrative and fiscal barriers that the Single Market is aiming to remove have not been accorded a central role in economic theories of trade and in economic integration. The primary emphasis has been on the removal of tariff and quota barriers. This is understandable since a high degree of political and administrative integration is required to remove the non-tariff barriers. A logical first step in the integration and free trade process is the removal of quotas and tariffs. Indeed, trade liberalisation theorists suggest that quotas be removed first, and that this be followed by a phased reduction in tariffs (Balassa, 1971).

In addition, it is possible that the economics literature has underestimated the costs of technical and other non-tariff barriers in terms of their impact on economic welfare.

A customs union or a common market embodies both free trade and protection elements. The members of the customs union remove quotas and tariffs in order to institute free trade between them. However, the customs union maintains a common external tariff against the rest of the world and therefore has protectionist measures. This explains why the Single Market, and indeed the EC, is seen as a move towards freer trade for Ireland and why, to the rest of the world, the EC might be regarded as a protectionist grouping. These features give rise to the concepts of trade creation and trade diversion.

Trade creation refers to the situation whereby, because of the customs union, the sourcing of a product switches from a high cost to a lower cost producer. For example, a member economy might have manufactured a product because it was protected by a tariff. Removal of the tariff would result in a more efficient member country supplying the product since it does not now have to compete with the tariff-protected domestic industry. The resources saved by the importing country can be transferred to more productive uses.

Trade diversion refers to the situation when 'imports from a more efficiently producing country are switched to a less efficiently producing country because of the customs union' (Sodersten, 1985). This will arise where country A imports from country C. Country C can deal with A's tariff because of C's relative efficiency. Country B, which is less efficient than C, forms a customs union with A. Hence, B has tariff-free access to A's market. Country C has to cope with the common external tariff that A and B impose on the rest of the world. This could allow B to displace C in country A, even though C is a more efficient producer. Trade has been diverted from country C to country B, a less efficient producer, because of the customs union.

The imposition of a common external tariff, therefore, can lead one member of a customs union to import products from a relatively high-cost fellow member, rather than from a formerly cheaper supplier now outside the customs union. This diversion of trade is a misallocation of resources. The freeing of trade within a customs union, therefore, need not lead to increased welfare.

Economic integration theory argues that competitive economies would gain more than complementary economies from forming a customs union. Competitive economies produce similar goods and have similar factor-resource endowments. Complementary economies produce different products — for example, an agricultural economy and an industrial economy.

Assume that we have two economies, one completely specialised in industrial production and the other specialised in agricultural production. Before the customs union, each country will have to import those goods that it requires but does not produce. When a customs union is formed, the resource allocation situation remains unchanged, although tariffs are removed. Of course, there may be trade creation or trade diversion if the industrial country had sourced its agricultural requirements from a country other than the one with which it had formed the customs union. The same would apply with the agricultural economy. If each country had imposed a uniform, non-discriminatory tariff before the customs union, there would be either trade diversion or no change in the source of supply. If discriminatory tariffs had been applied before the customs union, there is the possibility of trade creation.

If similar economies, two industrial economies for instance, form a customs union, there is greater scope for gains, because production is reallocated on the basis of efficiency. In this case, the customs union provides greater scope for a better allocation of resources. Economic integration gives rise to both static and dynamic effects. These are broadly equivalent to the direct and indirect effects defined in Single Market analyses. The mechanisms of the direct and indirect effects of economic integration are discussed in Chapters 4 and 10. We briefly shall outline the concepts here.

The static impact of the customs union is the effect on economic welfare of the removal of tariffs, assuming that other things hold constant. Dynamic effects, on the other hand, include the realisation of hitherto unrealised economies of scale, increased competition as markets are opened up, restructuring of industry in the context of the larger market and increased efficiency and innovation induced by the greater degree of competition. Dynamic gains from the Single Market are expected to be more important than static gains for the manufacturing sector (see Chapter 10).

These impacts have been seen as the 'stick and carrot' effects of international trade (Balassa and Giersch, 1986). The stick relates to the improved efficiency that the increased competition of international trade is expected to bring; the carrot refers to the opportunities of larger markets and economies of scale.

The effects of a customs union in economic theory are analysed primarily in the context of tariff reductions. As Chapter 1 noted, the EC has largely eliminated tariffs between member states. The Single Market programme is concerned with the removal of a large variety of non-tariff barriers or, as Emerson et al (1988) described them, cost-increasing barriers. The removal of these barriers is broadly similar to the effects of tariff removal. However, there is a difference when compared with the traditional theory of customs unions in its effect and on non-EC countries, described here as the rest of the world. One of the effects of the Single Market will be a unilateral reduction in trade barriers against the rest of the world. Consequently, instead of the integration process increasing protectionist tendencies, it reduces them against the rest of the world, without any corresponding reciprocal reduction. This comment assumes that technical regulations for the EC are not defined in such a way as to increase access costs for the rest of the world.

If the Single Market programme is implemented, barrier-free movement of goods and services will be possible between member states. The case of Japan exporting to the EC will illustrate the point. At present, a Japanese firm exporting to several or all EC economies bears the costs of barriers in entering the European Community. In addition, it then bears the costs of barriers in moving goods between the member states and/ or the costs of satisfying different national technical regulations. The Single Market is intended to eliminate these intra-EC costs. The cost of exporting to the Community is therefore reduced, provided that the rest-of-the-world exporter sells in more than one EC economy or crosses more than one EC frontier. There will be an absolute reduction in the cost of exporting to the EC without any reciprocal arrangement on the part of the rest of the world.

The effect is analogous in tariff terms to the following situation. There is a common external tariff against the rest of the world. Each member of the trade grouping also imposes additional tariffs on imports from both member states and from the rest of the world. These national tariffs do not discriminate between members of the customs union and the rest of the world. If the national tariffs are removed and the common external tariff is maintained, both the members of the trade grouping and the rest of the world benefit from the removal. The rest of the world, however, maintains its tariff levels against exports of the members of the trade grouping.

The removal of barriers may create trade diversion if EC producers alone get the benefit. Consequently, trade will be diverted from rest-of-the-world suppliers to EC producers (Neven, 1990, p. 19). However, as was argued above, rest-of-the-world suppliers are likely to benefit to some extent from the reduction in intra-EC barriers to trade.

The stages of economic integration outlined in Figure 3.2

above have come in for criticism. Pelkmans (1982 and 1984) argued that the role of government in modern economies is extensive, and many of these interventions create distortions and affect the competitive environment in each country. The traditional stages of economic integration, he argued, give very little role to the government sector and, hence, are not relevant for analysing integration in mixed economies.

Allied to this criticism is the distinction between negative and positive measures for integration (Pinder, 1968). It is argued that the traditional models of integration concentrate on the removal of barriers, i.e. negative integration measures. Even with the removal of trade barriers and obstacles to factor mobility, the extensive range of government interventions will ensure that competitive conditions are not equalised and that competitive distortions will exist between producers in different member states. The contention is that the remedy for this problem lies in measures of positive integration, such as harmonisation of government intervention and the creation of common policies. In other words, positive action must be taken to ensure that competitive conditions are equalised between members of the customs union or the integrated group of economies.

It is certainly the case, as the need for the Single Market programme shows, that the removal of trade restrictions and factor mobility restrictions on their own will not create a common market with broadly equalised competitive environments. The experience of the EC is testimony to this. On the other hand, trade integration theory has identified many forms of protection, ranging from quotas and tariffs to government subsidies, and the later stages of integration identify the need for a harmonisation of policies. Nevertheless, it has not focused extensively on the policy and institutional requirements for removing these forms of protection. The important contribution of Pelkmans and Pinder highlights the need for active measures to create a 'real' common market, rather than simply to remove the more obvious barriers. The Single Market programme is a major attempt to move in this direction, although full harmonisation of competitive conditions influenced by government would require complete economic integration.

However, even if economic integration occurred on the supply-side, there would not be a 'Single Market' in the full economic sense. Substantial differences on the demand-side, such as incomes and tastes, will remain between regions within the EC. In addition, even on the supply-side, substantial differences in external economies, such as concentrations of resources and expertise, will remain.

Outward-looking strategies

Outward-looking theories and strategies deal with the relationship between trade and industrial development; specifically, they examine the impact of trade liberalisation on development prospects. By and large the strategies focus on developing countries and deal with the transition from protection to free trade by means of the removal of tariffs and quotas. The Single Market is a level of integration that goes well beyond the removal of tariffs and quotas. It is also the case that Ireland is formally defined in international classifications as an industrialised economy. Despite this, a knowledge of the theories concerning outward-oriented development is helpful in understanding the Single Market's impact. There are three main reasons for this. The Single Market is a movement from a certain degree of protection to a situation of freer trade. In essence, therefore, it deals with the same issues as outward-looking theories. The underlying economic and trade theories and mechanisms are the same in both the Single Market process and the outward-looking theories. Finally, Ireland's level of indigenous industrial development differentiates it markedly from most of the industrialised economies. In effect Ireland is still trying to develop a solid, indigenous industrial base and is a late starter in the industrialisation process. The analysis that follows depends heavily on the theories of international trade that were outlined above.

Ireland began to introduce 'conventional' (see O'Malley, 1982) outward policies in the 1950s. This involved a phased movement to free trade, the attraction of direct foreign investment and a reliance on free market forces, aided by tax concessions, grants and other assistance, to develop indigenous manufacturing. The Irish economy had what McAleese (1975) calls a 'textbook progression' from inward to outward policies. McAleese also noted that, if outward policies were to succeed anywhere, they should have succeeded in Ireland.

There are two conflicting views about the effectiveness of the Irish outward strategy. One, pointing to the rapid growth and diversification of industrial structure and exports, which are usual performance indicators in such assessments, regards Ireland as another example of success. The second view maintains that the strategy has failed because of what is perceived to be the weak structure and export performance of indigenous manufacturing and the strong dependence on direct foreign investment for manufactured exports, manufacturing employment and the economy's presence in modern industries (see Chapter 10).

We shall now review the economic literature on outward-looking policies and the associated economic literature in the context of their predictions on industrial develoment and performance.

In the literature there are many definitions of what constitutes an outward strategy. McAleese (1975) referred to a set of policies aimed at export promotion and free trade. The World Bank (1987) defined 'outward' as being characterised by neutrality between incentives for domestic market production and exports. Balassa (1971) broadly agreed with this, but also noted that, given the costs and uncertainties of entering foreign markets, it might be desirable temporarily to provide additional incentives to the export of manufactured goods.

Approaches that do not include adherence to free trade have also been subsumed under the 'outward-looking' heading. Some developing countries have countered the bias against exports while still temporarily retaining protection. This approach is also consistent with the conventional outward policy prescriptions. In citing such countries as departures from the recommended commercial policies, critics of the outward approach have not taken account of the detailed transition recommendations which are an inherent part of outward policies. Michaely (1986, p. 52), for example, noted that 'the introduction of export subsidies, given the existence of import barriers, is considered part of a liberalisation policy' and that this could precede the first stage of import liberalisation. The implementation and phasing of outward policies are considered by their proponents to be complex. There is also general agreement that outward-looking policies should be carried out in stages. Keesing's (1979) first stage in the process focuses on export promotion. An extensive export promotion programme, aided by devaluation and government incentives, would be initiated, with no change in the protection of domestically produced importables. In Keesing's analysis, this first phase would be lengthy. His approach appears to be different from what are usually understood to be the main tenets of an outward-looking policy.

Balassa (1971a, p. 90) commented that 'policy formulation [in the implementation of outward-oriented policies] for individual countries would have to depend greatly on the particular circumstances of the situation'. In his view, factors to be taken into consideration include the existing industrial structure, the availability of human and physical capital, and the size of domestic markets. Balassa argued that there is a 'need for a spectrum of policies applicable to countries of different sizes with varying emphasis on import substitution and exports'.

It is clear from the literature on outward-looking policies that the movement to free trade is intended to occur over relatively long periods. The phasing is dependent on the specific circumstances of the particular economy, but the transition from inward to outward policies should not be hasty.

Outward-looking policies are expected to increase the competitiveness of exports and potential exports, encourage investment in export activities, and reallocate resources along comparative advantage principles. It is not expected that such measures automatically would generate manufactured exports, regardless of a country's stage of economic development. As Balassa (1987) noted, a country may export primary products and, thereafter, as skills and productive capacity increase, move on to low-skill manufactures. Outward policies do not allow a country to avoid the gradual raising of economic competence. Rather, they are expected to facilitate and accelerate this. A country must have a potential comparative advantage in a particular sector before outward-policies will enable this potential to be realised.

There are some cases, however, where the removal of protection could reduce exports. Krugman (1984) referred to the case where protection can assist exports — his 'protection as export promotion' argument. The basis of this argument is that producing more is good for the domestic firm, through marginal cost being inversely related to output and through a learning-by-doing effect. Having the domestic market allows a firm to operate at lower average costs; it can then compete more effectively with foreign suppliers on the export market. Opening up the domestic market to foreign competition would reduce the firm's level of output and adversely affect costs and competitiveness. Implicit in this argument, however, is the expectation that the firm is efficient and that the protected domestic market does not lead to a departure from market criteria. The argument is similar to aspects of the barriers-to-entry view, discussed below. Both require that there is efficient development of industry behind the protective barriers.

As will be noted in Chapter 10, protected firms might operate price discrimination between the domestic and export markets. Higher domestic prices could subsidise lower export prices. In such a case, movement to free trade and world prices in the domestic market could cause a reduction in exports because of its effect on firms' viability and profitability.

This 'growth-generated' export model — export performance comes after the economy has grown and developed to some minimum competence level — is argued by Ustunel (1972) and Maizels (1976) among others. Ustunel argues that a domestic (indigenous) engine of growth would have to be established to enable the exploitation of trade opportunities.

This view is not necessarily inconsistent with what might be regarded as the mainstream outward-looking approach, but it does introduce a cautionary note about the scale and speed of the positive impact on exports of outward policies. In fact, the growth-generated view is consistent with the learning effect requirement and with the argument that the type of exports will change (in terms of improvements in quality and technology) as economic development proceeds and income levels rise.

Indeed, one could accept the main elements of the two approaches. Where they do diverge, however, is on the emphasis given to the implicit time-scale involved in attaining 'good' industrial export performance. The growth-generated export approach implies the expectation of a relatively long period of time to establish an export capacity. The outward-looking approach, while it refers to comparative advantage and evolving economic skills and capacities, does not place much emphasis on, or even give attention to, the period needed to raise export capacity. Nevertheless, it does suggest that the movement to complete free trade would be relatively prolonged.

It must be emphasised, however, that outward-looking advocates do not expect a 'great leap forward' that is independent of basic economic comparative advantage. Rather, it is the case that these economic capacities (i.e. changing comparative advantage) are expected to evolve in a world prices regime primarily through market forces as economic development proceeds.

The 'conventional' outward approach encourages foreign investment as an aid to development. It is not very clear from the literature on outward-looking approaches what precise role is intended for foreign investment. Even in those countries that are taken as successful examples of outward approaches, the role of foreign investment varies greatly. A situation of almost exclusive reliance on foreign investment for industrial exports appears to be consistent with outward strategy expectations, as would a situation of a limited role for foreign investment. Domestic entrepreneurs may be incapable of mobilising the economy's resources or may be lacking in technical or managerial skills which can be provided by foreign investment.

Advocates of outward policies have identified the same type of dynamic (or indirect) factors as in economic integration theory referred to earlier in this chapter, which arise with outward policies (or which, at least, are absent under protection). It is argued that, because of the lack of competition, protected firms would have little incentive to reduce x-inefficiency and would not engage in product improvement and technical change (Vollrath (1985), Balassa (1971) and Michelapoulos and Jay (1973)). With outward policies and increased competition, one expects greater managerial enthusiasm for technical change. Even those who are not regarded as strict adherents of the orthodox outward approach acknowledge the role of competitive pressures, induced by exposure to the world economy, in stimulating technical innovation and a dynamic learning process.

An economy's supply capacity as a factor in determining export performance is emphasised by a number of studies.

Kennedy and Dowling (1975) commented that the establishment of an efficient economy, i.e. adequate infrastructure, education and technical and entrepreneurial skills is a prerequisite for a successful export performance. A minimum level of economic competence and resources is necessary for export performance. Kennedy and Dowling noted that the 'learning effect' of supplying the domestic market is important in developing entrepreneurial abilities, which then can facilitate export development.

The broad thrust of the outward approach is a reliance on market forces. It is always difficult to categorise degrees of intervention. The outward approach does not place exclusive reliance on market forces, but proposes incentives and aids to manufacturing. An extensive development effort — improving marketing competence, management and quality control — generally are included in outward-inspired development strategies for individual economies. The government's role in basic education, infrastructure and general industrial promotion is accepted. Government is expected to provide and promote a desirable business environment. However, outward-looking strategies do not recommend specific intervention by government at the firm or sectoral level.

Even within this broad analysis, there are exceptions. Keesing (1967), while generally following the outward-looking approach, pointed to the need for more extensive and specific intervention by government to develop an export capacity. Despite this, it is reasonable to characterise the outward-looking approach as relying primarily on market forces.

In summary, then, exports are expected to grow through the removal of the various disincentives that protection imposes and, as the level of industrial development proceeds, exports would become more skill- and technology-intensive, compared with initial labour-intensive, low-skill exports or primary commodities as dictated by comparative advantage. Technological change would be stimulated by the 'carrot and the stick' of foreign competition. Differences of emphasis arise about the significance of the learning period or period of evolution. In no such case, however, is it suggested that movement from low-skill or primary exports to 'higher order' exports can escape the constraints imposed by domestic supply conditions. In addition, the benefits of direct foreign investment are acknowledged and the market mechanism is deemed to be the most effective method of resource allocation.

The criticisms of the outward-looking approach, which are based on the structural difficulties facing newly industrialising or late industrialising countries, can be divided in two. It has been argued (O'Malley, 1982) that outward free market approaches will result only in easy-to-enter industries and low-skill, labour-intensive exports. This is because entry into more technologically advanced industries and exports is inhibited by barriers to entry such as economies of scale, technology, marketing and finance (see O'Malley (1982), Devine (1979), Telesis (1982) and Porter (1980)) which free market forces will not overcome. Consequently, industrial development will not proceed to the industrial activities of the advanced countries. Industrial development and export performance is limited, on this argument, to easy-to-enter industries. This view is of direct relevance for Ireland's prospects in the more integrated Single Market. It is of interest to note that economies of scale are, at one and the same time, a barrier to export development and a gain from trade.

However, as Dreze (1989) has argued

In relation to the producers of large countries, those of small countries suffer an absolute disadvantage in those sectors characterized by economies of scale, since they have to overcome the inherent imperfections of the international market in order to attain a profit-earning level of production. But the less imperfect the international market is, the less significant are these disadvantages; this is particularly the case when there exist fewer qualitiative differentiations between the demand of different countries. Hence lesser absolute disadvantages may be regarded as comparative advantages. Thus *small industrial countries enjoy comparative advantages in those sectors where international demand is standardised, whenever economies of scale are present.*

Alternatively, it is argued that, in those cases where the upward trend is observed — for instance South Korea — it is because of a significant departure from the general policy stance of the outward strategy, such as active intervention by government at sector and firm level, sometimes allied with protection. The continuation of protection is consistent with outward-looking policy proposals, but the reliance on selective and specific intervention would be a departure from the orthodox proposals.

The common thread running through both lines of argument is that adequate domestic technical and entrepreneurial skills are needed for industrial development and export performance. The barriers-to-entry view is that outward strategies will not be capable of breaching some minimum barrier. The outward-looking view acknowledges that higher quality exports require improvements in factors of production, but expects that this will be forthcoming as industrial development proceeds, or at least does not point to any structural constraint.

It is unlikely that even a staunch advocate of conventional outward policies would deny the existence of barriers to entry as a feature of industrial markets. Their role is illustrated by a casual observation of the existence of imperfect competition. The question then is whether barriers to entry constitute a continuous spectrum ranging from 'easy to enter' (i.e. free entry) to 'impossible to enter' (i.e. perfect barriers), with an infinite, or at least extensive, range of products in between with varying degrees of entry difficulty. If such is the case, then the gradual raising of domestic productive capacity (including management, technology and labour skills) will lead, step by step, to the ability to enter these industries.

Of course, this does not imply that outward strategies, even if successful, would be expected to result in a capacity to enter all industries. The size of the economy will influence industrial structure and partly determine which industries are appropriate. Consequently, the role of barriers to entry must be viewed in the light of the technically efficient range of choices open to an economy.

If there is a significant break in the entry conditions, where some industries (within what might be called the feasible range) are defined as easy to enter, but others are difficult (or almost impossible) to enter, then unless a specific firm or industrial structure exists, one can see how a limit to outward strategies could arise. This would imply that there is a discontinuity in the chain of industrial skills and activities.

An additional feature of the debate is the expectation of the development strategy. Entry barriers and comparative advantage will change continuously. As supply factors improve in developing countries, they will establish a comparative advantage in some manufactures hitherto held by the advanced countries. Equally, as technology advances and becomes more demanding, the advanced countries' comparative advantage will shift to these more 'difficult' activities. Thus, even though the developing countries' capacity to export will grow beyond the basic primary products or low-technology manufactures, it will still fall below the advanced country capacity, with consequent effects on the income gap.

Under this slightly different view of barriers to entry, export performance can improve and go beyond low-skill products, but the gap with richer countries will remain. The more extreme argument suggests that barriers to entry will prevent, under outward policies, evolution beyond easy-to-enter export markets. It is argued that market forces would not overcome these barriers. Consequently, governments should intervene to overcome them through selective and efficient intervention.

The above barriers can be divided into two separate, but often interrelated, issues. First, there are the barriers that inhibit the development of the efficient production of exportables, such as technical and scale economies. Secondly, there are the barriers that prevent successful exporting, even if efficient production is possible, for example marketing competence. Thus, even if scale economies and technology are sufficient to facilitate efficient domestic production, barriers to exporting may still exist.

It is important to emphasise again, however, that an outward-looking strategy envisages the gradual raising of entrepreneurial and technical competence to levels that permit the production and export of more and more difficult products. In the terminology of the outward approach, we are referring to different comparative advantages. A country with a weak research and development capacity or with low technology levels would not have a comparative advantage in the production of science-based products. Equally, a country with relatively high wage costs would not have a comparative advantage in the production of low-skill, labour-intensive products.

Nonetheless, despite the capacity of the outward theory to absorb the terminology of barriers to entry within its own paradigm, it appears to be reasonable to argue that the non-price factors have not commanded a central place in the analysis. There are probably two main reasons for this. First, there is the general tendency in economic analysis to focus on price factors, with only an acknowledgement of and passing reference to non-price factors. Secondly, the significant disincentives to and bias against exports was the most important issue to be corrected in most of the countries analysed in the course of developing the theory. Appropriate incentives would act as a necessary condition for all else to follow. Inappropriate incentives would ensure that economic activities would not be attempted.

One can distinguish between *market* criteria and *market-generated* (or *created*) criteria. Market criteria relate to the requirement that production should be efficient, that firms should be self-financing and competitive and should not require subsidies or sheltering. Market-generated or market-created refers to market forces generating or creating new economic activities. One can readily accept market criteria without believing that market forces automatically will generate the necessary economic activities. The two concepts are often confused. However, there is much evidence that market criteria are often not applied to economic activities that are not market-generated. This, of course, need not be so. Consequently, it is sometimes the case that proponents of market generation are primarily advocates of market criteria but they do not believe that one can have the latter without the former.

While orthodox outward-policy proponents advocate an equal incentives approach to the development of industry, they do allow for the possibility of special treatment to particular industries. It is argued that exceptions should be made only for well-established reasons, such as industries providing above-average external economies and technologically advanced industries (Balassa et al., 1982, p. 68). In Balassa's view, however, insufficient knowledge exists about the additional benefits that particular industries generate. Consequently, he argued that market principles and competition would produce better results than priorities decided upon by governments. It is apparent that outward-policy proponents are concerned that a detailed interventionist approach by government would not be pursued in an economically efficient manner, i.e. that special assistance and protection would not be soundly justified. Venables and

Smith's (1987, p. 658) view that 'any advocate of an interventionist policy must evaluate that policy in the light of how it will actually be applied rather than how it ought to be applied' is relevant here.

On the efficiency of a selective or targeted strategy, the World Bank (1987) noted that significant mistakes are made in promoting what turn out to be 'wrong' sectors. (At times winners are also missed.) This is not a conclusive criticism because market forces themselves do not guarantee that all investments will be profitable. The essence of market forces in the outward strategies is that some economic activities will decline and some will grow. Of course, what matters is the number of failures relative to the successes. The existence of failures, per se, is hardly surprising. It is also argued that the role of the Japanese Ministry of International Trade and Industry has declined since the 1960s and that South Korean import protection is less important now than in the 1960s. This feature, however, is fully consistent with the 'barriers to entry' and 'selective intervention' view. The purpose of selective intervention is to establish competitive firms and industries. When barriers to entry are overcome, and such firms and industries are established, the need for detailed selective intervention is ended or at least is much reduced. Ongoing restructuring and adjustment to competitive change would be based on a firm's own capacity and resources, with a much reduced role for intervention. Consequently, a reduction in such measures could be evidence of their earlier success and not disenchantment with their effectiveness.

The World Bank commented that (in some East Asian economies) 'the government's role as a coordinator and information clearinghouse was important'. It also argued that it included desirable features, such as time limits and maintenance of competition, and was carried out by 'strong and capable' governments. The worry is that developing countries that follow such a general policy prescription would not be so efficient.

In recent years there has been an increased interest in strategic trade and industrial policy in the larger developed industrial economies (Krugman, 1986a). The increased role of imperfect competition, economies of scale, learning curves, and technology in determining trade has prompted this interest. Krugman argued that 'the changing character of trade away from trade based on simple comparative advantage and towards trade based on a more complex set of factors has required a reconsideration of traditional arguments against trade policy'. As was noted above, the justification for intervention derives from the above-average returns available from certain sectors of industry and from external economies.

Despite the recognition of the rationale for intervention, Krugman was concerned with the feasibility of efficient intervention and argued that the identification of strategic sectors is not something that can be done with confidence. Balassa et al (1982) made much the same point about external economies.

The intervention that is suggested for the developed countries, while being selective and drawing inspiration from Japan's industrial policy experience, appears to fall short of the detailed intervention proposed by the barriers-to-entry view in the economic development literature. Nonetheless, the broad rationale is the same, in that market forces are not expected to produce an optimal allocation of resources.

Kennedy and Dowling (1975), without going so far as to suggest intervention on a detailed sectoral and firm basis, implied that reliance on the price mechanism alone to realise comparative advantage would be insufficient. They commented that 'even where a country has a price advantage in a particular product, exports will not take place automatically without a measure of entrepreneurial and marketing effort' (p. 112).

It can also be argued that orthodox trade theory, on which much of the outward-strategy theory depends, with its concentration on competitive markets and homogeneous products, ignores the significance of barriers to entry arising from the need to market products. With perfectly competitive markets, the only relevant marketing variable is price. Price and adequate quality are not sufficient to guarantee sales when markets are not perfectly competitive. Product differentiation and after-sales service are also significant. This relates back to the Kennedy and Dowling view that a price advantage will not generate exports automatically.

Outward-looking polices are generally proposed as one, if not the most, important of the elements of a broader liberalisation process, including the capital and labour markets. Krueger (1986, p. 27) commented that there is no instance 'where a country's trade liberalisation has been highly successful in the context of highly restrictive and enforced regulations surrounding the labour market'. Keesing (1988, p. 4) made the same point about the four East Asian newly industrialising countries: 'all four have given a major impetus to manufactured exports by creating or maintaining highly competitive labour markets with only weak unions and little job security'. Consequently, labour and wage conditions are an important factor influencing, inter alia, export performance under outward strategies. This is an important caveat about the potential of conventional outward polices.

The implementation of an outward strategy is seen by its proponents as a complex process which should be put into effect on a phased basis. The view that there is a single rigid 'conventional' outward approach is incorrect. The ultimate objective, of course, is always free trade. We have noted Balassa's argument that the particular implementation strategy and phasing will be different in each country and will depend on many economic factors.

Movement to free trade is just one part of a liberalisation process. A liberalised labour market is particularly important. One possibility in Ireland's initial response to outward polices is that costs, in particular, high labour costs, were mismatched with technological capacity, particularly because of the high degree of labour mobility between Ireland and the industrialised UK.

Even within the broad parameters of the outward approach, the pre-free trade competitive capacity of industry will be an important determinant of the success of outward policies. If the infant industry stage of development was inefficient and firms were far from a mature stage of performance, one would expect a poor export performance. This broadly appears to have been the case in Ireland. Consequently, time-lags before an efficient export activity is attained would be long because a substantial reorientation would be needed within existing firms or as a new generation of firms developed. This would occur even if outward approaches were the appropriate path, but it begs the question of how an economy ensures an efficient development of industry under a protective commercial policy.

The outward approach also would produce poor short-term results in manufactured exports if the bulk of existing industry was in the 'non-traded' sectors, where exports are expected to be relatively insignificant. This would occur even if such industries were as efficient as producers in other countries.

There are also other issues, the level of taxation for instance, that would affect economic activity. For much of the recent past (and also currently) taxation has been at levels that many economists consider adversely affect economic activity (Balassa and Giersch, 1986). Of course, whether this would specifically affect export activity is another question.

The outward-looking theory accepts a substantial role for government in providing an appropriate business environment. In particular, the provision of skills and training, in which there are substantial social benefits, are considered to be important.

As was indicated in the examination of the literature, the outward approach is presented as an industrial development strategy. It is not expected that an economy can escape the constraints of its technical, entrepreneurial and other productive resources. It does not assume that a great leap forward is possible, regardless of economic constraints. It is presented as a superior industrial development strategy.

Overall, the outward approach is a more complex and conditional set of policies than critics sometimes present. It also does not indicate the likely time-scale for the realisation of substantial gains. Nonetheless, despite the often forgotten complexities of implementing an outward approach, there are powerful intellectual arguments against some of its tenets. Some criticisms, in fact, are criticisms of what are assumed to be the features of an outward policy, rather than the actual features of such policies. In this context, we could include the advocacy of protection continuing for some period as liberalisation proceeds. We also could include the role of selective intervention where, and if, one can definitely identify significant external economies arising from specific sectors.

Despite this, however, it is reasonable to argue that the broad orientation of the outward approach reflects a belief in free market forces working with comparative advantage to push the economy towards a better economic and export performance. Krugman (1986) summed it up with the comment that the proposition that markets work so well that they cannot be improved upon has become untenable. The existence of economies of scale, the role of technology in determining trade flows, and the prevalence of product differentiation, imperfect competition and oligopoly are weighty intellectual arguments in the view that a more important role ought to be given to selective intervention in helping a newly industrialising economy to catch up. It is clear that entry to many higher order activities is not easy.

These factors, of course, are not new to the outward approach, but it is not thought that they pose specific or structural impediments to the industrial and export development process. They may be there, but they will be overcome. The view that selling on the domestic market is not the same as exporting is another strong caveat to the expectation that export performance will readily be forthcoming. Once again, however, the outward approach acknowledges that entry to world markets is a difficult process. It does not suggest that it is a fundamental or structural obstacle. The alternative view is that it does present major difficulties: the cost of selling and risks, marketing competence, and, possibly, the minimum efficient size of companies.

It is clear that there are substantial points of agreement between outward advocates and the barriers-to-entry critics. These include the need to promote exports, the ultimate desirability of free trade, the necessity for international competitiveness, the desirability of economic activities based on market criteria (if not based on market generation), the necessity for substantial government intervention (if not the degree and type of intervention) and that export performance must be related to basic economic resources and skills.

The substantial point of difference arises in the general acceptance of market forces as the best allocator of resources on the part of the outward approach. Critics argue that the production of exportables or exporting will not be developed substantially in the absence of specific sector and firm-level intervention. The distinction is not black and white. Some outward advocates recommend more extensive intervention than others; certain interventionists recommend less than others. Even the acceptance of the theoretical case for intervention can leave one short of supporting the implementation of the policy, unless there is relative certainty about the target sectors or firms.

The primary lesson from Ireland's experience is that Ireland's implementation of outward policies has not produced, after three decades, a strong indigenous manufacturing employment, output and export capacity. While it is true that the economy's export performance has been very good, this is due primarily to direct foreign investment (see Chapter 10). Part of the explanation for this poor performance is broadly consistent with the conventional outward approach.

The conventional outward view is that the structure and efficiency of industry will have a strong influence on the realisation of export gains. If the import substitution phase had been inefficient, with inappropriate industries and uncompetitive firms, the conventional view predicts weak performance. Substantial restructuring of firms or, in more extreme cases, a new generation of firms would be required. This new generation of strong indigenous exporters has not yet emerged. It would imply a substantial decline in the existing manufacturing base and a relatively long time-lag before the realisation of export gains. Obviously the more efficient and in tune with world market forces protected industry is, the greater and more rapid will be the gains from outward policies. By most accounts, indigenous industry in the 1950s and early 1960s was substantially non-competitive by world standards (CIO, 1965).

An interesting point in this context is how to ensure efficient industry under a policy of protection. By definition, a policy of protection suspends the impact of world market criteria. Industries can then develop, protected from world market criteria. This is broadly expected to be the case in the conventional approach. A tougher, more interventionist approach by government to protected industry could substitute for the absent world market criteria. By this is meant an identification of world efficiency levels and an assessment of progress to these levels by protected industries. Unsatisfactory progress would result in the removal of protection or the promotion of alternative firms. In this way the operation of market criteria, which is an essential part of the conventional view and which is suspended behind protection, can be brought to bear. In this context, the view that markets know better than governments no longer holds true. Thus the argument is that specific intervention is necessary in order to allow the conventional transition to outward policies to bear fruit.

The general view, however, is that protected industries are

inefficient (or are allowed to be inefficient) and that they do not provide much hope for export success. This seems to have been the case in Ireland.

Krueger's argument about labour markets is a most important caveat to the outward approach. One is not talking about marginal gains or losses in competitiveness between similar countries. The issue here is that very cheap labour provides a competitive advantage in exporting simple labour-intensive manufactures (e.g. from South Korea and Taiwan), subject to the availability of minimum technology and other industrial skills. This base can enable companies to grow and develop export capacities and progress gradually to more skill-intensive products. In other words, efficient companies with export capacities are established in relatively low-entry-barrier industries based on the availability of cheap labour. This appears to be the textbook progression expected under outward policies.

This path was less likely for Ireland. While Ireland's industrial competence was significantly lower than its major trading partner (UK) in the late 1950s and early 1960s, Irish wage levels were much closer to UK levels by virtue of, inter alia, the common labour market between the two countries. This would have led to the situation that Irish wage costs were too high to sustain efficient entry to labour-intensive manufactures and to develop strong companies, which would then evolve into more skill-intensive products. Irish industry would have been unable to avail of this experience. Entry to other industries where labour costs were less crucial as a determinant of success would have been difficult, given the technological and managerial limitations in Irish industry. Consequently, even without the selective intervention argument, Ireland would not have followed the South Korean experience. In this scenario, much of Irish industry would have been vulnerable and without basic competitive strengths in either low labour costs or high technological competence. This raises questions about the appropriateness of the 'simple' outward prescriptions for what might be called middle-cost economies such as Spain and Ireland, compared to low-cost developing economies. We should note, however, that Balassa argued that the outward strategy should take account of the economy's specific circumstances.

While the basic business environment in terms of grants and

fiscal framework has been favourable over the outward-looking period, some 'environmental' questions could have been operated more efficiently. These include adapting the education system to the needs of industry and to support industry.

The period from the mid 1970s to 1987 was dominated by concern about public sector borrowing and national debt. This did little to establish an environment of business confidence. Other elements of the Irish approach, e.g. maintenance of the inward period exchange rate until the late 1970s, also suggests a poor response within the predictions of the conventional outward approach. It is hard to see that improvements in these areas would have fundamentally transformed indigenous export capacity, given its weakness. It is reasonable to argue, however, that improvements in some of these areas would have contributed to a somewhat better performance.

It could also be argued, in the terminology of the conventional outward approach, that Ireland's comparative advantage probably lay with attracting direct foreign investment and with it the technology, marketing and management skills which were deficient in the indigenous manufacturing sector.

All this contributes to an understanding of why a strong indigenous sector has not emerged (or that it will only emerge after a very long time, if it is to emerge at all). It does not show how to achieve a more accelerated development of the indigenous sector. A feature of the Irish approach was the failure until recently to think in detail about the micro level requirements for indigenous exports such as adequate firm size or technology capacity, aspects which are not central parts of the outward literature. Indigenous exports did not prosper but this tended to be ignored because of the rapid growth of exports from foreign firms for the first two decades of outward policies. To paraphrase Balassa, it seems that insufficient attention was devoted in Ireland to the specific features of indigenous industry in implementing its outward strategy.

Conclusion

The theory of international trade is primarily concerned with the reasons why trade takes place, the gains made from trade, and which goods are imported and which are exported. The theory of comparative advantage shows that a country can gain from trade even if it is inefficient in the production of all goods. International trade and the specialisation which accompanies it allow factors of production to be allocated to their most efficient use. However, the pattern of specialisation induced by trade may not be desirable to an economy in that it may have consequences for income and growth prospects. For example, within the EC, Spain, Portugal and Greece would have a comparative advantage in the production of labour-intensive products because of their relatively low labour costs. Countries such as Germany and France have higher labour costs and relatively greater concentrations of human capital, advanced industrial skills and technology capacity. Equally, Ireland probably has a comparative advantage in low-level food processing and the attraction of direct foreign investment. The objective of government policy, however, is to raise industrial competence above labour-intensive production (with its relatively low productivity and income), above a dependence on direct foreign investment (with its limited potential for promoting economic development), and above limited food processing into higher value-added production. Consequently a reallocation along static comparative advantage principles is not an end in itself.

The more fundamental question for late industrialising countries such as Ireland, Spain, Portugal and Greece is whether or not the effort of raising industrial competence beyond existing capacities is helped or hindered by free or freer trade. In other words, how will an economy perform under outward-oriented policies. It is certainly the case that Ireland has not yet developed, after three decades of outward policies, an industrial capacity comparable in quality to the industrialised economies. There is the possibility that barriers to entry and structural difficulties will prevent this happening. If so, then the trade liberalisation accompanying the Single Market will not help. On the other hand, Ireland is now in a stronger position, in certain respects, to perform better under outward policies than in the past. Industrial policy is more focused on structural barriers. The remaining elements of indigenous industry are stronger than the indigenous industry of the 1960s. There is a better match between labour costs and managerial capacities. The optimistic view would be, not that outward policies do not work, but that Ireland did not operate them effectively or that other important conditions were not met. Improvements in these two areas will make the economy better able to realise the potential of free trade. However, it must be recognised that, even on this 'optimistic' assumption, the difficulties of reaching advanced industrial competence are great. Barriers to entry are extensive. The newer theories of trade emphasise the importance of imperfect markets, scale economies and product differentiation in determining much of the trade between the advanced industrial economies. These are the factors which operate as barriers to entry for prospective new producers.

The economic integration envisaged by the Single Market includes the removal of barriers to factor mobility. Part of the adjustment process may, therefore, include factor mobility. The trade models assume international immobility of factors of production. Resources released by sectors because of trade liberalisation may emigrate instead of ultimately being absorbed by growing sectors. Ireland's long-term economic development has been characterised by the inability of growing sectors to absorb labour released from declining sectors and new entrants to the labour force.

To the extent that international labour mobility raises labour costs in underdeveloped regions and economies (by causing wages to rise to prevent emigration of scarce skilled labour), their competitiveness will be reduced. On the other hand, to the extent that labour returns are lower in underdeveloped economies than in industrialised economies, scarce skilled labour will emigrate, thereby reducing the growth capacity of the underdeveloped areas.

It should readily be seen that trade and integration theory, despite the theory of comparative advantage, provides no guarantees that individual, and especially peripheral economies, must do well from the Single Market process. Ultimately, the realisation of potential depends on basic economic capacities and competitiveness, and sound economic management.

Note

1. Parts of this chapter are adapted from, and use material from, Foley (1989) and from material prepared by Foley as part of research for a doctoral degree under the supervision of Prof. D. McAleese of Trinity College, Dublin.

4

The Single Market and the Economy of the European Community

MICHAEL MULREANY

The twelve economies of the European Community, taken as a unit, comprise one of the world's major industrial and trading blocs. The EC economy's relatively poor performance, when compared to other major industrial and trading blocs such as the United States and Japan, gave rise to concerns that were an important driving force behind the proposals for the Single Market. These proposals were drawn up in the mid-1980s when the fragmentation of the EC member states stood in contrast to a seemingly monolithic Eastern Europe. Developments in 1989 and 1990, however, altered the traditional perception, as the EC moved toward greater integration and the old structures in Eastern Europe increasingly disintegrated. The EC must deal with the transformation of Eastern European states from centrally planned to market-oriented economies and, in particular, with the consequences of German reunification.

This chapter examines the performance of the EC economy and assesses its prospects for growth in the light of the Single Market programme. The EC economy is compared with the other two major industrial and trading areas: the United States and Japan. The consequences of German reunification for the EC economy are assessed. We conclude with an evaluation of the implications for the Irish economy of developments in the EC economy.

The EC Economy

In examining the performance of the EC economy, three distinct phases become apparent:

- the period up to 1973, during which the EC economy grew unprecedentedly
- the period from 1973 to the mid-1980s, during which there was a marked deterioration in the conventional measures of macroeconomic performance — GNP growth, unemployment and inflation
- the period since the mid-1980s, during which there has been an improvement in the main macroeconomic indicators.

Table 4.1 presents the main economic indicators for the EC economy over the period 1961–90; the three phases can be seen in these data.

The early phase can indeed be traced back to the 1950s. Table 4.2 shows that, over the period 1950–73, the rate of growth in major Western European economies and Japan, and to a lesser extent in the US economy, was historically high.

This accelerated rate of growth in Western Europe has been attributed to several causes, including an abundant and cheap labour supply, the availability of inexpensive technology, and more optimistic expectations among investors. The abundant and cheap labour supply was due to the movement out of agriculture and also to the availability of labour from Eastern and Southern Europe. Cheap technology, which enabled productivity to grow, was available from the US, an economy that had opened up a 'technology gap' between itself and the relatively more backward Western European economies. The optimism in the expectations of investors has been attributed to the establishment of a new post-war international economic order and to the growing belief that demand management by governments could control the business cycle (Boltho, 1982, p. 16).

The foregoing factors operated in conjunction with others, such as the availability of cheap and secure energy supplies and the development of improved communications, to produce unprecedentedly high rates of growth.

Table 4.1: **Main economic indicators, 1961–90 (EUR 12)[1]**

	1961–73	1974–81	1982	1983	1984	1985	1986	1987	1988	1989	1990	Ireland 1988
1. Gross domestic product — at constant prices	4.8	1.9	0.8	1.6	2.3	2.5	2.8	2.8	3.8	3.4	3.1	3.7
2. Gross fixed capital formation[2]	5.6	−0.4	−2.0	0.1	1.5	2.5	3.4	4.8	8.3	6.9	4.9	−1.7
3. Share of gross fixed capital formation in GDP[3]	23.4	22.1	20.2	19.6	19.3	19.2	19.0	19.2	20.0	20.6	20.9	17.0
4. Inflation (price deflator private consumption)	4.6	12.3	10.5	8.5	7.2	5.9	3.8	3.4	3.6	4.8	4.5	2.5
5. Productivity[4]	4.5	2.0	1.7	2.3	2.2	1.9	1.8	1.6	2.2	1.8	2.0	2.6
6. Real unit labour costs												
— Index: 1961–73 = 100	100.0	104.3	103.0	101.9	100.2	99.2	98.0	97.8	96.8	96.1	95.7	90.8
— Annual percentage change	0.1	0.4	−1.1	−1.1	−1.7	−1.1	−1.2	−0.2	−1.1	−0.7	−0.5	−3.2
7. Relative unit labour costs in common, currency against 9 other OECD countries[5]												
— Index: 1961–73 = 100	100.0	108.0	97.6	92.0	85.2	85.0	93.3	100.2	98.7	94.2	93.1	98.2
— Annual percentage change	1.0	−0.2	−6.5	5.7	−7.4	−0.2	9.8	7.3	−1.5	−4.5	−1.2	−4.6
8. Employment	0.3	−0.1	−0.9	−0.7	0.1	0.6	0.8	1.2	1.6	1.5	1.1	1.0
9. Unemployment rate[6]	2.2	5.5	9.5	10.0	10.8	10.9	10.8	10.4	10.0	9.0	8.7	17.8
10. Current balance[7]	0.4	−0.3	−0.7	0.1	0.3	0.8	1.4	0.8	0.3	0.1	0.3	2.0
11. Net lending (+) or net borrowing (−) of general government[7,8]	−0.7	−3.7	−5.5	−5.3	−5.4	−5.2	−4.8	−4.3	−3.6	−2.9	−2.9	−3.7
12. Gross debt general government[7,8]	:	39.8	48.0	51.2	54.4	56.9	57.9	59.6	59.3	58.6	58.0	116.6
13. Interest payments by general government[7,8]	:	2.8	4.1	4.4	4.7	5.0	5.1	4.8	4.8	4.8	4.8	9.5
14. Money supply (end of year)[9]	11.9	13.4	11.9	10.7	9.9	10.0	10.3	11.0	10.6	:	:	6.3
15. Long-term interest rate[10]	7.1	11.7	14.3	12.7	11.8	10.9	9.2	9.4	9.4	9.9	:	9.4
16. Profitability (index: 1961–73 = 100)	100.0	69.9	64.8	67.5	71.6	74.7	78.9	80.5	84.1	86.2	87.6	:

[1]1989 and 1990 data are forecasts. [2]At constant prices. [3]At current prices. [4]GDP at constant market prices per person employed. [5]Against 19 competitors for Ireland. [6]Percent of civilian labour force 1961–73: EUR 12 excl. Greece, Spain and Portugal. [7]Percent of GDP. [8]1974–81: EUR 12 excl. Greece and Portugal. [9]Broad money supply M2 and M3 according to country (M3 from Ireland) 1961–73: EUR 12 excl. Spain and Portugal. [10]Levels.
Source: Adapted from Commission of the European Community, *European Economy* No. 42 (November 1989).

Table 4.2: **Phases of GDP growth 1913–84
(average annual compound growth rates)**

	I 1913–50	II 1950–73	III 1973–84	Acceleration from Phase I to Phase II	Slowdown from Phase II to Phase III
France	1.1	5.1	2.2	+4.0	–2.9
Germany	1.3	5.9	1.7	+4.6	–4.2
UK	1.3	3.0	1.1	+1.7	–1.9
Japan	2.2	9.4	3.8	+7.2	–5.6
USA	2.8	3.7	2.3	+0.9	–1.4

Source: Adapted from A. Maddison (1987)

Of course, the factors just outlined are not exhaustive. Olson (1982), for example, argued that World War II had destroyed, in the defeated nations, old economic structures made rigid by regulatory complexities which repressed economic growth. According to this argument, the emergence of new economic structures that were more conducive to growth helps explain the post-war economic miracles in Germany, Italy and Japan.

Table 4.2 shows that there was a slowdown in growth in major Western European economies in the period 1973–84. Growth also slowed down in the US and in Japan, but the average growth rates in these two countries over the period exceeded those in the Western European economies. In general, the slow growth in major EC economies was accompanied by increasing unemployment, high inflation and a growth in public deficits.

There has been much theorising about the causes of economic slowdown. Beenstock (1983), for example, adopted a global perspective and attributed the general weakening of western economies to large transfers of capital to developing countries where rates of return were higher. However, in what follows a more narrowly European perspective is adopted.

The deterioration in Western Europe's economic fortunes between 1973 and 1984 is attributable to a number of factors. Following Lawrence and Schultze (1988), we can divide the causes into four categories. First, there was a changed structure of growth. In contrast to the preceding period, labour supply conditions were tightened as the movement out of agriculture slowed down; there was a more expensive and insecure system of oil supply; and there was a closing of the US-European technology gap, which meant that Western European economies had to move from the adoption of existing technology to the more difficult process of innovation. There were many other problems, too, including poor demand in traditional growth sectors of the economy, such as steel, ships and cars, and competition from Japan and from the newly industrialising Asian countries. The foregoing developments required that Europe's labour and capital markets be flexible, which they were not. On the contrary, there was a marked increase in trade union militancy during the period. Inflexibility was also present in the fragmentation of the EC economy into national economies, where governments could favour domestic suppliers in public procurement. The Commission of the EC tackled such barriers to economic growth in its proposals for a Single European Market.

A second contributory factor ascribed to Western Europe's poor economic performance in the 1973–84 period was the size and growth of state intervention. According to this argument, state intervention — by means of transfer payments, taxation, minimum wage legislation and other regulations — led to disincentives to work, the discouragement of employers and the stifling of competition. These market-suppressing effects of government intervention became known as 'Eurosclerosis'.

The emergence of relatively high real wages, compared to profits, formed a disincentive to investment and was seen as a third contributory cause of Europe's deteriorating economic performance.

A fourth contributory factor was the relatively restrictive stance of macroeconomic policy, particularly after the second oil price shock in 1978. The oil shocks of the 1970s exposed the fragility of economic growth and undermined the confidence of investors, which had been an important feature of the preceding phase. Previously important Keynesian policies lost favour for a variety of reasons, including fears about inflation and about imbalances in public finances.

The above-mentioned factors were present to a greater or lesser extent in the EC's own appraisals of economic slowdown. Albert and Ball (1983), in a report commissioned by the European Parliament, referred to the relatively high wages, the adverse effects on company profits and the decline in investment. They also adverted to the problems surrounding transfer payments and taxation in the EC and to the difficulties created by discriminatory public procurement and the general failure of the member states to act as an integrated economic unit. Throughout their analysis, Albert and Ball emphasised the relatively poor performance of the EC *vis à vis* the US and Japan.

The latter theme was again present in the EC Commission's assessment of the economic effects of the Single Market (Emerson, 1988). Emerson demonstrated the relative backwardness of EC industries in sectors where technical content is high and demand conditions favourable, and noted that EC output lagged behind the respective outputs of the US and Japan. The White Paper, *Completing the Internal Market*, was, at least to some extent, a response to the EC's relatively poor economic performance since 1973. Ironically, the EC economy has experienced a marked improvement since 1985.

Table 4.3 presents the main indicators of economic performance. It shows a rising trend in GDP growth, in employment and in investment, a decline in inflation, and improvements in the current account balance and in the net lending of general government.

Table 4.3: **Key indicators of economic performance in the European Community**

	1985 / 1980	1990[2] / 1985
Annual percentage change		
Real GDP	1.5	3.1
Employment	−0.4	1.2
Investment[1]	−0.6	5.7
Private consumption deflator	8.8	4.1
Annual average (percentage of GDP)		
Current account balance	−0.2	0.6
Net borrowing/lending of general government	−5.3	−3.7

[1]Gross fixed capital formation at constant prices
[2]Provisional forecasts, September/October 1989
Source: Commission of the European Community, *European Economy*, No. 42 (1989)

The EC Commission (1989) attributed the turnaround in growth to four factors: improvements in the profitability of fixed capital, changes in relative factor costs, the reorientation of budgetary policy, and a change in the structure of demand.

Profitability rose as a result of declining real labour costs (as real wages moderated compared to labour productivity); increasing capital productivity (as rates of capital utilisation improved) and gains in the terms of trade (as oil prices fell and the American dollar declined).

Moderation in real wages also altered relative factor costs. As a consequence, employment began to increase, particularly after 1985.

Budgetary policy in the 1970s and early 1980s reacted to the need to maintain both economic activity and the level of transfer payments by increasing expenditure. The extra taxation required to finance this expenditure impeded economic growth. The recognition of these problems led to a reorientation of budgetary policy by means of controlling government expenditure and reforming tax and expenditure to improve their contributions to economic growth. The latter has been accomplished through lower marginal tax rates and greater selectivity of expenditure, leading to improved work incentives and higher productivity.

A final cause of the turnaround in growth since 1985 was the shift in the structure of demand from exports to investment. As a result of this, the EC economy is less dependent on external factors, which naturally are outside its control.

In the following section, we shall examine the effects of the Single Market programme on the EC economy. The foregoing discussion provides a context, not only in its presentation of the ebbs and flows of growth, but in its identification of some of the many influences on the EC economy.

The Economic Effects of the Single Market

The EC Commission used both a microeconomic and a macroeconomic evaluation to arrive at an assessment of the economic effects of the Single Market. A brief review of these evaluations will illustrate not only how the assessment was formed but also will highlight key features of the Single Market programme.

Microeconomic Evaluation

Figure 4.1 shows the benefits flowing from the Single Market proposals. The removal of non-tariff barriers leads to a reduction in costs, which in turn brings about lower prices and higher profit margins. Falling prices set in motion a positive chain of events: an improvement in national and international demand, a growth in the volume of production of goods and services, and scope for the realisation of economies of scale and economies of learning-by-experience.

The effect of the Single Market programme on profit margins depends on market structure. There is a positive impact on the profits of competitive firms through reductions in costs. On the other hand, increasing competitive pressures reduce profit margins attributable to monopolistic practices (i.e. 'monopoly rents').

Competitive pressures also lead to the restructuring of industry, with investment in new plants and the closure of inefficient plants, and to a reduction in 'x-inefficiency' (i.e. inefficiencies in monopolistic firms which take the form of overmanning, excess stocks, and so forth).

Apart from costs and prices, various non-price factors, such as organisation structure, quality and range of products and innovation and technical progress, are important elements in business strategy. By reducing barriers to market entry and by promoting competition and growth, the Single Market facilitates innovation and technical progress, which further promotes competition.

It is important to draw a distinction between the static and the dynamic effects of the Single Market. Static effects have a once-and-for-all impact on the level of economic welfare. For example, the removal of barriers will reduce border delays and administrative costs. These beneficial effects operate over a period of years, but are once-and-for-all in that they do not raise the growth rate of the economy in the long run.

Dynamic effects, however, do raise the long-term growth rate. For example, innovation and technical progress, and also economies derived by learning-by-experience, have continuing and positive effects on the rate of economic growth.

The EC Commission's assessment of the economic impact of the Single Market recognised the role of both static and dynamic

Figure 4.1: **Microeconomic effects of the Single Market**

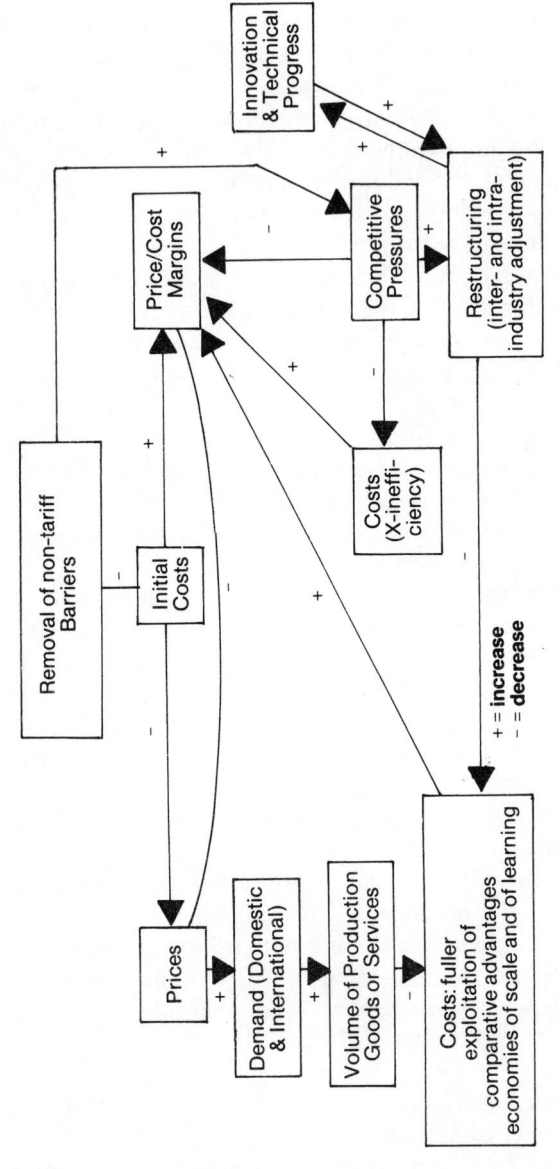

Source: Cecchini (1988)

effects and saw the former as more important in the initial stages and the latter as gradually gaining in significance. However, the assessment, while it did include the dynamic effects of some economies of scale, did not include estimates of some important, but hard-to-measure, dynamic effects, such as the beneficial effect on innovation. The assessment is also deficient to the extent that some non-tariff barriers will survive deregulation, perhaps by re-emerging in other forms; and to the extent that resources released in rationalisation will not be re-employed. Furthermore, the research was conducted for seven member states, accounting for 88 per cent of the European Community's GDP, and then was scaled-up, with all the attendant hazards, to give an estimate for the EC as a whole.

The Commission's research acknowledges these drawbacks in its assessment of the microeconomic effects of the Single Market. Within the time and resources available, the Commission was able to present estimates of the static and some dynamic gains. The gains from the removal of barriers and from market integration were put at between 4.3 and 6.4 per cent of GDP over the medium term. We shall comment on this estimate below, but before doing so we examine the macroeconomic evaluation that complements the microeconomic assessment.

Macroeconomic Evaluation

With the aid of econometric models, the Commission estimated macroeconomic effects attributable to four factors: the abolition of border controls, the opening-up of public procurement, the liberalisation of financial services, and the supply-side effects. Single Market proposals on each of these will have direct effects which will be amplified or moderated by the full workings of the EC economy.

Figure 4.2 presents an illustration of the macroeconomic mechanisms associated with the Single Market. The abolition of intra-Community border controls leads to job losses among customs staff, forwarding agents and administrative personnel in exporting firms. On the other hand, there are reductions in costs associated both with the proposals on border delays and

Figure 4.2: **Macroeconomic mechanisms of the Single Market**

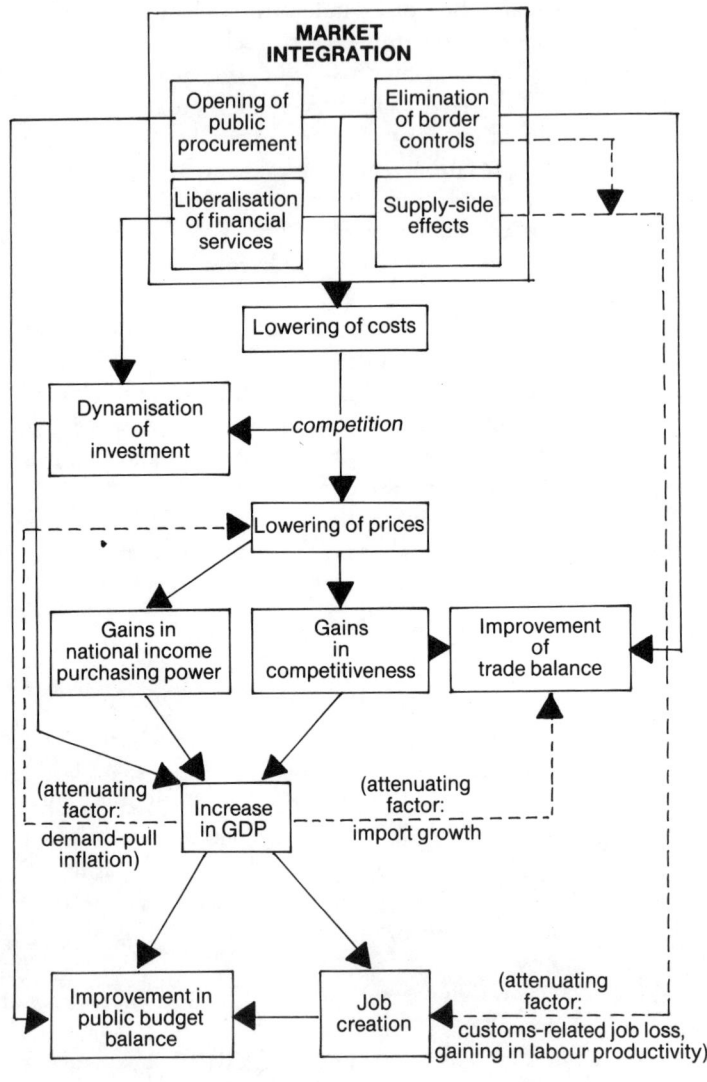

Source: Cecchini (1988)

on administrative formalities. The cost reductions enable prices to be reduced which, first, displace imports from outside the EC with intra-EC imports and, secondly, favour imports from other member states at the expense of domestic production. Thus, there would be terms-of-trade gains for member states and balance-of-trade gains for the EC economy *vis-à-vis* the rest of the world. These latter gains would entail increases in the European Community's GDP.

The opening up of public procurement leads to falling prices for public purchases and to increasing intra-Community trade. The latter will lead to industrial restructuring and productivity gains; the former will yield budget savings and lower production costs for public enterprises. The ultimate macroeconomic effect depends on the options that are exercised after gains have been realised. Budget savings could be used to reduce debt, to reduce taxation, or to reflate the economy. Economies in public enterprises can be used to increase profits, to increase wages, or to reduce prices. We shall return to these options below.

The liberalisation of financial services leads to price reductions. The falling cost of credit promotes investment and hence growth. The effects of the Single Market on financial services are particularly important; first because the highly protected nature of this sector suggests significant gains from liberalisation, and secondly because of the organic role of financial services throughout the entire process of production.

Microeconomic supply-side effects also work through to the macroeconomy. For example, free movement of capital and labour enables more efficient resource allocation and higher factor productivity. The latter promotes growth and checks inflation, but creates short-term job losses; these, however, may be recovered as the economy grows. Economies of scale resulting from the removal of non-tariff barriers can also work through to the macroeconomy, either through the mechanism of higher factor productivity or through increased intra-Community trade resulting from the expansion of the most efficient enterprises. Supply-side effects take the form of increased competition, which not only reduces 'x-inefficiency', or wastefulness, but also increases the need for innovation and restructuring. The macroeconomic effects of the exploitation of economies of scale and of increased competition take the form of growth in GDP, anti-inflationary pressures and higher employment in the medium term.

Taking together the four channels for macroeconomic effects, the EC Commission estimated that, on average, the Single Market measures would increase growth by 4.5 per cent, depress consumer prices by 6.1 per cent, improve budgetary balances and external balances by 2.2 per cent and 1.0 per cent respectively, and create 1.8 million jobs representing a growth in employment of approximately 1.5 per cent, all in the medium term. Moreover, if there were to be accompanying economic policies that capitalised on the Single Market-induced benefits to budgetary and external balances and to inflation, then the Commission estimated that, in the medium term, Community GDP could grow by 7 per cent and employment by 5 million.

Assessment of the Commission's evaluation

Almost inevitably, particular aspects of the Commission's evaluation have come under critical scrutiny. Indeed, the Commission repeatedly acknowledged drawbacks in its analysis. We have already noted its concerns about over- and under-estimation due to the neglect of dynamic effects, to scaling-up errors and so forth (see Emerson, 1988, pp. 201–02); there is even a caveat: to use 'all due caution' in dealing with the estimates (Emerson, 1988, p. 218). Indeed, some of the estimates are subject to a margin of error of approximately 30 per cent. However, temporarily leaving aside these reservations, the estimates do have the benefit of being built on a consistent framework and are useful in indicating rough orders of magnitude.

The highest of the Single Market-induced growth rates postulated by the Commission, at over 6 per cent in the medium term, is still relatively modest. If the medium term is taken as six years (see Catinat, Donni and Italianer, 1988, p. 568), then the most optimistic projection translates into an annual growth rate of approximately one per cent, which is insufficient to bring the EC growth rate up to that of Japan. Moreover, growth rates of this magnitude seem relatively muted, compared to the dramatic nature of the Single Market proposals.

In fact, the Single Market raises fundamental questions about

THE SEM AND THE IRISH ECONOMY   101

the nature of economic growth and illustrates that there are important disagreements about the determinants of growth. In order to organise some brief comment on the determinants of economic growth, it is useful to use a production function framework in which real output is related to the input of capital, the input of labour, and a residual factor that includes innovation, technical progress, education, attitudes to work and so forth.

Taking the labour input first, economic growth is related to changes in labour productivity. An increase in labour productivity occurs for two main reasons: transfers from lower to higher productivity occupations, and the effects of learning-by-experience. As we have seen, the former was an important factor in an earlier phase of EC economic growth as labour transferred from agriculture to manufacturing. The effects of learning-by-experience were omitted from the Commission's estimates of economic benefits.

The role of capital input in economic growth has been the subject of considerable discussion in economic literature. The essential argument is that economic growth is related to increasing net productive investment (i.e. gross productive investment less depreciation). More precisely, higher growth rates are related to increasing net productive investment/GNP ratios. This argument remains powerful despite claims that economic growth causes increasing net productive investment/GNP ratios and not vice versa. The Commission's assessment envisaged higher investment leading to economic growth (see Figure 4.2). It has been argued that part of the increase in investment in the EC in 1988 was due to Single Market effects and that, over a five-year, medium-term period to 1993, these effects will raise private investment in the Community by roughly one per cent (Commission of the European Communities, 1989, p. 201–02).

Turning to the residual factors, the role of technical progress has been prominent since the efforts of Solow (1957) to explain variations in output per head by separating the contribution of technical change from that of increased capital per head. The Commission's assessment, while recognising the role of technical progress, omitted an estimation of its dynamic effects in the process of completing the Single Market.

In general, the Commission's assessment focused on the static effects and neglected some important dynamic effects. In so doing, it allowed for a once-and-for-all increase in growth, but not for an increase in the long-term rate of growth.

Baldwin (1989) took issue with the Commission's assessment, not only for its failure to account for permanent long-term growth effects but also for its neglect of medium-term effects. The latter are due to positive knock-on effects, which occur as the previously discussed static efficiency gains of the Single Market raise savings and investment, which in turn increase the capital stock. Thus, there is a virtuous cycle of growth which, before petering out, raises EC economic growth in the medium term. In addition to this 'medium-term growth bonus', Baldwin argued that there will be a 'long term growth bonus' because, contrary to what traditional theorists had argued, capital can grow continuously and can permanently raise the economy's underlying growth rate.

According to Baldwin's self-admittedly crude calculations, the inclusion of these new growth effects could raise the possible range for Single Market-induced growth to between 11 and 35 per cent in the medium term.

It therefore appears that the Commission's assessments underestimate the likely impact of the Single Market measures. However, all estimates of the effects of the Single Market must be considered imprecise. In assessing macroeconomic effects — for example in the opening up of public procurement — much depends on the behaviour of governments and public enterprises. Governments can choose between using budget savings for reflation, for debt reduction or for tax reduction. Similarly, public enterprises can choose to use surpluses to increase profits, to increase wages or to reduce prices. The behaviour of consumers and investors is also important. Consumer loyalty and differing consumer preferences will continue to form a special type of barrier that may restrain growth in intra-EC trade. Uncertainty about the future may restrain investment in sectors where the achievement of economies of scale requires large sunk costs. Thus, once again the growth effects of the Single Market may be hampered.

Pelkmans and Winters (1988, p. 20) noted that the attainment of currently unexploited economies of scale can take place only in certain circumstances. Their argument is based on a firm in one EC member state that hopes to serve the rest of the Community, but is currently underpriced by imports from outside

the EC. For such a firm, the removal of barriers in the Single
Market must be sufficiently great to enable it to sell at prices
below imports from outside the EC. If not, then the firm will
not win markets and the economies of scale will remain
unexploited.

The benefits of the Single Market could be limited also by
impediments to competition in the form of monopolistic practices
or of government intervention to protect domestic markets. To
prevent such obstructions, the Commission is emphasising an
effective competition policy (Emerson, 1988, p. 178–80).

The ultimate growth effect of the Single Market will also
depend significantly on developments and reactions in the rest
of the world. These will be examined in the following section.

The EC economy and the world economy

The world economy is important to our evaluation in several
ways: the growth of the world economy affects the EC economy;
the growth of other trading blocs in the world economy affects
the relative performance of the EC economy; and reactions by
other trading blocs to the Single Market influences their
effectiveness.

Table 4.4 shows growth performance in the OECD between
1980 and 1988 and gives projections up to 1990. In general, there
has been growth in the main OECD countries since 1983. The
US led the global recovery after the recession of the early 1980s.
By the end of the decade the EC was challenging and indeed
surpassing the US as the major 'western' source of world growth.
From 1988 onwards, it seems likely that the Single Market

Table 4.4: **Growth of real GNP/GDP in the OECD area**
(Percentage changes from previous period)

	1980	1981	1982	1983	1984	1985	1986	1987	1988	1989	1990
United States	−0.2	1.9	−2.5	3.6	6.8	3.4	2.7	3.7	4.4	3.0	2.3
Japan	4.3	3.7	3.1	3.2	5.1	4.9	2.5	4.5	5.7	4.8	4.5
West Germany	1.5	0.0	−1.0	1.9	3.3	1.9	2.3	1.7	3.6	4.3	3.2
EC	1.4	0.1	0.8	1.7	2.5	2.4	2.6	2.7	3.7	3.4	3.1
Total OECD	1.5	1.7	−0.1	2.7	4.8	3.4	2.6	3.5	4.4	3.6	2.9

Source: OECD, Commission of the EC

measures have been responsible for at least some of the growth (see Commission of the European Community, 1989, pp. 201–02).

The US in the World Economy

The pre-eminence of the United States economy from the 1950s was based on the large size of its market, high levels of disposable income, the superiority of its technology, a skilled workforce, and high productivity. Other industrial nations, however, have eroded these advantages, though the US still dominates in terms of size. By the end of the 1980s, the US was labouring under deficits in the budget and in the balance of payments on current account which, paradoxically, had helped the world economy to recover from the recession of the early 1980s. The budget deficit developed out of ambitious tax cuts and high levels of expenditure, notably military spending. The growing balance of payments deficit exposed an apparently structural trade deficit with Japan.

The US twin deficit problem created major uncertainties in the world economy. There were fears that the dollar would fall, necessitating sharp increases in US interest rates which would lead to a world recession. However, these fears abated as the deficits shrank as proportions of GNP. Moreover, it was recognised that the increasing integration of world capital markets, and the mobility of capital, allowed countries to sustain large balance of payments deficits.

A legacy of US concern over balance of payments deficits since the 1970s has been friction with other trading blocs. The United States took issue with the EC for protecting shipbuilding and aircraft manufacture. The EC and the US have accused each other of protecting steel and textiles. Most importantly, there have been mutual recriminations over agricultural trade policies (Ginsberg, 1989). For example, the US has contended that the EC dumps subsidised surplus production on world markets, thereby depressing prices and hurting US exporters. The EC has countered that the US also has subsidised food exports.

The upshot of US concern over international trading problems with the EC and with Japan was the enactment of a protectionist Trade Bill in 1988 which developed upon Section 301 of the 1974 Trade Act and allowed the US to retaliate against perceived unfair trade practices. However, retaliation may feed on itself and lead to a protectionist world with a lower volume of trade. Protected industries may become inefficient. If the aforementioned happens, some of the gains to the EC from a Single Market could be negated. Fortunately, influential commentators (Dertouzos, Lester and Solow, 1989) have emphasised that there are other ways of correcting US trade difficulties, such as better productive performance, leading to improved international competitiveness.

Japan in the World Economy

Of the three major world trading blocs, Japan's economic performance exceeds that of both the US and the European Community. Figure 4.3 shows that, in the period since its entry to the OECD in 1964, Japan outperformed the other two trading blocs in economic growth, and in controlling unemployment and inflation.

Figure 4.3: **Comparative economic performance**

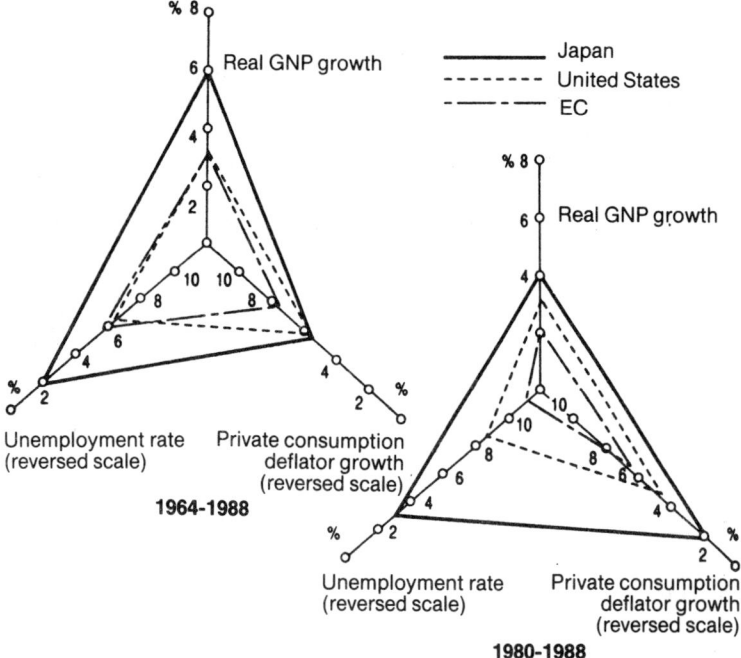

Source: OECD

To some extent, the counterpart to the US balance of payments deficit is Japan's trade surplus. The OECD (1989(b)) noted that, since 1970, Japan's share of world merchandise exports rose from 7 to 10 per cent and its share of merchandise imports remained relatively stable at between 6 and 7 per cent. The strong export performance can be attributed variously to price competitiveness, high product quality, adaptability to changes in world demand, flexibility in the labour market, and specialisation of exports in limited product markets. Japan's exports to the US and to Western Europe (predominantly the EC) between 1985 and 1988 grew by 37 and 122 per cent respectively. In 1986 alone, the country's exports to Western Europe grew by 49 per cent.

Japan's comparatively low ratio of imports to GNP, at approximately 10 per cent, has been attributed to such factors as market-entry difficulties (for example, the preferences for long-term trading relationships and close links between distributors and producers) and import barriers. However, the OECD (1989(b)) has argued that import barriers are more likely to be decisive in agriculture than in manufacturing.

This favourable import and export performance led to balance of payments surpluses on current account. In 1988 the surplus was 2.8 per cent of GNP, having been as high as 4.4 per cent in 1986. Against this background of Japanese trading strength, EC businesses welcomed the proposals for an integrated EC economy in that the removal of barriers would permit concentration at the level of the large internal market and facilitate the maintenance or recovery of market share.

Nevertheless, there have been indications of a weakening in Japan's trade performance as the accumulation of wealth in the 1980s has led to increasing consumption and imports. Moreover, Japan has tried to open its economy in order to boost the role of domestic demand in economic growth and, in so doing, to restrain protectionist sentiments elsewhere in the world. Still, this opening up to imports may be halted because of growing protectionist policies elsewhere in the world or if the fall in the yen that occurred in 1989 and 1990 continues and causes imports to fall and exports to rise.

A continuation of world growth?

We have already noted that there has been a sustained period of world economic growth since 1983. Most EC member states shared in this growth. The Padoa-Schioppa report (1987, p. 110) saw lack of economic growth as creating political difficulties for the Single Market programme. Not only has there been economic growth in the period since the Single Market programme was commenced, but there are grounds for optimism that this growth will continue.

Many previous growth periods faltered because inflation led to a tightening of monetary policies. With some exceptions, inflation rates appear relatively stable, although they are higher than optimal. The deflationary aspects of the Single Market programme are helpful in this regard. However, of greater importance is caution in wage settlements in the major industrial economies.

Progress on budgetary and trade imbalances are also important for continuing world growth. If, for example, the US balance of payments deficit proves unsustainable, then earlier fears of a recession may be realised.

Other important influences on growth arise in the sphere of international cooperation. The General Agreement on Tariffs and Trade (GATT), in its 'Uruguay Round' of talks on liberalising world trade, may have important influences on growth. The Uruguay Round commenced in 1986 and has been dealing with US proposals for reducing distortions to agricultural trade and with issues relating to textiles, services and intellectual property. Reductions in agricultural trade distortions would mean a reform of the Common Agricultural Policy and would have negative implications for Ireland which benefits considerably from financial transfers under the CAP. However, looking beyond national self-interest, there are important implications for the world economy. Failure of the talks to achieve agreement could lead to greater protectionism.

Yet another influence on world growth will be the reforms in Eastern Europe.

Eastern Europe and the EC economy

The transition from centrally planned to market-oriented economic management in Eastern Europe poses a question about the eventual size of the EC economy. This is most easily seen in the case of East Germany. The West German Treaty of

Accession to the European Community permits automatic entry for East Germany to the EC should reunification occur. Other East European countries may also seek EC membership. If some members of the European Free Trade Association (EFTA) such as Austria and Norway also seek to join, then in due course the EC conceivably could consist of up to 20 member states.

Eastern European economies suffer from inter-related problems of poor infrastructure, uncompetitive industry, undiversified commodity trade structure, obsolete plant and machinery, and environmental degradation. Furthermore, the price system has been distorted by subsidies; artificially low prices raise demand, reduce supply and create shortages. The consequences of distorted relative prices include rationing, high savings due to the lack of consumer goods, latent inflation attributable to the artificially reduced prices, and budget deficits — that reflect the costs of subsidies. Further details in the picture of economic underdevelopment include overvalued exchange rates, unconvertible currencies, and a highly administered banking system with no proper interest rate mechanism to allocate credit.

Clearly, in the transition to a market-oriented system, the Eastern European economies will require Western support. This may take the form of private or official investment or of easier access to Western European markets. In the case of the EC, the latter would take the form of reduced quotas on Eastern European exports.

The European Community's most immediate concern is with East Germany and the implications of German reunification. In discussing East Germany we shall discuss factors that could also apply if other Eastern European countries were to join the EC. East Germany suffers from most of the economic problems outlined above, and to some extent these difficulties are heightened by comparison with West Germany, one of the world's most powerful economies.

The unification process must contend with dramatic differences between the two economies. For example, productivity in East Germany is roughly 40 per cent, and wages are roughly 33 per cent of West German levels. Comparing real GNP, the West German economy is approximately nine times the size of its neighbour's.

Monetary integration is an initial stage in the reunification process. Before the agreement on monetary integration, the market rate of exchange was at least 7 Ostmark to 1 Deutsche Mark. However, the success of monetary integration to a large extent depends on the new conversion rate between the Deutsche Mark and the Ostmark. Too high a rate, such as one-to-one conversion, would make East German industry uncompetitive and dispel some of the advantages to Western investors of the low wage levels in East Germany. Indeed, this uncompetitiveness, combined with poor infrastructure, would fuel unemployment. In addition, too high a rate would increase the debt servicing burden on East Germany's national and corporate debt.

Too low a rate, on the other hand, would re-emphasise the considerable differentials in wages and social security benefits and would create an economic incentive to migrate to West Germany. Such an incentive also exists in the form of greater employment opportunities and greater consumer choice in West Germany.

The reunification process has given rise to fears about inflation. Savings by the East German household sector are estimated at approximately 170 billion Ostmarks. A favourable conversion rate with the Deutsche Mark could boost East German consumer spending in West Germany and cause inflationary pressures. To counter this, the Bundesbank could be expected to raise interest rates. Other EC member states might be forced to follow suit in order to prevent capital outflows and this may lead to strains on the EMS at an important time in the evolution of EC monetary integration.

However, fears of inflation may be exaggerated. Inflationary restraining actions could be taken in the form of constraints on the disposal of savings, or else by introducing convertibility in stages. Alternatively, East Germans might be given an opportunity to use their savings to buy assets such as state-owned housing or bonds. In any event, East Germans may not be quite so eager to spend their savings. Because of the underdeveloped nature of the monetary sector and the lack of a capital market in East Germany, there was no real alternative to savings. Savings therefore comprise the bulk of wealth holdings by East Germans and are unlikely to be dissipated.

The terms of the intergovernmental agreement on monetary union takes into account some of the above-mentioned concerns.

It allows each East German to convert 4,000 Ostmarks of savings into Deutsche Marks at a favourable one-to-one rate. All other conversions of savings will be at a two-to-one rate. Wages and pensions will be convertible into Deutsche Marks at the one-to-one rate and corporate debts will be convertible at the two-to-one rate.

Judging the effects of reunification on West Germany must take account of several factors. The West German birth rate is low and the country's population is aging. An influx of young people will help to correct this imbalance. Moreover, West Germany suffers from a skills shortage, which can also be allayed; but it must be noted that some of the influx of labour possesses skills in services, such as teaching, that are not in short supply. The new investment opportunities in East Germany are also a positive influence on the West German economy.

Yet inflationary pressures are a negative influence, particularly in view of the traditional antipathy of West Germany to price instability. While fears of inflation may be exaggerated, nonetheless they exist in the form of increased demand for consumer and investment goods in an economy that already is operating close to capacity. Any rise in productive potential after unification is unlikely to match the increased demand, so some upward pressure on prices seems unavoidable.

The West German economy grew at over three per cent a year at the end of the 1980s. A continuation of this growth could help to smooth the process of unification. Costs to the public sector, such as grants and subsidies for industrial restructuring, assistance to infrastructural measures, and transfers to social security funds, could be financed through higher tax revenues. Economic growth could provide these revenues at existing tax rates. Lack of economic growth, however, would lead to high taxes and attendant social frictions.

The process of German reunification raises a number of issues for the European Community. Initial fears that reunification would cause West Germany to lose interest in the European Community and in the Single Market programme have been defused by official West German statements. There are also fears that inflationary pressures on West Germany will lead to strains on the EMS. Clearly, too, if reunification slows down the West German economy, then the EC economy will be affected. However, this is unlikely, as we shall see below.

Other problems exist in the form of uncertainties about whether EC rules on such matters as product safety, subsidies or the environment will apply in East Germany. Furthermore, there are important trade links between East Germany and other Eastern European states which may prove difficult to disentangle. The general issue of the security of the EC's economic frontiers with non-member states also arises. Finally, it is important to note that, as an underdeveloped region, East Germany will require regional aid. West Germany will fund most of this, though other member states will also contribute. The poorer regions — Ireland, Spain, Portugal and Greece — are unlikely to bear any direct costs of this regional aid.

There are positive aspects for the EC in German reunification. The West German economy should receive a stimulus to growth as reunification increases consumption and investment. Economic growth in West Germany would benefit other EC member states. A positive factor also exists in as much as the introduction of modern plant and machinery to East Germany should lead to improved productivity and a growing economy that provides an expanding market for the EC member states.

The opening up of new markets in East Germany and elsewhere in Eastern Europe can be seen as a potential benefit for Ireland. Nevertheless, there are difficulties. The increasing demand on regional funds could reduce the amount of future structural funds allocated to Ireland and indeed to other peripheral member states, but the allocation to Ireland up to 1993 of £2.86 billion in structural funding will not be affected. Another source of concern for Ireland is the competition, particularly in textiles and in agricultural products, that could emerge as a result of easier access for East Germany and other Eastern European economies to EC markets. Moreover, reunification could make it more difficult to attract increasingly eastward-looking West German industry to Ireland. Nevertheless, it should be noted that factors such as the poor infrastructure in East Germany, and the relatively slow adjustment process to the institutions and processes of market-oriented economies might make West German industry somewhat wary.

Adverse effects for Ireland also could arise out of any inflationary pressure caused by German reunification. A counter-inflationary interest rate increase in West Germany could be difficult for Ireland to withstand. A particular factor which limits the ability to withstand West German interest rate increases is the proportionately high holding of Irish government securities by West German investors. A failure to match a rise in the West German interest rate could lead to a withdrawal of West German investors from the Irish market.

Conclusion

This chapter has examined the performance of the EC economy and has assessed the potential for economic growth of the Single Market programme. We also examined the EC economy within the world economy. Finally we considered the implications of development in Eastern Europe, and in particular the process of German reunification, for the European and the Irish economies.

The EC Commission discovered fairly modest benefits in its quantification of some of the economic effects of completing the Single Market programme. In the microeconomics evolution, gains were estimated at between 4.3 and 6.4 per cent of GDP over the medium term. Of the four causes of these gains, the two major ones were the removal of trade barriers (such as discriminating public procurement practices and differing standards and regulations) and the exploitation of economies of scale (since existing capacity is more fully used and restructuring enables the achievement of more efficient scales of production). Improvements in business efficiency resulting from intensified competition was another important source of economic growth in the Commission's assessment. Reductions in border delays were seen as the least significant cause of economic growth. The Commission's estimate included some dynamic factors, such as the effects of economies of scale and increased competition, but omitted others, such as increased innovation. Baldwin (1989) evaluated some effects that were missing from the Commission's quantification, and raised the estimate of benefits. Forecasts of Single Market effects are hazardous and should be treated cautiously. However, it seems that the Single Market will have more significant effects on economic growth if the long-run growth of the EC economy is affected.

However, it is important to place the anticipated growth

in perspective. The gains forecast by the Commission would be insufficient to raise EC economic growth to that of Japan, and although the EC rate of growth in 1989 exceeded that of the US, this had much to do with the slowing of the US rate of growth and relatively little to do with Single Market effects.

Baldwin's more optimistic estimates entail a dramatic increase in the EC's comparative economic growth rate. However, it is likely that the comparative unemployment rate will remain high. In 1989, estimated unemployment rates were 9 per cent, 5.5 per cent and 2.3 per cent respectively in the EC, the US and Japan. The reaction of trading partners is also an important part of a comparative perspective (Catinat, 1989). The elimination of non-tariff barriers in the Single Market is a unilateral action. Without reciprocation in other trading blocs, there is a danger that external competition in EC markets will lead to a displacement of indigenous EC firms' production by non-EC firms and, in certain circumstances, to a reduction in the EC trade balance.

The Single Market programme should not be viewed in isolation from developments in the world economy. Since the White Paper, *Completing the Internal Market*, was published in 1985, there have been significant developments in the world economy, such as the fall in oil prices in 1986, the decline in the dollar from 1985, the increase in protectionist sentiment in the US, and the continued progress of the newly industrialising economies, such as Hong Kong, South Korea and Taiwan. These developments affect economic growth in Europe and provide an important context for analysing the effects of the Single Market. On the other hand, the Single Market programme affects the world economy by providing a new dynamic to economic integration in the EC and by leading to a re-evaluation of international cooperation.

Yet another important perspective is to consider how the benefits of the Single Market are to be shared. The gains and losses will not be shared equally within and between member states. These matters are discussed in detail in Chapters 2, 17 and 18.

The EC economy is heterogeneous: it contains large and small economies, early and late industrialising economies, and open and less open economies. The Irish economy is one of the most open to trade in the developed world and is in marked contrast to some of the less open EC member states, such as West Germany. Ireland's Gross Domestic Product per capita is approximately one-third less than the EC average. Ireland's economic performance differs from the EC average in several ways. Table 4.1 shows that in 1988, the latest year for which there are settled data, Ireland performed well compared to the EC average on economic growth, inflation and the balance of payments on current account, but that government debt and unemployment were comparatively high.

Since 1985, but independently of the Single Market programme, the Irish economy had benefited from a fall in oil prices and a strong recovery in world trade. Fiscal imbalances have improved and the punt has appreciated. However, fiscal imbalances remain serious and the underlying growth of the Irish labour force creates difficulties for the alleviation of unemployment. The Single Market programme must be viewed against this background.

The effects of the Single Market on Ireland's economic performance depend on such factors as the ability of indigenous manufacturing industry to export (see Chapter 10) and Ireland's attractiveness as a location for foreign direct investment (see Chapter 14).

Irish firms must be competitive if they are to gain from Single Market opportunities. Gains in competitiveness can trigger a virtuous circle of growth as higher exports lead to increased investment and thence to improved productivity and further gains in competitiveness. Gains in competitiveness are of particular importance in attracting foreign direct investment. However, such benefits will be forfeited if, through lack of competitiveness, Ireland does not seize the export opportunities in the Single Market.

The Single Market also has implications for the management of the national economy. One implication is a loss of indirect tax revenue (see Chapter 7). Moreover, there is the question of whether Single Market-induced gains to consumers and producers will be taxed and, if they are, to what use the revenues will be put. The ultimate effect on the Single Market on the Irish economy will depend to some extent on decisions, such as these, that are made in Ireland. Much will also depend on the amount of, and the use of, structural funds. The renegotiation of the funds in 1991 will determine the amount of the funds after 1993. The issue of structural funds is discussed in Chapter 17.

The EC member states, though heterogeneous in size and openness, are increasingly interdependent as a result of intra-Community trade and the integration of labour and capital markets. Remaining discretion by member states to protect domestic markets by altering exchange rates will disappear under monetary union. The implications of monetary union are examined in Chapters 5 and 6. The interdependence of member states means that failure to take account of policy actions in other member states can lead to domestic policy problems. For example, a member state with a small open economy may encounter unexpected balance-of-payments problems if it decides to reflate its economy in ignorance of a policy decision by another member state to contract its economy. Futhermore, a policy that is effective for a member state acting alone might be ineffective if simultaneously pursued by all member states (Krugman, 1987, pp. 134-36). Member states of the EC must take account of such interdependence in the management of their economies. The implications of the Single Market for the management of the Irish economy is the subject of the next chapter.

5

The Implications of the Single Market for Economic Management

SEAN CROMIEN

Economic management

In recent decades there has been lively debate about the exact role the state should play in the economy. In the 1960s the tendency was to look to the state to remedy all economic ills. More recently, as laisser-faire economic philosophies have influenced governments — particularly those in the USA and the UK — more emphasis has been placed on reducing the state's economic role. Still, there is probably general agreement that the state has a role to play in managing the economy. Governments, even those of the USA and the UK, are criticised by their electorates if unemployment or inflation increases or if the balance of payments goes into deficit. They are expected to do something about it.

Economic theory usually assumes that the market system works perfectly, that its operations are fully coordinated to produce a desirable equilibrium. In the working of economies, however, this does not happen. At times, there can be a disequilibrium in the economy which causes higher unemployment or inflation or perhaps difficulties with the balance of payments. Certain extreme theoreticians claim that, eventually, markets will correct themselves and a desirable outcome will be achieved, but most economists accept that such an automatic adjustment would be too prolonged and that the consequences would be disruptive of commercial activity and too severe in human terms. Instead, they prefer to see governments stepping in and taking action to help restore the necessary equilibrium.

Governments can do this by using instruments at their disposal to influence economic activity. They can use monetary policy (changing interest rates and/or setting money supply targets) or fiscal policy (varying taxes and public expenditure). They can change the exchange rate, adjust tariffs or exchange controls, or, if they are unconstrained, pursue incomes policies. The range of policy instruments available varies from one country to another, depending on factors such as the nature of the economy, the extent of the particular nation's trading links with other countries, its membership of an economic bloc, and so on. The government's political philosophy also may play a part. Some countries focus on monetary policy and claim to spurn everything else. Others believe in substantial state intervention, using every available instrument to influence economic activity.

In performing this stabilisation function, most countries nowadays prefer to operate within a medium-term strategy. This can be related solely to the state's own financial transactions, such as setting medium-term budgetary targets, or it may cover the economy as a whole. Many countries, Ireland being one, see the role of the government as not just to create the conditions necessary for sustained long-term economic growth but actively to promote such growth. Since the success of the First Programme for Economic Expansion in 1958, there has been an expectation in Ireland that the state will set a medium-term perspective that will allow the various groups in the private sector to coordinate their economic decisions. In particular, successive governments since the early 1980s have produced medium-term programmes for the economy, setting a broad framework within which the private sector can be expected to operate. Targets are established for the public finances, over which the government has most control, but indications are also given of such objectives as higher economic growth, employment and the control of inflation.

Irish government policy, therefore, can be seen as having a dual function: to achieve stabilisation in the short-term and, so far as this lies within its power, to create conditions in which the national objectives of economic growth and increased employment can be achieved in the medium-term.

Present constraints on action

The full implementation of the Single Market (SM) will undoubtedly reduce the number and scope of instruments that the Irish government will be able to use to influence economic policy. However, it has to be said that even now, before the SM is achieved, the use of the instruments of macroeconomic policy is constrained for a small open economy such as Ireland's. Theoretically, one instrument of policy that governments can use is to impose tariffs against the goods of foreign countries. Ireland's membership of the European Community, however, precludes the use of this instrument since tariffs have been removed on trade by the member states, and a common tariff exists for foreign countries.

We cannot go too far with fiscal policies because the balance of payments acts as a constraint. Likewise, we must take account of movements of interest rates abroad. For many years, during the period when the Irish pound was linked to sterling, Ireland had to follow British interest rates, even when the vicissitudes of that economy required a rise in rates while Irish circumstances may not have warranted it. In more recent years, following Ireland's entry into the European Monetary System (EMS) and the subsequent break with sterling, the country's economy has been linked more closely with the Deutsche Mark. During 1989, interest rates in Ireland were raised on a number of occasions because of increases in German rates. Ireland was not alone in this, of course. The increase in German rates in May 1989 was immediately followed by increases in France, Italy, Belgium and the Netherlands. Even the big players, the United States, Japan and West Germany, have to take account of each other's economic policies.

Since 1979 Ireland has been a member of the EMS. This has constrained the country's freedom to amend exchange rates, since membership is intended to encourage the stability of these rates, and changes can be made only with the agreement of other members of the EMS. Thus membership has meant some diminution of Ireland's sovereignty, but this has been a modest price to pay for the substantial benefits that have accrued. Uncertainty for traders and investors has been reduced. Membership has provided an anchor for the Irish currency, with consequent gains in the form of lower interest rates. It has also helped to reduce inflation.

One aspect of administration where governments are still theoretically sovereign is taxation. Nevertheless, even here, countries have not got full freedom to do as they wish. If the Irish government is considering a rise in indirect taxes (VAT or excises), it has to take into account the level of taxes in Northern Ireland. If not, it will tend to lose business to shops in Northern Ireland or, to the extent that this loophole has been closed in recent years by the '48-hour rule' (which confines the benefits of duty-free allowances to those who have been outside the jurisdiction of the state for 48 hours or more), to smuggling, which develops on a large scale if price differentials are too great between Northern Ireland and the Republic.

A similar constraint, but for different reasons, operates in relation to income tax. High income tax rates in Ireland encourage voluntary emigration, particularly among young people, who, because of the increased freedom to travel, may prefer to move to countries where income tax is low.

Effect of completion of the SM

How precisely will the instruments available to the Irish government for economic management be constrained as a result of the completion of the SM? This question can perhaps best be answered by taking for illustration the two key areas of monetary policy and fiscal policy.

Interest rates and monetary policy

The completion of the SM has obviously important implications for the conduct of interest-rate policy and monetary policies in general in Ireland. Perhaps the most significant development here is the liberalisation of capital movements. Ireland does not have to phase out exchange controls fully until the end of 1992. There has already been a considerable relaxation of controls, however, and this, as expected, has led to marked outflows of capital as Irish investors have adjusted their portfolios in the light of the new options open to them. On the other hand, non-resident investors have been purchasing Irish government bonds on a much larger scale than heretofore. This increased two-way flow of funds is likely to become a permanent feature of financial markets, and Ireland will have to offer sufficiently attractive returns to maintain a satisfactory balance between inflows and outflows.

A stable exchange rate is the central plank of Ireland's policy on its currency, and membership of the EMS has reinforced this policy stance. This stability has been a key factor in influencing outside investment. The external discipline that the system imposes on Ireland is welcomed because it helps to strengthen the economy. If the Irish pound was still tied to sterling, the country now would be experiencing higher interest rates and high inflation.

Fiscal policy

One of the inevitable consequences of the integration of national markets will be that intra-Community trade flows will increase. Consequently, the degree of 'openness' of all economies, including the Irish economy — currently one of the most open — will be accentuated. This will have important implications for the conduct of budgetary policy, in that the balance of payments is likely to become a more immediate constraint, though not necessarily a more acute one. This means that Ireland's already restricted 'freedom' in relation to running budget deficits to stimulate demand will be further curbed. The coordination of economic and budgetary policies among the member states, which is analysed below, will institutionalise that constraint. Yet, though greater openness limits the impact of budgetary policy on domestic demand and activity, as Ireland knows from experience, paradoxically it also controls more effectively the balance of payments. It will become more important to move quickly to correct undesired trends in domestic demand, but correcting them will require smaller adjustments in the fiscal stance.

The SM, of course, will have a bearing on the evolution of taxation, quite apart from its role in influencing demand through the budget balance. The constraints on freedom of action in regard to taxation, to which I have referred, are likely to be greatly increased in the SM. The removal of barriers to free movement of persons, capital, goods and services will inevitably have significant effects. Free movement of persons obviously will have a bearing on levels of income tax. The removal of exchange controls will affect the way the member states tax income from savings: funds will tend to move to where the tax rates are low.

However, indirect taxation is where the effect of the SM is likely to be greatest. Harmonisation of indirect taxation is essential to the development of the SM. If taxes were to differ widely in a Community where goods were able to be freely traded across frontiers, there would be gross distortions of trade. This would be totally at variance with the principle of freeing markets in the interests of more efficient production. Therefore, a degree of approximation of taxes is necessary to allow goods and services to move naturally from one country to another.

How exactly will the new arrangements for taxation in the SM operate? This is difficult to foresee. While in many aspects of the SM it has been possible to make considerable progress in moving towards 1992, probably least progress has been made in taxation policy. The reason may be that proposals here represent a restriction in a very sensitive aspect of sovereignty — the taxation of a country's citizens. Ministers for Finance prefer to have a wide range of policy instruments available and are understandably concerned if that range is reduced and their room for manoeuvre is limited.

This being said, it is obvious that the SM will not operate properly without a considerable degree of harmonisation of taxes, whether this is achieved by member states deciding to limit their rates of VAT and excises to specific agreed ranges or, as another proposal suggests, by having agreed minimum rates. Even in the case of the latter, governments would still find that their freedom to raise taxes is constrained because in a situation where there were no frontier controls, which is the essence of the SM, they could not raise their rates more than 1 or 2 percentage points above those of bordering member states.

There has already been considerable discussion and controversy about the EC Commission's proposals for the approximation of rates of VAT and excises. Detailed discussion of these is outside the scope of the present chapter. There is little doubt, however, that these proposals raise major issues for Ireland, given the country's traditional reliance, for financial, economic and social reasons, on high indirect taxes. Whatever agreed solutions may emerge, this aspect of the Single Market will act as a major constraint on Irish governments in their use of indirect taxation.

Why 'convergence of economic policies'?

Of course, the completion of the Single Market also will limit the room for manoeuvre of other member states in influencing domestic activity. This will be happening at a time when the ever closer integration of the Community economy brings the risk that unsuitable economic policies will have destabilising effects outside a member state's own borders. The increasingly urgent question is therefore being asked: how can the economic policies and performance of member states be coordinated? In Community terminology, this is described as the need for 'convergence'. Why is such convergence necessary? The answer lies in the nature of the Community.

With a population of over 320 million people, the European Community represents the largest economic body in the industrialised world. The combined output of the member states is equivalent to about one quarter of total world production — greater than that of the United States, which is roughly one-fifth of the total, or Japan, which is about one-tenth. The total imports of the Community are larger than those of any other single economy in the world.

Yet despite its global economic importance, and its effective dominance in some respects, the economy of the European Community has not got a single authoritative core that is responsible for developing economic policy. In this respect, it is at a disadvantage compared to Japan and the United States. It is not at present capable of developing a Community economic policy commensurate with its potential and comparable with that of the other major trading blocs.

This lack of a single core of authority has serious consequences for economic management in member states. Given the now very high degree of economic interdependence between members, macroeconomic policy measures implemented in one member state inevitably have effects in others. The impact of policy adjustments 'leaks out across national frontiers'. For example, measures designed to stimulate domestic demand in any of the smaller and more open economies of the Community lead quickly to a rise in imports, with an adverse effect on the balance of payments, and any immediate benefits are at least partly offset. Recent experience — for example, that of France between 1981 and 1983 — suggests that even the larger economies of the Community cannot remain insulated from the effects of an uncoordinated expansion of domestic demand.

Completion of the internal market in 1992 will increase greatly the interdependence of member states and make even more urgent the need for a closer convergence of economic policies. Effective coordination of economic policy between the separate national authorities is essential if the gains of the wider market are to be maximised. Any attempt by an individual member state to pursue an independent economic policy will be translated quickly into exchange rate pressures, which will undermine the effectiveness of the SM.

Policy coordination to date in the Community

In recognition of the increasing interdependence of the economies of member states, in 1974 the Council produced a 'convergence decision', which was intended to ensure that the budgetary policies of members would be coordinated. This decision required that the Council should establish 'guidelines' for economic policies in the member states, including the main aggregates of budgetary policy (budget deficit, expenditure, revenues) in quantified form.

Experience in subsequent years revealed a fundamental weakness in implementing this decision, namely, that, since the Council is composed of the same ministers who have national responsibility, the guidelines merely tended to reflect current national policies. Moreover, it proved difficult for ministers responsible to national parliaments to commit themselves to specific fiscal policies at EC level which would have to be reviewed twice or three times a year. There was in effect no political will among members to implement the decision in anything but a half-hearted way. It is now widely accepted that this cannot continue and that the SM calls for substantial changes in the formulation of the economic policies of the member states.

Economic and monetary union

In this connection, recent decisions that the Council has taken in a different but related field, Economic and Monetary Union (EMU), are significant. The ultimate logic of the SM is that the Community should establish a full Economic and Monetary Union. In June 1988, the European Council decided to appoint a committee, chaired by the President of the European Commission, Jacques Delors, to study and propose concrete stages that would lead to EMU. In April 1989 the committee published its report, which formed the basis for the decision of EC heads of state in June 1989 to move progressively towards EMU (Delors, 1989).

The committee recommended that movement towards this goal should be in three stages. *Stage One* would seek convergence of economic performance through a closer coordination of economic and monetary policies within existing institutions. This would necessitate the replacement of the 1974 Council decision on economic convergence by a new procedure, which would provide a comprehensive framework to assess the consequences and consistency of the economic and fiscal policies of member states. On the basis of the assessment, *non-binding* budgetary and economic guidelines would be issued in respect of each country. In particular, the committee envisaged that a revised version of the 1974 decision on convergence would:

- establish a process of multilateral surveillance of economic developments, based on agreed indicators
- set up a new procedure for budgetary coordination, with precise quantitative guidelines and recommendations for the medium term
- provide for concerted budgetary action by member states.

Stage One would also see all members of the EC becoming full members of the EMS.

The committee envisaged that in *Stage Two*, macroeconomic policy guidelines, including precise but *not yet binding* rules relating to the size of annual budget deficits in member states, would be adopted by a majority decision of the Council of Ministers. During this stage, the margins of fluctuation in the EMS exchange rate mechanism would be narrowed in preparation for the final stage.

Stage Three would start with an irrevocable move to locked exchange rates. Rules governing coordination in the macroeconomic and budgetary spheres of policy would become *binding*.

The Council has agreed to implement Stage One of EMU and has approved two decisions designed to strengthen co-ordination of budgetary and monetary policies. These decisions are scheduled to come into force on 1 July 1990 and should have an important influence on actions by governments by the time the SM is completed. The task of economic policy coordination will be the primary responsibility of the Finance Ministers Council (ECO/FIN), which will be strengthened by the participation of the Chairman of the Committee of Central Bank Governors at the appropriate Council meetings. The essence of the proposals is that the ministers of the member states, with the assistance of the Commission and of committees of officials, will monitor jointly all aspects of economic policy and the performance of members states' economies in terms of price stability, stable public finances and monetary conditions, sound balance of payments and open competitive markets. Where policy or performance is judged inadequate or detrimental to commonly set objectives, policy consultations will take place within the Community and recommendations may be formulated with a view to promoting the necessary corrections in national policies.

Conclusion

Closer economic and monetary integration, even before it arrives at the full union envisaged in the Delors Report, will impose stronger disciplines on all member states. The advantages for a small country such as Ireland are stability and association with a large and economically strong Community. Against this is the danger that the more intense competition, and the scope for freer play of market forces — which, of course, are the source of the 'economic benefits' of the creation of the Single European Market analysed in the 'Cecchini Report' (Commission of the EC, 1988) — may work to the disadvantage of those regions of the Community which, by reason of location or history, have the lowest productivity and income levels. If adequate arrangements are put in place to strengthen the economic structures of these regions, and to alleviate the particular difficulties they already have and that are likely to arise for them in the process of creating the SM, the opportunity will certainly be there to close the gap in employment prospects, in productivity and, ultimately, in living standards.

Turning this opportunity into reality poses a considerable challenge to Irish society, to government, to policy-advisers and, indeed, to all actors on the economic stage. It is true that Ireland shall lose some flexibility in economic and financial management, but, as for all small and open economies, the room for manoeuvre on this front is, in any event, quite limited.

Notwithstanding the additional constraints on macroeconomic policies, the balance of advantage for Ireland is towards greater economic and monetary integration. The size of the 'plus' will depend crucially on how the country responds to the challenges, and, in particular, on the approach adopted in the broad field of microeconomic policies — all those activities of government that impinge on the efficiency with which we use the resources of land, labour and capital at our disposal. The shape of Ireland's microeconomic policies probably will exert a far more decisive influence on its long-term economic prosperity and its ability to provide jobs at home for Irish people than macroeconomic policies ever could hope to. In a more integrated Community, production and jobs increasingly will be drawn to those regions that offer the best balance between costs and productivity. At present there are inefficiencies in the economy inevitably created by taxation and subsidies and by the pursuit of non-economic objectives or resulting from poorly designed policies. In addition, the operation of competitive markets is inhibited by traditional practice and arrangements. The SM will accentuate greatly the cost of all such inefficiencies in the operation of the Irish economy.

The costs, direct and indirect, associated with taxation are considerable, and it is clear that the economic cost of unfavourable tax differentials will be accentuated by market integration. Since taxes are for the most part raised to fund public services, the pressure to ensure that Irish producers are not unduly disadvantaged necessarily will have implications for the level and quality of the country's public services.

There is a final point, made by Dermot McAleese in an article in *Seirbhis Phoibli*:

> Loss of autonomy in economic policy-making is an inevitable accompaniment of closer integration. But this is not a conclusive argument against it. Even by 1992 Irish general government expenditure is unlikely to be much less than its present 54 per cent of GDP. That leaves plenty of scope for domestic discretion, if it is used properly. (McAleese, 1989)

The essential point is that, even with close coordination of macroeconomic policy within the Community, the Irish authorities will still retain a decisive role. Ireland's government, by levying taxes on a great variety of activities, by carrying out many key functions itself and by providing certain funding to businesses and households, and, last but not least, by providing a legislative framework within which economic agents must function, will still play a central role. It will, as now, have a great deal to say about the how, the when and the where of the millions of decisions that are made daily in the economic system: what to buy, what to produce, how to organise production, whether to invest here or elsewhere, and so on. While the glamour attaches to the big budgetary and monetary decisions, it is being realised increasingly that it is the quality of the small decisions that differentiates the successful economies from the unsuccessful.

This is a role that we shall be free to exploit to our advantage or not. It is a misunderstanding to assume that convergence of macroeconomic and fiscal policies after 1992 will transfer all key decision-making functions from the Irish authorities. In fact we are not being let off the hook. Within the Community's macroeconomic and fiscal policies, the key decisions that will determine the success of the Irish economy are ours and shall remain so after 1992.

European Monetary Integration

PETER BACON and MARY BATEMAN

It is timely to consider the evolution of the process towards monetary integration in Europe. The moment is opportune, not only because we now have the benefit of a decade's experience within the European Monetary System (EMS), but also because of the likely impact of initiatives such as the growing liberalisation of capital movements, the establishment of a united European market for goods and services, as well as the study by the Delors Committee on concrete steps towards the realisation of economic and monetary union in Europe.

Moves towards greater monetary integration, and the ultimate goal of European Monetary Union, must be seen in the perspective of the completion of the internal market. While monetary integration is not in itself a specific feature of the proposals for a Single European Market, many developments taking place within the context of the completion of the internal market will impinge on the process towards monetary integration within Europe. Indeed, developments with respect to the liberalisation of financial markets, the removal of exchange controls and the harmonisation of taxes, will all have direct implications for the process of monetary integration. In this chapter, we provide an update on the progress of the movement towards monetary union in Europe and examine the principal features and implications of European Monetary Union. We also discuss the implications of the Single Market proposals for monetary integration. The impact on Ireland of these developments are considered together with some thoughts about the prospects for the future.

1969–79

been a by-stander at EC summits and Monetary union h..wledged but not taken too seriously. As meetings, always EC Heads of State, at a meeting in the far back as 19..t a plan should be drawn up with a view Hague, agree..in stages, of an economic and monetary union to the crea..mmunity. The plan for the attainment of such a within th.. presented in the Werner Report, prepared in 1970. union .. In March of the following year, the member states expressed th..r political will to establish an economic and monetary union. Several important moves followed: in 1972, the 'snake' was created; in 1973 the European Monetary Cooperation Fund (EMCF) was set up; and in 1974 the Council's decision on the attainment of a high degree of convergence in the Community was adopted. By the mid-1970s the process of integration had lost momentum, largely as the result of divergent policy responses to the economic shocks of the period; and moves towards greater monetary convergence had stalled or gone into reverse.

1979–88

However, in 1979, the process of monetary integration was relaunched, with the creation of the EMS and the European Currency Unit (ECU). Within the framework of the EMS, participants in the exchange rate mechanism have succeeded in creating 'a zone of increasing monetary stability' at the same time as gradually relaxing capital controls. The EMS has served as the focal point for improved monetary policy coordination and has provided a basis for multilateral surveillance within the Community. However, the EMS has not fulfilled its full potential. Firstly, a number of member states — namely Greece, Portugal and the UK — have not yet joined the exchange rate mechanism and one country, Spain, is allowed wider margins of fluctuation. Secondly, the lack of sufficient convergence of fiscal policies, as reflected in large and persistent budget deficits in certain countries, has remained a source of tension and has put a disproportionate burden on monetary policy. Thirdly, the transition to the second stage of the EMS and the establishment of the European Monetary Fund, as foreseen by the resolution of the European Council adopted in 1978, have not been accomplished.

The 'Basle/Nyborg' agreement of September 1987, the most recent step in monetary coordination, marked the beginning of a new phase for the EMS. With the progressive integration of financial markets and the objective of the abolition of the remaining capital restrictions, in line with the completion of the internal market by 1992, the exchange rate mechanism of the EMS required some reinforcement to meet increased or new strains on the system. The agreement comprised a combination of technical improvements and moves towards greater coordination in monetary policies. There was agreement to exploit the scope for a more active, flexible and concerted use of the instruments available, i.e. foreign-exchange market interventions; exchange rate movements within the fluctuation band; and interest rate changes. In addition, the agreement permits the financing of intra-marginal interventions in certain circumstances, which is both an important technical and a practical step forward, and it was agreed to strengthen the joint monitoring of economic and monetary developments and policies by the Committee of Governors of Central Banks. Although the experience acquired in managing the system since 1987 has been of short duration, it has been varied concerning external factors, such as the dollar, the yen and the G7 accord to stabilise exchange rates. Interest rate differentials have become the main weapon used to combat tensions in the parity grid. The appropriate width of these differentials has been reached at times by way of changes in the levels of interest rates in both strong and weak currency countries without endangering anti-inflation strategies. This more balanced and more efficient management of the system has increased confidence in the stability of the parity grid. However, it remains to be seen whether the new procedures and methods will be sufficient to meet the challenge represented by the complete liberalisation of capital movements.

The success of the EMS in promoting its objectives of internal and external monetary stability contributed to further progress on European integration, as reflected in the adoption of the internal market programme and the signing of the Single European

Act (SEA). In January 1985, the Commission proposed the achievement of the objective of a market without internal frontiers by the end of 1992. The detailed measures for the removal of physical, technical and fiscal barriers were set out in a White Paper that specified the precise programme, timetable and methods of creating a unified economic area in which persons, goods, services and capital would be able to move freely. This objective was embodied in December 1985 in the SEA.

The SEA marked the first significant revision of the Treaty of Rome and introduced a number of changes in the Community's strategy for advancement of the integration process. It greatly simplified the requirements of harmonising national law by limiting harmonisation to the essential standards and by systematic adoption of mutual recognition of national norms and regulations. Most importantly in the present context, it reaffirmed the need to strengthen the Community's economic and social cohesion in order to enhance the EC's monetary capacity with a view to economic and monetary union (EMU). However, although the SEA has given treaty status to the monetary capacity of the EC, by mentioning both the EMS and ECU, it is not clear that it has in any way extended the competence of the Community. Indeed, any institutional developments in the monetary area will require further amendment of the Treaty.

1989

The European Commission has now established its commitment to pursue the idea of developing monetary cooperation even further, with the goal being full European Monetary Union. The recent Delors Committee's *Report on Economic and Monetary Union in the European Community* has greatly increased the pressure for movement towards monetary union and is the first detailed blueprint to emerge from the current debate of the steps towards monetary union. The Delors Committee sees the move towards economic and monetary union as, in many respects, a 'natural consequence' of the committment to creating a market without frontiers but representing a 'quantum jump' which goes beyond the Single Market programme. As we shall discuss later, EMU does imply far more than the Single Market programme and will require further major steps in all facets of economic policy.

The Delors Report, submitted to the European Council in April 1989, envisages three stages in the process of integration. The first stage is to be a period of convergence in economic and monetary performance, with a strengthening of the element of cooperation within the Exchange Rate Mechanism and the possible creation of a European Reserve Fund. This involves strengthening the existing Central Bank Committee in an attempt to work out agreed, although not identical, monetary guidelines for member countries, all of which would join the Exchange Rate Mechanism. In Madrid, at the end of June 1989, the European Council agreed on the date of 1 July 1990 for the launch of the first stage of the Delors plan. The Council also decided to entrust the Community's finance ministers and other key monetary authorities with the task of organising an inter-governmental conference to lay down the subsequent stages. Stage two would establish the basic structures for monetary union, with the creation of a European System of Central Banks, aimed at establishing a single monetary policy across Europe. The third and final stage would be the move to irrevocably locked exchange rates and the passing of key monetary powers to European institutions, away from the individual national authorities, together with constraints on the freedom of fiscal action by national governments. As part of this third stage, a single European currency eventually would emerge. No timetable has been suggested yet for these later stages.

World trends in financial market integration

The movement towards an internal market for financial services marks a major new departure in integrating the economies of the EC. However, this movement is taking place against a background of greater internationalisation of financial markets. Financial markets in the major industrial countries during the past decade have expanded rapidly and have undergone extensive structural change. The unification of the internal market in financial services will add another dimension to the forces already impelling these changes. Before examining the implications of the 1992 programme for the financial services industry and monetary integration, it is worthwhile taking a brief look at how the financial services sector has evolved in more recent times, not only because countries have embarked on the initial stages of integration, but also because of the changes that are taking place anyhow within the global economic system.

Financial services have attracted considerable attention because of the unprecedented speed at which structural change has occurred in this sector of the world economy. Ireland is no exception to the rapid change in financial markets. Underlying the rapid change in the financial system of many countries have been important changes in the economic environment, as well as the policy reactions to them. In particular, the rapid growth of international trade and the expansion of multinational corporations have provided a strong stimulus to the globalisation of financial markets. Where regulations permitted, commercial and investment banks have extended their networks internationally. Advances in technology have facilitated the creation of new financial instruments, brought about strong competition in financial markets and also stimulated large investment in the industry. Structural changes in the sector have also resulted from increasing uncertainty surrounding the economic environment, which has increased the demand for risk management.

A major policy response to the structural changes outlined above has been the liberalisation of regulatory controls in major countries. Financial markets are the most regulated of all economic activities in industrialised countries. The rigidities produced by such a regulatory environment have forced governments worldwide to examine their policies towards the financial sector. There has been a dismantling of interest rate and price cartels in domestic oligopolistic markets, including brokerage commissions, such as that which occurred during the deregulation of the London Stock Market in 1986, the 'Big Bang'. The latter had a strong influence on the Irish financial markets which, until recently, tended to be regulated much like their UK counterparts. There have been moves worldwide to open up markets to foreign competition, including the admittance of international institutions to local financial markets and the liberalisation of cross-border financial flows. Regulatory changes have allowed the various financial institutions to compete against each other in more integrated financial markets. It is clear that all participants in the financial services market have been facing a rapidly and radically changing environment, irrespective of developments within the context of the Single European Market.

In Ireland, the financial services sector also has grown rapidly over the past decade. The share of the financial sector (financial institutions and insurance) in total value added in Ireland is slightly below five per cent (Table 6.1). The financial markets in Ireland have been dominated by the large credit demand of government, and at the same time this structure has been influenced heavily by differential regulation and tax rules. However, the situation has changed for a number of reasons. A significant improvement in the government budget balance since 1987 reduced demand in financial markets. Therefore, over the past two years, the Irish financial system has been adjusting to the reversal of these flows, with the public sector's appetite for funds declining and the balance of payments moving into surplus. Furthermore, traditional structures are being challenged by market forces arising from the globalisation of financial activities, in addition to the schedule of changes proposed under the Single Market programme. Advances in technology have brought about strong competition and facilitated the introduction of new services; for example, a new future and options market has started to operate in Dublin since May 1989. These developments, together with innovations in financial instruments, have made markets more 'liquid', increasing the speed with which external and internal shocks are transmitted.

Completion of the EC internal market

The creation of a single market confers a new dimension on the process of financial integration within the EC. As we have seen, the existing regulatory system in financial markets worldwide has been challenged by developments such as the globalisation of financial markets and innovation in financial instruments. This tendency in Europe will accelerate with the establishment of an integrated internal market in 1992.

While it is recognised that monetary integration is not in itself a specific feature of the Single Market programme, there are many proposals that will impinge on monetary integration. It is beyond the scope of the present chapter to discuss all these developments in detail. However, we highlight a number of major fields in which the Single Market proposals will contribute to the process of monetary integration within the EC. These include the liberalisation of the financial services industry, tax harmonisation, and the removal of exchange controls, each of which is discussed below.

Table 6.1: **Share of the financial services industry in GDP***

	1975	*1980*	*1985*
Ireland	**3.4**	**4.9**	**4.8**
United States	3.9	4.6	4.8
Germany	4.5	4.5	5.5
Austria	5.1	5.6	6.2
Canada	1.9	1.6	1.8
Denmark	3.4	2.7	2.8
Finland	3.0	3.4	3.9
Iceland	3.2	4.2	4.3
Netherlands	3.8	4.7	5.1
Norway	3.0	3.2	3.2
Spain	—	5.9	6.4

*Includes financial institutions and insurance
Source: OECD, National Accounts

Liberalisation of EC financial markets

The programme for the completion of the EC internal market includes 43 legislative proposals to create a common market for services. Of these, 24 relate directly to financial services — banking, insurance and transactions in securities. A further three relate to the liberalisation of capital movements, and another five relate to new technologies which provide the 'conduit' for the vast majority of internal financial services transactions. In addition to these legislative proposals which relate directly to financial services, capital movements and information technology networks, there are a further 11 legislative proposals relating to company law, five relating to direct taxation, and 25 relating to the removal of fiscal barriers (VAT & Excise). Almost one-third of the total package of approximately 300 legislative enactments required to complete the EC internal market relate directly to finance, or to the legislative and fiscal environment in which financial transactions take place. In addition, there are many other enactments that will affect financial transactions directly, including regulations relating to public procurement, the protection of intellectual property, competition policy, and regulations regarding state assistance to business.

The Commission used two main approaches in attempting to achieve an integrated market in financial services. The first relates to freedom of establishment, while the second is freedom to trade in services without establishment. The new approach by the Commission represents a shift in emphasis from the freedom of establishment to the free movement of financial products and services across frontiers. This new strategy developed by the Commission towards the integration of the European financial services sector is based on the principle of mutual recognition of standards. Therefore, an essential feature of the Community's regulatory changes is that once a financial institution is authorised in its home member state, it will be free to conduct business in any other member state without the need for additional authorisation.

The present types of regulatory barriers to integration which exist can be illustrated by considering the barriers to establishment and to operating conditions in the banking sector. While in each member state there is freedom of establishment for foreign banks, the conditions under which this may be done differ markedly from country to country. Barriers to establishment relate to areas such as restrictions on the legal form banks may adopt, or limitations on the number of domestic banks. Barriers to operating conditions in banking include the need to maintain separate capital funds, differences in the definition of own capital funds, and the need to maintain certain capital asset ratios. A range of different types of barriers exists in relation to insurance and securities.

In the banking sector, the Commission aims to achieve greater integration with a directive providing for a single banking licence; this allows a bank to provide a range of banking services anywhere in the EC. While the single licence establishes a very liberal framework, the transformation of the twelve member states' banking systems into a Single Market requires the harmonisation of many national regulations to ensure a proper competitive environment. In the area of mortgage lending, proposals provide for the freedom of establishment and the freedom to supply services in the field of mortgage credit in a host country in accordance with the financial techniques permitted in the home country. Transactions in unit trusts and equivalent products require only home country authorisation. Another directive covers investment services in the securities field, by providing a system of authorisation for anybody wishing to offer a range of investment services in respect of transferable securities covering investment advice, broking, dealing and portfolio management. The directive provides for home country authorisation and supervision, subject to harmonised minimum requirements and, once authorised, for freedom to provide services throughout the EC.

There can be little doubt that, when the EC proposals are implemented, some overseas suppliers of financial services will attempt to obtain an increased share of the Irish market. The real challenge here relates to the ability of overseas suppliers to trade without establishment. In Ireland, competition is likely to come from the UK as the result of the common language and communications and of the constant movement of people on business and personal visits. The possibility should be considered of overseas suppliers implementing a marginal pricing policy in Ireland. Many of these overseas competitors may be subject to more lenient tax or regulatory regimes and the implications of this need to be taken into account. In the event of increased penetration of the Irish financial services market across borders, the government may be faced with the difficult choice of reducing certain taxes and regulations or witnessing the shift of part of the financial services sector offshore.

The completion of the internal market in financial services is also dependent upon the removal of all exchange controls between EC countries, an issue that we shall examine later. The principles of mutual recognition and home-country control are likely to increase competition, not only among firms across the EC but also between the different national regulatory systems. There will be great pressure on these systems to converge since they are a crucial factor in the ability of the financial service businesses to compete internationally. The liberalisation of financial services will also limit the monopoly rents which the segmentation of the Community market into so many national markets currently provides. Together with the free movement of capital, it would lead also to a better allocation of financial resources, ensuring that the most worthwhile investment projects are undertaken and can be financed smoothly.

In a larger, integrated financial market system, investors will have access to a wider range of markets and financial instruments, and will be able to diversify their portfolios accordingly. In particular, the investor will be able to obtain a given return on financial investments for a lower risk, or if a certain risk is acceptable, to obtain a higher return. Similar benefits will be available to the borrower.

Thus, the liberalisation and further integration of financial markets across Community borders are important not only because of their effect on the efficiency of the sector itself but also on the efficiency of resource allocation of sectors using financial markets. It will also influence the conduct of macroeconomic and monetary policy, especially when taken with exchange rate commitments, as in the EMS (see Chapter 5). It is appropriate to view all these moves towards financial integration and harmonisation as being mutually supporting and representing an important part of the wider process of EC monetary integration. On the assumption that the movements towards financial integration are paralleled by greater monetary integration, the additional effects are likely to contribute further economic gains to the member states.

Tax harmonisation

Taxation is one of the main areas of difficulty in determining how best to ensure balanced competition between the financial institutions of the member states. The formation of a unified financial market also will require major changes in tax systems that impinge on the financial area. At present, the treatment of interest and dividend income, securities transactions, capital gains and bank deposits varies greatly from country to country. Capital gains taxes range from zero in Belgium to 50 per cent in Denmark. Stamp duties range from zero to one per cent of the value of stocks and bonds. The variety of practice in regard to the taxation of interest and dividend income is shown in Table 6.2.

With the completion of the internal market there will be great pressure on these tax systems to converge since they are a crucial factor in the ability of financial service businesses to compete internationally.

Table 6.2: **Withholding taxes in the EC member states (percentage of interest and dividend income)**

	On interest paid to		On dividends paid to	
	Residents	*Non-residents*	*Residents*	*Non-residents*
Belgium	25	25	25	25
Denmark	0*	0*	30	30
France	**	0–51	0	25
Germany	0***	0***	25	25
Ireland	**32**	**0**	**0**	**0**
Italy	12.5–30	12.5–30	10	32
Luxembourg	0	0	15	15
Netherlands	0*	0	25	25
United Kingdom	25	25	0	0
Greece	****	49	42–53	42–53
Portugal	30	30	12	12
Spain	20	20	20	20

Rates indicated are subject to restrictions and exemptions

*	Banks report interest income to the tax authorities.
**	Recipients can choose to pay 27% or 47% depending on the savings instrument, or to lump interest income with other income. Banks report interest income to the tax authorities
***	Banks do not report interest income to the tax authorities
****	Corporations pay 25%; individuals pay 8% plus an amount linked to graduated rates applicable to income taxes.
Source:	Ireland in the European Community: Prospects and Strategy, NESC No. 88, 1989

A major factor in the retention of differences in taxation has been the existence of exchange controls. Their removal will require changes in the tax regimes of the member states. The 1988 EC directive on capital liberalisation required the Commission to produce proposals aimed at 'eliminating or reducing risks of distortion, tax evasion and tax avoidance linked to the diversity of national systems for taxation'. In February 1989, the Commission published its proposals, which included the application by all member states of a 15 per cent withholding tax on interest income and a strengthening of mutual assistance between member states' tax administrations in order to facilitate measures to counter tax evasion. Such a proposal would limit the extent to which the flows of capital will be motivated by differentials in tax treatment.

Harmonisation of company taxation will be necessary if the liberalisation of capital movements is to achieve its full impact. Major differences in company taxation between member states can distort investment decisions regarding the siting of a company's operations, the location of its administrative headquarters, and decisions by individual shareholders and investors on where to place their funds. Furthermore, the removal of all restrictions on capital movements also could lead to an increase in tax evasion. Since investors will be able to have their investment income paid to bank accounts held outside their country of residence, there will be an increasing likelihood of the income not being declared. This is particularly likely in the case of interest income, since many member states either do not deduct tax at source or they exempt non-residents.

Therefore, since many overseas competitors are subject to more lenient tax or regulatory regimes, there will be increased pressure on the government to review taxation on financial services since there is considerable doubt whether many forms of taxation will be sustainable after the liberalisation of exchange controls. The completion of the internal market places a heavy onus on the Irish taxation and regulatory authorities to ensure that they provide an appropriate environment within which the financial services industry can operate competitively. In addition, the different tax treatments between banks and other financial institutions domestically will need to be standardised. The tax rules currently applying to financial institutions in Ireland are both complicated and not very transparent. This is partly because the authorities imposed additional tax measures to offset existing distortions instead of removing these distortions. In its analysis of the tax treatment of Irish financial institutions, the NESC has concluded that 'the ad hoc nature of the taxation of financial institutions in Ireland, through a basic regime plus levy in the case of banks, levies on general insurance companies and levies on the products of life assurance companies, will have to be replaced by a more rational form of taxation, underpinned by the principles of good taxation practice and designed not to handicap financial institutions in a single financial market.'

The Commission has drawn up proposals, mainly in the area of indirect taxation, on the harmonisation of the rates and structures of taxation, in accordance with the Single Market programme. These are not intended as measures of tax reform, still less are they aimed at achieving an optimum tax system for the Community. They merely seek, taking the present differences between member states in the structures and rates of taxes, to ensure that tax harmonisation will make it possible to abolish fiscal frontiers and speed up the process of integration. The final form that tax harmonisation in the Single Market will take still remains uncertain. Nevertheless, the benefits of removing tax frontiers are inseparable from those resulting from the removal of all the other barriers to the completion of the Single Market. The various barriers reinforce each other, especially where they are a shelter from market segmentation practices, as can be seen from the large differences that occur between member states. Within the overall movement towards monetary integration, the harmonisation of capital taxation is particularly important since the elasticity of capital movements in relation to differences in taxation will increase very significantly as those movements are liberalised.

Free movement of capital

Increased monetary integration requires the removal of all obstacles to financial integration and increased cooperation in, and the coordination of, monetary policies. The removal of restrictions on movements of capital is clearly an essential precondition to the establishment of an integrated financial system. Member states are working towards the achievement of complete liberalisation of capital movements in the EC by the end of 1992. The basic argument for having free movement of capital is one of resource allocation. Controls inhibit the movement of resources to the areas where they would be most productive. The price mechanism fails to function efficiently and real interest rates in different countries are able to diverge. Despite this argument, capital controls continue to be used. Although free movement of capital would be globally optimal, individual countries can lose because of lower investment. Furthermore, controls allow greater policy autonomy within individual member states.

To some extent, a country with relatively low investment opportunities, and therefore low rates of return, will get into deeper and deeper trouble as exchange controls are prolonged over time. The longer controls last, the greater the chance of funds leaving the country at the time of their removal. There is consequently a myopic incentive for countries to retain exchange controls. In the longer term, however, such a policy can be positively harmful. Those countries that are not open to international competitive forces will have little incentive to improve the productivity of their capital and will suffer slower growth rates, lower profitability and more severe balance of payments constraints.

The aim of abolishing all capital and exchange controls by 1992 is therefore entirely consistent with the aims of a Single Market. It would be difficult for any one country to argue that it should be entitled to maintain exchange controls and would certainly not be within the spirit of a free market for Europe. A return to the use of capital controls almost certainly would be interpreted as a major setback for the supporters of an integrated Europe, apart from it leading to an inefficient allocation of resources and a lowering of net welfare. The objective of complete liberalisation of capital movements in the EC by the end of 1992 has been partly achieved. The UK has already (in 1979) abolished all exchange controls, as have Germany and the Netherlands. The position varies in other member states, but all countries have been making progress towards complete liberalisation.

As a member of the sterling area, Ireland maintained extensive foreign exchange controls during the post-war period. On Ireland's accession to the EMS in 1979, these controls were extended to other members of the sterling area in order to protect the Irish pound from undue turbulence, against the background of Ireland's close economic ties with the UK. Exchange controls were aimed mainly at restricting capital outflows, with both foreign portfolio investment and the holding of foreign currency balances by Irish residents restricted. With the improvement in domestic economic performance, especially the strengthening of the fiscal position and the reversal from deficit to surplus on the current account of the balance of payments, the government implemented a series of liberalisation measures concerning the restrictions on capital outflows as a step towards the elimination of all controls on cross-border capital movements.

This process of relaxing exchange controls began in January 1988. Irish residents previously did not have automatic access to foreign exchange for direct investment, portfolio and real estate transactions abroad. Such investments were generally financed with either the proceeds from the sale of assets abroad or by authorised foreign currency borrowing. Foreign currency financing requirements have been relaxed considerably since January 1989. For example, Irish residents are now permitted domestic currency financing for the acquisition of foreign currency securities of at least two years' maturity at issue and, in the case of non-EC countries, for 25 per cent of the cost of direct investment and 25 per cent of the cost of personal property valued at up to IR£50,000. Certain restrictions still remain, principally on short-term capital movements to all countries and on real estate operations in, direct investment in, and certain personal capital movements to, non-EC countries.

Experience has shown that complete liberalisation of movements of capital results, in the first instance, in portfolio adjustment on the part of residents taking advantage of new forms of investment previously barred to them. In theory this is a once-off effect. Another, more lasting, consequence is obviously the potential increase in flows of short-term capital induced by expectations of exchange-rate changes or by interest-rate differentials. At the time of writing there is insufficient official data available to enable us to assess the full implications of the January 1989 liberalisation. However, while it is difficult to gauge the extent of the response very accurately, we can comment on some developments that have occurred.

Clearly, in a post-exchange controls environment, domestic residents will have a wider choice of competing bonds. Prior to January 1989, the use of back-to-back facilities, which enabled the conversion of Irish currency into foreign assets, and the manner in which foreign investment abroad was permitted, enabled foreign market exposures to be achieved but not the desired net foreign position. Following the relaxation of controls, it appears that back-to-back facilities were unwound during the early months of 1989, involving a reduction in foreign currency borrowings and a fall in the banks' net external liabilities. It is estimated that total private and residual outflows of almost £1.5 billion took place during the first six months of 1989 (Figure 6.1). While portfolio reallocations were probably the main reason for the outflows in the first quarter, we expect these effects to have been largely completed by the middle of the second quarter. It is also likely that there was a sharp increase in direct external investment, partly associated with industry's preparations for 1992. Purchases of foreign securities by Irish residents using Irish currency in the period January to August 1989 are estimated at £550 million. Thus, while portfolio adjustment, subsequent to the liberalisation of exchange controls, may account for some of the outflows, there still remains a large unidentified component.

Figure 6.1: **Ireland: Private and residual flows**

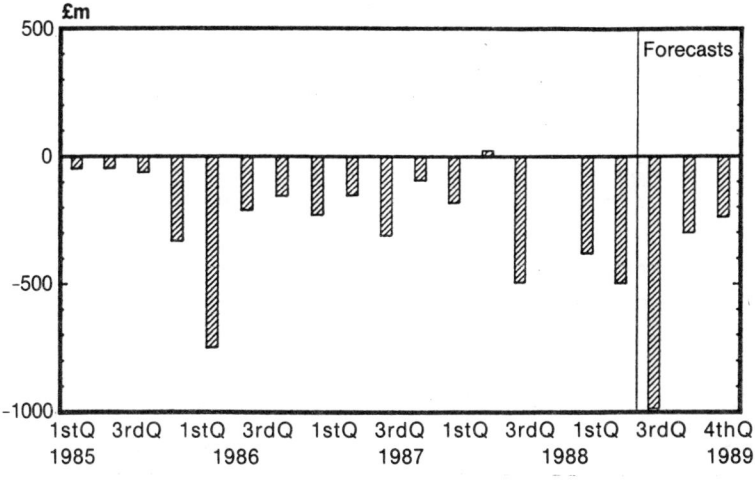

The UK's experience in the early 1980s also demonstrates some of the short-term problems associated with an abolition of exchange controls. The interpretation of economic develop-

ments in the UK over this period is complicated by a number
of factors, including a change in the policy regime in 1979 and
the rapid growth of North Sea oil production. However, the
removal of exchange controls was associated with a sharp rise
in outward direct investment, as is shown in Figure 6.2. This
reflected in part the higher returns available on investments in
other countries. In addition, the sharp appreciation of the
exchange rate in 1980 was not considered to be sustainable. This
implied that foreign capital would rise in value in sterling terms
when sterling, as anticipated, depreciated. Paradoxically, the
removal of exchange controls probably benefited the UK in the
short term. The outflow of capital kept the exchange rate lower
than it otherwise would have been, and therefore helped
ameliorate some of the worst effects of the recession.

Figure 6.2: **Net UK outward direct investment**

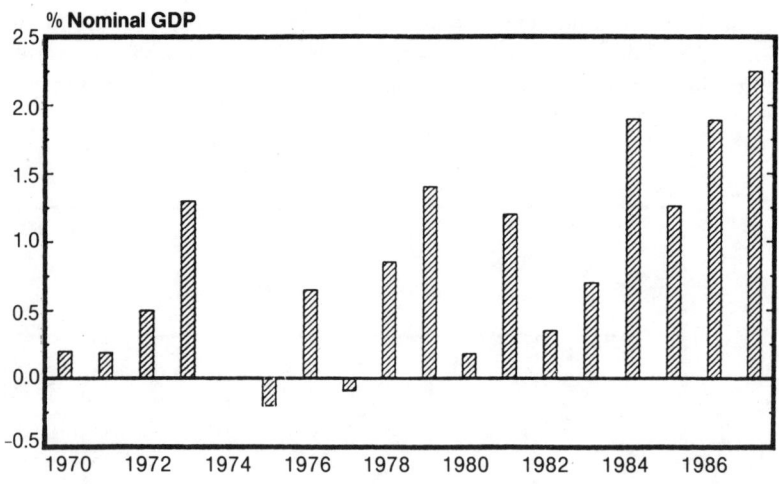

The process of financial integration, while bringing benefits,
also brings certain dangers, with the greatest risks undoubtedly
attaching to the removal of controls. There is a risk that the
benefits of removing controls may accrue essentially to the
member states that are most advanced economically and
financially. In such an event, the gaps between member states
would widen. In particular, if movements in short-term capital
are completely unrestricted, speculative transfers of funds would

be free to follow expectations regarding exchange rates, short-term economic differences or even expectations arising from political factors. Rapid changes in such expectations could exert pressures on exchange rates, forcing them away from their underlying levels. Thus, massive flows of short-term capital, resulting from portfolio adjustments, transmitted by the international financial markets, will be critical in determining variations in exchange rates. This in turn could threaten the stability and even the survival of the EMS.

Thus, doing away with exchange controls places a heavy burden on monetary policy. Monetary policy will have to cope with the 'increasing' mobility of capital and maintain exchange rate parities within permitted margins. To a large extent, these dangers already exist, in that capital movements are free in certain member states and financial markets have become more internationalised. However, the effects will become greater with the liberalisation of exchange controls by 1992. Thus, in a situation of total deregulation, member states could be confronted with massive short-term capital flows, causing major upheavals in the conduct of monetary policy. The Commission has proposed a special safeguard clause designed to enable member states to deal with such situations by controlling short-term movements. The liberalisation of capital movements, while playing an essential part in achieving integration and the benefits expected, nevertheless constitutes a potential cause of instability.

In summary, amongst the different effects that the integration of European financial and capital markets will have on the economy is a competition-induced reduction in the cost of financial services. Moreover, capital market integration will force interest rate equalisation since capital will be free to locate wherever the rate of return is highest. As we have seen, this effect will be relative rather than absolute, because there is already a substantial degree of capital movement within Europe. The Cecchini Report (1988) estimated that, as a result of the liberalisation of financial and capital markets, long-term interest rates will fall by about 0.5 per cent below the levels that would otherwise obtain, with similar reductions in other interest rates.

In the context of a fixed (or semi-fixed) exchange rate system, the integration of financial markets, and notably the elimination of controls on capital flows between countries, intensifies the need for a higher degree of convergence and coordination in monetary and exchange control policy. As the Padoa-Schioppa Report argued, this means in practice that the EMS will need to be progressively reinforced as financial markets are integrated and capital controls dismantled. However, as was discussed earlier, a step in this direction has already been taken by the finance ministers of the EC in the Basle/Nyborg agreement. Thus, with the planned creation of an integrated financial market and with free movement of capital, a basic component of monetary union also exists. As we shall see in the next section, full monetary union offers further economic gains of a directly financial nature, such as the elimination of exchange rate transaction costs and economies in the need for external reserves.

The final objective of monetary integration:
economic and monetary union

Any examination of the process of European monetary integration is now inextricably bound up with the consideration of economic and monetary union. With the inception of the EMS, the EC has made considerable progress in the field of monetary policy cooperation. In conjunction with the measures to establish an integrated financial area and the planned establishment of the SEA, the perspective of an economic and monetary union now appears in a very favourable light. Economic and monetary union would mark the end of a process, but one which, despite all the considerable progress that has been made, would still take some time to achieve.

Economic union involves:
- freedom of movement of goods and services, capital and labour
- a high degree of policy coordination
- the reduction of regional disparities.

Monetary union, the final stage in the process, would require, in addition, the irreversible fixing of exchange rates. These objectives require commitments which far exceed those made in joining the EMS and in ratifying the Single European Act.

Above and beyond the integration effects of a Single European Market, a monetary union provides a number of additional economic advantages. Firstly, the irrevocable fixing of parities means that the exchange rate risk associated with the intra-Community exchange of goods, services and capital is eliminated. This fosters, in particular, the integration of the financial market and the strengthening of competition. Secondly, there is a saving in transaction costs since market participants are increasingly willing to accept partner currencies or a 'common currency' without taking recourse to hedging operations, and to hold them as a means of payment or investment in the place of national currencies. Thirdly, the creation of a monetary area with a greater weight internationally, entails advantages in transactions with non-EC countries since the international acceptance of the Community currencies would grow. Furthermore, the Community becomes less susceptible to external shocks and is able to represent its monetary policy interests more effectively at the international level. While, in principle, national currencies can be retained in a monetary union, the introduction of a common currency would allow full advantage to be drawn from these benefits.

Another important aspect of the dynamic process of integration is the nature and timing of the costs and benefits of monetary integration. The adjustment costs to monetary or currency integration are private, borne by specific individuals and groups, and are incurred almost immediately in the short-term. By contrast the benefits of monetary integration are spread very widely and, furthermore, many materialise only in the long run. This combination clearly raises the possibility of concerted resistance to currency integration and, of course, raises a question about the desirability of economic and monetary union (Pelkmans, 1982).

On the European front, opinion is divided on the strategy for EMU as defined in the Delors Report. The British government, while supporting the first stage of the process, has not committed itself to the following two stages. Indeed, the British position is that it will not join the exchange rate mechanism until its inflation rate is much closer to the European average and until after the EMS has shown that it can survive the removal of exchange controls by France and Italy scheduled for July 1990. Germany has also cast some doubts on the idea of transferring sovereignty over monetary policy to a European central bank. The French have been the main proponents of EMU.

In conclusion, considerable progress has been made in the EC in the field of monetary policy coordination, particularly since the inception of the EMS. In conjunction with the latest measures to establish an integrated financial area and the planned establishment of the Single European Market, the prospect of greater monetary integration comes closer. In particular, capital liberalisation will further strengthen financial links between member countries and could act as a powerful force for monetary integration. The process of economic and monetary integration in Europe is both desirable and in many respects inevitable, even though it is one which will undermine the capacity of member states, including Ireland, to pursue independent economic policies. The arguments for or against the Delors approach to monetary integration are far from clear cut. The economic prerequisites for a monetary union that is characterised by fixed exchange rates between the participating countries will probably not exist for the foreseeable future. There is a necessity for further progress in the direction of greater convergence in a large number of macroeconomic as well as structural fields. Monetary integration cannot be imposed but will have to evolve over time. Isolated steps in the monetary field could very well overburden monetary policy in political terms and jeopardise the credibility of unification in the longer term.

The capacity of the Irish economy to perform well in the context of free capital mobility and increased monetary integration depends on its fundamental economic competitiveness. As noted above, there is a risk that the benefits of free capital mobility may accrue to the more economically advanced economies and regions. Capital will flow to the areas of greatest return. Consequently, while monetary integration reduces the capacity to pursue an independent approach in many areas of economic policy, it increases the need to exploit and develop the basic economic comparative advantages of a particular region. This requires, at the national level, efficient microeconomic policy and at the EC level an effective regional policy. The immediate short-run effect of free capital mobility for Ireland may be a further increase in capital outflow as portfolio adjustment continues. Even after this stock adjustment, there is likely to be a longer run increase in capital outflows than would otherwise occur because investment funds can avail of increased choice.

In other words, there will be an increase in the share of the Irish capital flow invested overseas. Equally, however, there will be an improved inflow. The relative scale of both these changes depends on the economic attractiveness of investing in the Irish economy.

7

The Impact of the Single Market on Indirect Taxation Rates and Receipts

RODNEY THOM

The harmonisation of indirect taxes and the abolition of economic frontiers are central to the European Commission's proposals for completion of the internal market by January 1993. Tax harmonisation under the EC Commission's original proposals implied that the rates of excise duties applicable to goods such as petrol, alcohol and tobacco would be equalised across member states and that each country will operate two rates of value-added tax (VAT) within the ranges 4 to 9 per cent and 14 to 20 per cent. The abolition of economic frontiers, on the other hand, requires the removal of administrative impediments to intra-Community trade, to enable the uncontrolled movement of goods and services between member states.

From an Irish perspective, these proposals have far-reaching implications. With the exception of Denmark, Ireland has the highest rates of indirect taxes in the European Community. For example, Irish taxes on alcohol range from fifteen times the proposed levels for wine to approximately twice the proposed level for spirits. Hence, full implementation of the Commission's proposals must result in large changes in tax rates, prices and exchequer revenues in Ireland. The purpose of this chapter is to assess the extent of these changes. The following section sets out the proposals for tax rates and assesses their impact on the prices of the goods that are most affected. Section 3 presents estimates of exchequer revenue changes. Section 4 briefly discusses alternative estimates. Conclusions are presented in the final section.

Two points must be stressed from the outset. First, this chapter focuses on *indirect* taxes only and does not deal with possible proposals for income and corporate taxes. Second, all estimates are based on the Commission's proposals to operate two VAT rates, with no zero-rating, and to harmonise excise duties to Community averages. Recent negotiations on VAT rates suggest that Ireland may be given a derogation on zero-rating which, if it is implemented, will alter the revenue estimates. Furthermore, detailed negotiations on the extent and timing of excise harmonisation have yet to be concluded. Any significant changes in the Commission's proposals would require a revision of the revenue estimates given below. At the time of writing the EC Commission is reconsidering its proposals. The analysis in this chapter should be useful in assessing the final outcome.

Tax rates and price changes

This section considers the implications of the Commission's proposals for the structure of indirect taxation and prices in Ireland.

Tax rates

In common with other member states of the European Community, Ireland operates a system of indirect taxation based on two types of tax — VAT and excise duties. VAT is a percentage imposed on the selling price of goods and services; excise is a specific tax imposed on each unit sold. The operation of these taxes can be explained best by the current method for taxing petrol. As of April 1989, petrol was subject to an excise duty of 30.35p per litre and VAT at 25 per cent. The net-of-tax price of a litre of premium petrol (i.e. the amount retained by the distributor and retailer) was approximately 17.65p, resulting in a selling price inclusive of excise of 48p, and a retail price of 60p per litre, the latter being the selling price plus 25 per cent VAT. More generally, we can express the relationship between retail price and tax as:

$$P = (1 + v)(Ps + x)$$

where P is the retail price, v is the VAT rate (0.25 in the above example), Ps is the net of tax price, and x is the per unit excise duty. however, it is more convenient here to combine VAT and excise into a composite tax rate and redefine the above relation as:

$$P = (1 + t)Ps$$

where t is the composite tax rate. Since total tax per unit sold is the difference between P and Ps, the tax rate t is given by:

$$t = \frac{Ps + T}{Ps} - 1 = \frac{T}{Ps}$$

where T denotes the sum of VAT and excise. Hence, for petrol, the 1989 tax rate is 42.35/17.65, or 2.40. The section below uses this definition of a composite tax rate to project possible revenue losses and gains that might result from the harmonisation programme. Before undertaking that exercise, it is necessary first to outline the proposed changes in tax rates, prices and expenditure patterns.

Proposals for VAT

In 1989, Ireland operated a standard VAT rate of 25 per cent and a reduced rate of 10 per cent. Goods such as alcohol, tobacco, petrol and consumer durables are taxed at the standard rate, while fuel, adult clothing and hotel accommodation are taxed at the reduced rate. However, in common with the United Kingdom, Ireland has a range of goods — principally food, children's clothing and pharmaceutical products — that are zero-rated for VAT. The Commission's original proposals would require each member state to operate two VAT rates: a standard rate within the range 14 to 20 per cent and a reduced rate within the range 4 to 9 per cent. For political reasons, it is possible that Ireland and the UK may be permitted to continue zero-rating for 'essential' goods. However, given the possible revenue implications of the harmonisation legislation, I shall assume that Ireland will end zero-rating and that goods previously in this category will be subject to 4 per cent VAT, with other goods taxed at a standard rate of 20 per cent.

In addition to changes in the rates of tax, the Commission also proposed to change the method by which VAT is imposed on intra-industry trade. Table 7.1 presents an illustration of how

Table 7.1: **Alternative VAT systems**

| | IR£100 of exports from UK to Ireland | |
	Present	Proposed
Export price	IR£100	IR£115
Plus VAT	25	0
Import price	125	115
Selling price	200	200
Plus Irish VAT	50	50
Retail price	250	250
Total VAT	75	65
Reclaimed VAT	25	15
Net Irish revenue	50	50

Note: Irish VAT 25 per cent, UK VAT 15 per cent.

the proposed system differs from the current system. This example assumes exports of IR£100 from the UK to Ireland. Under the present system, these goods would be zero-rated for export from the UK but subject to 25 per cent VAT on importation into Ireland. Given a selling price of IR£200 (the price charged by the Irish distributor/retailer), the price to the consumer would be IR£250 inclusive of VAT at 25 per cent. Gross VAT revenue is IR£75. However, since the import VAT can be reclaimed, the net revenue is IR£50. Under the proposed system, the exports would be charged to UK VAT at 15 per cent but would be zero-rated on importation into Ireland. At the same selling price of IR£200, consumers would be charged Irish VAT at 25 per cent, giving a retail price of IR£250. Total revenue collected by the Irish government is IR£50. The IR£15 VAT collected in the UK is refunded to the importer by the Irish government, which can reclaim the tax from the UK government via a VAT 'clearing house'. Hence, for a given set of tax rates, the proposed change has no long-term effect on revenue accruing to the Irish government.

Proposals for excise

Together with the removal of economic borders, the proposals for harmonising excise taxes were the most far-reaching of all the proposals for the Single Market. Unlike VAT, no variation in duty levels was to be permitted, so that excise taxes, measured in ECUs, were to be identical in all member states — with the rates of duty being approximately equal to existing Community averages. The reason for this uniformity in excise duties is to minimise the dispersion of prices that may result from flexibility in VAT rates within the Community. From an Irish perspective, these proposals have important implications because, with the exception of Denmark, Ireland has the highest rates of excise duty in the EC, with duties on beer, wine, spirits and tobacco in excess of twice the Community average. Table 7.2 gives a summary of excise taxes in the Community, together with those proposed by the Commission, and highlights the extent to which Irish excise duties are out of line with those in other member states. Note that the proposed rates are set in ECUs, so that a change in the Irish parity within the European Monetary

Table 7.2: **Excise taxes (ECUs) (April 1987)**

	Spirits (litres)	Wine (litre)	Beer (litre)	Petrol (litre)	Cigarettes* Excise	AV (%)
Belgium	5.01	0.33	0.10	0.261	2.5	66.4
Denmark	14.00	1.57	0.71	0.437	77.5	39.3
France	4.60	0.03	0.03	0.369	1.3	71.1
Germany	4.69	0.20	0.07	0.256	27.3	43.8
Greece	0.19	0.00	0.10	0.349	0.6	60.4
Ireland	**10.89**	**2.79**	**1.13**	**0.362**	**48.9**	**33.6**
Italy	0.92	0.00	0.17	0.557	1.8	68.6
Luxembourg	3.37	0.13	0.06	0.636	1.7	63.6
Netherlands	5.18	0.34	0.23	0.340	26.0	35.7
Portugal	0.99	0.00	0.09	0.352	2.2	64.8
Spain	1.24	0.00	0.03	0.254	0.7	51.9
UK	9.93	1.54	0.68	0.271	42.8	34.0
Proposed	**5.08**	**0.17**	**0.17**	**0.340**	**19.5**	**52.54**

Notes: Excise is per 1,000 cigarettes. AV(%) is percentage Ad valorem tax.

System would alter the IR£ value of the common excises. If, for example, the UK decided to participate in the EMS before 1993, then Ireland might opt for a devaluation of the IR£ against the ECU; this would raise the levels of excise duties measured in domestic currency.

Proposals to fix common excise rates for all member states imply that national governments no longer would have the freedom unilaterally to vary taxes on goods such as alcohol and tobacco. However, political considerations aside, there are important economic reasons for questioning the complete harmonisation of tax rates throughout the Community. For example, if consumer tastes and preferences for individual goods differ significantly within the Community, efficiency considerations might require that tax rates should differ accordingly. For example, there seems little justification for taxing wine at the same rate in both Ireland and France. On the other hand, the practice of some member states using high taxes as a form of protection is clearly a matter of concern throughout the Community. For example, high Irish taxes on wine, all of which is imported, have similar effects to tariffs, which are illegal for intra-Community trade. Such 'pseudo-tariffs' distort the pattern of trade within the Community and give a degree of protection to domestic industries that produce substitutes for imported goods.

Price changes

Given the magnitude of the VAT and excise changes outlined above, it is clear that they will result in significant price changes within Ireland. Table 7.3 presents estimates of possible price changes for the goods most affected — petrol, beer, spirits, wine and tobacco products. The methodology underlying these estimates is as follows. First, a typical 1989 price is assumed for each good: 60p per litre of premium petrol, £2.80 per litre of beer (approximately £1.60 per pint), and so on. Second, the rates of VAT and excise duties are those given in the 1989 budget. Third, the net of tax price, denoted Ps, is the retail price less all taxes, and is assumed to be constant in the face of tax changes. This assumption implies that the total tax change is passed to the consumer and is reflected fully in the retail price, so that the incidence of the tax is borne by consumers only. In most

Table 7.3: **Price changes**

	1989 £	New £	Change (%)
Petrol per litre			
Retail price	00.60	00.530	−11.7
VAT	.120	.088	
Excise	.303	.265	
Tax revenue	.423	.353	
Ps	.176	.176	
Tax rate	2.400	2.010	−16.2
Beer per litre			
Retail price	2.80	1.73	−38.2
VAT	0.56	0.29	
Excise	0.93	0.13	
Tax revenue	1.49	0.42	
Ps	1.31	1.31	
Tax rate	1.14	0.32	−71.9
Spirits per litre[1]			
Retail price	16.00	10.48	−34.5
VAT	3.20	1.75	
Excise	8.03	3.96	
Tax revenue	11.23	5.71	
Ps	4.77	4.77	
Tax rate	2.53	1.19	−49.4
Wine per litre			
Retail price	8.00	5.39	−32.6
VAT	1.60	0.90	
Excise	2.04	0.13	
Tax revenue	3.64	1.03	
Ps	4.36	4.36	
Tax rate	0.83	0.23	−73.3
Cigarettes per 20			
Retail price	2.00	1.80	−10.0
VAT	0.40	0.30	
Excise	0.81	0.31	
Ad valorem	0.27	0.67[2]	
Tax revenue	1.48	1.28	
Ps	0.52	0.52	
Tax rate	2.85	2.46	−13.7

Notes:
[1]40 per cent alcohol.
[2]Assumes 20 per cent VAT rate, with VAT equal to 16.67 per cent of the retail price and Ad valorem 37.3 per cent.

cases it would be expected that the tax incidence will be borne by both producers and consumers, with the actual change in retail price being determined by the price elasticities of demand and supply. Generally the more responsive supply is to price changes, the greater the change in retail price resulting from a specific tax change. However, since we have almost no information on supply elasticities, I assume that the supply of each good is perfectly elastic at the current market price. That is, producers will supply any quantity demanded at the market price. Hence the price changes estimated in Table 7.3 are likely to be in excess of the actual price changes.

Revenue changes

Methodology

The previous section discussed ways in which the Commission's proposals on excise duties and VAT rates might affect the structure of indirect taxation and retail prices in Ireland. Given the relatively large changes in indirect taxes that are likely to result from the tax harmonisation programme, the Commission's proposals have obvious implications for exchequer revenues. Since Irish excise duties are the second highest in the Community, it is certain that full implementation of the programme will result in a decline of government tax revenue.

However, it must be stressed that a loss of government revenue does not imply a loss to the Irish economy. On the contrary, most of the revenue lost to the exchequer will be a gain to Irish consumers; that is, a transfer of purchasing power from the public to the private sector. Nevertheless, if government expenditure is to be maintained at current levels, then barring the unlikely event that the Commission will 'compensate' Ireland, this revenue loss will have to be made good from other sources such as taxes on income. Since Irish income taxes are already relatively high, such a switch will prove to be politically and financially difficult. This problem would be compounded if food and other zero-rated goods were charged to VAT. Hence, although the revenue lost to the exchequer should not be considered as a loss to the economy as a whole, the switch to harmonised tax rates would lead to significant political and budgetary problems for the government. It is therefore of considerable importance to assess the possible revenue changes that might result from implementation of the Commission's proposals.

Since these proposals imply significant changes in the relative prices of goods and services, it is essential that assessments of potential revenue changes should account for the way in which the pattern of consumer expenditure may vary as a consequence of tax-induced price changes. To illustrate: consider a case where the Commission's proposals result in a fall in the retail price of a given good or service. At a constant seller's price (wholesale price plus retailer's margin), a cut in the rate of taxation, in the form of a change in VAT or excise duty, will affect exchequer revenue in two distinct ways. First, at any constant volume of sales, a reduction in the tax rate unambiguously will reduce revenue. Second, since the tax cut may reduce retail price, the quantity purchased by consumers may increase, leading to a rise in revenue from additional sales. Since these effects work in opposite directions, the total effect on revenue will be ambiguous. Generally the net effect of a change in the tax rate will depend on the product of the price elasticity of demand and the proportion of tax in the final price (i.e. the price elasticity of demand multiplied by the proportion of tax in final prices). If the absolute value of this product is less than unity, then revenue will fall (rise) as the tax rate falls (rises). Conversely, if the absolute value is greater than unity, then revenue will increase (decrease) as the rate of taxation increases (decreases).

Although the proof of this result is somewhat technical, the intuition can be got from the following example, which relates to the taxation of petrol in Ireland. Table 7.3 presents the breakdown of the price of a litre of premium non-leaded petrol in April 1989. The first column gives the actual breakdown, while the second gives the hypothetical breakdown that would have existed if the Commission's proposals had been in place at that date. In computing the new price, it is assumed that both the wholesale price and the dealer's margin are constant; this enables us to compare like with like. Using the methods of the previous section, the actual tax rate applying to petrol in April 1989 was 2.40; that is, the ratio of tax per litre (42.3p) to the sum of the wholesale price and the retail margin (17.6p). With the Commission's proposals in place and a 20 per cent VAT rate, excise tax would have been 340 ECUs per 1,000 litres which, at an exchange rate of IR£ = 1.28 ECUs, gives excise duty of 26.5p per litre and a tax rate of 2.01. With annual sales of, say, 1,200m litres, these figures imply a fall in revenue from £508m. to £417.m., with a revenue loss of £91m. However, because the retail price would fall by approximately 12 per cent, it is unrealistic to assume that the annual petrol sales would remain constant.

The extent to which petrol sales might rise as the rate of tax is reduced depends on the responsiveness of the demand for petrol to changes in the retail price. The price elasticity of demand, defined as the ratio of the percentage change in sales to the percentage change in price, is a measure of sales responsiveness to price changes. If, for example, elasticity is 0.5, then a one percentage reduction in price will lead to a 0.5 percentage rise in demand; a 12 per cent price cut will increase sales by 6 per cent. Hence, starting from a sales base of 1200m litres per annum, a 12 per cent price reduction would increase consumption by 72m litres, giving additional revenue of £25m. and a net loss of £66m. Clearly, so long as demand is sensitive to price changes, then projections of revenue changes that assume constant sales are likely to be misleading.

The above example considers only revenue from a single good, whereas total revenue from VAT and excise is the aggregate of revenues over all goods and services. Consider, for example, two goods, A and B. If the rate of taxation on A is reduced and its price elasticity is less than unity, the revenue derived from A will decrease. However, if A and B are complementary goods, then sales of B will increase as the price of A falls, so that the revenue loss from A will be offset at least partly by revenue gains from B. For example, if the tax on gin is reduced, we might expect increased sales of both gin and tonic water, so that any revenue loss from the former will be offset partly by increased revenue from the latter. If, on the other hand, A and B arc substitute goods, then *ceteris paribus* a tax-induced fall in the price of A may reduce sales of B, with the consequence that revenue from both goods may decline. Therefore, to evaluate the revenue consequences of a change in the tax rate on A, we need to know both its price elasticity of demand and the response of the other goods to a change in the price of A. Further, if the tax rate applied to B is also changed, then an estimate of the overall revenue change requires knowledge of the price elasticity of demand for B and the response of the demand for A as the price of B changes.

More generally, a comprehensive assessment of potential revenue changes requires a prior estimate of the way in which consumer expenditure patterns respond to tax-induced changes in relative prices. One method of obtaining such an estimate is to specify a 'demand system' which relates the consumption of each good or service to consumer prices and other determining variables such as real income. Estimates of the system's parameters then can be used to project the variations in consumption patterns and revenue change that may follow any given set of price changes. For example, Thom (1988) estimated such a system over eleven goods and services and projected a revenue loss of approximately £350m., or 13 per cent of total VAT and excise revenues, relative to actual revenue from personal consumer expenditure in 1985.

The estimates for revenue changes presented in this section are slightly less ambitious. Rather than covering the entire spectrum of consumer expenditure, I concentrate on the principal goods affected — beer, spirits, wine, cigarettes and goods that are zero-rated for VAT under the present system. Taken together, these goods represent the major sources of excise revenues in Ireland and constitute a significant proportion of the expenditure base which is subject to VAT at the standard rate. Although there will be revenue changes for goods taxed at reduced rates, these are likely to be relatively small. Further, for other goods that carry significant excises there are not yet specific proposals. The most important case of an excluded good is automobiles. Even if the Commission does not move to harmonise taxes on automobiles, Ireland still will be faced with a problem because of the significant tax and price differentials, currently in the region of 15 to 20 per cent, relative to the UK, including Northern Ireland. In the absence of a narrowing of tax differences, the abolition of economic frontiers will mean that such price differentials will not be sustainable after 1992. Any attempt to maintain higher taxes in Ireland will be thwarted by Irish purchasers buying in the UK. Hence if market pressures, as opposed to the harmonisation programme, force Ireland to reduce taxes on automobiles, it is possible that the government may respond by substituting a 'registration fee' to maintain its revenue. That is, rather than have excise duties in excess of UK levels, the government may impose a domestic registration charge on automobiles regardless of where they are purchased. If such a registration tax is not applied, then 1993 may see a significant fall in revenue from this source, together with a serious contraction in the domestic automobile trade.

Revenue projections

Estimates of changes in revenue can be computed as follows. Denoting the number of units sold by Q, the total revenue from any good is defined as:

$$R = TQ = tPsQ$$

where t (the composite tax rate) and T (revenue per unit) are defined as earlier in this chapter. Since PsQ (or seller's revenue) must equal total expenditure (the product of P and Q) minus tax revenue, then:

$$R = t(E - R)$$

where E denotes total expenditure. Rearranging gives:

$$R = tE - tR$$
$$\text{or } R + tR = tE$$
$$\text{or } R(1 + t) = tE$$
$$\text{or } R = \frac{t}{1 + t} E$$

Hence revenue can be computed from two bits of information: the tax rate, and consumer expenditure on any given good or service.

Current (1989) and proposed tax rates for the principal goods affected are given in Table 7.3 above. Unfortunately, disaggregated data on Irish consumer expenditures are available with a two-year lag. I therefore use the Central Bank of Ireland's 1989 estimate for total consumer expenditure (£12,862m.) and apportion it to petrol (5.6 per cent or 1200m litres at 60p per litre), alcohol (11 per cent, allocated to beer 60 per cent, spirits 30 per cent and wine 10 per cent), tobacco (4.5 per cent) and currently zero-rated goods (30 per cent). The last category, principally food, is assumed to be taxed at 4 per cent VAT under the harmonisation proposals. Part A of Table 7.4 gives the estimated expenditures on each good, together with the 1989 tax rates and the projected revenues. Hence an expenditure base of £720m. and a tax rate of 2.4 for petrol would generate total revenue, VAT plus excise, of £508m., or approximately 70 per cent (2.4/3.4) of expenditure (i.e. $R = (5/1 + t)E$).

Part B of Table 7.4 gives estimates of revenue from each good in 1989, assuming that the Commission's proposals are in place and that the volume of sales remains constant. This is equivalent to assuming that the price elasticities of demand are zero, so that the percentage change in expenditures equals the percentage change in prices. The aggregate revenue loss is £485m. relative to the estimated revenue for 1989, or 28 per cent of total.

However, these projections fail to account for changes in expenditure patterns resulting from tax-induced price changes. Hence Part C of Table 7.4 gives revenue projections based on the assumption that the quantities purchased vary inversely with price changes. The own-price elasticities of demand used to compute the expenditure figures in Part C are derived from the results reported by Thom (1984 and 1988). Note that these elasticities approximate the response of quantities to price changes, so that an elasticity of, say, –0.6 implies that the volume demanded will rise by 0.6 per cent for each one per cent fall in price, with the consequence that expenditure will decline by 0.4 per cent. For example, with a price elasticity of –0.47, an 11.7 per cent decline in the price of petrol will increase sales by approximately 5.5 per cent (0.47 times 11.7) but will reduce expenditure by 6.2 per cent. Hence, starting with an expenditure of £720m., an 11.7 per cent decline in the retail price of petrol will reduce expenditure by almost £45m. to £675m. With a reduced tax rate of 2.01, approximately 67 per cent, or £451m., of this expenditure will be tax revenue, implying a decline of £57m., as compared to £83m. when elasticities are assumed to be zero. Allowing for the responses of demand to tax-induced price changes gives an estimated revenue loss of £286m. relative to the estimate for 1989, or 17 per cent of the total revenue, as compared to 28 per cent when quantity responses are ignored.

However, there are several reasons why the estimates given

Table 7.4: **Estimated revenue changes: 1989 (IR£m.)**

	Expenditure	Tax Rate	Revenue	Revenue Change
A: Current Tax Rates				
Petrol	720	2.40	508	—
Beer	849	1.14	432	—
Spirits	425	2.35	298	—
Wine	141	0.83	64	—
Tobacco	579	2.85	428	—
Zero-rated	3859	0.00	—	—
Total			1730	
B: New Tax Rates: Constant Quantities				
Petrol	636	2.01	425	–83
Beer	525	0.32	127	–305
Spirits	278	1.19	151	–147
Wine	95	0.23	18	–46
Tobacco	521	2.46	370	–58
Zero-rated	4013	0.04	154	154
Total			1245	–485
C: New Tax Rates: Varying Quantities				
Petrol	675	2.01	451	–57
Beer	719	0.32	174	–258
Spirits	469	1.19	255	–43
Wine	168	0.23	31	–33
Tobacco	538	2.46	382	–46
Zero-rated	3936	0.04	151	151
Total			1444	–286

Notes:
[1]Part A gives estimates based on total consumer expenditure of £12,862m. and actual tax rates in 1989.
[2]Parts B and C use the tax rates computed in section 2 and assume that goods currently zero-rated for VAT are subject to VAT at 4 per cent.
[3]Elasticities used in Part C are derived from Thom (1984, 1988). Elasticities are: Petrol –.47, Beer –.60, Spirits –1.30, Wine –1.60, Tobacco –.30, Zero-rated goods –.50.

in Table 7.4 must be treated with caution. First, the estimates for consumer expenditures certainly will need revision once the actual data become available in 1991. Second, they are based on own-price elasticities only and ignore cross-price effects, although in many cases these are likely to be relatively small. Third, and most important, the magnitude of the price changes considered are untypical of anything that has occurred in the past. Therefore, it is by no means certain that the price elasticities used in Part C, and estimated from previous price and quantity data, can be taken as being representative of consumer responses to a situation in which prices may change by over 30 per cent.

Alternative estimates

Given these reservations, it is useful to compare Table 7.4 with the 'official' estimates produced by the Department of Finance. Full details on the range of goods, statistical techniques and elasticity estimates used in official studies are not, unfortunately, in the public domain. However, the National Economic and Social Council (1989) reported Department of Finance estimates of revenue loss at £508.7m., with constant quantities, and £481.3m. after consumption effects are taken into account. These 'official' estimates are close to those given in Table 7.4 when consumption effects are ignored, a difference of only £24m. using Part B, but differ widely when these effects are permitted, a difference of £195m. using Part C.

Since full details of the official study are unavailable, it is difficult to comment on these divergences. However, the closeness of the constant quantity estimates, together with the difference in the varying quantity estimates, suggest that the set of elasticities employed in the official study are significantly different from those used in this chapter.

Conclusions

This chapter has examined the impact of the Commission's tax harmonisation proposals for Irish tax rates, prices and government revenues. These estimates must not be taken as a definitive guide to the actual changes that will occur in January 1993. Apart from the fact that both Irish taxes and the Commission's proposals may change over the next three years, the estimates must be treated with caution for two important reasons: they do not account for supply responses in computing price changes, and the price variations considered are so untypical of previous experiences that consumer responses cannot be assessed precisely. Hence the estimates given in Table 7.4 should be taken as being largely illustrative of the divergent results that can be derived from different assumptions regarding the responses of consumers to price variations.

What these results do show is that any estimate of revenue changes based on unchanged consumption patterns is likely to be misleading, especially when the tax-induced price variations are relatively large. However, taking full account of demand changes requires good quality data on individual spending patterns for a large number of individuals, and involves relatively refined statistical analysis. While the latter does not present an insurmountable problem, the former is not readily available to private users in Ireland. The elasticity estimates used in Part C of Table 7.4, for example, are derived from aggregate time series data, which are probably unsuitable for deriving the type of micro information required.

Finally, and perhaps most important, it must be remembered that a fall in exchequer revenues does not necessarily imply a loss to the Irish economy. If, on balance, the government sector loses income as a result of the Commission's proposals, then the other sectors in the economy will gain. Whether or not the economy as a whole gains is a much larger question and its answer is well beyond the scope of this chapter. However, it is clearly a mistake, often made in the mass media, to equate the economic welfare of Ireland with that of its government. Consequently, it would be unfortunate if our attitude to the Commission's proposals were to be dominated by their implications for exchequer revenues alone.

8

Technical Barriers to Trade

EWING PATERSON

As Chapters 1 and 2 made clear, technical barriers to trade will be removed as part of the Single Market programme. Different national technical standards prevent free movement of goods or impose extra compliance costs before cross-border trade can occur (Groupe MAC, 1988). The achievement of the free exchange of goods is based on the principle that if a product is lawfully manufactured and marketed in one member state, there is no reason why it should not be sold freely throughout the Community. This principle has evolved in recent years and has been used to replace the earlier concept that the removal of technical barriers required the establishment of common product standards, such as euro-bread, euro-chocolate, euro-beer, and so on. It had become well recognised that this concept was not capable of providing agreed solutions and also that it would be unpopular if it resulted in the removal of a diversity of products. In May 1985 a major element of the Community's preparation for the Single Market was a 'new approach' to product standardisation. In fact, the groundwork for this new initiative had been laid as far back as 1973.

Section 2 of this chapter outlines the background to the development of the harmonisation process, and explains the specific elements. Section 3 examines the extent of technical barriers for Ireland and for the Community at large. When considering Ireland, one must deal with those technical barriers that have acted as protection in the home market, and the foreign technical barriers that make exporting difficult. Section 4 presents conclusions and assesses how Ireland will be affected by the removal of technical barriers to trade.

The harmonisation of European standards

From the establishment of the European Community in 1958 the issue had to be considered of diverse national standards restricting trade between countries. The restrictions on the sale in Germany of French-made television sets and electrical appliances were examined from the late 1960s. The German government insisted that these electrical goods had to be safe; their safety had to be tested and certified in German laboratories. This problem was eventually dealt with in 1973 when all the EC governments, which by then included Ireland, agreed to implement common legislation known as the 'Low Voltage Directive'. For the first time the member states agreed that common technical standards could be the basis for ensuring that products were safe. Rather than defining safety requirements in the form of government regulations, it was now possible for industry to draw up technical standards that were free of government involvement, on the basis that, once they had been agreed for all EC countries, these standards could be used for testing the safety of electrical goods. An independent body in each member state was designated to test and issue approval certificates showing that the electrical equipment complied with the agreed safety standard. The manufacturer was then able to place a recognised national mark on his goods. In Ireland this introduced the Irish Mark of Electrical Conformity (IMEC), which is accepted in the other member states as evidence that the product is electrically safe.

An important feature of the Low Voltage Directive was that, for the first time, non-government standards bodies were asked to cooperate in removing a trade barrier.

Another important disagreement between France and Germany led to a milestone in the strategy for removing technical trade barriers. The product concerned, 'Cassis de Dijon', gave its name to a legal case that the French government initiated against Germany. Cassis de Dijon is a fortified fruit wine and its sale was prohibited by the German government on the doubtful grounds that its low alcoholic content would result in increased alcoholism in Germany. The German stance was based on the hypothesis that drinkers of Cassis de Dijon eventually would change over to stronger drinks, which they would consume in large quantities. In 1979 the European Court of Justice in Luxembourg ruled that the German prohibition was not justified. The Cassis ruling established that products accepted as safe for use in one member state must be considered safe in all the others — and that restriction on the sale of goods between member states can be permitted only on the grounds of health and safety.

These two approaches, the Low Voltage Directive and the Cassis de Dijon judgment — established the role of agreed technical standards in health and safety regulations drawn up by non-government bodies. Within two years it was decided to follow a new course of action based on this link. Four important measures implement this action:

Information on national standards and regulations

Although the enforcement of national standards is based on cooperation between the national bodies within and without the Community, until recently most of the technical work was directed to the needs of national interests, and in effect controlled by national industries. Within the EC it was considered necessary to increase the emphasis on cooperation at the European level to facilitate the removal of technical barriers.

The means of bringing this situation under control was the Information Directive — 83/189, approved by the member states in 1983. Since 1984 both governments and standards bodies in the EC have been required to provide each other with advance information on proposed technical standards and regulations concerning products other than food, and agricultural and pharmaceutical goods. Since January 1989, the directive applies to all products. The directive sets out to stop the development of any further technical trade barriers. This is achieved by other member states, which may be adversely affected, raising objections. The operation of the directive is monitored by the EC Commission in consultation with the member states through their Departments of Industry. Often the Commission forms an opinion that a proposed regulation would create a barrier to trade and advises the originating government that a change is necessary to comply with the Treaty of Rome.

In addition, the Commission dealt with the need for action to provide uniform harmonised technical standards in order to improve the trade in specific products. This is made possible by the direct involvement of the standards bodies that are recognised by the Information Directive. In fact the European organisation of the standards bodies, known as CEN/CENELEC, in which Ireland participates, has been commissioned to organise the exchange of data on standards on behalf of the Commission. From the time of its implementation in 1984, the Information Directive has been used by the Commission to reduce the number of trade barriers in the form of national regulations and to develop a wide range of new European standards to replace different national product standards.

The 'new approach' to harmonisation of standards

At the time when the information directive was ready for implementation, the member states set up a working party to review the operation of the Low Voltage Directive and to develop from the ten years' experience of its operation a 'model directive' that could be applied to other products. The objective was to restrict the legislative element to a general safety duty of government, and to establish technical requirements by reference to standards. As far as possible, these would be harmonised European standards but the absence of such standards could be overcome temporarily by mutual acceptance of national standards. In addition, the basis for manufacturers to demonstrate conformity of their products to safety requirements would be established for a wide range of goods. Furthermore, the extent to which the manufacturer's claims would require a form of independent testing would be defined.

By the end of 1984 when the EC Council of Prime Ministers met in Dublin under the Irish Presidency, the work on the model directive was complete and the Council agreed to 'take steps to complete the internal market, including implementation of European standards'. In its final form, this became the 'new approach' to harmonisation, which henceforth would apply in those sectors where technical barriers result from justified national regulations concerning the health and safety of citizens, consumer protection and environmental protection. From now on, legislative harmonisation affecting governments is confined to laying down the essential requirements. Products conforming to these requirements are entitled to free movement within the Community. The task of providing harmonised technical specifications is entrusted to European standards, which are published as national standards by the members of CEN/CENELEC. In 1985 the internal rules of CEN/CENELEC were changed so that qualified majority voting applies to the acceptance of a harmonised European standard; once the standard is accepted, each national body is required to publish it and to withdraw conflicting national standards.

With the publication in June 1985 of the White Paper *Completing the Internal Market* (EC, 1985), the Commission set out a programme for applying the 'new approach' to the development of directives in specific sectors where trade barriers exist.

In addition to setting out in the directives the essential requirements of the products to ensure health and safety, the principle of 'reference to standards' results in a major programme of work, involving the drawing up of harmonised European standards (EN) by the CEN/CENELEC technical committees. These committees are composed of national delegates representing the industrial and other interests of the individual member states. In Ireland, the National Standards Authority, which is part of EOLAS, provides the focal point for participation in the technical committees of CEN, nominating delegates and arranging the distribution of draft standards for comment before providing the Irish vote on their acceptance as European standards. Involvement in electrical standards is provided in CENELEC work by the Electrotechnical Council of Ireland, whose staff is provided by the National Standards Authority of Ireland.

Besides the programme of 'new approach' directives, comparable action has been taken to provide European standards for information technology, and telecommunications. It combines directives aimed at opening the market in equipment previously purchased on a national basis by government telephone authorities with an extensive programme of standards linking network requirements and equipment specifications. In support of this work, a third European standards body was created in 1988. The

European Telecommunications Standards Institute (ETSI) is associated with CEN/CENELEC and provides comparable consultation at national and industrial level.

Public procurement policy

In general, governments tend to operate public procurement policies which favour domestic suppliers. This fragments the EC market (Atkins, 1987).

To the extent that public procurement is based on technical specifications for a wide range of goods, one of the ways to improve access by suppliers throughout the EC is to strengthen the responsibility of government to specify supplies in tender documents by reference to European standards, where they exist. In the absence of such standards, the procurement authority is required to consider products that provide equivalent levels of safety and quality when judging offers of supply to tenders.

A 1988 case involving the Irish government concerned a contract given for the supply of a pipeline in Dundalk. The judgment of the European Court of Justice on a complaint made by the EC Commission, supported by the Spanish government, emphasised the importance of considering alternative suppliers within the Community. It was stated that, where a national standard is used to specify goods, it is essential to include the proviso 'or equivalent' to allow for the consideration of any other goods offered.

Until now the major contract sectors of energy, transport and water (in addition to telecommunications) have not been subject to rules on open procurement, but proposals are being prepared to bring these sectors within the scope of the concept of a Single Market. This will be done by ensuring that there is transparency in the tender documents, and in particular by establishing harmonised technical specifications and standards.

Harmonised testing and certification

The fourth element in the strategy for removing technical barriers is the matter of testing for conformity to regulations and standards. The basis of this will be a system for the mutual recognition of product tests and certification; this will eliminate the wasteful duplication of tests, which in some sectors is the rule rather than the exception.

During 1988 and 1989 'A Global Approach to Certification and Testing' was developed and the Commission submitted it to the Council of Ministers in July 1989. This is a major initiative and is considered to be an essential extension of the 1985 adoption of the 'new approach' to harmonisation. On 21 December 1989 the Council of Ministers agreed on a Council Resolution (90/C 10/01) which adopts throughout the EC the main elements of this 'global approach' to the assessment of whether products conform to the proper standards. It covers the groundwork required to create confidence in the competence of testing laboratories in any of the member states. The basis is a series of agreed European standards known as the EN 45000 Series, which lays down codes of operation that now apply to laboratories whose test reports will be accepted in all member states. These laboratories may be operated by manufacturers, private test bodies or government authorities. Provided that their operation complies with EN 45000, the laboratories will be accredited by national supervisory authorities, and products tested there will not be subject to retesting when they are traded between member states.

Similarly, bodies in each country which issue product approval certificates must operate in accordance with EN 45000, and their certificates will be recognised throughout the Community. This arrangement will apply particularly in conjunction with a new EC product mark that will be placed on products to indicate their conformity with the related directive requirements. The new mark is based on the letters 'CE'; it is intended as far as possible that the manufacturers will apply it to their products. An important aspect of this is that, by doing so, the manufacturer accepts responsibility for a claim of compliance. In order to define the basis for the manufacturer's claim, the 'global approach' introduces a series of 'conformity assessment modules' which will apply to a wide range of products. These modules are structured to cover both the product design (e.g. type examination) and the quality control of full production. Consequently, it is recognised that the international standard for the manufacturer's quality system, ISO 9000, will facilitate product control. At the request of the Commission, this standard has been adopted as a harmonised European standard under the number EN 29000, and is now published by the national standards bodies in each member state, where it is used both voluntarily by manufacturers and also for independent audits. In Ireland the importance of this standard was recognised some years ago when it was published as Irish standard IS 300, and already more than sixty companies have received the registration of the National Standards Authority. So these companies are already prepared for the new European policy on product quality control, and they will be joined by many others during the next two or three years.

An important element of the strategy devised for product testing and certification is the introduction of a supervising body that will include representation from each country, as well as certification and testing bodies. This body will not be involved in the day-to-day operation of mutual recognition. Its role will be to establish the arrangements that will apply in different sectors of industry and to reconcile their various requirements for efficient trade with a uniform set of practices.

Completing this strategy will be the final step in the formation of a single unified European Standards Organisation, and negotiations are already in progress to achieve this by further integration of the existing bodies, CEN, CENELEC and ETSI. The general view that the future structure should be based on national representation within a single organisation is opposed by some, who prefer a federation that would ensure the continuation in their present form of the three existing bodies. The resolution of this matter may take several years and it may be necessary to allow it to develop by the evolution of the present close relationship, which is based on a commonality of procedures.

Existing technical barriers

The extent to which national technical barriers operate within each member state varies considerably, but nonetheless these barriers exist primarily to the advantage of home manufacturers in their national market. Experience in Ireland and elsewhere has shown that technical barriers in Germany provide the greatest obstacle to exports.

In manufacturing industry, the most siginificant experience of German technical barriers has been in Irish-based computer companies, such as Digital Equipment Corporation, Wang, Prime and Data Products, where customers in Germany sought protection from the legal obligations of a general safety law that required installed computer equipment to be safe. Consequently, the customers insisted that the products should be tested and certified as safe to German national standards by tests conducted in Germany. The testing insisted that radio interference be limited, and this had to be approved in Germany. The complexity of this situation (which is not untypical of the technical barriers in Germany) requires that significant resources be devoted to obtaining approval. The prototype units have to be shipped to the German test house and, in the past, there have been delays in the testing, primarily because of the large volume of work in the test laboratories. The test results often would make it necessary for the manufacturers to make design modifications.

Fortunately, the Irish manufactuerers were part of multinational companies with resources and experience available to deal with the technical barriers. During the last five years test houses have been developed in each member state to enable them to grant national approvals. This applies to German requirements too.

More recently the same companies have encountered another technical barrier in Germany; this relates to the ergonomic requirements of terminals and keyboards. The German authorities intend these requirements to provide a level of health and safety to equipment operators. However, in the absence of harmonised European standards, the German requirements operate as a technical barrier.

The same companies are affected by similar Spanish trade barriers. These take the form of a number of royal decrees promulgated in December 1985 to introduce compulsory testing and certification in Spain for imported computer equipment. It is significant that Spain's entry to the European Community took place on 1 January 1986, after which it would have been impossible to introduce such legislation. The impact of the Spanish royal decrees was sufficiently serious for one Irish manufacturer to withdraw from the Spanish market, despite having potential customers there.

Regulations operated by the governments of both Belgium

and France have resulted in technical trade barriers against the products of a number of leading Irish manufacturers of medical devices. In these countries, the products were required to undergo tests for sterility, although the Irish factories carry out tests on the products to the recognised sterility standards of the European industry. It was possible for one of the companies to arrange for the re-test to be done for the French market in their associate factory there, but for the Belgian market it was necessary to establish a duplicate laboratory facility in Belgium, resulting in an additional cost of approximately £100,000 per annum to be set against their sales income from exports to Belgium.

Although the close link between Ireland and the UK market has led to a large commonality of technical standards, technical barriers have obstructed the access of some products. Some years ago an Irish company developed a 13AMP electric plug intended for moulding onto the mains leads of domestic appliances. However, in order to be acceptable for fitting by manufacturers of the equipment, it was necessary to have the combined wire and plug unit approved by the recognised certification body in the UK. In turn, the Irish cable had to be approved in the UK by the recognised certification body for electrical cables, BASEC. The cable was already certified to European safety standards by the IIRS (the predecessor of EOLAS), but this approval was not accepted by BASEC. Efforts made by the IIRS to reach agreement with BASEC were unsuccessful. Consequently, the Irish manufacturer was required to obtain similar approvals in both countries, thus duplicating the costs. In addition, the time taken to negotiate this, added considerably to the product's development costs.

In general, Irish manufacturers have found it advantageous in recent years to seek UK approval for products because, since 1982, there has been a general policy by the British government to rely on compliance with British standards as an indicator of quality. While such a policy is not itself a technical trade barrier, from time to time its use in public procurement contracts had the same effect. Sometimes this has had a positive result where Irish manufactuers have raised the quality of their products to meet higher standards.

However, some Irish manufacturers have had their products excluded from established UK markets by the standards' policy.

One such case was the supply of electrical household cable to the Northern Ireland Housing Executive, where some years ago there was a changeover in standards that resulted in the loss of business to Irish manufacturers.

One interesting result of this emphasis by large UK purchasers that products be approved by bodies such as the British Standards Institute (BSI) has been that some Irish manufacturers chose to have their products approved only in the UK, rather than both there and in Ireland. The respective sizes of the potential markets make this an appropriate decision, but do nothing to project the image of quality Irish products.

Of course, it would be dishonest and naive not to include examples of the use of technical barriers in Ireland. For many years the technical requirements of Irish standards published by the IIRS were based entirely on Irish-made products in order to differentiate them from imports. That this was dealing with a small-scale economy is illustrated by the fact that by 1978, after thirty years of operation, only 200 standard specifications were required. Since Ireland joined the EC, this situation gradually has changed in response to the country's industrial development. In recent years approximately 200 standards have been published in a single year, but it has to be said that most are harmonised international and European standards used by Irish companies that are manufacturing for export.

As noted above the EC Commission challenged the use of IS 188 as the specification for the supply of pipes for a water scheme in Dundalk. Their complaint was based on the fact that this restricted the contract to one supplier, Tegral Pipes of Drogheda. In a subsequent judgment, the European Court of Justice ruled that the contract should have allowed for pipes made to an equivalent standard to IS 188. It has become established as general practice to allow 'equivalent standards' for public contracts in Ireland — and indeed throughout the EC, where the Dundalk case was seen to have wide implications for the prevention of technical barriers.

Nonetheless, it must not be assumed that manufacturers now have licence to dictate to their customers the specifications and standards applied to their products. In 1988 both Ireland and the UK were permitted to impose tight controls on the manufacture and sale of 13AMP electrical plugs. These controls were accepted in the EC on safety grounds. They apply to all manufacturers irrespective of the country of origin.

This highlights an important aspect of the Single Market. Technical barriers must be objectively justified, and the rules that apply to them must not unfairly discriminate between manufacturers within the EC.

All the above examples have been subject to investigation and consultation with the legal authorities of the Commission in order to determine the extent to which the technical requirements impose trade barriers that are illegal under particular Articles of the Treaty of Rome. Not every complaint made by exporters and importers about specifications and certificates required in member states is judged to be illegal or contrary to the spirit of the Treaty.

Ireland appears to be unique within the EC in that almost all complaints about trade barriers operating to protect Irish manufacturers are initiated by Irish companies. In the other member states there seems to be less interest in exposing trade barriers which may be in place to protect national industries.

In the other countries, complaints and investigations have to be undertaken by the export manufacturer and this is usually a more difficult situation from which to establish the operation of a trade barrier against the product. Indeed, the victimised exporter often is unwilling to make a formal complaint, for fear that some form of retaliation may restrict future sales in the importing country.

The White Paper, *Completing the Internal Market*, identified a number of products where technical barriers were significant. The Commission set targets for the harmonisation of standards for the following products:

Simple pressure vessels
Toys
Construction products
Machinery (plant and processing)
Electromagnetic interference of products
Electromedical equipment
Gas appliances
Personal protective equipment
Mobile machinery
Weighing machines

In future, products will be added to the list as the Commission considers it necessary to promote free trade by the harmonisation of standards.

Implications for Irish industry

Since 1973 there has been a gradual attack on technical trade barriers. The difference now is that, within the Single Market, there is a much more structured attack on the issue. As demonstrated above, this is being accomplished by comprehensive legislation which covers technical standards, national regulations, and specific restrictions on the use of public procurement for the purpose of unfairly encouraging national suppliers. The implications for Irish industry are very serious and require immediate action in all sectors, and at all levels of activity, no matter how small. Firms must find out what is planned and how it will affect their businesses.

The construction sector will be particularly affected by the removal of technical barriers (see Chapter 13). The Commission has granted a major programme to CEN and this is now the responsibility of 46 technical committees, with a further five being formed. Irish interests participate in the technical committees as designated delegates of the National Standards Authority of Ireland, the national CEN member. As would be expected, the subjects cover all aspects of materials (e.g. doors, windows, lighting columns, cement, tiles, fire safety, thermal insulation and timber), and consequently are of vital importance to Irish manufacturers. In addition, CEN is harmonising construction codes in a series of 'Eurocodes'. Irish participation in this process includes contractors, engineers and consultants.

Irish manufacturers now find it is essential to allocate staff experts to attend the meetings of CEN committees and working groups established to draw up proposed standards. The number of companies taking on this commitment is growing every day and includes Irish Cement Ltd, Moy Insulation, Spollen Concrete, Readymix Group, Medite, Irish Roofing Felts, Gypsum Industries, Tegral, Sanbra Fyffe, and Wavin. No company can afford to ignore the CEN programme, which will result in the changeover of most British and Irish standards used in the construction industry to new European standards.

The Department of Environment is directly involved in the implementation of the changes. Recent changes made for public procurement contracts mean that future construction tenders are subject to EC-wide rules, which among other things require that materials and equipment are specified by reference to nationally published European standards wherever available, and in their absence to agreed national standards only where equivalence of requirements is available. Indeed, it is possible for a national standard of one member state to be agreed as an interim equivalent standard, with which established Irish products do not conform.

The major instrument of change in the construction sector is the Directive on Construction Products (reference 89/106/EEC) and each government in the EC is required to have it fully implemented by July 1991.

The rules on public procurement were amended during 1988 with changes to two directives. The Public Supplies Directive (reference 88/295/EEC) was adopted by the Council of Ministers on 22 March 1988 and governments have been required to comply with it since 1 January 1989. The associated Public Works Directive (reference 89/440/EEC) was adopted by the Ministers on 18 July 1988, to come into force in national legislation by July 1990.

A second important sector affected by this is the Irish health care sector, where Ireland has a very important export industry, primarily composed of branches of foreign firms. This sector will benefit from the removal of trade barriers. In this case, the particular work on European standards has been strongly influenced by Euromed, the association of European manufacturers. With the Commission's further support, a programme of harmonised standards is being drawn up by 16 technical committees and special task forces of CEN. Once again Irish representation, in the form of NSAI delegates, involves major companies such as Abbott Laboratories, Becton Dickinson, Smith and Nephew, Howmedica and Baxter Health Care.

It is significant that these two sectors, construction industry and health care, represent important portions of the Irish economy with contrasting impact on both the trade balance, and the technology base, but nonetheless are enormously affected by the common developments of CEN work on technical standards. Within CEN these are both major programmes for which separate 'technical boards' have been formed to coordinate the work. Similarly, in Ireland, all the participation in technical work is coordinated through two sectoral consultative committees of NSAI. The Construction Industry Standards Committee (CISC) has been formed to work alongside well-established committees for the concrete and timber industries. The Health Care Standards Committee (HCSC) was formed five years ago with a modest task of encouraging greater use of existing international standards, but now it finds its work transformed as a result of the Single Market.

Because of the well-established use of international standards, the electrical sector is not as significantly affected as others. However, in both the information technology (IT) and electromedical equipment fields, there are significant developments. The major aspect affecting Ireland's IT industry is the improved arrangement for mutual recognition of test results which is inherent in the Commission proposals (reference COM(89)209). This aims to remove trade barriers caused by the product testing required for each country. Companies such as Apple Computer, Digital, Dataproducts, Prime and Wang will derive enormous benefits from this change to single-product testing based on agreed harmonised standards. These companies participate directly in the work being conducted in committees of CEN, CENELEC and ETSI. The coordination of Irish interests is provided in the NSAI Advisory Group on IT Standards, where these companies, together with others including Bord Telecom, exchange views with the Department of Industry and Commerce and the Department of Communications.

In the field of electromedical equipment, which is the subject of a proposed directive from the Commission, Irish interest is predominantly from users such as the Department of Health, the regional Health Boards and hospitals. This is coordinated in a committee of the Electrotechnical Council of Ireland (ETCI) which, although independent of NSAI, provides a national consultative committee for the standards work of CENELEC.

A major sector affected by the harmonisation programme is the general engineering industry, where the variety of products covered is very wide, and where the work being carried out by CEN is extremely diverse. Companies such as Irish Steel, CPV Ltd, Liebherr, Timoney Group, Donnelly Mirrors, Crown

Central and others link into the programme through the Engineering Industries Association within the CII, which has established a formal contact within the NSAI to exchange information on the specific work of the CEN technical committees.

Besides these four or five major sectors, there is almost no part of manufacturing industry that is not likely to become subject to changes in standards. NSAI provides access for Irish companies to the committees dealing with the formation of these standards at European level. A number of other sectoral consultative committees covering gas safety, fire safety, food industry and quality assurance provide a forum for the national discussion of Irish interests.

Conclusions

The effect on the Irish economy of the harmonisation of technical standards and regulations is difficult to quantify — and will never be clearly known whatever the consequences of the Single Market after 1992. During the past two years the change in Europe has been presented as both an opportunity for and a threat to Ireland. The threat in the field of technical standards can be overcome by effective planning and action.

It is essential to bear in mind that suppliers from the other member states are planning to gain additional business in Ireland when the barriers are removed and, in particular, are likely to respond aggressively to public procurement opportunities. It should be noted that an important element of these public procurement tenders is that they require to be notified in every member state at the same time as in Ireland through a computer database known as Tenders Electronic Daily. Naturally this operates to the advantage of Irish companies that are actively seeking business in the larger market, but only if their products meet the new European standards.

The widespread effect of the changes can be seen from the fact that the future business of established Irish importers is also affected, particularly those buying products from non-EC countries. In all the new directives, those importers have placed on them the legislative responsibilities of manufacturers, and will be held responsible for the products conforming to European standards. In many cases this will involve the products being labelled with the 'CE' Mark, which of course does not refer to the country of origin.

Taking into account Ireland's industrial development especially in the period since 1973, there is reason to be optimistic that the country can gain more through the benefits to high technology exporting industries than will be lost in the increased competition in the home market.

When comparing knowledge on the way technical trade barriers have been operating in other countries, it seems reasonable to conclude that, with a small number of exceptions like the Dundalk water pipe case, in recent years Ireland has operated as an open market. Perhaps it is proper to record that protectionist measures have been associated with the country's older industries which operated on a more favourable home market before 1973 when Ireland joined the EC and accepted the provisions and philosophy of the Treaty of Rome.

One potential benefit can be fairer access to the UK. This may arise because of Ireland's close technical link to the codes, practices and standards of the British Standards Institute. Until now the use of British standards has been followed by Irish industry as recognition that they represented good engineering practice and the IIRS (now EOLAS) could not hope to improve on the experience and knowledge on which they are based. In many instances this had the beneficial effect that products then could be marketed directly in Britain, and advantage taken of larger sales volumes. However, following the UK government's 1982 White Paper, *Quality, Standards and Competition*, British purchasers have laid more emphasis on technical specifications in both the public and private sector. With uniform interpretation of fair trading imposed by Community directives, there will be less opportunity for British-made products to be favoured against Irish products that are manufactured to the same quality. It is important that sales representatives of Irish manufacturers operating in Britain and the other member states be aware of the limited scope now available to potential purchasers to operate an unofficial protectionist policy in favour of home products.

An important matter for Irish manufacturers is to establish the conditions required for marketing products with the 'CE' mark. NSAI can advise on the requirements, and can arrange for any testing and certification that the manufacturer requires, particularly for exports.

The greater use of standards — particularly in imposing strict quality requirements, will improve the competitiveness of Irish companies. It will also increase the likeihood that multinational companies will 'source' more of their requirements from indigenous suppliers.

In this way the Single Market imposes valuable disciplines on the Irish economy.

9

Transport

TOM FERRIS

Transport is a very significant issue in the context of the Single
European Market. Its importance arises because of (i) its role
in facilitating the free movement of goods and persons, a primary
objective of the Single Market, and (ii) its size and scale as an
industry, and its crucial linkages with other economic sectors.
There are, therefore, two principal elements in this discussion
of Irish transport. The first is the present and future Irish transport
infrastructure (having regard to both physical infrastructure and
legislative framework) and how it can perform in a cost effective
way in facilitating access to markets. The second is the future
that faces the Irish transport industry. Even assuming that the
physical infrastructure is adequate, will Irish or foreign transport
enterprises provide the bulk of Irish transport services?

The importance of transport and the need to remove non-
tariff barriers to transport services were recognised in the Treaty
of Rome, which established the European Community. Article
3(e) indicated that the activities of the Community should include
the inauguration of a common transport policy. That article (and
the separate chapter on transport in the Treaty) recognised that
freedom for goods and persons to move without obstacles and
barriers was fundamental to the achievement of a true common
market.

As an island trading nation at the periphery of Europe, Ireland
requires efficient, economic and speedy transport links with its

trading partners in the Community, with the minimum of administrative formalities and border controls. In the 1990s Ireland will not only have to operate in a truly single market, it will also have to do so as the only island nation in the Community. Once the Channel Tunnel between Britain and France is open, Ireland will be the only member state of the EC without a land connection to the rest of the Community.

The significance of transport in Ireland and Europe

Transport's share of both total output and total employment has remained relatively constant at around 6 to 7 per cent since 1970 in Ireland and other EC member states. While transport's share of output and employment has varied somewhat in individual member states, the proportionate changes have been only marginal. Table 9.1 summarises the relevant proportions for 'transport and communications services' in 1970 and 1984 (the latest year for which data are available) for Ireland and a number of other member states.[1]

Table 9.1: **Proportions of output and employment in transport and communications services, 1970 and 1984**

Member State	Transport and communications output as % of GDP		Transport and communications employment as % of total employment	
	1970	1984	1970	1984
Belgium	7	8	6	7
Denmark	8	8	7	7
France	6	5	6	6
Germany	6	6[a]	5	6[a]
Ireland	6	5[a]	6	6
Italy	6	7	5	6
Netherlands	8	6	7	7
United Kingdom	6	6	7	6

Sources: Eurostat, Transport and Communications Yearbook, 1970–1986, Statistical Office of the European Communities, Luxembourg, February 1989; Department of Finance *Economic Review and Outlook: 1989,* Pl 6764, Dublin, November 1989.
(a) Year 1983

The output and employment shares in the foregoing table provide measures of the size of the transport sector. Some other statistics point up sharply the scale of the transport sector in the EC (Toomey, 1989).

- transport's share of the gross domestic product of the Community is greater than that of agriculture, 6 per cent compared with 5 per cent
- the number of workers employed in transport is estimated at 6 million; over a million work for the railways alone
- capital expenditure in transport is estimated to represent 11 per cent of total private investment in the Community
- as much as 40 per cent of public investment is pumped into the transport sector
- the Community owns about 24 per cent of the world's merchant fleet (over 30 per cent if one includes Community ships that sail under a flag of convenience)
- nearly 40 per cent of the world's container fleet sails under a Community flag.

Another measure of the significance of transport can be gleaned by looking at the share of final energy that the transport sector consumes. Recent EC data show that transport consumed between a quarter and a third of final energy consumption, in the 1980s, in the different member states. Ireland's share is around 28 per cent, which is in line with the average. As can be seen from Table 9.2, some EC member states consume slightly higher proportions than the EC average (mainly the states distant from the centre of the Community), while others (mainly the central member states) consume slightly lower proportions that the average. Between 1980 and 1986, transport's share of final energy consumption increased in all the member states, with the exception of Ireland, which recorded a slight decrease (from 28.3 per cent in 1980 to 27.7 per cent in 1986). The foregoing statistics show that Ireland is not exceptional in the significance of transport in overall output, in overall employment and in energy consumption. However, these statistics tell only part of the story. Other statistics should be considered before the full significance of transport in Ireland can be appreciated.

Table 9.2: **Transport sector's share of final energy consumption, 1980 and 1986**

EC member states	Transport sector as % of final energy consumption	
	1980	*1986*
Belgium	17.8	22.4
Denmark	20.7	28.3
France	24.8	28.7
Germany	22.3	24.9
Greece	36.8	41.6
Ireland	28.3	27.7
Italy	25.4	30.9
Luxembourg	16.7	20.7
Netherlands	19.8	21.3
Portugal	35.2	37.8
Spain	32.5	36.3
United Kingdom	26.1	28.5
EC average of 12 states	24.6%	28.0%

Source: Eurostat, Transport and Communications Yearbook, 1970–1986, Statistical Office of the European Communities, Luxembourg, February 1989.

The transport sector in Ireland consumes a considerable amount of national resources in enabling people to travel and goods to be moved. The fact that around 14 per cent of total annual household expenditure is spent on transport in Ireland (CSO, 1989), and that transport currently accounts for around 5 per cent of Irish Gross Domestic Product, gives some idea of the amount of resources that the sector consumes annually. Moreover, there are also indirect costs associated with the use of transport, and particularly the use of the road system, such as policing, the treatment of accidents and general administration (NESC, 1980). The commitment to transport in terms of human resources is equally significant. The Irish transport sector is estimated to account for about 6 per cent (or 66,000) of the total number at work in the economy, with the state transport companies employing over 25,000 persons in Ireland. The transport employment figure of 66,000 refers to direct employment in the 'transport, communications and storage' sector, but considerable numbers are employed within other economic sectors, whose main functions are of a transport nature. Indeed, the Confederation of Irish Industry has estimated that the total number employed in Irish transport could be as high as 150,000, because sectors other than 'transport, communications and storage' employ people in a transport function, such as manufacturing and distribution (CII, 1989).

Ireland has a relatively greater dependence on transport than most other EC member states because of its peripheral and island location, which leads to a heavier reliance on air and sea access transport services. In 1988 merchandise exports represented 58 per cent of GDP (and merchandise imports represented 48 per cent). In tonnage terms, the sea accounts for 81 per cent of total merchandise trade. Tonnage crossing the land frontier with Northern Ireland accounts for nearly 19 per cent of trade, while traffic by air represents less than 1 per cent of total merchandise trade. Table 9.3 illustrates the composition of Irish merchandise trade tonnage in 1988 by main markets and by key transport modes. It shows that the UK continues to be Ireland's main trading partner (it takes 55 per cent of Irish exports and provides 43 per cent of Irish imports). Other member states take 36 per cent of Ireland's exports and supply 25 per cent of the country's imports.

Besides *direct* trade with the UK, a considerable volume of Irish traffic is also shipped *indirectly* through the UK — using what is known as the 'landbridge' route to other countries, including Continental EC countries. Some of the landbridge shipments go through Northern Ireland; others go by sea and air to and from Continental Europe via Britain. For example, the total number of freight units to and from Ireland's ports (North and South) was over 923,000 units in 1988, with 58 per cent going through Northern ports and only 42 per cent going through the ports of the Republic of Ireland. The share enjoyed by Northern Ireland ports is over twice as great as would be expected on the basis of the relative scale of Gross Domestic Product in Northern Ireland *vis-à-vis* that of the Republic of Ireland. In other words, a 30 per cent share of 'All-Ireland GDP', suggests that Northern Ireland should carry only 277,000 units through its ports. This, in turn, suggests that Northern Ireland is gaining up to 260,000 extra units of traffic destined for or originating in the Republic of Ireland. However, this may be an overestimate. A reported study estimated that the deflected traffic may amount to only 125,000 units (Dublin Port, 1989). Whatever the true figure, it is clear that the Republic's competitiveness relative to Northern Ireland leaves much to be desired.

Table 9.3: **Ireland's merchandise trade tonnage, 1988**

	Imports		Exports		Total	
	mn. tonnes	%	mn. tonnes	%	mn. tonnes	%
A. *Trade origin/destination*						
United Kingdom	7.99	42.6	4.84	54.8	12.83	46.5
Other EC	4.70	25.0	3.05	35.5	7.75	28.1
Non-EC	5.47	29.2	0.93	10.5	6.40	23.2
Unclassified trade	0.61	3.2	0.01	0.1	0.62	2.2
Total	18.77	100%	8.83	100%	27.60	100%
B. *Trade by mode*						
Sea	15.91	84.8	6.46	73.2	22.37	81.0
Land frontier	2.83	15.1	2.35	26.6	5.18	18.8
Air	0.03	0.1	0.02	0.2	0.05	0.2
Total	18.77	100%	8.83	100%	27.60	100%

Source: CSO, 'Analysis of Exernal Trade by Ports in 1988', June 1989.

As regards inland transport in Ireland, over 90 per cent of all freight tonne-kilometres is carried by road, with only 10 per cent travelling by rail. It is generally true to say that, as far as inland transport is concerned, the geographically peripheral member states are more dependent on road transport than the central member states, which tend to rely more heavily on railways. As a result, the former tend to favour deregulation of road transport, whereas the latter attach more priority to uniform conditions of competition (Abbati, 1987).

As regards passenger movements to and from Ireland, two-thirds of the passengers now travel by air and only one-third by sea. Air, which accounted for 50 per cent of the passenger market in 1983, increased its share to 66 per cent by 1988, reflecting a very positive market response to the lower air fares which came into effect during that period. In the case of inland passenger movements, it has been estimated that over 96 per cent of all passenger kilometres are by road and only 4 per cent by rail (Government of Ireland, 1989a).

Single market proposals on transport

Obstacles to transport

The development of a common policy in transport is essential to the completion of the internal market. Yet many obstacles still have to be overcome before transport operators have a genuine integrated market in Europe. For example, the removal of restrictions in the road transport sector is likely to lead to greater competition and a more efficient use of transport equipment. The present permit system and the prohibition of 'cabotage'[2] in road haulage up to now are reflected, among other things, in the cost of empty moves. A study by Ernst and Whinney has estimated the cost of empty moves in the Community at some 1.2 billion ECU, of which 20 per cent may be related to regulatory restrictions (Commission, 1988).

While many key measures have been adopted in the transport sector, it is clear from the 1985 EC White Paper on completing the internal market that the Council must take many more decisions before transport services can be provided without restriction throughout the EC. Indeed, about 15 per cent of the measures listed in the White Paper relate either directly or indirectly to transport.

Progress in the development of a common transport policy has been slow during the past three decades. It must be recognised, however, that the EC institutions have had to contend with a range of very diverse national transport policies, often with conflicting objectives. Furthermore, the sheer scale of the sector and the different modes within it have made it difficult to package transport into a single 'common' policy. The fragmented development of transport in the member states has been exacerbated by the fact that road, rail and waterway infrastructure networks, as well as ports and airports, have continued to be developed predominantly on the basis of national priorities and the availability of national resources. As a consequence, the member states' networks are far from homogeneous and many contain 'transport infrastructure gaps' particularly at frontier areas and in less developed regions. In an effort to fill these 'gaps' and to achieve a more integrated European transport infrastructure, the EC Commission has been attempting for many years to get the Council of Ministers to establish a transport infrastructure fund that would provide financial support for the implementation of transport infrastructure projects of Community interest. Obviously, such a fund would be of particular interest to Ireland, especially if it applied to access transport services and infrastructure (given Ireland's dependence on sea and air services for access to European markets).

The European Council so far has failed to adopt the Commission's programme for Community Action on Transport Infrastructure, despite the Commission's arguments that, in context of a larger and more open transport market, improvements will have to be made to the transport infrastructure linking different member states in order to facilitate movement, reduce blockages and avoid creating environmental problems. Indeed, the Commission has categorically warned that, without such improvements, the completion of the Single Market for transport services will be severely hampered (Pena, 1988). To date, the European Council has only noted the Commission's proposals. However, it should be pointed out that, under ad hoc arrangements, the EC has given a limited amount of financial support during the past decade to a number of selected transport infrastructure projects of Community interest, including Irish road infrastructure projects.

Deregulation

As regards the organisation of the EC transport markets, it is true to say that there is increasing evidence that the regulation of Europe's transport services is ceasing to be a matter reserved to national governments. As in other sectors, the balance of power is shifting and, increasingly, transport is being regulated by legislation adopted at an overall EC level (Commission, 1989a). The rationale behind the EC's centralisation of decision-making in relation to transport is simple. The Community cannot, on the one hand, advocate the virtues of the free movement of goods and persons and, on the other, allow member states to restrict their transport markets. It is hardly surprising, therefore, that the Commission has consistently emphasised the vital role to be played by a liberalised transport industry in its attempts to bring about a Single Market by the end of 1992. The position of the Commission was strengthened considerably when, in 1985, the European Court of Justice, ruling on a case brought against the Council of Ministers by the European Parliament, instructed the Council to fulfil its obligations under the Treaty of Rome and adopt measures to ensure the creation of a common transport policy.[3] In the absence of an effective Community transport policy, other economic sectors will not be able to derive maximum benefit from the Single Market.

The Council's concern with a common transport policy has not just arisen in the context of the Single Market. In fact, the Council adopted a number of important measures over the first three decades of the Community's existence, including the application of the Treaty rules on competition (Articles 85 and 86) to inland transport; the introduction of certain social regulations for road transport governing driving hours and rest periods; rules which reduce the potential for hidden subsidies to inland transport; public service obligations and railway costing and accounting; criteria and conditions for entry into road freight and road passenger operations; the establishment of a Community quota system for the carriage of goods by road between member states, and the introduction of a first phase of the authorisation of 'cabotage'. These measures included some useful steps in the harmonisation of competition rules both between transport operators in the different member states and between the transport modes themselves, and for improving the functioning of the transport market. Still, the practical impact of the isolated steps taken was limited and several important proposals remained deadlocked (Toomey, 1989).

Reference has been made to the European Court of Justice

ruling of 1985, whereby the EC Council of Ministers was instructed to fulfil its obligations under the Treaty of Rome and to adopt measures to ensure the creation of a common transport policy. This, together with the qualified majority voting procedures introduced by the Single European Act, has resulted in an increased momentum in the present decade. Agreement has been reached over the past four years on a number of significant transport matters: liberalisation in maritime transport (December 1986), air transport (December 1987) and road freight transport (June 1988). The decisions that have been taken in recent years have allowed most modes of transport to expand their trans-frontier activities. Nevertheless, at the time of writing, decisions of particular significance for the completion of the internal market remain to be taken. For instance, agreements on 'cabotage' in road-passenger services, which would open up national markets to non-resident road-passenger operators, and on further liberalisation in air transport have yet to be achieved. It is hardly surprising that a recent Commission report admits that the EC Council still has a long way to go to implement the Treaty and to correct the shortcomings in its activities noted by the Court of Justice (Commission, 1989a).

Modal developments

A number of developments are planned in the different modes of transport.

Air Transport: For nearly three decades, since the establishment of the EC, the airline industry was effectively immune from any action being taken against restrictive practices because it was held that the competition rules of the Treaty of Rome did not apply to the air transport sector. However, a European Court of Justice judgment in April 1986 (commonly referred to as the 'Nouvelles Frontieres' judgment) confirmed that the general rules of the Treaty of Rome, and in particular those on competition, in fact do apply to air transport, in the same way as to the other modes of transport. This paved the way for the first steps to be taken towards a more liberalised regime in civil aviation

(O'Mahony, 1988). Accordingly, in December 1987 the Transport Council adopted a series of measures covering air fares, capacity, access to routes and the application to civil aviation of the competition rules of the Treaty of Rome. These measures were designed to override less liberal provisions in bilateral agreements between member states. They have already enabled Irish airlines to expand their operations significantly. New routes and new fifth freedom services[4] have been inaugurated to points in the UK and mainland Europe. Lower fares have been introduced as a result of the new procedures for fare determination. The market has responded well to the lower fares. In 1988 alone, air passenger traffic to and from Ireland (excluding transit traffic) increased by nearly 24 per cent over the previous year and growth continues to be very buoyant.

The second stage of the completion of the Single Market in civil aviation is to be introduced during 1990. In December 1989 the Transport Council agreed the set of principles that would be included in the next stage of air transport liberalisation. The principal objective, in so far as Ireland is concerned, is to move as far as possible towards a fully liberalised system. The major emphasis will be on relaxed capacity controls, lower fares, less restrictions on fifth freedom rights, improved access to new routes, and increased capacity and liberalised arrangements governing air freight transport. A third stage leading to the completion of the internal market in civil aviation is to be tabled by the Commission in 1992. At present the Commission is formulating proposals for the harmonisation of the conditions of competition, including flight-time limitations for crews, · harmonisation of personnel licensing arrangements and airworthiness standards. These measures are to be designed to accompany the liberalisation process. As regards air traffic control, steps are being taken to ensure that the airspace congestion problems that have been growing in Europe in recent years do not frustrate the potential benefits of a fully liberalised civil aviation regime.

Road haulage: Road freight transport has provoked bitter debates between EC Transport Ministers over the years. The issue that frequently has been at the centre of these debates has been whether liberalisation (the removal of restrictions on road haulage) should be preceded by harmonisation (the creation of equal opportunities for hauliers in all member states), or vice versa.[5] Nevertheless, the EC Council did make considerable progress with the decisions it took in relation to road haulage in June 1988. Then, it decided that multilateral and bilateral quotas would be abolished on 1 January 1993 and that thereafter access to the market would be governed by a system of Community licences, issued on the basis of qualitative criteria only (professional competence, good repute and financial standing). The measures necessary to implement this decision are expected to be introduced not later than 30 June 1991. Since the emphasis in international road freight in future will be on qualitative rather than on quantitative aspects, the focus at Community level will shift to revising the existing criteria for access to the professions of road freight operator and road passenger operator. Indeed, new conditions of professional qualification were agreed in principle by the Council in March 1989. A proposal on the specific conditions of access to the market is to be published in 1990. Similarly, the Commission has proposed the full freedom of pricing in the road haulage sector.

The Transport Council decided at its December 1989 meeting to allow hauliers registered in one member state to operate transport services wholly within another member state (cabotage) on a limited basis and with certain safeguard provisions, in order to avoid excessive penetration of any particular market or geographic zone. Under this transitional arrangement for 'cabotage', there will be a quota of 15,000 EC authorisations, each valid for two months (but convertible to monthly authorisations). Ireland will have a quota of 585 such authorisations. This interim scheme will come into effect on 1 July 1990 and will run until the end of 1992, as a prelude to complete 'cabotage' (the details of which will have to be agreed before implementation on 1 January 1993).

Substantial progress has already been made on the maximum lorry weights and dimensions. By 31 December 1998, Ireland's national limits will be in line with most of the limits so far adopted by the Community, following the derogations granted to Ireland and the United Kingdom on 5 June 1989. To cater for heavier lorries, the programme 'Ireland — Road Development: 1989 to 1993' included financial provisions for the strengthening of roads and bridges to carry heavier lorries

(Government of Ireland, 1989a). Decisions still have to be taken on harmonisation of vehicle-related taxes, so the impact on Irish road haulage is not yet clear. However, it appears that the deregulation of road haulage, together with the benefits of the removal of non-tariff barriers, should create opportunities for professional haulage firms and own-account transport firms in Ireland to develop their businesses to a much greater extent. In addition, exporters should benefit from the availability of less expensive transport and a wider range of transport options.

Road passenger: Very little progress has been made on the deregulation of road passenger services. Yet two significant proposals affecting this sector currently are under consideration in the context of the completion of the Single Market. The proposals are in the form of two draft regulations. One relates to common rules for the international carriage of passengers by coach and bus; the other contains 'cabotage' conditions, under which non-resident carriers may operate national road passenger services within a member state. The Council of Ministers is still discussing these proposals. They will have major implications for Irish bus operators, in the public and the private sectors, and in both the domestic and international markets. The Government of Ireland has decided to introduce new legislation to replace the Road Transport Act, 1932, which regulates access to the domestic bus passenger market. The new legislation will contain provisions for greater liberalisation of the licensing system.

Rail: The EC's main objectives for rail transport will continue to be the improvement of the competitive position of rail *vis-à-vis* road transport, and the financial reorganisation of the railways. The EC does not propose measures of liberalisation for rail transport. It should be pointed out, however, that the completion of the Single Market at the end of 1992, combined with the opening of the Channel Tunnel, will create new opportunities for international rail passenger and rail freight traffic between the United Kingdom and continental Europe. The Tunnel could also have an impact on Irish rail passenger and rail freight movements.

Shipping: Agreement was reached in December 1986 on four regulations in the maritime transport sector which marked a first stage towards the development of a common policy in shipping trade. The key regulation liberalised the EC's international trade and by 1993 will ensure freedom to provide shipping services to, from and between member states. The other three regulations enable the EC to take concerted action to combat protectionism by non-EC countries, to counter unfair pricing, and to establish a competitive regime for shipping in the EC. The Council has made no further progress on the proposals to allow 'cabotage' services, since the adoption in December 1986 of the package of measures guaranteeing the freedom to provide shipping services. In the context of its proposals of 31 May 1989, concerning 'positive measures', the Commission has been taking new initiatives to maintain and develop a competitive and efficient shipping industry and to ensure the supply of competitive shipping services in the interests of Community trade.

Inland waterways: The proposal on 'cabotage' for inland waterways has made no progress. It is linked politically with 'cabotage' in road haulage, and the decision taken at the Transport Council in December 1989 should open the way for the adoption of the proposal on inland navigation. This mode of transport has little or no effect on trade emanating from Ireland.

Frontier checks: Many steps already have been taken to make trade across EC frontiers easier. The elimination of customs duties between member states has been one of the foundations of the common market. Less obvious, but nevertheless important, has been the continuing process of administrative harmonisation and simplification that gradually is bringing into line member states' arrangements. For example, the Single Administrative Document (SAD), introduced in January 1988, has simplified customs documentation. The planned computerisation of the processing of this documentation in Ireland should speed up the completion of customs formalities and help to reduce costs. By the end of 1992 the EC plans to abolish frontier checks on vehicles and goods circulating internationally within the Community. This should further reduce delays at frontier border posts (and this in turn should be reflected in somewhat lower transport costs).

Fiscal barriers: The EC fiscal proposals are being revised at time of writing and it is not possible to say precisely how Irish transport will be affected. A few broad statements can be made. Both passengers and shippers could face higher charges for air and sea transport if the Community proceeds to implement its fiscal proposals on four main transport matters: if it is decided to apply VAT on both intra-EC passenger fares and freight rates; if VAT is applied to ships' and aircraft supplies; if excise duty is applied to ships' fuel; and if duty-free sales are abolished. However, to the extent that shippers provide their services to VAT-registered businesses that reclaim VAT, these charges would not have major long-term implications for industry, although there could be short-term cash flow effects. If the sale of duty-free items is abolished, passengers would be allowed to bring unlimited quantities of duty-paid goods across national borders within the EC. However, the abolition of duty-free sales would have very adverse effects on the profits of airlines, airports and ferry operators. It could also discourage growth in Irish tourism to the extent that air and sea fares would be increased as a consequence of duty-free purchases being abolished. Of course it would not be just Irish tourism that would be adversely affected. At present no member state charges VAT on international fares, so they too would be affected by the EC proposals (Quigley, 1988). Accordingly, the tendency for intra-EC travel costs to rise in the wake of the Commission's tax harmonisation proposals seems unavoidable (Fitzpatrick, 1989). Furthermore, an anomaly arising from the EC proposals is the fact that the imposition of VAT on passenger transport would result in a situation whereby intra-EC travel would be discriminated against by comparison with extra-EC travel. Against this background, the National Economic and Social Council has recognised that the implications of the EC proposals on Irish transport must be taken into account when devising an appropriate response to the Commission's indirect tax proposals (NESC, 1989).

Vehicle-related taxes: The EC has made harmonisation proposals for motor tax and fuel tax. Discussions are continuing on a draft Directive on motor tax which may require Ireland and a number of other member states to calculate it for heavy goods vehicles according to laden weight (not unladen weight as at present) by 31 December 1992. The Community is considering the question of harmonising tax rates for heavy goods vehicles. There are two possible options. Tax rates may be harmonised so as to meet infrastructure costs generated by heavy goods vehicles using public roads in the member states. Alternatively, vehicle tax rates may be harmonised on the basis of the average of the existing tax rates of member states. The former would be likely to result in very substantial increases in road taxes on heavy goods in Ireland (Quigley, 1988). At present, the prospects of achieving agreement on road tax harmonisation remains unclear.

As regards fuel tax, the Commission has submitted proposals for harmonising vehicle excise duty on diesel and for increasing the amount of diesel that can be imported without duty. Harmonisation of transport-related taxes is still under consideration in the Council of Ministers in the context of overall tax harmonisation proposals.

Ireland's transport infrastructure

Poor transport infrastructure can be just as much a barrier to trade as high tariffs. Indeed, the quality of transport infrastructure influences not only the cost of access to foreign markets, but the efficiency of the Irish economy in both traded and non-traded sectors. There are gaps in Ireland's transport infrastructure and systems and these are the proper subject of structural policy investments in the run-up to the Single Market.

In March 1989 the Irish government submitted its *National Development Plan: 1989–1993* to the European Commission. The plan placed considerable emphasis on transport developments. Over the five-year period, the government intends to develop an adequate internal transport structure that will be fully integrated with improved access transport services. The plan highlighted the importance of ensuring the maximum integration of services in Ireland with the European transport network (Government of Ireland, 1989b).

In competing with other member states, Ireland has to overcome a double disadvantage: its distance from major markets and its isolation by sea. Accordingly, Irish producers have to face much higher transport costs, both on imported materials and on exported products, than their counterparts in the central member states. There is no doubt that transport costs are a significant factor affecting the competitiveness of the Irish economy, both at domestic and at international levels. The *National Development Plan* pointed out how Ireland suffers from major cost disadvantages vis-à-vis other member states because of the generally poor quality of the internal transport network and Ireland's peripheral and island location. The small size of the Irish market — less than 1 per cent of the EC population — compounds the problem of Ireland's peripherality because it makes producers relatively more dependent on exports.

Ireland's relatively high transport costs can be illustrated by two sets of estimates. First, a 1987 study, using survey data, estimated that the Irish road haulage industry suffered a relative cost disadvantage of some 16 per cent vis-à-vis the Northern Ireland road haulage industry (CITI, 1987). Secondly, it was estimated in the 1989 *National Development Plan* that Irish exporters to Europe have to meet transport costs which represent between 9 per cent and 10 per cent of export sales values and that such costs were approximately twice those incurred by EC countries trading with one another on the European mainland. The Confederation of Irish Industry has produced very similar statistics. It concluded that the transport cost element of Irish exports is 9 per cent, compared with an EC average of 4.5 per cent (CII, 1989). The transport cost penalty applies to the great bulk of Ireland's international trade; not only exports, but imports of materials and capital goods.

The *National Development Plan* went on to argue that the most significant reason for the high Irish transport costs is the deficient state of the national roads and the access roads to the principal ports and airports.[6] The importance of improving Ireland's road infrastructure has been recognised for some time. Since the 1970s a number of studies of road development needs, most of them concentrating on Irish national roads, have highlighted serious deficiencies. In 1981, the NESC argued that there are, 'very strong reasons for improving the Irish road system which does lag behind that of broadly comparable nations' (NESC, 1981). During 1987 the Department of the Environment carried out a review of road development needs, covering an evaluation period of twenty years, which identified long-term road needs for the entire network, costing about £9 billion. To remedy the deficiencies, the Irish government submitted a road development programme to the European Commission in March 1989; this provided for the detailed implementation of the road development strategy outlined in the *National Development Plan*. The programme envisages a total expenditure on roads of almost £1 billion over a five-year period. The CII agrees that priority should be given to roads investment in Ireland, but it claims that much more is required than is currently envisaged — 'current road planning means we will not reach EC standards for twenty years' (CII, 1989). The EC, while recognising the importance of road investment, nevertheless envisages a somewhat smaller level of expenditure on roads than that set out in the *National Development Plan*. Specifically, the EC has included £876 million for roads in the Community Support Framework for Ireland, under the measures announced in October 1989 to offset the effects of peripherality (Commission, 1989b). According to the Framework, such road expenditure is expected to be financed partly by way of Community support (£447 million) and partly by way of national public financing (£429 million).

The provision of a road system that is comparable with that of our trading partners is not sufficient of itself to ensure that the Irish economy can compete successfully in a Single Market. The fact that Ireland has to export such a high proportion of its output places a great onus on the quality of access transport services. The government recognised in the *National Development Plan* the importance of developing an adequate internal transport structure which would be fully integrated with improved access transport services. For Ireland, investment in air and sea links is equivalent to investment by the mainland member states in cross-border links and road and rail links to other member states. Over £440 million was included in the plan for the development of four main areas of access transport: seaports, sea freight services, airports and air services. The £440 million also includes provisions for bus and rail infrastructure and services. The EC, in the Community Support Framework, envisages a somewhat smaller level of total expenditure on access transport and inland transport. A sum of £391 million has been included in the

Community Support Framework, with £94 million of the total expenditure to come from Community support and £297 million to accrue from national public financing. In addition, subject to the results of a feasibility study, investments in sea and air freight shuttle services will be considered (Commission, 1989b).

In the absence of the detailed breakdown of the likely expenditure on the different segments of transport under the Operational Programme for Transport, it is useful to look at the arguments in favour of developing access transport — the question upon which the *National Development Plan* concentrated particular attention. The four main aspects of access transport are looked at briefly.

First, for seaports, the intention is to provide appropriate berthing facilities and to improve loading and handling facilities, particularly at the ports of Dublin, Rosslare, Waterford and Cork. The importance of Ireland's seaports can be seen from the fact that they handle 81 per cent of total merchandise trade in volume terms and about one-third of passenger movements.

For sea freight services, the plan discusses the urgent need to concentrate freight traffic for different destinations at specified ports and the need to establish fast sea freight shuttle services from Dublin Port to the west coast of Britain and from Rosslare Harbour to Le Havre, Cherbourg and Rotterdam. The importance of good freight links with Britain and the Continent, in terms of sufficient capacity and frequency of service, must be seen against a background where three-quarters of Ireland's seaborne trade *in volume terms* is with the other member states.

The third aspect is the development of airports, comprising state and regional airport developments. As a result of the increase in traffic numbers, there is now an urgent need for an accelerated capital investment programme at the state airports.

The fourth matter is what the plan describes as the development of air channels with mainland Europe, as part of the determined drive to improve access for Irish exporters to their principal European markets. The EC's Community Support Framework for Ireland points out that, subject to the results of a feasibility study, investments in sea and air freight shuttle services may be considered for additional investment assistance (Commission, 1989b).

Before leaving the proposed developments of access transport, it is necessary to refer to the likely implications for Ireland of the Channel Tunnel, between Britain and France, due to open in June 1993. There is no doubt that the Tunnel will have an impact on the patterns and levels of passenger and freight movements to and from Ireland. This conclusion stems from the economic theory of transport: while the demand for transport is almost always indirect, induced or derived, the actual mode or route chosen by passengers or freight depends on the fares or rates charges and the quality of service offered, compared with competitor services. Different groups of passengers and types of freight are likely to be affected differently by the Channel Tunnel. For convenience, traffic movements can be broken down into four broad groups — two passenger and two freight — and the implications for the different groups can be summarised as follows (Ferris, 1988):

- *Car passengers:* The 'landbridge' routes via Britain to the Continent are likely to capture some share of the market, particularly from the present *direct* access transport services to the Continent
- *Rail passengers:* The growth of the rail passenger market with the Continent via Britain could be greater than the car passenger market growth, but only if attractive rail packages can be devised, with good rail services that have the minimum of inter-rail connecting in Britain
- *Roll-on/Roll-off freight:* a redirection of some freight traffic from the direct sea crossing between Ireland and the Continent, to those of the UK 'landbridge' and the Tunnel, is likely to occur
- *Unaccompanied freight traffic:* The real growth of freight traffic through Britain is likely to take place in unaccompanied freight traffic, i.e. lift-on/lift-off container traffic and unaccompanied roll-on/roll-off freight, travelling through Britain to the Channel Tunnel by train.

Overall the Channel Tunnel can have a positive impact on Ireland's freight and passenger movements to the Continent in terms of reduced journey times and transport costs and the ease of delivering goods. This view is supported by the main conclusion of a recent study: that the Channel Tunnel is likely to provide a huge social benefit through substantially lower prices for passengers and freight (Kay, Manning and Szymanski, 1989). But the extent of the positive impact on Ireland is dependent on the quality of road and rail links between the Tunnel and west British ports. Obviously, the benefits will be all the greater to the extent that more integrated rail and motorway links to the Channel Tunnel are put in place. The Channel Tunnel should help reduce the cost of access to European markets for Irish exporters. However, the main economic benefits from the Channel Tunnel for Irish exporters and importers are likely to stem more from service improvements than from rate reductions. The real challenge for Ireland is to do everything possible to ensure that efficient, economic and speedy routes are provided to allow Irish traffic to capitalise on the Channel Tunnel (Ferris, 1989).

In addition to having to meet higher transport costs per se, Irish exporters also have to surmount a series of indirect costs. Moreover, the growing trend towards 'just in time' delivery of raw materials and finished goods magnifies the disadvantage of distance and increases the importance of efficient transport in the logistical system. While transport is only one element in the system, it must be closely related to other elements, such as inventory management, materials handling and information processing.

Irish transport industry

Investment in transport infrastructure can make a positive contribution to increasing Ireland's economic potential for growth by assisting the movement of freight and commercial traffic and by providing mobility for tourists and the workforce. However, transport policy must encompass not only investment in transport infrastructure but also the efficient management of major transport facilities.

The success of the Irish transport industry in the 1990s will depend not only on the quality of the transport infrastructure that is then in place, but also on the competitiveness of Irish transport operators *vis-à-vis* their foreign counterparts. This point was made in a report to the European Commission: 'For example, the improvement of accessibility only, via the building of roads, railways or airports, may have the effect that foreign producers will profit from a reduction in long distance transportation costs and will thereby be able to become even more competitive in the backward regions' (Commission, 1986).

The challenges of the Single Market facing Irish transport are likely to be felt in all modes of transport, to a greater or lesser extent. The liberalisation in *air transport* should provide further opportunities for Irish airlines to develop their businesses. In order to compete on equal terms with their larger foreign rivals, Irish airlines must not be confined to Irish markets. It is vital that they be allowed to serve other markets in Europe, especially the major markets, so as to achieve the economies of scale necessary to be competitive (NESC, 1989). Irish airlines will have to be even more vigilant in the future and take appropriate steps to ensure that they are not disadvantaged in a marketplace that is increasingly being dominated by mega-carriers and airlines that are forming global alliances. Irish airlines also will have to respond to the potentially negative effects of the removal of fiscal frontiers after 1992.

The Single Market will pose both challenges and threats to the Irish *road haulage* industry. Córas Tráchtála (Irish Export Board) points out that the new rules for road haulage will offer the possibility of faster and more economic distribution to European markets; furthermore, Irish hauliers will be able to 'backload' freely. In effect, they will be free to operate throughout the Community, picking up and delivering loads wherever they wish (CTT, 1988). However, the potential for expansion of the Irish road haulage industry must be seen against the cost disadvantages under which it operates at present. The Irish international haulier has to compete for a share of the international freight market with hauliers from Northern Ireland, hauliers from other countries, own-account operators and shipping companies who operate haulage services. From an analysis of data for 1984, the Chartered Institute of Transport in Ireland (CITI) has concluded that Irish registered vehicles held just over a quarter of the roll-on/roll-off traffic market travelling directly by sea (to and from Britain and to and from continental Europe) and just over half of the cross-border traffic (Chartered Institute of Transport in

Ireland, 1987). Dublin Port has highlighted the fact that the haulage industry in the Republic of Ireland faces keen competition from Northern Ireland hauliers. In particular, Dublin Port has pointed out that the lower standby and running costs of the Northern Ireland haulage industry enable it to market its services successfully in the Republic, thus capturing traffic for Northern Ireland ports, particularly Larne, at the expense of ports in the Republic (Dublin Port, 1989).

While the introduction of 'cabotage' from 1 July 1990 will allow Irish hauliers to reduce 'empty-running' on return journeys from overseas, British and continental hauliers will also be able to avail of 'cabotage' opportunities within Ireland. The future competitiveness of the Irish road haulage industry depends on decisions (still only at the proposal stage in the EC) regarding the taxation of vehicles and fuel. It also depends on certain domestic decisions. As the NESC study pointed out, if domestic haulage companies are to compete with international firms, the domestic environment that impinges directly on their competitiveness must be critically examined and any identified handicaps should be immediately rectified (NESC, 1989).

As regards the competitiveness of Irish sea operators, they should benefit from the EC policy which aims to ensure freedom in providing shipping services to, from and between member states, while at the same time allowing the Community to act against unfair pricing by shipowners from non-EC countries. A development of possible benefit to Irish exporters is the extension to shipping of the competition rules of the original EC Treaty, which prohibit any abuse of a dominant position that might have a detrimental effect on trade between member states (CTT, 1988). However, against the background of positive measures, the Irish shipping industry has to face one potentially negative development: the impact of fiscal harmonisation, in terms of the application of VAT on shipping services, the extension of excise duties to ships' fuels and the abolition of duty-free sales. The EC still has to decide on these matters.

In relation to the competitiveness of Irish ports, it was pointed out above that a considerable volume of freight traffic destined for or originating in the Republic of Ireland travels across the border and through ports in Northern Ireland. The significance of these data is highlighted by the fact that a considerable portion of trade through the Northern Corridor (e.g. Larne-Stranraer) is potentially Central Corridor (e.g. Dublin-Holyhead) trade. The NESC argued that the access ports must have the capacity to handle freight and passengers efficiently and competitively (NESC, 1989). Dublin Port has pointed out that the loss of traffic to Northern Ireland ports reveals certain competitive disadvantages under which ports in the Republic of Ireland, serving the Central Corridor, operate at present (Dublin Port, 1989).

As regards Irish airports, Aer Rianta, the state airports authority, has been responding to the increase in air passenger traffic by developing an accelerated capital investment programme at the state airports. In planning for the 1990s, attention will have to be paid to redesigning terminal buildings, to allow intra-EC traffic to be handled as domestic rather than as international traffic (if immigration controls are completely abolished for intra-EC air traffic). Account will also have to be taken of the loss of duty-free sales. It has been argued that the absence of duty-free sales revenue will require compensatory measures, e.g. increased landing charges in the case of airports, which will be passed on to customers in the form of dearer air tickets (Fitzpatrick, 1989).

As regards passenger transport in Ireland, the private motor car is now the primary mode of travel and its dominance is growing. While long-distance scheduled bus services and, to a lesser extent, the railways have experienced some growth in demand, city bus services are used less frequently.

The EC proposals, in conjunction with the proposed legislation, if adopted, will provide for a more liberal system for the licensing of the private bus industry and for greater competition and increased flexibility in the range of services. In particular, the EC proposals will have major implications for Irish bus operators, in the public and the private sectors, and in both the domestic and international markets. In turn, Irish railways are likely to have to face sharper competition from road passenger operators.

Conclusion

The degree of openness of the Irish economy and its island nature explain why transport is of relatively greater importance for Ireland than for central EC member states. The Irish transport system is an amalgam of the different modes of transport, each having a definite role to play in the provision of an efficient and effective transport system. It has been argued that 'the internal arteries of transport must dovetail with access ports — both air and sea. Those access ports must have the capacity to handle the freight and passenger movement efficiently and competitively. Sea and air capacities must also be sufficient to move goods competitively and speedily' (NESC, 1989).

The completion of the Single Market is likely to stimulate more trade and travel and that in turn is likely to generate a demand for more freight and passenger transport services. The opening of the Channel Tunnel should help to improve access to European markets for Irish exports. But, for all the improvements the Single Market and the Channel Tunnel are likely to bring, it must be recognised that transport improvements are symmetrical. Just as the outward flow of exports may be improved by the introduction of better transport infrastructure, so too the inward flow of imports will be improved. In this regard it can be argued that the improvement of transport infrastructure pursued in isolation could do more harm than good: 'It is vital that, simultaneously with the improvement in access to foreign markets, the ability of domestic firms, and individuals, to respond to market opportunities is enhanced by industrial and other policies' (NESC, 1989).

It was in the context of achieving the national and Community aim of greater economic and social cohesion that the Irish government submitted its *National Development Plan* to the European Commission in March 1989. The plan set out the measures that Ireland proposed to implement over a five-year period, in conjunction with the European Community structural funds. As has been pointed out above, the plan placed considerable emphasis on transport developments. The thrust of the action proposed by the government for the transport sector is to develop an adequate internal transport structure that would be fully integrated with improved access transport services. The EC Community Support Framework, in response to the plan, envisaged expenditure of £876 million on roads. This level of investment, which is to be spread over a five-year period, must be seen against the long-term requirement of about £9 billion for the entire road network. It is the view of the CII that Ireland will not reach EC road standards for twenty years under current road planning proposals (CII, 1989).

The EC's Community Support Framework Plan includes £391 million for inland transport and access transport investment. In addition, funds might become available for the upgrading and development of transport, if an EC programme for Community Action on Transport Infrastructure is adopted. However, the EC Council so far has failed to adopt such a special programme for assisting transport infrastructure. Of all the member states, Ireland has a strong case to make for having such a programme adopted, as a way of helping to reduce the disadvantages of the country's peripheral location and inadequate internal transport infrastructure.

It is very important that Ireland's transport infrastructure and access services are improved at the earliest opportunity, particularly as the movements to make trade easier across EC frontiers gather pace throughout the member states. The direct effect of the removal of customs barriers will be a reduction in costs caused by delays and administrative procedures. The liberalisation of transport is likely to make most modes of transport more competitive and to allow them to expand their trans-frontier activities (including the opening up of national transport markets to non-resident operators). However, if the EC proposals to apply VAT to both passenger fares and freight rates and to remove duty-free sales are adopted, then, ironically, transport costs could increase. On the other hand, to the extent that the final tax harmonisation package includes lower fuel and vehicle taxes, Irish transport will benefit and that, in turn, should enhance the competitive position of Irish exporters generally. It must be recognised, however, that the impact of reduced transport costs on the relative profitability of Irish industry (which is the main determinant of industrial output) will be limited to the extent to which there is a greater reduction in transport costs in Ireland than in other countries (O'Sullivan, 1989). However, since harmonisation of transport-related taxes is, at time of writing, still under consideration, it is not possible to say whether Irish transport costs will be reduced (or increased) relative to existing costs.

The Irish transport sector will have to ensure that it is equipped to meet the challenges and opportunities that the Single Market will present and that the sector is adequately developed to allow Irish industry to compete effectively in Europe. The government has presented its development plan to the EC Commission to ensure that Ireland is better equipped to meet the challenges posed by the completion of the internal market and that it obtains the maximum possible assistance from the EC in financing the plan. But action at government level is not sufficient. The economic sectors also have roles to play. The opportunities presented by the EC's Single Market and by the Channel Tunnel must be harnessed by Irish producers and exporters if Ireland's relative economic position within the EC is to be improved. At the same time, Irish transport operators must ensure that Ireland has efficient, reliable, high quality and cost-effective transport services to meet the needs of its trading sector.

Notes

1. Transport data are published by the EC only at the level of the 'transport and communications services' sector. However, the bulk of the activity in this sector relates to the transport industry per se.
2. The movement of goods by road within the EC is partly restricted and there are differences between the national regulations on capacity and tariff control. Hauliers are required to apply for a limited number of licences to enable them to move goods between member states and within member states. The right of non-resident hauliers to pick up and deliver goods within another member state is known as 'cabotage'.
3. The practical result of the European Court of Justice decision in the case of the European Parliament versus the Council of the European Communities (Case No. 13/83; 22/5/85) has been the passage of a considerable amount of far-reaching legislation and the certainty that more is on the way.
4. The 'fifth freedom right', under an air transport agreement relating to scheduled international air services, is the right of the airlines of one country to carry traffic from a second country with which it has an agreement, to a third country.

5. The EC now proposes to facilitate the development of road transport by both 'liberalisation' of the road transport sector, and 'harmonisation' of competitive conditions for road hauliers.

   'Liberalisation' will involve: the removal of restrictions on international road haulage, and the opening-up of domestic road haulage markets to transport by non-resident hauliers ('cabotage').

   'Harmonisation' of competitive conditions for road hauliers will involve the creation of equal opportunities for hauliers in all member states by harmonising: road conditions, with financial assistance from the European Community; maximum lorry weights and dimensions; vehicle-related taxes; and social conditions.

   The other noteworthy point is that the Commission has proposed a change from the present 'nationality' principle of taxation (under which vehicles pay road tax only in their country of registration) to the 'territoriality' principle of taxation, under which road hauliers would contribute towards the cost of road infrastructure in the member states traversed. This proposal is still under discussion in the Council of Ministers.

6. In addition to the need for competitive road costs, the *National Development Plan* also recognised the importance of rail costs comparing favourably with those in other member states. The Plan pointed out that rail freight infrastructures require improvement to maintain the competitive position of the rail mode and that new rail and bus passenger services are essential to cope satisfactorily with the mobility needs of large populations where in certain western suburbs of Dublin there is very high unemployment. The plan envisaged expenditure on investment programmes for rail and bus infrastructures and services of £45 million over a five-year period. The specific expenditure on these transport modes will be announced with the publication of the Operational Programme for Transport.

10

Indigenous Manufacturing

ANTHONY FOLEY

This chapter examines the implications of the Single Market for indigenous or Irish-owned manufacturing. The emphasis is on non-food manufacturing because the food industries are discussed in Chapter 11. However, some references to food are included where data limitations do not permit disaggregation and to provide a context for non-food manufacturing. Section 2 outlines the mechanisms through which the Single Market could affect manufacturing. Section 3 is an examination of the structure and performance of indigenous manufacturing. Section 4 assesses the possible impact of the Single Market on indigenous manufacturing. Conclusions are presented in section 5.

While the broad concept of indigenous manufacturing, as distinct from the multinational component of Irish manufacturing, is clear, there are definitional and data difficulties in examining the concept. By focusing on the indigenous component, one ideally is dealing with firms that have evolved from the industrial and entrepreneurial capacities of the Irish economy. These can be contrasted with the multinational or direct foreign investment firms which have emerged from the capacities of their home economies and which have located elements of their operations within the Irish economy.

Irish Distillers and Lake Electronics, for example, are significant companies that emerged from the capacities of the Irish economy. They are now foreign-owned. Consequently, defining industry by nationality of ownership, as is done in the

Census of Industrial Production (CIP), and by the Industrial Development Authority, would underestimate the indigenous contribution, according to our concept of 'indigenous'. Córas Tráchtála defines 'indigenous' in terms of location of marketing control in Ireland. This definition could include multinational firms that have their marketing function in Ireland and which use CTT's services, thus overestimating the sense in which they are truly indigenous.[1]

These definitions are important in assessing indigenous manufacturing. The most comprehensive data set on indigenous manufacturing is that published in the CIP. This uses the nationality-of-ownership definition. The Irish government's indigenous export target (National Development Plan, 1989) for the first phase of the Single Market, up to the mid-1990s, is based on the CTT definition. The following analysis mainly uses CIP data but makes occasional use of IDA and CTT data. Throughout the chapter the terms 'Irish-owned' and 'indigenous' are interchangeable unless stated otherwise. The terms 'multinational' and 'foreign-owned' are treated as interchangeable. The term 'Irish manufacturing' refers to total manufacturing in Ireland.

The Single Market and manufacturing

The scope of the measures to create the Single Market have already been outlined in Chapter 1. This analysis focuses on the Single Market's impact on manufacturing. The intention is that the movement of goods between member states would become as easy as it currently is within each member state. This will be achieved by the removal of all physical, technical and fiscal barriers to the movement of goods. One of the main motivations for, and hopes of, the Single Market is that the competitiveness of EC industry would be improved relative to the world and, in particular, relative to the United States and Japan. The removal of non-tariff barriers to trade within the EC is not expected, by itself, to be the main determinant of improved competitiveness. It is expected that their removal will facilitate a number of consequential changes that will improve the structure and performance of EC manufacturing.

It is argued that the Single Market will facilitate the restructuring of EC manufacturing and will result in improved productivity and competitiveness through a greater realisation of economies of scale. It is also argued that innovation and efficiency will be encouraged by the increased competition and dynamics of the Single Market. The removal of the many barriers to trade is seen as a necessary condition to enable these other effects to be realised. As we shall see below, the manufacturing gains resulting from the direct reduction in costs (a consequence of the removal of non-tariff barriers) are substantially less than the gains resulting from the indirect effects of economies of scale, increased efficiency and improved product and process innovation. This process will result directly in a reduction in costs and increased competition, and this will lead indirectly to restructuring, greater economies of scale, more efficiency and more innovation.

This classification of direct and indirect effects, as used in Emerson et al. (1988) and NESC (1989), is similar to the static and dynamic concepts of the effects of a customs union in economic integration theory. The removal of tariffs, i.e. the static gain in a customs union, is similar to the removal of the cost-increasing barriers in the Single Market programme. The dynamic gains of a customs union — such as increased innovation and economies of scale — are the same as the indirect effects as defined by Emerson et al. (1988).

The effect arising from the removal of cost-increasing barriers is short-term in nature. The indirect effects are primarily medium and long-term. The distinction between direct and indirect effects is important when examining the impact of the Single Market. It might be the case that an economy could gain from the removal of non-tariff barriers to exports, but in the longer term it could lose because of the economies-of-scale effect of integration.

Cecchini, for example, pointed out that smaller firms face proportionately higher costs from customs-related paperwork and that, therefore, small firms have more to gain from the ending of customs controls (Cecchini 1988, p. 10). Even if this was also the case for the other non-tariff barriers, it does not necessarily mean that the full Single Market process, i.e. allowing for the indirect effects as well as for the removal of the non-tariff barriers, would be good for small firms.

The mechanisms through which the market integration process will work are summarised in Figure 10.1. The elimination of non-tariff barriers, such as the physical, fiscal and technical barriers, directly reduces costs and increases market access and hence competition. The lower costs will influence prices, demand and margins and will spread through reductions in the cost of inputs. At the same time there is an increase in both competitive pressures and in the size of the market. These facilitate the realisation of economies of scale. The economies of scale arise from the impact of the increase in output volume and the restructuring, induced by increased competition and by access to larger markets. Competitive pressures should lead to greater efficiency to protect margins. They also will have non-price effects, such as improved management, better quality and range of products and increased product and process innovation activity.

The effects of the Single Market will not be the same for each industry within the manufacturing sector. The relative importance of direct and indirect effects will vary between industries. For example, the economies-of-scale impact will be important in chemicals but not in clothing because of the different size structure of the industries and the different degrees of integration already achieved. While all industries will be affected by the removal of administrative barriers and frontier delays, the removal of technical barriers and public procurement barriers will be more significant in some industries than in others. Public procurement is important in industries such as pharmaceuticals and telecommunications, but not in food. Technical barriers are of significance in food and telecommunications, but not in clothing and textiles. The impact of the Single Market will also depend on the size of firm. Large firms are more affected than small firms by public procurement barriers and restrictions. Small firms are more concerned than large firms with transport regulations (Nerb, 1987). Estimates of the direct costs of customs formalities show that the cost burden is highest for small and medium-sized firms. Cost per consignment was 30% to 45% higher for firms of under 250 employees than for larger firms (Ernst and Whinney, 1987). Indigenous Irish industry is overwhelmingly in the small and medium-size category. The differential impact of the Single Market on small and large firms is, therefore of some importance.

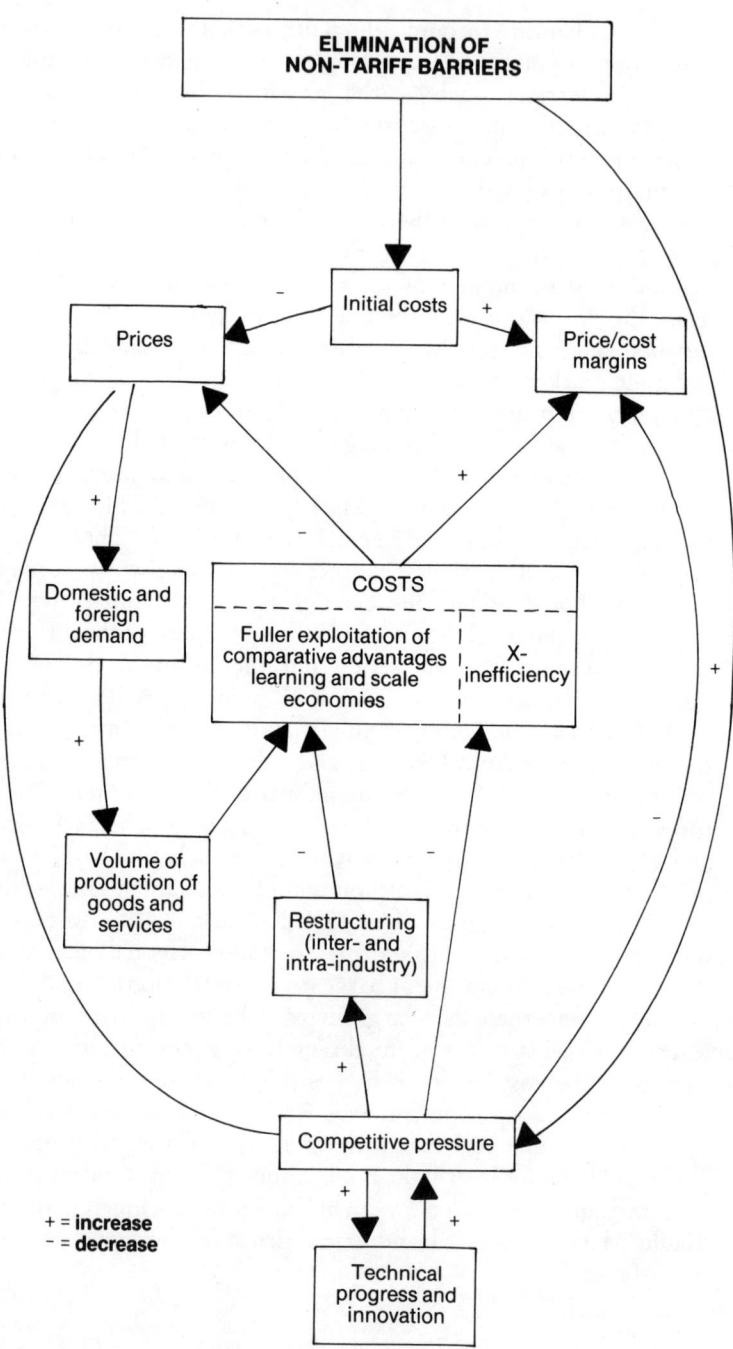

Figure 10.1: **Single Market effect**

Source: Reproduced from Emerson et al. (1988)

The direct costs of the barriers, as derived from EC-wide business surveys, range from less than 1% of turnover (mineral oil refining, office machinery, data-processing machinery and rubber products) to 3.3% (man-made fibres) and 3.5% (the production and preliminary processing of metals).

Emerson et al (1988) classified the gains from the Single Market into four stages. These are listed in Table 10.1.

Table 10.1: **Classification of the gains from the Single Market**

Effects of removing barriers

Stage 1	Effects of removing barriers affecting goods traded between countries within the Community.
Stage 2	Effects of removing barriers affecting goods produced in the Community, whether traded or not.

Effects of market integration

Stage 3	Effects of economies of scale associated with increased output, as well as with the restructuring of output among plants, firms and member states.
Stage 4	Effects of increased competition through the elimination of X-inefficiencies and monopoly rents.

Source: Emerson et al. (1988), pp. 227, 228.
Note: It should be noted that the content of stages 1 and 2 in this estimation of costs/gains is slightly different from that described on p. 196 of Emerson (unnumbered table)[2]

The stage 1 effect derives from the removal of barriers which result in an imported good being priced higher than the price in the member state that produced it. Thus they reflect the barriers-induced costs of exporting within the EC. These barriers include customs and administrative barriers and technical and public procurement barriers. Stage 2 measures the reductions in costs that arise from liberalisation in financial, transport and other inputs that are experienced across the Community even where the product is not traded. Once stage 1 barriers are removed, i.e. the cost of intra-EC exporting, the Community is effectively a single economic unit relative to the rest of the world. Stage 2 cost savings will improve competitiveness with the rest of the world.

Stages 3 and 4 refer to the dynamic impact of the Single Market, i.e. its market integration effect. Stage 3 is concerned with economies of scale and stage 4 refers to inefficiencies, such as overmanning or excessive overheads. Increased competition will reduce or eliminate these and will also reduce or eliminate monopoly rents earned because of lack of competition.

Ideally, there should be a fifth stage dealing with the impact 'on innovation and technological progress and on the strategic behaviour of EC enterprises in relation to European and world markets' (Emerson, p. 200). However, since the Emerson study could not quantify these effects, they were not included.

The source of gains is significant for individual economies and industries. Gains arising from economies of scale, for example, are not likely to assist small firms. It is informative, therefore, to examine the sources of the expected gains for manufacturing its component industries. The empirical estimates of the gains should be treated as indicating broad orders of magnitude rather than precise measurement. As was already noted, it was not possible to measure the impact of the innovation effect. Moreover, it is difficult accurately to predict the impact of the indirect effects.

In quantifying the impact of the Single Market, the Emerson and Cecchini studies made a range of estimates. Variants A and B relate to different data sources for calculating stages 1 and 2. Variants I and II relate to different methodologies for evaluating the market integration effects. These alternative approaches produce substantial differences in the sources of gains. These differences are smaller for manufacturing than for other kinds of economic activity. Variant B produces higher estimates for stages 1 and 2 than variant A. Variant I produces substantially greater market integration gains than variant II. Hence variant IA is the estimate that accords greatest importance to the market integration effects and, at the other extreme, variant IIB is the estimate that gives a greater role to the direct effects. If the reduced role of market integration effects includes a correspondingly reduced role for scale economies, estimates based on IIB suggest a somewhat more positive impact for an economy such as Ireland, with its relatively small scale of firms, than would variant IA. Unfortunately, variant II does not separately identify the effects of stage 3 and stage 4 (see Table 10.2).

Table 10.2: **Distribution of gains from Single Market: total, manufacturing, other**

	Total Billion ECU	%	Manufacturing Billion ECU	%	Other Billion ECU	%
Variant IA						
Stages 1 & 2	64.8	37.9	22.4	19.5	42.4	75.4
Stages 3 & 4	106.0	62.1	92.2	80.5	13.8	24.6
TOTAL	170.8	100.0	114.6	100.0	56.2	100.0
Variant IB						
Stages 1 & 2	79.8	56.5	31.9	34.1	47.9	100.0
Stages 3 & 4	61.5	43.5	61.5	65.8	0	0
TOTAL	141.3	100.0	93.5	100.0	47.9	100.0

Source: Derived from Emerson et al. (Table A.8).
Note: Totals do not always add to 100 because of rounding.

Under variant IA, the market integration effects for all sectors amount to 62.1% of the full gains. This falls to 43.5% under variant IIB. The change is due to the fact that Variant IIB is based on the assumption that there are no market integration effects for non-manufacturing.

Within manufacturing, the market integration effect drops from 80.5% under IA to 65.8% under IIB; the effect of barrier removal almost doubles from 19.5% to 34.1%. The main manufacturing gain under both methodologies comes from the market integration or dynamic effect.

The manufacturing sectors that will experience the relatively lowest impact from the Single Market (as estimated in variant IA) are ores and metals; metal articles; non-metallic minerals; meat; other food and beverages; textiles, clothing and leather; timber and furniture; paper, and rubber and plastics. Of these sectors, the highest impact is in ores and metals at 11% of value added. However, even the lowest sector in the group, timber and furniture, will experience an impact equivalent to almost 5% of value added. At the other end of the scale, relatively strong effects will be felt by chemicals, office machinery, electrical goods, vehicles and transport products, dairy products and tobacco. Among these sectors the lowest impact is on chemicals — at around 20 per cent of value added.[3] The remaining two sectors, mechanical engineering and 'other manufactures', have an impact of around 16 per cent of value added.

The sources of the gains in these sectors within manufacturing, as estimated in variant IA, are illustrated in Table 10.3. The role of the market integration effect would be even greater if the innovation and strategy effects had been quantified.

Table 10.3: **Percentage distribution of Single Market gains (Variant IA)**

| | Removal of Barriers Stages 1 & 2 | Market Integration Effects | |
		Stage 1 Economies of scale	Stage 2 Inefficiencies/Rent
Ores metals	16.1	83.9	0
Non-metallic Minerals	11.5	73.1	15.4
Chemicals	18.7	51.3	30.7
Metal articles	17.4	71.7	8.7
Mechanical engineering	19.5	33.1	46.6
Office machinery	23.9	25.4	53.7
Electrical goods	13.8	28.2	58.5
Motor vehicles	12.7	27.1	60.2
Other transport	29.3	44.8	24.1
Meat preserves	31.3	56.3	12.5
Dairy products	20.8	45.8	33.3
Other food	20.0	51.7	30.0
Beverages	21.1	47.4	26.3
Tobacco	11.8	29.4	52.9
Textiles/ Clothing	51.6	19.4	25.8
Leather	53.8	23.1	23.1
Timber and furniture	50.0	28.6	21.4
Paper and products	12.0	58.0	30.0
Rubber and plastics	12.5	67.3	20.8
Other Manufactures	53.8	15.4	30.8

Source: Derived from data in Table A.8 of Emerson (1988)[3].
Note: Columns do not add up to 100 because of rounding, which in some totals produces figures substantially different from 100[3].

As columns 1 to 3 indicate, the gains arise primarily from the market integration effects. Of the twenty sectors listed in Table 10.3, the stage 1 and 2 gains are greater than the market integration gains in only four — textiles and clothing, leather, timber and furniture, and other manufacturing. In fourteen sectors the stage 1 and 2 gains account for less than one-quarter of the total gains. Economies of scale provide over half of total gains in eight sectors and in only three do they provide less than one-quarter of the industry gains.

Buigues and Ilkovitz (1988) examined manufacturing at the more detailed NACE three-digit level of classification (i.e. the 'nomenclature générale des activités economiques dans les Communautés Europeenes' general industrial clarification of economic activities within the European Communities). At this level of disaggregation, manufacturing is divided into 120 industries. All industries will be affected by the removal of customs-related barriers. Buigues and Ilkovitz, however, identified 40 of these industries that will be affected significantly by the Single Market. The industries were identified on the basis of the existence of non-tariff barriers, price discrepancies between member states, concentration patterns and potential for economies of scale. The 40 industries are grouped into four categories. Group 1 is composed of high technology industries, where public procurement restrictions are significant. Group 2 is composed of industries in which trade is a relatively small proportion of total output, partly due to non-tariff barriers. Group 3 industries already have a relatively high level of trade with non-EC countries and so are more exposed than group 2 industries. Group 4 includes industries in which a high degree of trade already occurs between member states but in which non-tariff barriers are important. The impact of the Single Market is expected to be greatest for group 1 and 2 industries and lower for groups 3 and 4.

O'Malley (1989) adapted this list for the Irish economy, taking account of features of certain industries specific to Ireland. Consequently, some industries were excluded from the list, one was added and some were moved to other groups. O'Malley's list of Irish industries that will be affected significantly by the Single Market is presented in Table 10.4. There are six changes from the Buigues and Ilkovitz list of 40 industries.

The selection of industries by Buigues and Ilkovitz in some respects may seem surprising. For example, clothing is included, albeit in the least affected category. This industry is described as having moderate non-tariff barriers and a high degree of import penetration. Industries with these characteristics were not described as 'significantly affected' if price discrepancy between member states was less than 10%. On this basis, clothing was included since its price discrepancy was greater than 10%. Notwithstanding this, clothing products (along with textiles) are subject to import restrictions in the member states because of the operation of national quotas under the Multi-Fibre Arrangement, through which clothing and textile imports from developing countries into industrialised countries are regulated.

While one could argue with the specific selection of industries, it seems reasonable to use the Buigues and Ilkovitz list as a starting-point for the identification of 'sensitive' or significantly affected industries.

The fact that an industry is significantly affected by the Single Market at the Community level or in individual member states does not necessarily mean that the Irish part of that industry should be affected equally. Industries, even at the relatively disaggregated three-digit level, are composed of a variety of products. For example, glass and glassware (NACE 247) includes both mass-produced glass and craft-intensive glassware such as that produced by Waterford Crystal. The wool industry (NACE 431) includes mass-produced garments as well as individual hand-made products. Telecommunications equipment (NACE 344) ranges from large-scale telephone exchange equipment to 'niche' type pieces of equipment. Consequently, the expectation that an industry will be affected significantly by the Single Market does not necessarily mean that all products within that industry classification will be so affected, or will be influenced by the same types of gains.

In his revision of the Buigues and Ilkovitz list of industries, O'Malley in some cases allowed for this. He excluded boilermaking because the Irish boilermaking activity was substantially different to the Community-level industry. Pharmaceutical products were changed from Group 2 to Group 4. It is likely that further adjustments could be made within industries, i.e. including some components and excluding others in arriving at the indigenous components of manufacturing that will be affected significantly by the Single Market. It is less

Table 10.4: **Irish industries that will be affected significantly by the Single Market**

Category	NACE Code	Industry
Group 1	330	Office and data-processing machinery
	344	Telecommunications equipment
	372	Medical and surgical equipment
Group 2	362	Railway and tramway rolling-stock (including repairs)
Group 3	341	Insulated wires and cables
	342	Electrical machinery
	361	Shipbuilding
	417	Spaghetti, macaroni
	421	Cocoa, chocolate and sugar confectionery
Group 4	247	Glass and glassware
	248	Ceramic goods
	251	Basic industrial chemicals
	256	Other chemical products, mainly for industrial and agricultural purposes
	257	Pharmaceutical products
	321	Agricultural machinery
	322	Machine-tools for working metal
	323	Textile machinery
	324	Machinery for food, chemical and related industries
	325	Plant for mines, iron and steel industry
	326	Transmission equipment for motive power
	327	Other machinery for specific branches
	345	Radios, televisions, consumer electronics
	346	Domestic electric appliances
	347	Electric lamps and other electric lighting
	351	Motor vehicles
	364	Aerospace equipment (including repairs)
	413	Dairy products
	427	Brewing and malting
	428	Soft drinks
	431	Wool industry
	432	Cotton industry
	438	Carpets and floor coverings
	451	Footwear
	453	Clothing
	455	Household textiles
	481	Rubber products
	491	Jewellery
	493	Photographic and cinematographic laboratories
	494	Toys and sports goods

Source: Eoin O'Malley (1989)

likely that there would be activities in indigenous manufacturing that are not included in the Buigues and Ilkovitz list, and which would be sensitive to the Single Market programme. Such activities would have been in the Buigues and Ilkovitz list since they would have been affected by the direct and indirect effects of integration. Thus we can regard the O'Malley list as a maximum estimate of the indigenous industries likely to be significantly affected by the Single Market. The relative importance of these industries in indigenous manufacturing is examined in the following section.

Structure and performance of indigenous manufacturing

This section briefly examines the industrial composition of indigenous manufacturing, the export and domestic market shares of output, the commodity composition and geographic destination of indigenous exports, and the size structure of indigenous establishments. It also briefly examines the performance of indigenous manufacturing in 1988 and 1989. These aspects are of importance in assessing the impact of the Single Market. We have seen that the impact of the Single Market will not be the same for all industries. Consequently, the impact on indigenous manufacturing will depend on its industrial composition. The Single Market will improve market access. This will result in increased competition in the domestic market and easier, and less costly, access to export markets. Other things being equal, therefore, the lower the domestic market dependence and the greater the dependence on exports, the more beneficial will be the market access impact.

However, domestic market dependence may arise precisely because exporting in some industries is prevented or severely limited by the barriers that the Single Market will remove. Substantial export potential may exist in these industries and may be realised by the liberalisation of markets. In such industries, therefore, a pre-Single Market domestic market dependence will not be indicative of weak gains from the removal of barriers. As we shall see below, there is little evidence to suggest that this is the case for significant parts of indigenous manufacturing. Nonetheless, it remains the case that the Single Market will make commercial life easier for exporters and potential exporters and more difficult for suppliers who are dependent on the domestic market. It is necessary, therefore, to examine the domestic market and export market features of indigenous manufacturing.

The impact of the Single Market on indigenous manufacturing depends to a great extent on whether the constraints on exporting are exogenous or endogenous. Exogenous constraints include the various technical and other barriers imposing compliance and transactions costs on exporters. Endogenous constraints refer to the marketing capacity and competitiveness of indigenous manufacturing, i.e. supply constraints. If exogenous constraints are dominant, then the removal of barriers will facilitate a good supply response. If endogenous constraints are strong, the removal of barriers, while a necessary condition to generate a good supply response, will not be sufficient.[4]

Structure of indigenous manufacturing

There is a very strong presence of foreign firms in Irish manufacturing. As Table 10.5 indicates, indigenous firms provide only 57.6% of total manufacturing employment and only 51.3% of non-food manufacturing employment. The indigenous shares in the main industrial sectors vary greatly. The indigenous employment share is highest in timber and furniture (91.8%) and lowest in chemicals (24.7%). The indigenous shares in the other sectors are paper and printing, 85.7%; food; 81.4%; non-metallic minerals, 71.6%; clothing and footwear, 66.1%; miscellaneous, 52.1%; metals and engineering, 41.4%; textiles, 33.5%; and drink and tobacco, 31.8% (see Table 10.5, columns 1 and 2).

Within metals and engineering, the more technologically advanced industries tend to be dominated by foreign firms to a much greater extent than for metals and engineering as a whole. Foreign firms provide 97% of employment in data-processing equipment, 93% in instrument engineering and 75% in electrical engineering.[5]

The distributions of indigenous and foreign employment are outlined in Table 10.5 (columns 3 and 4). Food, drink and tobacco account for 29.3% of indigenous employment and 9.1% of foreign employment. Metals and engineering provide 22.3% of indigenous and 42.7% of foreign employment. The indigenous component has a relatively large proportion of employment in paper and printing, and timber and furniture (18.2%), as compared with the foreign component (3.3%).

Table 10.5: **Indigenous and foreign employment classified by manufacturing sector (1988)**

	Share of sectors' employment		Distribution of employment by sector	
	Indigenous	Foreign	Indigenous	Foreign
Non-metallic minerals	71.6	28.4	7.4	4.0
Chemicals	24.7	75.3	3.0	12.5
Food	81.4	18.6	29.3	9.1
Drink and tobacco	31.8	68.2	2.4	7.0
Metals and engineering	41.4	58.6	22.3	42.7
Textiles	33.5	66.5	3.2	8.5
Clothing and footwear	66.1	33.9	8.8	6.1
Timber and furniture	91.8	8.2	7.5	0.9
Paper and printing	85.7	14.3	10.7	2.4
Miscellaneous	52.1	47.9	5.4	6.7
Total	57.6	42.4	100.0	100.0

Source: Derived from IDA data in Ruane and McGibney (1990).
Note: Totals do not always add up to 100 because of rounding.

Indigenous manufacturing has a relatively large share of employment in food and a relatively small share in metals and engineering, compared with the industrial structures of the small industrially advanced EC economies (see Table 10.6).

The indigenous share for a sector is defined as 100 in Table 10.6. The equivalent share for each of the other two countries is expressed as a percentage of this. Consequently, a foreign figure of less than 100 indicates a smaller share than in indigenous manufacturing. A figure of more than 100 indicates a higher foreign share. Indigenous manufacturing has higher shares than both countries in non-metallic minerals, in food, drink and tobacco, and in clothing and footwear. It has lower shares than both countries in chemicals and in metals and engineering. A somewhat surprising aspect is the relatively large presence in Denmark of both timber and wooden furniture, and paper and printing. Their shares of Danish manufacturing are slightly greater than of Ireland's indigenous manufacturing.[6]

Table 10.6: **Irish indigenous manufacturing structure compared with Belgium and Denmark (1986)**

	Irish Indigenous	Belgium	Denmark
	Sector share 100	Belgium sector share relative to indigenous	Danish sector share relative to indigenous
Non-metallic minerals	100	52	47
Chemicals	100	310	148
Metals and engineering	100	201	233
Food, drink, tobacco	100	39	62
Textiles	100	154	58
Clothing and footware	100	68	53
Timber and wooden furniture	100	69	106
Paper and printing	100	62	108

Source: Indigenous CIP (1986); Belgium and Denmark EC Industrial Yearbook (1986), Commission of the European Movement (1989). The Belgian and Danish data refer to all persons employed, whereas the Irish indigenous data refer to persons employed in establishments of at least three persons.

In examining the sectoral composition of indigenous industry it is useful to distinguish between traded goods (exportables and importables) and non-traded goods. Non-traded goods refer to goods where transport costs (e.g. concrete blocks), product features (e.g. fresh bread) or necessity to be close to customers (e.g. simple metal fabrication, printing or joinery) provide an element of 'natural protection' to domestic producers.

International trade would be limited in such sectors. There is obviously a grey area between what are traded products and non-traded products. Ultimately, if cost factors so dictate, all products are importable. Furniture is sold across frontiers, although generally it would be considered to be a non-traded industry. Technology changes can increase an industry's trade orientation; for example, by extending the life of food products. One expects lower export ratios in non-traded products than in traded products.

Two sources, the EC Business Survey and the Expert Services of the EC Commission (see Nerb, 1987 and Emerson et al., 1988) have identified the importance of technical barriers by industry. From these sources we can identify the relative significance of non-food indigenous industries that are affected by technical barriers. Industries are said to have high technical barriers if they scored 50 or above in the Business Survey and are classified as having barriers of 'great' importance by the Commission.[7] There are four such non-food industries: electrical engineering; mechanical engineering; pharmaceuticals; and precision and medical equipment. Industries with low barriers are defined as having a score of below 50 and a Commission classification of 'less important'. There are eight industries in this category: plastics; wood and furniture; metals; textiles; clothing and footwear; oil refining; paper and printing; and artificial fibres. There are no indigenous output data for oil refining and artificial fibres and these are excluded from the analysis below. This will not significantly affect the overall picture because indigenous employment in these industries was less than 350 persons in 1987. The results of the exercise are presented in Table 10.7. The EC data refer to value added. The closest indigenous indicator for which data are available is net output.

There is a very low indigenous presence in the high technical barrier industries compared with the Community as a whole. Only 9% of indigenous non-food manufacturing net output is provided by these industries, compared with 28% for EC manufacturing. At the other extreme, low barrier industries provide 45% of indigenous non-food net output, compared with 30% for EC manufacturing. Thus, indigenous manufacturing has a low presence in high barrier industries and a high presence in low barrier industries relative to EC industry. The consequence of this conclusion are discussed below.

Table 10.7: **Role of industries with high and low technical barriers**
Non-food manufacturing — indigenous and EC

	Percentage of indigenous net output in non-food manufacturing, 1986	Percentage of EC value added in non-food manufacturing, 1985
High technical barrier industries (non-food)	9	28
Low technical barrier industries (non-food)	45	30

Source: Derived from 1986 CIP and data in Emerson et al., 1988 and Nerb 1987:
see text for details and definitions.
Notes: 1. Leather is included with clothing and footwear as a low barrier
industry, although it has a 51 score in the EC Business Survey.
However, the Commission ranks it as 'low'. Drink and tobacco are
not included in non-food manufacturing in this table.
2. Manufacturing is defined as per CSO CIP definition.

There are, of course, other mechanisms through which
industries could be affected by the Single Market. The industries
that were defined as being significantly affected by the Single
Market were listed in Table 10.4. The relative importance of
these industries is outlined in Table 10.8. It is worth re-emphasising
that some Single Market measures will affect all industries. The
industries referred to here mainly deal with activities that will
be influenced by effects other than the usual customs/
administration costs. As Table 10.8 shows, these significantly
affected industries account for 36% of indigenous manufacturing
employment. This compares with about 50% for EC manufacturing as a whole. They provide 42% of employment in indigenous
non-food manufacturing and 23% of employment in the indigenous
food industry.

Within the category of non-food 'affected industries', five
industries — clothing, glass and glassware, aerospace equipment
and repairs, railway and tramway rolling stock, and jewellery
— account for 50% of the category's total employment. The
other 31 industries provide the remaining 50% of employment.

The affected industries are heavily concentrated in group 4
(the non-food component includes the drink industries). This is

the group in which the Single Market impact is expected to be weakest. Of the non-food indigenous industries listed in Table 10.4, 29 out of 36 are in group 4. These account for 82% of the employment in non-food indigenous manufacturing that will be significantly affected by the Single Market. The higher impact groups 1 and 2 provide 11% of employment in the affected industries.

Table 10.8: **Industries significantly affected by the Single Market as a percentage of indigenous employment (1987)**

Indigenous manufacturing	Indigenous non-food manufacturing	Indigenous food
36	42	23

Source: Derived from IDA Employment Census (1987) and CIP (1986) for the railway industry, which is not included in the IDA census.

As was discussed above, the proportions in Table 10.8 represent maximum estimates of the indigenous industries affected by the provisions of the Single Market. For example, in railway rolling stock about two-thirds of the output is repair work, with only one-third being manufacture of equipment. The repair element is not likely to be significantly affected by the Single Market. Within glass and glassware, the craft glass activities of Waterford Crystal will not be significantly affected by Single Market provisions because the barriers are not significant for their products.

Overall, 42%, at maximum, of indigenous non-food employment is in industries defined as being significantly affected by the Single Market provisions. The great majority of this (82%) is in group 4 industries, i.e. those with the lowest level of impact of the significantly affected industries. A relatively low proportion of employment in significantly affected industries has both positive and negative economic consequences. On the positive side it implies that the impact of increased competition on the domestic market will be relatively weak. On the negative side it implies that potential export gains will also be weak. The greatest export opportunities will arise in those industries that are significantly affected by the removal of non-tariff barriers. In short, the smaller the role of significantly affected industries, the weaker the threat of potential competition and the weaker the export potential arising from the Single Market.

Export and domestic market shares of output

Manufacturing industry in Ireland is substantially export-oriented. However, the high export propensity is mainly due to foreign firms. Indigenous manufacturing is still heavily dependent on the domestic market and indigenous non-food manufacturing is even more dependent on this market. The details of export and domestic market orientation are presented in Table 10.9. The data are from the latest CIP and refer to 1986. The CIP indigenous export propensity is less than that indicated by the IDA's Irish Economy Expenditure Surveys. Since the IDA source is a survey, it is less representative than the CIP. Indigenous export performance has been impressive in 1988 and 1989. The export proportion, therefore, is likely to have improved since 1986.

Table 10.9: **Export and domestic market shares of output in Irish manufacturing: total, foreign and indigenous (1986)**

	Total manufacturing	*Foreign*	*Indigenous*	*Non-food indigenous*
Percentage of output exported	54.9	83.2	26.6	23.6
Percentage of output absorbed by the Irish market	45.1	16.8	73.4	76.4

Source: CIP (1986); CSO (1989).

For manufacturers as a whole, 54.9% of manufacturing output is exported. The foreign component of Irish manufacturing exports 83.2% of output, while the indigenous component exports only 26.6% of output. The export proportion of non-food indigenous manufacturing is 23.6%. The domestic market absorbs over three-quarters of non-food indigenous manufacturing output.

It is clear from the data that indigenous manufacturing is

heavily dependent on the domestic market. The argument that, because Ireland is an exporting economy, it must benefit from measures to promote freer trade and improved market access does not apply in its simple form to the indigenous manufacturing sector. However, it may be the case that measures to remove barriers to trade will facilitate an improvement in indigenous export performance. On the basis of the 1986 data, every 1% drop in non-food indigenous domestic market sales caused by increased competition arising from the Single Market must be offset by a 3.2% increase in export sales to keep overall sales constant.

Details of exports and domestic market sales for the nine industrial groups are presented in Table 10.10. The export

Table 10.10: **Export and domestic market shares of output in non-food indigenous manufacturing, by sector (1986)**

	Exports as percentage of output	Domestic market sales as percentage of output	Percentage in indigenous exports to compensate for 1% loss in indigenous domestic sales
Non-metallic minerals	28.1	71.9	2.6
Chemicals	25.0	75.0	3.0
Metals and engineering	31.4	68.6	2.2
Drink and tobacco	7.5	92.5	12.3
Textiles	54.3	45.7	0.8
Clothing and footwear	31.8	68.2	2.1
Timber and wooden furniture	11.4	88.6	7.8
Paper and printing	7.5	92.5	12.3
Miscellaneous	15.8	84.2	5.3
Non-food indigenous manufacturing — average	23.6	76.4	3.2

Source: Derived from unpublished data from the 1986 CIP, supplied by the Central Statistics Office.

proportions range from 54.3% in textiles to 7.5% in paper and printing, and drink and tobacco. Five of the nine groups have export proportions that are above the average of 23.6. These are non-metallic minerals; chemicals; metals and engineering;

textiles and clothing; and footwear. The other four have relatively low export proportions. The sectors with the above average domestic market dependence are drink and tobacco; timber and wooden furniture; paper and printing; and miscellaneous. The export growth needed to compensate for a 1% drop in domestic market sales ranges from 12.3% for drink and tobacco and paper and printing to 0.8% for textiles.

The indigenous export propensity hides the fact that some firms do not export any output. Consequently the exporting firms will have a higher export proportion than total indigenous manufacturing. Firms that do not export will experience increased competition in the domestic market but can only benefit from improved and less costly export market access if they become exporters. Firms that already export will immediately benefit from improved and less costly export market access to offset, to some degree, the increased domestic market competition.

Table 10.11: **Exporting establishments, export and domestic market shares of output, indigenous manufacturing**

	Non-exporting establish- ments' output share	Exporting es- tablishments' output share	Exporting es- tablishments' proportion of output exported	Exporting es- tablishments' proportion of output on domestic market
Indigenous manufacturing	42.5	57.5	46.3	53.7
Non-food indigenous manufacturing	42.9	57.1	41.3	58.7

Source: CIP (1986), CSO (1989) and unpublished CIP (1986) data.

Table 10.11 presents details of the role of exporting establishments and non-exporting establishments. The non-exporting establishments account for just over 40% of indigenous non-food manufacturing output. If they continue to be non-exporters, the market access effect of the Single Market will be negative, i.e. increased competition from other EC producers will reduce their sales. The magnitude of this negative effect will depend on the types of industry and on the pre-Single Market protective barriers. If the industries are primarily non-traded activities and/or have limited technical barriers and preferential public procurement provisions, the effect of increased competition will be correspondingly small. It will be negative, nonetheless, since the reductions in transport costs and removal of frontier customs related costs improve the capacity of other countries to export to Ireland.

The exporting establishments account for just under 60% of indigenous output (57.5% for total indigenous manufacturing and 57.1% for indigenous non-food manufacturing). These establishments also have a substantial dependence on the domestic market. Indigenous non-food exporting establishments export 41.3% of output and dispose of 58.7% on the domestic market. These establishments are in a much stronger position to avail of the better export market access that the Single Market will provide. The impact of the better market access made possible by the Single Market on the exporting establishments depends partly on the degree of pre-Single Market protection enjoyed on the domestic market and consequential possible discriminatory pricing between the domestic and export markets. If the domestic market is sufficiently protected to allow higher than competitive market prices, these could be used to 'subsidise' exports. The Single Market should result in the domestic market price moving to the competitive level. Of course, this would remove the subsidisation possibility and adversely affect the viability of the enterprise.

If, however, domestic market price is close to the competitive level because non-tariff barriers are relatively weak, the impact of the Single Market on exporting establishments could be favourable. Competition in the domestic market nonetheless would increase through the impact of reduced customs and administrative barriers. This would affect almost 60% of the output of exporting establishments.

There are substantial sectoral differences in the role of exporting establishments. These are set forth in Table 10.12.

Exporting establishments account for over 50% of output in all sectors except drink and tobacco (no data are available for timber and wooden furniture). Of these seven sectors, the proportion of output exported by exporting establishments is relatively low in paper and printing (17.0%) and in chemicals

(32.2%). The same indicator is relatively high in textiles (61.7%) and in metals and engineering (55.0%). Of the eight sectors, there are only two in which exporting establishments export more than they sell on the domestic market. These are metals and engineering, with 45.0% of output sold on the domestic market, and textiles (38.3%).

Table 10.12: **Exporting and non-exporting establishments; non-food indigenous classified by sector (1986)**

	Non-exporting establishments' output share	Exporting establishments' output share	All establishments' total output	Exporting establishments' proportion of output exported	Exporting establishments' proportion of output on the domestic market	Exporting establishments' total output
Non-metallic minerals	32.5	67.5	100	41.6	58.4	100
Chemicals	22.5	77.5	100	32.2	67.8	100
Metals and engineering	42.9	57.1	100	55.0	45.0	100
Drink and tobacco	65.8	34.2	100	21.8	78.2	100
Textiles	11.9	88.1	100	61.7	38.3	100
Clothing and footwear	29.8	70.2	100	45.3	54.7	100
Timber and wooden furniture	Not available for reasons of confidentiality					
Paper and printing	43.9	56.1	100	17.0	83.0	100
Miscellaneous	36.8	63.2	100	43.1	56.9	100

Source: Unpublished data from CIP (1986), supplied by Central Statistics Office.

Geographic destination and commodity composition of indigenous exports

Table 10.13 contains the details of the geographic destination of indigenous exports.

Table 10.13: **Indigenous exports classified by sector and market**

| | Percentage of exports in each market | | | | |
	UK	Other EC	USA	Rest of the World	Total
Non-metallic mineral products	26.1	1.1	70.2	2.6	100
Chemicals	49.1	27.7	8.6	14.6	100
Metals and engineering	50.4	26.5	13.7	9.3	100
Food	55.7	15.3	5.3	23.6	100
Drink and tobacco	22.9	17.9	53.7	5.5	100
Textiles	70.1	11.1	13.4	5.4	100
Clothing, footwear and leather	60.0	30.3	6.4	3.3	100
Timber and wooden furniture	(Not available for confidentiality reasons)				
Paper and printing	85.7	4.1	8.9	1.3	100
Miscellaneous	84.3	10.0	3.3	2.4	100
Total Indigenous	55.2	16.5	11.5	16.7	100

Source: CIP (1986), unpublished data supplied by Central Statistics Office.
Note: Totals do not always add up to 100 because of rounding.

The UK Market absorbs 55.2% of indigenous exports; 16.5% go to the rest of the EC, 11.5% go to the USA, and 16.7% are sold in other markets. It should be noted that the data in Table 10.13 refer to the sectoral distribution of exports. They do not indicate the relative magnitude of each market. Percentage shares for individual markets therefore, can refer to quite small monetary amounts. Total exports of clothing, footwear and leather was IR£74.6m in 1986. The 'rest of the world' exports from this sector, at 3.3%, were therefore only £2.5m. The total chemical exports were £93.2m. The other EC exports amounted to about IR£26m.

It can be argued that the improvement in market access for indigenous manufacturing created by the Single Market will be relatively greater in the non-UK Community markets than in the UK market. Technical barriers against Irish exports are less significant in the UK than elsewhere. A low proportion of output exported to the non-UK Community markets could be indicative of the impact of these barriers. Equally, however, it might be the case that failure to export to these markets could reflect weaknesses in the marketing capacity of indigenous industry. In this case, the removal of the various barriers would not facilitate significant growth of indigenous exports in the non-UK Community markets.

As Table 10.13 shows, the share of total indigenous exports going to non-UK markets of the EC is only 16.5%. The share of exports going to all markets other than the UK, i.e. to more difficult markets, is 44.8%. Three sectors — clothing, footwear and leather; chemicals; and metals and engineering — each sell over one-quarter of their exports in the non-UK Community markets. Two sectors have extremely low export shares in this market. Only 1% of non-metallic mineral exports goes to the rest of the EC. This partly reflects the impact of Waterford Crystal which is substantially focused on the US market. Paper and printing sells only 4.1% of exports to the rest of the EC market; 85.7% is sold on the UK market. Since paper and printing is not a sector that would be affected substantially by technical barriers to trade at present, the low share of exports going to the non-UK EC market is not likely to be influenced by the direct impact of the Single Market. It is likely to be related to marketing and structural factors.

Census of Industrial Production information is not available for wood and furniture. The trade statistics, however, suggest that this sector's exports are heavily dependent on the UK. In wooden office furniture, 82% of exports go to Britain. Similarly, 98% of wooden kitchen furniture exports go to the UK, 86% of bedroom wooden furniture exports go to Northern Ireland, and 90% of other wooden furniture exports are sold in the UK, most of them in Northern Ireland.

Data in Foley (1989) show that indigenous manufacturing exports are dominated by food, which provides 59.1% of total exports (CIP, 1986 data). Metals and engineering exports are 14.1% of the total. Non-metallic minerals, chemicals and textiles each provides around 5% of the total. The other sectors are around 3% to 4%, except for drink and tobacco which is 1%. The dominant role of foreign firms is illustrated by their share of exports: chemicals 92.7%; metals and engineering 91.9%; drink and tobacco 89.9%; miscellaneous 82.1%, and non-metallic minerals 70%.

Size structure of indigenous manufacturing

The details of the size structure of indigenous manufacturing, as indicated by the 1986 CIP, are presented in Table 10.14.

Table 10.14: **Size structure of indigenous manufacturing, including food (1986)**

Size category (persons engaged)	Number of establishments	Percentage of establishments	Percentage of employment	Percentage of gross output	Percentage of net output	Average size of establishment
Under 20	2630	68.0	20.7	14.4	15.7	9
20–49	700	18.1	19.5	17.3	17.5	30
50–99	302	7.8	18.7	18.9	16.9	68
100+	235	6.1	41.1	49.4	49.9	192
Total	3867	100.0	100.0	100.0	100.0	28

Source: CIP (1986)

Table 10.14 shows that 235 establishments, or 6.1% of the total, employ one hundred persons or more. The average size within the largest size category is only 192. The average size within the 50-99-person size category is 68, i.e. below the mid-point of the size class. Establishments of below 100 persons account for 93.9% of total indigenous establishments, 58.9% of employment, 50.6% of gross output and 50.1% of net output. The CIP does not provide details of the size distribution of the '100-and-over-person-establishments', but the average size of only 192 persons indicates that there are few very large establishments in this category. Overall, then, indigenous manufacturing is relatively small-scale and is dominated by small and medium-sized establisments.

Exporting establishments are also relatively small, although somewhat larger than non-exporters. Only 7.0% of exporting establishments employ 100 persons or more.

Table 10.15: **Size structure of exporting establishments: indigenous manufacturing (1986)**

Size category	Exporting establish- ments	Size dis- tribution of exporting establish- ments %	Exporters as percen- tage of total establish- ments	Average size (persons engaged)	Percentage of total exports	Percentage of total output exported	Percentage of expor- ters' out- put exported
Under 20	1089	65.3	41.4	8	8.2	15.3	38.4
20–49	283	17.0	40.4	32	11.2	17.2	42.9
50–99	178	10.7	58.9	70	20.2	28.4	44.8
100+	117	7.0	49.8	236	60.4	32.5	49.0
Total	1667	100.0	43.1	35	100.0	26.6	46.3

Source: CIP (1986)

The average size of the exporting establishments in the 100 and over person category is 236, compared with 192 for all establishments and 147 for non-exporters. The other size categories have much the same average size for both exporters and non-exporters. The 7.0% of establishments in the largest size category accounts for 60.4% of total exports and these establishments export 49.0% of their output. The smallest size category accounts for 65.3% of all exporting establishments but provides only 8.2% of total exports.

A large proportion of establishments export; around 40% in each of the two smallest categories, almost 60% in the 50-99 person category and nearly 50% in the largest size category. Equivalent data for other countries are not available. It is likely to be the case, however, that these proportions, especially in the smaller size-categories, are relatively high, compared with other countries.

Indigenous firms are relatively small compared with companies in other industrialised EC economies, which imposes a signficant competitive disadvantage on indigenous firms. This situation exists even before the impact of the Single Market, which is expected to result in increased concentration and larger firm size in the Community. It could be argued, therefore, that the competitive position of indigenous firms will be worsened because of the impact on firm size of the Single Market. However, indigenous firms, by and large, are already so small by international standards that they are not likely to be viable or strong in products that can benefit from substantial economies of scale. There may be some marginal firms that are just viable within the existing size structure and that will cease to be competitive in the Single Market as larger firms emerge in other member states with increased recourse to economies of scale. If, however, indigenous firms in general were to become vulnerable to the scale effect of the Single Market, it is likely that they were already vulnerable because of their small size and were producing in sectors where their small scale was already a disadvantage. In brief, indigenous firms are relatively small and the scale effect of the Single Market will worsen their competitive position. However, effectively it makes a bad situation slightly worse rather than introducing significant new problems for indigenous firms.

Performance of indigenous manufacturing

Indigenous manufacturing has performed badly over the period of Ireland's EC membership. This has been particularly the case for medium and large firms in the traded sectors. Employment in medium and large firms declined from 120,000 in 1973 to 72,000 in 1988, a decline of 40%.[8] Total indigenous employment declined by 21% between 1973 and 1988. Indigenous employment declined each year between 1980 and 1988.[9] Domestic market share of Irish manufacturing declined from 86% in 1970 to 43% in 1987.[10] Export performance by indigenous firms did not improve sufficiently to compensate for a decline in their share of the domestic market.

However, there were some signs of better performance in the last years of the decade. Employment in indigenous manufacturing rose in 1989, but this growth was made up of increases in small firms and a continuing decline in medium and large firms.[11] Indigenous export performance improved substantially in 1988 and 1989, compared with previous years.

Using the CTT concept of 'indigenous', there was a growth of indigenous exports in value terms of 23% in 1988 and 13% in 1989.[12] The growth performance in 1989 was substantially below that of 1988, but 1988 was a particularly good year. Up to 1987, export growth from indigenous firms averaged about 5% per year. The 1988 indigenous export growth was greater than total export growth and foreign firms' export growth. The 1989 indigenous growth was less than the growth of total exports. Consequently, even though indigenous export performance, as defined by CTT, improved substantially in the final years of the 1980s, multinational firms retained their dominance in export performance. Indeed, such is the dominance of foreign firms in the economy's export performance that, even if the indigenous export target of the National Development Plan is met, indigenous exports still will contribute a relatively small share of manufactured exports.

The 1987 Programme for National Recovery had an indigenous export target of £3 billion for 1990. This was reached in 1989, a year ahead of schedule. The National Development Plan (1989) set an indigenous export target of £4.5 billion for the 'mid-1990s'. This represented an increase of 80% on the then estimated 1988 total of £2.5 billion (since revised to £2.65 billion). At the time of writing in early 1990, it seems probable that this target will be met, and even exceeded, if domestic competitiveness is maintained and if external conditions are reasonable. This expectation is reinforced by the anticipated export impetus of the Single Market, the good performance in 1988 and 1989, and the increased policy focus on developing indigenous exports. As was noted above, however, even this level of success will not fundamentally alter the dependence of the economy on foreign firms for manufactured exports.

Impact on indigenous manufacturing

In assessing the impact of the Single Market, two separate but related issues are considered. First, the impact on existing firms is examined. Second, there are brief comments on how the Single Market will affect the task of developing indigenous manufacturing to the level of the industrialised economies. We have already seen that Irish indigenous industry has a relatively limited presence in high technology sectors, compared with the richer EC economies. We concentrate on the Single Market effects rather than deal with the various national and international developments that may affect manufacturing.

It is possible, in most cases, to identify the direction of the effects of the Single Market. Unfortunately not enough data is available to identify the magnitude of these effects, even in those areas that, in principle, could be quantified. A Cecchini-type assessment of the cost of barriers and of the Single Market impact has not been undertaken for Irish indigenous manufacturing. However, the data presented in this chapter provide us with material on which to make judgments. Some conclusions and issues have been identified earlier. These are drawn together in the overall assessment. A EC-wide survey was undertaken as part of the research programme for the Single Market. However, the Irish part of this survey is not broken down between indigenous and foreign firms.[13]

The Europen Bureau has also examined attitudes to the Single Market and has undertaken a number of sectoral studies on its impact (Europen Bureau, 1989a, 1989b, 1989c, 1989d). By and large, however, these analyses have been constrained by the lack of detailed quantification of the effects of the Single Market (to the extent that quantification is possible). In general, these, and other assessments of the Single Market impact, fall short of the NESC's recommendation for 'industry specific analysis' involving 'deep industry-specific knowledge' (NESC, 1989, p. 281) and ultimately leading to detailed industry-specific action programmes.

The Single Market will affect both absolute and relative prices and costs. The removal of barriers in foreign markets will reduce the transactions costs and compliance costs of exporters. This will assist indigenous exporters and will improve their competitiveness vis-à-vis the domestic producers in foreign markets. This improvement also will be achieved by all other exporters in the Community. There are, therefore, two stages in the process. All EC exporters to a particular economy will experience an improvement relative to domestic producers. The scale of the improvement will not be the same for the exporters of each member state. It will depend on the relative influence of barriers such as customs and technical barriers and on the impact of transport costs and other input cost reductions. Irish indigenous exporters will improve their position in a particular export market relative to domestic producers. However, Irish indigenous exporters in a particular export market may improve or disimprove their position relative to other EC exporters in that market.

The impact of the Single Market on transport costs, which are high for peripheral economies, and the significant Irish dependance on small firms for which barriers are believed to be relatively high, suggest that Ireland's exporters may improve their competitive position relative to other EC exporters. In other words, these two factors will reduce the costs of exporting for indigenous firms to a greater extent than for other EC exporters. On the other hand, maintenance of barriers in the Irish insurance sector, which provides inputs to exporters, could result in other EC exporters experiencing greater cost reductions for this input than Irish exporters.

The UK is Ireland's most important export market. While indigenous exporters will improve their position relative to UK producers because of the Single Market, there are grounds for expecting a disimprovement in this market relative to exporters from the rest of the EC. This disimprovement arises from Single Market measures and from the impact of the Channel Tunnel. Ireland's technical standards are closer to the UK than to any other member state. Consequently, the harmonisation of standards will produce greater cost reductions for other member states exporting to the UK than for Ireland. Indigenous exporters cross only one frontier in selling to the UK. Some exporters from the rest of the EC have to cross more than one frontier in exporting to the UK. The removal of customs and administrative barriers, therefore, will have a proportionately greater beneficial effect on those exporters than on indigenous exporters.

The same argument could apply to the impact of transport costs on the UK market, notwithstanding the expectation that transport cost reductions will be more beneficial to peripheral economies. The Channel Tunnel, while not part of the Single Market programme, will reduce substantially the cost of transport to mainland EC exporters serving the UK market. It will improve their position relative to UK producers but it will also improve their position relative to indigenous Irish firms exporting to the UK. The tunnel will reduce access costs for other EC exporters but, of course, will not affect the access cost of Irish indigenous exporters selling in the UK market.

However, as will be noted below, the magnitude of the direct impact of barrier removals is relatively low, at between 0.5% to 3.5% of turnover, with relatively small effects on the mechanisms discussed above.

The NESC Report (1989) dealing with Ireland's membership of the EC commented that the extra cost imposed by custom checks 'falls heavily on Irish manufacturers because a high proportion of their output is exported and access to European markets can involve crossing several borders' (p. 279).

This is not the case for indigenous manufacturing. Indigenous manufacturing is substantially dependent on the domestic market; it exports a relatively small proportion of output and sells relatively little in the non-UK markets of the EC. Every 1% drop in domestic market sales requires an increase of 3.2% in exports to maintain a constant level of indigenous sales. Further analysis showed that establishments that are completely dependent on the domestic market account for 42.9% of indigenous non-food output. Exporting establishments sell almost 60% of their output on the domestic market. Firms that sell all their output on the domestic market will also experience some cost reductions because the transaction costs of their imported inputs will be reduced by the Single Market and other costs may also decline. On the whole, however, one expects that the Single Market will reduce the competitiveness of firms selling on the domestic market since market access is improved for foreign producers. The firms that concentrate on the domestic market can gain from improved market access only if they become exporters.

The scale of the disimprovement depends on the pre-Single Market level of protection provided to indigenous industry by non-tariff barriers. Administrative and customs barriers provide some protection for all producers. Public procurement and technical barriers will have different effects on each industry, potentially ranging from no effect to a significant effect. It is generally argued that the roles of public procurement and technical barriers are relatively low in the Irish economy compared with other EC economies (McAleese and Matthews, 1987 and Chapter 8 of this book). These barriers, it is argued, provide relatively little protection to domestic producers. Consequently, the impact of their removal on indigenous industry would be relatively limited. Despite this general conclusion, there are, or have been, examples of technical barriers (see Chapter

8 above) and public procurement items such as army clothing, furniture and stationery. The loss of preferential public procurement, therefore, could have a impact on particular firms, although not on total indigenous manufacturing.

Competition on the domestic market will increase because of the direct effect of removing barriers and because of the indirect effect of firms changing their business strategies. For the EC, the direct impact of the removal of barriers is estimated at between 0.5% to 3.5% of turnover (Emerson et al., 1988, and Nerb, 1987). It would represent a larger proportion of value added and would have a very large impact on profits. Nonetheless, firms should be able to cope with this reduction in competitiveness, especially since import costs should be reduced. Between March 1989 and March 1990, for example, the exchange rate with sterling appreciated by 15%. This had a greater impact on competitiveness relative to UK producers than the direct effect of barrier removals (0.5 to 3.5%) would be likely to have. Indeed, because of the low incidence of technical and public procurement barriers in Ireland, the loss in competitiveness from the removal of barriers probably would be less than for the EC as a whole.

A greater competitive impact will arise from the indirect effects of the Single Market. The extensive public discussion, publicity, awareness programmes and preparation measures that have accompanied the Single Market programme in each member state have heightened business awareness of the full EC market. Even without the specific changes to improve market access, these general awareness measures would have encouraged firms to adopt 'EC market' strategies, to export more, and to compete more vigorously in markets other than their hitherto traditional markets. In effect, the Single Market is likely to cause (and already has caused) a shift in competitive behaviour. Thus, even with unchanged costs, the awareness and other measures will increase competition in the EC.

The main potential gain for indigenous manufacturing arises from improved export opportunities. These, in turn, arise from the removal of public procurement restrictions and technical barriers in foreign markets and the reduced costs of exporting. The export gains would arise from non-exporting firms becoming exporters and from existing exporters increasing their export sales. While economic theory would predict that both of these changes will happen, there are grounds for doubting that a substantial export increase will occur easily. First, we have already noted the possible situation in the UK market. Secondly, a very large proportion of firms already export. The current non-exporters presumably could have begun already exporting to the relatively easy-to-enter UK market with its common language and its similarities in culture, taste and technical standards. The fact that they have not must have something to do with marketing and product characteristics, as well as with the barriers-induced difficulties of exporting. It is also expected that the opening up of foreign public procurement will not confer significant opportunities on indigenous industry (McAleese and Matthews, 1987). The relatively small size of indigenous firms and the type of sectors in which they are involved suggest that substantial new opportunities will not emerge in public procurement. The removal of technical barriers, while important for some sectors, will not have a substantial impact on total indigenous non-food manufacturing. First, indigenous manufacturing is substantially concentrated in industries where technical barriers are not significant, such as timber, clothing and paper and printing. Secondly, if technical barriers in non-U.K. markets were the major constraint, one would have expected a relatively good indigenous export performance in the UK market. This has not been the case over the period of Ireland's EC membership.

While it is the case that indigenous exporters sell relatively little to the non-UK Community markets, it is not the case that non-tariff barriers are the only significant reason for this. Cultural and marketing barriers, and differences in language and tastes, are also part of the explanation, and these will continue to exist.

The change in business behaviour and awareness of foreign markets induced by the Single Market presumably will also have a positive impact on the export decisions of the indigenous firms, although substantial supply constraints still exist. Changes in business behaviour also will increase competition from other EC exporters in export markets through the same process as was discussed above for the removal of barriers.

However, we have seen that indigenous export performance was impressive in 1988 and 1989. To the extent that this reflects a substantial and lasting improvement in indigenous export capacity, and is not a temporary phenomenon, it suggests that indigenous manufacturing may be better placed to avail of the improved export opportunities provided by the Single Market. Improved export capability probably would have occurred, even without the Single Market impetus, as part of the raising of industrial competence as economic development proceeds and as a result of the greater focus of industrial policy on indigenous exports. However, the impact of the Single Market will strengthen and intensify export capability. This suggests a better indigenous export performance in the future than would have been predicted on the basis of the pre-1987 performance.

The Single Market is likely to result in increased firm size and additional innovation activity. Indigenous industry is already disadvantaged in its scale and innovative capacity. As the Programme for Industrial Development (1990) noted, the bulk of indigenous industry is characterised by 'major scale diseconomies, poor capability in general management, in marketing expertise, technology and quality control' (pp. 8 and 9). The Single Market may widen the gap between indigenous firms and EC firms in scale and technological capacity. However, as was argued above, the gap is already so wide that a slight increase in not likely to have a significant effect on indigenous firms.

Raising indigenous manufacturing to advanced country standards is an extremely difficult task and one in which Ireland has not yet been successful. In particular, it is very difficult to develop medium-to-large indigenous firms in traded activities, as the Telesis report recommended (Telesis, 1982). Longer-term indigenous industrial development ultimately depends on exports. As the Single Market reduces the costs and difficulties of exporting, particularly for small firms, it is likely to make the export development task of industrial policy easier. The main constraints will continue to be endogenous, however, and the solution to these supply difficulties will not be provided by the Single Market.

The development of relatively large indigenous exporting companies is possibly made somewhat more difficult by the scale and innovation effects on the Single Market. It is already very difficult to develop such companies and the specific impact of the Single Market will not significantly increase these difficulties. A substantial problem may emerge from changes in business strategy induced by the Single Market. Foreign takeovers of indigenous firms are more likely in the Single Market. While this already occurs, the Single Market will intensify the practice. In particular, small, promising, high technology companies may be likely targets for takeover. This would have a substantial influence on the possibilities of developing large indigenous firms.

The Irish government has operated an extensive awareness campaign on both the overall and sectoral implications of the Single Market. This has been supplemented by the effects of development agencies, industry associations and trade unions. In addition, national and sectoral analyses of the impact of the Single Market have been undertaken. The government also has an extensive array of industrial policy instruments and programmes to promote industrial competence. Within this environment, it is broadly expected — on the principle that individual firms know best — that firms will prepare an adequate response to the threats and opportunities of the Single Market. While industrial competence has increased since 1973, the comments in the Programme for Industrial Development (1990) on 'poor capability in general management' must raise doubts about the readiness of indigenous firms to deal with the Single Market. It was probably the expectation in 1973 that indigenous firms had prepared themselves as well as possible for EC membership. The performance of medium and large indigenous firms since 1973 indicates that, even allowing for domestic economic factors, this expectation was not justified.

It is recommended, therefore, that a more active effort should be made to ensure that individual firms are prepared adequately. This would be a logical development from the broader national and sectoral awareness and preparation programmes that already have been implemented. The Company Development Programme provides a model. In effect it would be a 'Single Market Company Preparation Programme'. As with the Company Development Programme, the intention would not be to replace the specific market knowledge of the firm and its management but to supplement it with a direct customised focus on the impact of the Single Market. Obviously this would not save firms that have poor commercial prospects. Equally there are many indigenous firms that are well prepared for the Single Market and which would not need this programme. However, it would increase the firms' awareness of the threats and opportunities presented by the Single Market and increase the possibilities of their being adequately prepared. There are resource constraints in dealing with each of the thousands of indigenous firms. However, according to the most recent Census of Industrial Production data (1986), there are only 235 indigenous manufacturing establishments (and a smaller number of firms) employing one hundred persons or more. These establishments provide 41% of employment, 50% of output, and 60% of exports. Indigenous manufacturing's response to the Single Market depends heavily on these firms. Of these establishments, 118 do not export and 117 are exporters. The response of the 118 non-exporters is of particular relevance in terms of the threats posed by the Single Market. The response of the 117 exporters will significantly determine the exploitation of the opportunities. The proposed Single Market Company Preparation Programme could focus, at least initially, on the 235 relatively large establishments. In effect, it would involve the state agencies and industries' associations going to companies in a coordinated manner, providing what information is available, obtaining what is not available and assisting in the preparations for the Single Market.

Conclusions

This chapter has examined the impact of the Single Market on indigenous manufacturing. Indigenous manufacturing has a relatively low presence (compared with EC manufacturing) in industries that will be affected significantly by the Single Market. For example, only 9% of indigenous non-food output is in industries with high technical barriers, compared with 28% for the EC as a whole. The direct removal of barriers will increase domestic market competition and will improve access to export markets. However, the cost of barriers at the EC level amount to between 0.5% to 3.5% of turnover, depending on the particular sector. Because of Ireland's relatively low dependence on such barriers, the levels of protection enjoyed by indigenous firms are probably less. It is reasonable to argue that, given suitable competitiveness and an appropriate domestic economic environment, indigenous firms should be capable of coping with the removal of barriers without major losses. Nevertheless, it should be pointed out that the cost of barriers represents a substantially higher share of value added and profits. Even so, indigenous firms should not be affected significantly by the increased competition caused by the direct removal of barriers.

The reverse side of this argument is that one should not expect dramatic improvements in export performance because of the direct removal of barriers in foreign markets. The impact of the removal is relatively small — between 0.5% to 3.5% of turnover. Indigenous manufacturing has a relatively low presence in those industries in which market access will improve most. Exporters from other EC countries will also experience improvements in the major market for indigenous firms, the UK. In fact, while indigenous exporters will improve their position vis-à-vis UK producers in the UK market, their position vis-à-vis other EC exporters to the UK will probably disimprove because of the Single Market and because of the Channel Tunnel. The size structure and product mix of indigenous manufacturing suggests that export gains in public procurement will be difficult to achieve. The improved export access, particularly for small firms, will make exporting easier and cheaper. This, however, has to be balanced against the other issues discussed above. In addition, there are significant endogenous constraints on indigenous exporting, such as marketing capacity, linguistic ability and product mix. The Single Market will not affect these.

The indirect effects will arise from changes in business strategy, economies of scale and innovation. This chapter has argued that the increase in domestic market competition arising from changes in business strategy, i.e. an increased perception by EC firms of the Community as a unified market, is likely to be greater than that arising from the direct removal of barriers. The Single Market effects on scale and innovation are not likely to have a significant negative impact on indigenous industry. This is because of the essentially negative argument that indigenous firms are already weak in their size and innovative capacity. Firms that are likely to fail because of the increased scale effect of the Single Market would be already vulnerable to pre-Single Market competitors. In effect, the scale and innovation effects of the Single Market on indigenous industry make an already bad situation worse, but they do not fundamentally alter the existing situation.

Indigenous industry is heavily oriented towards the domestic market. Each 1% decline in domestic market sales must be offset by a 3.2% increase in exports simply to maintain constant sales by indigenous firms. Indigenous non-food firms that do not export account for almost 43% of total non-food indigenous output. Relatively small proportions of output are exported, notwithstanding the improvement since 1988 and the likelihood that the government's mid-1990's indigenous export target is likely to be achieved. Only 17% of indigenous export sales go to the non-UK Community markets. This poor export performance is not due only to the Single Market barriers. Consequently, removal of the barriers will not transform the situation automatically.

It is recommended that a more direct and active Single Market focus on individual companies be implemented. This could concentrate on the 235 establishments that are in the 100-person and over category or at least on the 117 establishments in this category that do export. The objective would be to provide specific information and to encourage preparation for the Single Market. This chapter argued that it is not sufficient to hope, or expect, that individual firms will correctly anticipate, or prepare for, the threats and opportunities of the Single Market. While one could argue that firms know best, the experience of medium to large companies since EC membership suggests that a more active involvement by the development agencies could produce a better result from the Single Market than was experienced from EC membership since 1973.

Notes

1. There are degrees of foreign participation varying between, on the one hand, indigenous owned and generated firms and, on the other hand, branches of foreign multinationals. Among the types of foreign participation we can include foreign entrepreneurs setting up companies in Ireland and partnerships between foreign and indigenous companies. Consequently, classifying industry by ownership is not a perfect indicator of indigenous industry capacity. Nor is foreign ownership always to be equated with branches of multinationals. The data used in this chapter predate the ownership changes in both Lake Electronics and Irish Distillers. Other companies which have changed from Irish to foreign ownership earlier than this include Navan Carpets, Youghal Carpets, Arklow Pottery and Murphy Brewery (see Ruane and McGibney (1990)). It should also be noted that the economist's concern is not with ownership, per se, but with the different economic characteristics of indigenous and foreign companies.

2. In page 196, Stage 1 barriers refer only to export barriers such as administrative and customs barriers. Technical and public procurement barriers are included with Stage 2. However, in the empirical estimation

of the barriers by Emerson, et al, Stage 1 includes technical and public procurement barriers.

3. These are minimum estimates of the sectoral impact of the Single Market. They were calculated using Emerson's estimates of cost reductions which were calculated for only seven EC countries, and the value added data in Emerson which refers to the twelve EC countries. Consequently, the actual impact will be higher than these estimates. The seven EC countries account for just under 90% of total GDP in the EC. On average then, the gains would be around one-tenth higher. The overall sectoral rankings and general magnitudes would be broadly unchanged and are adequate to indicate the general impact of the Single Market on sectors and the relative position of sectors.

The data in Table 10.3 were derived from the individual columns and totals of Table A8 in Emerson et al. Because of rounding, the stages' totals, as presented, do not in some cases add to 100. We retained the totals as presented and hence the per cent distributions are in some cases substantially different from 100.

4. The description of endogenous and exogenous constraints was suggested by Frances Ruane.

5. Table 9.2 (p. 264) of NESC Report No. 88 gives details of foreign share of employment in metals and engineering industries. These do not appear to be correct in, for example, metal articles which is shown as having no foreign presence. The data for the sub-sectors of metals and engineering referred to in this chapter are from the CIP and refer to 1986.

6. We are comparing indigenous Irish manufacturing with total Danish and Belgian manufacturing which is, of course, also composed of their indigenous and foreign sectors. It would be more correct to compare with indigenous manufacturing in Belgium and Denmark but data are not available.

7. The Commission classified technical barriers into three categories; the lowest being "less important" and the highest being of "great importance" (see Emerson et al, 1988).

8. Data from McHugh (1989).

9. Data from Ruane & McGibney (1990).

10. Data from McHugh (1989) and Irish Goods Council (1988). The domestic market share refers to total Irish manufacturing, including both foreign and indigenous. Methods of calculation are not given in McHugh (1989) and Irish Goods Council (1988). Consequently, there may be different methods of calculation used in the two sources. Even allowing for this, however, there has been a steady and substantial decline in the share of the domestic market held by Irish manufacturing firms. McHugh refers to a domestic market share of 63% in 1985. This would suggest an unlikely decline between 1985 and 1987 if the IGC data are correct.

11. Data from IDA (1990) and additional detail provided by IDA.

12. Data from CTT (1990).

13. The survey covered 149 firms with 37,000 persons employed. 50 of the firms employed 200 persons or over. These 50 firms employed 29,000 persons. However, we do not know the indigenous and foreign details of these.

11

The Single Market and the Common Agricultural Policy: their Impact on Agriculture and the Food Industry

DENIS LUCEY and MICHAEL KEANE

Since the establishment of the European Economic Community in 1958, the greater part of the European Communities' legislative activity has been devoted to the Common Agricultural Policy (CAP) and to the processed food and drink sector. Similarly, agriculture and fishing have been the subject of the bulk of EC expenditure over the years, even though the share of the Community's budget devoted to the CAP has been declining steadily as expenditure on newly developing programmes, notably the Social Fund and the Regional Fund, increased in recent years (Table 11.1).

Table 11.1:**Structures of European Communities budget**

	Shares in total expenditure			Shares in Community GDP		
	1972	1980	1986	1972	1980	1986
Agriculture and Fishing	76.2	73.6	65.5	0.42	0.61	0.64
Social Fund	2.9	4.7	7.2	0.02	0.04	0.07
Regional Fund	—	6.7	6.8	—	0.06	0.07

Source: NESC, Report No. 88, p. 469

Over the past thirty years, then, one would have expected substantial progress already to have been achieved in the creation of a Single Market in agricultural and food products. All customs duties and quantitative restrictions (quotas) on trade had been eliminated. Common (i.e. community as opposed to national) organisation of the market applied to practically all agricultural products of significance. A community organisation of the market applies, for example, to all significant Irish farm products except potatoes. Moreover, there had been substantial progress in harmonising the rules for trade among Community member states and, in many instances, EC standards had been agreed for many products and commodities.

Common price support mechanisms had been applied to nearly all important agricultural commodities. Typically, a community market organisation involves the fixing of a target price, which the Community deems to be a reasonable level of recompense to farmers for the particular farm product. The market price of the product is generally supported relative to the rest of the world by means of a variable levy, which ensures that the product cannot be imported to the Community at less than a threshold price. This threshold price is fixed so that the product can be sold in the internal Community markets only at a price equal to or greater than the target price.

The Community thus, typically, has a common level of external protection relative to other countries. This, however, may not be sufficient to ensure that Community market prices approximate to the target price. The internal supply-demand balance, for example, may be such that market prices might fall substantially below the target price, e.g. for those products for which Community farmers would be prepared to supply quantities considerably greater than those that Community consumers would be prepared to purchase at the target price.

In an attempt to provide a floor on the extent to which market prices could fall below target prices, the Community has intervened in the internal Community market. Three forms of intervention may be identified. The Community itself (through a national intervention agency) may act as an additional purchaser of the commodity at a buying-in price, which might be 90 per cent or more of the target price. These are the well-known intervention purchases. The Community then would bear the cost of disposing of those purchases either on the world market at the (generally much lower) prices available in third-country markets, or by bearing the cost of channelling those products into alternative lower return uses within the Community — endeavouring, of course, to ensure that the product could no longer be recycled into the higher priced Community-supported market (by means of various types of denaturing procedures).

Secondly, the Community may offer to subsidise traders either to export the product at the lower prices available outside the Community, or to denature the product for alternative use. The Community payments in this case are the familiar export refunds (restitution) and denaturing premia. These, in effect, act as deficiency payment mechanisms to 'top up' the prices available from external markets or from alternative lower-return uses of the product, so that a gross payment approximating that which might have been paid by the intervention agency if it had purchased the product would be available to the trader concerned. The use of the term 'refund' or 'restitution' is associated with the concept that these payments, which bring Community price down to world price, are the mirror-image of the import levies that raise world price to Community price for that product when it is imported to the Community.

Thirdly, the Community may intervene by offering payments to traders to store products for periods of, say, three to six months before selling them on internal markets. These 'aids to private storage' schemes are essentially intended to alleviate undue seasonal price decline in situations where at the time seasonal production peaks exceed consumption levels.

Detailed sets of regulations are elaborated from time to time regarding the scope and level of each of these three types of intervention. In general, Community activity has become less open-ended in recent years, and the support offered has become less attractive. This arises not only because of a downward drift in the level to which the various intervention payments bring the price as a percentage of the target price, but also through other mechanisms. These include quantitative restrictions on the volume of product covered, extended payment delays, tougher quality standards for the product, and limitations on the availability of market support to various times of the year or to periods of persistent low market prices, either throughout the Community or in certain countries.

The CAP has several aims, among which is one of securing adequacy of food supplies to consumers at reasonable prices. It can, indeed, be demonstrated that the CAP operated in the mid-1970s to hold down Community prices at a time when world grain prices, for example, reached exceptionally high levels. This was achieved by putting the Community import levy mechanism into reverse, so to speak, and charging an export levy that held Community prices down near the target prices.

Nevertheless, it would be agreed generally that the main thrust of CAP activities has been to improve and stabilise the incomes of those engaged in the farm sector — largely through market support mechanisms, but with some actions oriented towards improving farming productivity and structural adjustment within the farm sector.

Fundamental to an understanding of the relationships between the CAP and the food industry is the realisation that when the Community decided to intervene in various markets in order to support farmers' prices, it could not do so by intervening directly in the market for the products that farmers actually sold. This was primarily because of the perishability of the farm products, but also because of the large number of potential participants dealing in relatively small volumes.

The Community, instead, generally intervenes at the first stage of the processing of those farm products that it wishes to support. Thus, instead of intervening in the fresh milk market, the Community intervenes in the markets for butter, for skimmed milk powder, and so on. Instead of intervening in the market for live cattle, the Community enters the market for, say, frozen hindquarters or forequarters of beef. However, it gives export refunds for live cattle that are exported to third countries. (These, of course, incorporate the various transport, sorting and marketing costs associated with assembling animals into export lots.) Instead of intervening in the market for grapes, the Community, for example, might subsidise the distillation of wine.

The Community therefore depends on the results of its various interventions in the market working their way back from the processing stages to enhance or support the demand for the original farm products. In fact, in fixing the various prices and payments applying to those processed food products, the Community has to keep in mind the imputed or estimated costs of providing the processing or marketing services between the farm gate and the stage of the food business chain at which the Community intervention takes place. The extent to which the effects of the Community interventions are actually transmitted backwards into farmers' prices depends, therefore, on the structure, organisation and efficiency of those stages of the food processing and marketing sectors that lie between the locus of Community action and the farmers producing the relevant farm produce.

These Community intervention activities thus introduce a new 'choice-set' for decision-makers in food-processing firms by providing a range of outlets for the supported food products which can be more attractive than those available from the conventional purchasers of the products. Thus, food processors have to decide on their individual or joint behaviour in response to the Community-influenced 'choice-set'. One difficulty arises from the situation in which a particular farm product may be processed into several alternative food products, only a limited number of which attract EC support, thus altering the opportunity costs or relative risk/uncertainty balance inherent in manufacturing the unsupported food products. The decision of some food processors to concentrate on the manufacture of EC-supported food products has been the subject of comment and criticism for many years. Thus, van Dijk and Mackel (1982), in a paper to an OECD symposium, comment:

> Where control mechanisms have intervention as the buyer of last resort we see that access to selling markets is no longer a necessity. There are clear examples in various EEC countries that groups of firms formulate agreements to the effect that one or more firms per group sell for intervention on behalf of the group. In the beef sector in the Netherlands we see a situation which is even worse: firms procuring carcasses which are just prepared for the intervention requirements.

A further complication orginating from the direct EC involvement in the markets for certain processed food products arises from the possibility that those products eventually may be used as ingredients in the manufacture of further processed, or higher value-added, products. So, even though the CAP, as defined in Article 38(1) of the Treaty of Rome and listed by product in Annex II to the Treaty, was confined to agricultural products, defined as 'products of the soil, of stock farming and of fisheries and products of first stage processing directly related to those products', the European Community soon found that it had to introduce regulations governing import levies, export refunds or other trade provisions for a large number of other processed food products, such as biscuits or processed meats, that incorporate CAP-supported products as ingredients. Complicated sets of coefficients may be used to reflect either the notional ingredient proportions or the costs of incorporating the supported product in those other manufactured products. In other cases, individual manufacturers' confidential ingredient recipes form the basis for negotiating levies and refunds for a range of complex food products.

It should be obvious by now that the CAP-mechanisms have a complex series of interrelationships between the markets for farm products and the markets for manufactured food products at various stages of the food business chain. The complexities of these relationships have been the subject of succinct comment by Harris et al. (1983):

> There will be occasions when the farm and food industry lobbies are at one, and seemingly similar situations when their interests diverge. Thus Scottish raspberry growers have complained about imports of cheap raspberry pulp for making jams from Eastern Europe. The Food Manufacturers Federation, however, objected to the import of cheap marmalades and jams but wished to have access to low priced fruit pulps.
>
> There is in fact a curious duality of interest that pervades the sector. On the one hand the industry in general shares the interest of the farm sector in having a large, protected, European market and even aspires to the vocation of manufacturer of processed export products. On the other hand each firm, wishing to minimize its own costs, objects to the level of raw material prices within the EC. The lobbying against the imposition of high import levies and tariffs on imported goods — be it 'strong' breadmaking wheat, long grain rice, or dehydrated onions — is particularly marked.
>
> It is in this respect that the difference in position between the first stage and second stage processors is most marked. Basically the former have a secure outlet for their production,

in intervention, no matter what the volume, at a fixed and relatively risk free price. When intervention prices are raised, so are processing margins although processors have to pay a higher price to farmers. Thus, as a broad generalisation, it can be said that it is in the joint interest of first-stage processors and farmers to seek higher intervention prices.

By contrast, second stage processors are in a very much less favoured position as a result of the CAP. Some of their purchase prices — those for supported CAP products — are firm and subject to little negotiation, whereas their output of manufactured food products must be placed in a highly competitive retail market. Thus food manufacturers have found themselves caught between the rigidities of CAP supported raw material prices on the one hand, and the pressures from retailers on the other.

Ireland and the CAP

The fortunes of and prospects for the Irish farming and food processing sectors recently have been evaluated in NESC Report No. 88, which also draws on a number of other studies. Three fairly distinct phases appear in respect of Irish agriculture. Initially, from Ireland's entry in 1973 to the end of the transition period to full EC membership in 1978, substantial increases occurred in gross output, gross product and average farm incomes. This was followed by a severe drop in farm incomes for several years because input prices rose much faster than farm product prices. The volume of gross output did not reach its 1978 level again until 1982. The revival of 1983 and 1984 was short-lived since a combination of poor weather and an increasingly restrictive approach in the CAP resulted in gross output declining in 1985 and 1986, with associated falls in real farm incomes. A third phase, characterised by a more sustained recovery of farm price, gross output and farm income levels, has been apparent since 1986, so that average farm income levels are again approximating those that obtained in 1977 and 1978.

Sheehy (1988) has demonstrated the volatility of real farm price levels attained in Ireland relative to other member states. To comprehend the nature of these price changes for farm produce and farm inputs, it is necessary to understand that all CAP prices are now fixed in European currency units (ECUs), which replaced an earlier system of European units of account (EUAs). The manner in which CAP prices translate into any national currency thus depended on the exchange rate between that currency and the ECU or EUA. If a national currency were devalued relative to the EUA or ECU, CAP prices in that currency would increase proportionately, and vice-versa in the case of a revaluation.

To all intents and purposes, therefore, it was as if the domestic floor prices of farm products that were supported by CAP were determined in a 'foreign currency' (the EAU or ECU), with any exchange rate change having an instant effect, as if the entire output of the farm sector actually were being exported to the territory of that 'foreign currency'! It was precisely this feature of the CAP pricing mechanisms that led to the EC to establish a system of 'green' rates of exchange between the EAU and national currencies, following the devaluation of the French franc in August 1969 and the revaluation of the German mark later in the same year, in order to slow down the speed with which the currency exchange rate changes otherwise would have translated themselves into higher farm prices in France and lower farm prices in Germany.

Simultaneously, a system of Monetary Compensation Amounts (MCAs) or border taxes had to be invented in order to prevent farm produce being moved from weak currency countries, which did not also devalue their 'green' rate, to stronger currency countries, to be sold into intervention there at prices that would yield a much higher return in the weaker currency when converted back at the commercial exchange rate. Alternatively, such flows of produce could drive market prices downwards in the stronger currency area when in competition with local produce.

Negative MCAs involve such taxes payable on exports from weakening currency countries which have not fully devalued their 'green' rate values of exchange, with corresponding subsidies on imports to those countries. Positive MCAs involve subsidies payable on exports from strengthening currency countries which have not fully revalued their 'green' rates of exchange with corresponding taxes payable on imports to those countries. This mechanism keeps farm prices in countries with positive MCAs higher than they would have been if 'green' rates had adjusted more rapidly to the actual currency exchange rate changes.

During the mid- to late 1970s, Ireland succeeded in obtaining several 'Green Pound' devaluations; these resulted in Irish farm prices keeping pace with the then rapid rate of inflation. In 1979, Ireland entered the newly formed European Monetary System and this significantly curtailed the scope for such 'Green Pound' devaluations. Irish farm prices in effect were now rising at the same rate as prices in other EMS countries, despite the fact that Irish inflation rates continued to be substantially in excess of the rates in those other EMS countries. However, farm input prices were not subject to the same restraint, so a severe cost-price squeeze hit Irish agriculture between 1979 and 1986.

Meanwhile, attention was being focused on the distorting effect that persistently positive MCAs were having on EC production and consumption patterns and on the EC budget. Keane and Lucey (1984) estimated that persistently positive MCAs at the then current levels, especially in Germany and the Netherlands, would account in the long run for an annual increase of about 5 per cent in the EC milk supply, a reduction of about 1.25 per cent in EC milk products consumption, and be responsible for about 30 per cent of the EC milk surplus.

Subsequently, in the mid-1980s the EC agreed to eliminate newly created positive MCAs by means of a 'switchover' system, which in effect allows for 'green' devaluations to occur in currencies other than those that have revalued. Thus, scope for Irish 'Green Pound' devaluations has re-emerged in recent years. Keane (1990) shows that, while the EC target price for milk (and associated support prices) has remained unchanged in ECU per 100 kg, five 'Green Pound' devaluations between 1985 and 1989 resulted in a 14 pence per gallon increase in support for milk prices in Ireland.

Turning to the food industry, the NESC Report No. 88 refers to 'the disappointing progress in developing Ireland's food processing industry'. Several commentators have referred to the roles of CAP in this regard. Lucey (1984), at a Conference for Cooperative Leaders, referred to the Irish food industry 'having to rely on . . . CAP to channel our extra farm output in traditional commodity forms to destinations outside the EC rather than have it further processed into food for the European or other markets?'

Recently, similar concerns were expressed much more bluntly by Matthews and O'Connor (1987):

The Common Agricultural Policy was designed to support farm prices (and incomes) but in many ways it has been antipathetic towards the food processing industry; high prices for farmers mean expensive raw materials for processors. This would not matter to any great extent if there were common agricultural prices in the EEC. But because different prices are allowed in different states, with inadequate border tax protection (MCAs) on many processed products, exporting countries like Ireland are often at a competitive disadvantage for many processed foods compared with importing countries like the UK whose objective is to keep market prices as low as possible, e.g. through the variable premium and through arrangements for the import of cheap meat from third countries for direct consumption and for processing. There have been short periods when the MCA system worked to Ireland's advantage, but these have been exceptional. In face of these disadvantages, it has been almost impossible for Ireland to develop a vigorous food processing industry. It has taken years to sort out some of the more blatant MCA anomalies. And it looks as if it will take many more years to wipe out the remaining impediments, including the UK variable premium scheme.

NESC Report No. 83 and NESC Report No. 88 both point to the necessity of securing 'better synchronisation between food industry supplies and market needs'. NESC places considerable emphasis on 'redressing the problems of seasonality among primary producers'. Irish milk and beef cattle production are highly seasonal, associated with the relatively low cost of farm production systems based on feeding summer grass to cows and cattle. Food processors, however, would have much greater scope for developing higher value food products and guaranteeing regularity of supplies of those products if they had access to a more even supply of farm produce throughout the year.

Individual farmers and processors exercise choices regarding their particular product mix and production process in the light of the market signals facing their own particular segment of the food business chain. The development of relationships that will make it worthwhile for farmers both to develop compatible strategies that maximise the benefits to the farm sector and to the food processing sector is one of the most daunting challenges facing Ireland's food industry, farmers and government leaders.

The issues are quite complex. Keane (1986) provides an extensive analysis of seasonality issues, concluding that the long-term benefits of all-year-round milk supply for the dairy industry's existing mix of products would not be sufficient to compensate farmers for the extra costs of providing that all-year-round milk supply. He also presented preliminary analyses which demonstrated that some types of cheese were unlikely to yield market returns sufficient to compensate farmers for the extra costs, while other cheeses were likely to do so. Undoubtedly, this is a subject deserving of much further research, in respect of both milk and cattle production.

A single European food market

Quite apart from the myriad of CAP-induced regulations of the market for a range of food products extending considerably beyond the level of first-stage processing, there has been an increasing tendency to adopt rules and regulations to which products must conform to be allowed on to the market — because of increasing concern with health and other consumer protection issues. These rules and regulations cover such maters as permitted contents, denomination, additives, processing conditions, packaging, storage, and labelling. 'Unfortunately', to quote Garvey (1988), 'a great deal of this legislative activity has taken place at national level, resulting in a mass of different national rules which have effectively partitioned the supposedly Common Market into 12 separate markets with disastrous consequences for the productivity and development of the food processing industry in Europe.' As Garvey subsequently noted in the same paper: 'in the processed food sector, trade between Member States only accounts for some 6 per cent of Community consumption'.

Garvey went onto explain the earlier EC strategy for building a single market in the food industry:

> ... the strategy adopted in the Community two decades ago to redress the fragmentation was that of harmonization — viz. the replacement of different national regulations by one Community regime. This approach to harmonization was

however non-selective in the sense that the Commission made proposals for directives seeking to harmonize not only the health, safety or horizontal aspects of national rules but also specific composition laws in vertical directives. The non-selective approach to harmonization was as unsuccessful with Council as it was popular with certain elements of the media which to this day seem determined to see all harmonization in terms of Eurobeer, Eurobread or Eurosausages. In fact the proposals which were adopted were those which dealt with general horizontal harmonization such as additives, labelling and so on. Of the 50 proposals in that original programme only 14 were ultimately adopted. The conclusion was that Member States were prepared to agree to the adoption of general rules concerning health, safety and fair trading but they had differing views when it came to the adoption of compositional criteria for individual products and successive enlargements of the Community made increasingly difficult the search for acceptable solutions.

Obviously, despite the elimination of customs duties and quantitative restrictions on trade, despite the common price support mechanisms of the CAP and despite what progress had been made in harmonising Community standards, a single market could not be said to have existed in farm products or in manufactured food products, because many non-tariff barriers to trade still existed. 'Indeed', to quote Dowling (1988), 'in many cases the incidence of such barriers had increased since the mid-1970s as Governments increasingly resorted to national measures to protect vulnerable sectors and the momentum towards further integration and harmonisation had slowed down.'

By 1985, as a result of its frustrating attempts at harmonisation, and influenced by the European Courts of Justice in the 'Cassis de Dijon' and subsequent judgments, the Commission (1985) had adopted a new approach and recommended to the Council and to the European Parliament that EC food legislation be confined to:

- public health protection
- food inspection
- consumer information
- fair trading

The underlying principle was to be that any product legally made and commercialised in one member state should be allowed free circulation in all other member states, unless imperative reasons justified the imposition of special restrictions by the importing member state. The goal had changed from product harmonisation to mutual recognition, thus offering greater consumer choice.

Non-tariff barriers to European food trade

The EC Commission retained the MAC Group to study the completion of the internal market in the foodstuffs industry by 1992. The Group studied ten product sectors in downstream areas of the food and drinks sectors, such as bread, cereals, confectionery, beverage and other grocery products. They did not study meat, fish, fruit and vegetables, dairy products or eggs so as to avoid focussing on CAP issues.

In the sectors studied, the MAC Group identified over 200 non-tariff trade barriers and confirmed the view that recent years had witnessed an increase in the number of such barriers. The Group offered a very useful five-part taxonomy of these barriers:

(1) Specific Ingredient Restrictions

These barriers prohibited the consumption of a product containing specific ingredients, such as additives, pesticides, residues or vitamins. An example of this type of barrier, which is generally erected by a country under the auspices of protection of consumer health, is the restriction of aspartame in the French soft drinks industry. Another example is provided by the pasta purity laws of Italy, France and Greece.

(a) Aspartame
Aspartame is a non-nutritive sweetener used in the 'diet' segment of the soft drink industries of North America and most EC countries. It is the active ingredient covered by the trade-name 'nutra-sweet'. Aspartame cannot be used in France, so a mass 'diet' segment does not exist in the French soft drinks industry. The MAC Group estimated that, if the

ban were removed, such a segment would ultimately capture
10–15 per cent of the French soft drinks market.

(b) Pasta purity law in Italy

Pasta can be made from combinations of two different kinds
of wheat — durum (hard) and common (soft) wheat. Pasta
for sale in Italy may be made only from durum wheat. In
other countries, pasta made either from durum wheat or from
a combination of durum and soft wheat may be sold. Soft
wheat is generally about 10–15 per cent cheaper than durum
wheat. The MAC Group suggested that industry experts
believe that if the Italian law were removed, the penetration
of the soft wheat/durum combination could reach 10–20 per
cent of total pasta consumption, reaching 2 billion ECU by
1992. The Group suggested that the direct cost savings from
the substitution of a less costly ingredient could be 20–60
million ECUs in 1992.

(2) Content/Denomination Regulations

These barriers prevent a producer from using a generic name
unless his product conforms to certain content requirements. The
most widely known content law is the *reinheitsgebot*, or beer parity
law, in Germany. Another example is that all EC countries except
the UK, Ireland and Denmark disallow the use of 'chocolate'
if the product contains vegetable fat other than cocoa butter.

(a) Beer purity law in Germany

Since 1516 the *reinheitsgebot* has prohibited the manufacture
of beer from ingredients other than hops, malted barley, yeast
and water. The law was designed to protect consumers.
'Impure' beer could not be imported to Germany and sold
under the name 'beer'. Foreign producers, especially the
Dutch, Belgian or French breweries, could sell beer as 'beer'
in Germany only if they changed their recipe. The European
Court of Justice has ruled that this law may not prohibit
the sale of other foreign beers as 'beer' in Germany. However,
German beer must still be made according to the traditional
formula.

(b) Vegetable fat in chocolate

United Kingdom and Irish chocolate manufacturers use
vegetable fat to counteract softening caused by the use of

substantial quantities of milk solids. Such chocolate may not be sold in continental member states, except Denmark, as 'chocolate'. This particularly inhibits UK exports of milk chocolate to Germany and France.

(c) Vegetable fat in ice cream

France and Germany disallow the sale as 'ice cream' of any frozen milk-based dessert product containing vegetable fat. This regulation was designed to protect consumers, but it prohibits the use of some vegetable fats that may be cheaper than animal fats. The MAC Group estimates that the cost savings from allowing ice cream containing vegetable fat to be sold in Germany would amount to 50–60 million ECU.

(3) Packaging/Labelling Laws

These laws affect all aspects of packaging, including the shape, materials, sizes, recycling and disposal of packages/containers, as well as labelling requirements.

(a) Danish law provides for soft drinks, beer and mineral water to be sold only in bottles, which are refillable and correspond to Danish bottle specifications, with the added requirement that bottles be shipped back to the bottling plant. The MAC Group shows that, between 1970 and 1986, Denmark had the lowest level of beer imports of any member of the EC and argues that the transportation costs of two-way bottles make them uneconomic at distances of over 200 km — a distance easily surpassed when exporting to Denmark.

(b) Labelling laws

Despite the EC labelling directive (79/112/EEC), several member states require additional labelling information. In Spain, labels must contain a health registration number. This forms a subtle but effective barrier to a potential new entrant to the Spanish market, while being merely an irritant to a trader who already has an established position there.

(4) Fiscal Discrimination

Some tax laws are capable of disadvantaging an importer relative to a local producer. These are distinct from trade barriers arising from actual differences among countries in rates of excise tax or VAT.

(a) 'Wort' excise tax

Five member states levy excise tax on their beer producers, based on the fermentation volume or 'wort', minus a pre-set wastage allowance, which is 10 per cent in Belgium, the Netherlands and Italy and 6 per cent in the UK and Ireland. Excise tax on beer imported into those countries is based on the actual volume of the final beer product. If a domestic beer producer routinely can overcome the wastage factor, he may derive a cost advantage relative to the importer of beer, by paying a lower average excise tax per unit of beer actually produced.

(b) Differential tax in France

According to the MAC Group, French rum is taxed in France at a rate that is about 60 per cent of the French tax levied on Spanish rum.

(5) Specific Importing Restrictions

This group of barriers captures many of the diverse and subtle types of discrimination that a producer/exporter must undergo before succeeding in the cross-border commercialisation of goods. The MAC Group quotes a barrister as referring to this category as all the barriers that 'make life difficult for the producer/exporter': import licence requirements, health registration requirements, border inspections and product testing.

Pitts and Simms (1988) applied the MAC taxonomy of barriers to trade in dairy products. They say that 'we have found over 30 barriers specifically affecting dairy products and feel the true figure is at least twice as high.' Their categorisation of those barriers into the MAC Group taxonomy is shown in Table 11.2. Many of the barriers arise from the existence of extensive food laws, especially in Germany, that rigidly define individual products in the name of consumer protection and quality guarantee.

Pitts and Simms selected three barriers for extensive analysis, since their potential removal was thought to be of most significance to the Irish dairy industry. These are the UK ban on liquid milk imports, the prohibition in several countries of manufacture and trade in dairy substitutes, and the barriers to imports of live animals imposed as a protection against the spread of foot-and-mouth disease. Removal of the first two might create some export opportunities for Irish dairy firms, while potential removal of the third has been a cause of grave concern in the meat trade. If a vaccination policy was to be introduced as a Community-wide means of containing foot-and-mouth disease, in contrast to the slaughter policy in use in Ireland, the UK and Denmark, it is feared that Ireland would lose its 'white-listed' status and access to certain markets based on the country's foot-and-mouth free status. Alternatively, if other EC countries were also to adopt a slaughter policy, they too might gain 'white-listed' status and compete with Ireland in those markets!

Table 11.2: **Classification of non-tariff barriers affecting dairy trade**

Specific ingredient restrictions	4
Content/Denomination regulation	14
Packaging/Labelling	9
Fiscal discrimination	2
Specific import restrictions	10
Total	39

Source: Pitts and Simms (1988)

In the meat sector, many of the impediments to the development of high value-added activities by Irish meat processors have been related to the Common Agricultural Policy. These include different incentives to various stages of processing and the operation of the Monetary Compensatory Amount System. Industry sources tend to be less sensitive to technical barriers, except in relation to minced meat, where the EC has not yet adopted its proposed directive. One notorious non-tariff barrier some years ago was the '3 kilo rule', by which certain countries prohibited the import of vacuum-packed cuts of beef, that were less than three kilograms in weight. This directly affected the export from Ireland of smaller prime cuts, e.g. fillets less than 3 kg but, more importantly, since 3 kg cuts were greater than consumer portions, any such exports of vacuum-packed cuts had to be opened on the Continent, cut into consumer portions and then repackaged for retail sale.

The Single Market, Irish farming and the food industry

The effects of completion of the Single Market on Irish farming and on the Irish food industry will be interwoven with the effects of two other developments — restructuring the Common Agricultural Policy (CAP) and the Uruguay Round of negotiations on the General Agreement on Tariffs and Trade (GATT).

Broadly speaking, the CAP will continue its evolution towards more emphasis on gearing farm and food-manufacturing sectors more closely to market requirements, with less emphasis on Community market support, especially for farm products persistently in surplus. This will be accompanied by relatively more support for rural development by measures other than merely promoting the development of full-time commercial farming. These measures will need to be genuinely cross-sectoral, to accommodate the part-time characteristics of local rural labour markets.

The GATT negotiations potentially could alter much of the framework within which the CAP and other countries' farm and food policies may be framed. Some countries have argued either for relatively unrealistic zero-support options or for the conversion of border supports to conventional tariffs. However, it is likely that some form of general understanding on a scheduled reduction in support levels will emerge, with the CAP surviving more or less in its existing form.

Both these developments (CAP evolution and GATT negotiations) would be consistent with the increasing market orientation of farm and food production, which would be consistent with the necessity for careful evaluation of the potential gains from completion of the internal market. In other words, the interrelationships among the three factors may have a synergistic effect potentially greater than the sum of the individual effects if the three features were not occurring together over the next few years.

Direct benefits arising from the removal of non-tariff barriers are threefold:

- use of less expensive ingredients
- reduction in labelling/packaging costs
- elimination of red tape.

Indirect benefits would also result to the Community as follows:

- a broadening of consumer choice
- significant trade increase in some products servicing similar market niches in several countries
- improvement in efficiency in certain processing sectors, arising from scale economies in marketing and distribution and industry — restructuring and consolidation.

The MAC Group estimates that the direct annual cost savings in the sectors it studied to be of the order of 500–1000 million ECU, about 2 to 3 per cent of industry value added, or one to two years gain in productivity.

Irish farmers should expect cost savings as a result of cheaper farm input prices. Similarly, the food industry should expect similar savings in fuel, transport, insurance and finance costs.

National production quotas, and even quotas linked to land in the case of milk production appear, at this stage, to be regarded as consistent with the subsequent free movement of the produce throughout the Community.

Abolition of the UK ban on liquid milk imports may create some trade opportunities for Irish milk processors, and Irish dairy firms may also be able to apply their experience of the dairy spread business to good effect on the removal of the prohibition on the sale of such products in several continental countries.

While it is not formally part of the 1992 agreement, there is a Commission commitment to remove all MCAs by 1992, although the problem of how to cope with future currency realignments within the EMS still would have to be resolved.

It is not yet clear whether border restrictions on plant and animal movement for disease-control purposes eventually will be resolved by levelling-up or levelling-down arrangements, though these too form part of the GATT discussions. Irish negotiators will be endeavouring to ensure that any relaxation of animal movement restrictions will be accompanied by measures to minimise the risk of importing diseases such as foot-and-mouth disease or classical swine fever.

One important potential feature of the Single Market has been referred to by Josling (1989), who expects what he refers to as 'the cosy relationship between agriculture and the food industry' to come under strain. Josling expects that weaker EC intervention arrangements, freer cross-border trade as a result of the Single Market, and the trend towards multi-country food firms, will force food firms, including first-stage processors, to develop 'more of an interest in seeking out the lowest cost source of supply'. Farmers may again learn to appreciate their cooperatives after 1992!

Restructuring the food industry

One of the more interesting features of the MAC Group report is its analysis of the extent to which global food firms are emerging because of the acquisitions of increasingly larger firms. It shows how United States food firms have pursued a twofold strategy in their own domestic market during the 1980s: (a) becoming the dominant brand in a product sector and (b) achieving nationwide coverage. The logic underlying such a strategy is straightforward. Within any product sector,the profitability of brand leaders is generally much greater than that of 'second-tier' brands. Nationwide coverage maximises the volume over which fixed costs (including R & D, marketing and promotion) can be spread.

In pursuit of this two-pronged strategy, most American food groups have been re-evaluating their product portfolios. Rather than dominating a region with a diverse range of unrelated products, the large firms are generally focusing on achieving nationwide penetration with a narrower product range. Many firms have been 'swopping' business units in order to achieve their similar objectives.

Few European-based firms in the food industry follow a Community-wide strategy. The MAC Group showed that, out of a sample of 46 large EC-based food firms, exactly half have a presence in two or less of the five major member states. Only about one in ten of the main EC food firms has a presence in all five major EC countries! It is obvious, therefore, that EC food companies by and large have remained nationally focused, which, in the broader context of the Single Market, translates into regional coverage. In contrast to the strategic behaviour of large American food firms in recent years, their counterparts in the Community still tend to diversify into new product sectors within their own home country, instead of penetrating across Europe in a limited number of product categories.

Very few major European food firms enjoy high brand strength and wide geographic coverage within the Community. Obviously, taste and cultural and linguistic factors contribute substantially to the prevailing national focus, but various kinds of trade barriers and subtle forms of 'protection' of domestic firms have also played a role. As these latter barriers decline, we can expect EC food companies more and more to seek to increase both their brand strength and their geographic coverage. We can expect a major consolidation and restructuring of Europe's food industry, with many mergers and 'swaps' occurring both within countries and across national borders. The MAC Group expresses the fear that US-based firms, with their greater experience of this strategy, may be able to grasp the opportunities presented by the Single Market more readily than EC-based firms, which thus run the risk of getting left behind.

How do Irish firms rate in this new scene? The Irish food industry has experienced a substantial degree of concentration in recent times. The sector has many Irish firms, both cooperative and investor-owned, which are among the largest Irish manufacturing companies. Many of these firms operate several processing plants. Indeed, with some exceptions, it is generally true that the scale of Irish food-processing plants is comparable to that of the plants of leading EC food firms. This has been acknowledged, for instance, in NESC Report No. 88 (p. 262).

It is, however, essential to distinguish clearly between the size of an entire enterprise (or firm) and the scale of any particular production plant which that enterprise operates. Existing global food firms and the emerging EC-wide food firms will tend to focus on economies at the level of the enterprise such as advertising and marketing expenditure. These economies help firms to capture the high margins from strong brand identity, transnational distribution, and also to support the high costs of research and development of new and improved food products.

By these criteria, even the largest Irish food firms are relatively small. A recent tabulation by Hadleigh Marketing Services Ltd of Europe's leading food firms based on 1988 turnover shows Nestlé, based in Switzerland, as the largest, with a turnover of over $25,000 million; followed by Unilever, based in the UK and the Netherlands, with a turnover of $14,000 million; Dalgety, from the UK with $7,500 million, BSN Groupe from France with $6,700 million, and Eridiana from Italy with $6,300 million. The first Irish food firm to feature in that tabulation is An Bord Bainne, the Irish Dairy Board, which appeared in the forty-first position, with somewhat more than $1,000 million, followed in forty-seventh position by Goodman International, slightly under $1,000. An Bord Bainne is a second-tier dairy cooperative which handles the export marketing function on behalf of its members — several individual Irish cooperatives which, in turn, are engaged in processing milk produced by their farmer-members. Even if one considers dairy product sales in isolation, An Bord Bainne is not large by world or even by European standards. The Dutch Produktschap voor Zuivel lists An Bord Bainne as tied with three other firms for positions 22 to 25 among the biggest dairy product marketers in the world. That listing features 15 EC-based firms among the world's top 25 dairy firms.

In many respects, the greatest opportunity facing Irish food firms is being provided by the new scope to restructure, in order to take advantage of the marketing, distribution and product development economies that will emerge from the Single Market opportunities. Two broad optional strategies face decision-makers in the Irish firms. One is to combine with other Irish firms to establish a sufficiently large strategic entity to have a significant presence in the European food market. The alternative is to establish similar arrangements on a transnational basis, with complementary firms located in other member states, thereby establishing market strength across the Community by another route. A variant of the second approach involves potential linkages with medium-sized American food firms that might be interested in associating with an Irish partner to supply some specialised niches in EC food markets.

Obviously, the prospects for strong brand penetration of the EC by Irish food firms are limited. McCrea (1988) suggests that Irish food firms carefully evaluate seven non-branded routes, based on 'Business to Business' sales, as a strategy for exploiting the Single Market opportunities.

In general, while Irish dairy and meat firms have adopted a product portfolio which emphasised sales to intervention agencies or commodity-type sales to third-country markets, it appears that Irish dairy firms have recently been devoting relatively more financial and human resources to the development of newer, more consumer-oriented products, which seem capable of generating higher earnings from sales to other European food firms or even to European consumers. The dairy industry therefore may be in a better position than the meat industry to achieve steady rather than spectacular development in the process of selling food into Europe and switching steadily from low to higher margin items.

Finally, as CAP restructuring brings production levels closer to consumption levels and as internal non-tariff barriers are eliminated, transport costs may be expected to play a greater role than heretofore in determining the spatial patterns of farm production and food processing throughout the European Community. Relatively more research in this field may be expected in the future from European food economists and food marketing specialists, almost akin to the greater emphasis that spatial analysis has received in recent decades in the United States. Current research, for example by Keane and Lucey (1990), involves modelling the extent to which milk quota reductions may cause Irish trade to move to a greater extent towards internal Community markets and involve a product mix less concentrated on dried products.

Traditional spatial theory suggests that in a large single market area, a homogeneous farm product from the peripheral regions will tend to be processed into less perishable, storable, transportable, cheaper commodity-type foods, in contrast to the fresher, more perishable, less transportable, higher margin consumer-oriented food products, which will tend to be processed from the same farm product coming from farming areas closer to the large-scale centres of consumption. Consumers in Europe's large population centres, however, are steadily increasing their demand for high-quality products in line with rising income levels; they are also demanding greater variety in their food and more foods that can be served quickly.

In that case, all farm produce of a particular kind in the Single Market may not be homogeneous in terms of consumers' perceptions of quality! Can the peripheral regions (including Ireland) convince the food consumers at the centre that Irish farmers will provide cleaner, higher quality farm products from an environmentally conscious farming system than those that are available from other EC locations, where agricultural activities have reached or exceeded the limit of what is ecologically tolerable? Can we organise marketing activities to identify these high-margin food niches, arrange the necessary timely distribution and high-quality processing and assembly services in such a manner as will yield a consistently higher payment to Irish farmers? If so, such higher payment must make it worthwhile for them to incur the higher costs necessary to produce year-round the consistently high-quality 'environmentally friendly' farm produce, rather than the production choices that it has paid them to make in recent years.

Ireland's success in selling more food into the Single Market will depend on whether the country can ensure consistent signals at each stage of the food business chain, so that sufficient decision-makers in the farms and firms at each stage can be expected to make product choices and business decisions that are in harmony with one another. We must not underestimate this challenge.

12

Indigenous Services

JOE DURKAN

Service industries in Ireland are quantitatively more important than production industries, both in terms of output (i.e. value added) and of employment (see Table 12.1).

Table 12.1: **Service sector: employment and output 1988**

	Percentage Share of National Total
Employment	57
Output	53

Source: National Income and Expenditure 1988; Central Statistics Office, *Labour Force Survey* 1988

While this has been the case for a number of years, the services sector has not received the detailed statistical analysis or comment that has characterised the agriculture, manufacturing and construction sectors. Consequently, it is possible to provide only broad-brush analysis, based primarily on employment data. Table 12.2 illustrates broad subsectors of the service sector. As can be seen, since 1979 there have been significant increases in the numbers employed in wholesale distribution, in the financial sector, in personal services and in professional services. The numbers employed in retail distribution and public administration have remained relatively stable, and there has been a decline in the numbers of those employed in the transport and communications sector.

The data in Table 12.2 make no distinction between aggregate public sector and aggregate private sector employment or between market and non-market services. In 1988 there were some 200,000 public sector employees in non-market services (Civil Service, Gardai, Defence Forces, Local Authorities, Education and Health) out of a total of 320,000 in Public Administration, Professional Services and Personal Services. Thus the bulk of market services are to be found in the wholesale and retail trade and the financial sector, with the remainder distributed among a wide number of activities. The next section examines the impact of the Single Market on distribution. The following two sections examine other market services.

Table 12.2: **Subsectors of service industry 1979–88**

	Employment (000s)	
	1979	1988
Commerce	161.2	172.3
— wholesale distribution	38.0	45.5
— retail distribution	123.2	126.8
Insurance, finance and business	36.6	49.7
Transport and communication	68.5	63.8
Public administration and defence	70.1	70.1
Professional services	148.5	184.3
Personal services	57.1	65.3
Other*	16.8	20.2
	558.8	625.7

Source: Central Statistics Office, *Labour Force Surveys* 1979, 1988

Distribution

In this section separate treatment is given to the wholesale and the retail components of distribution. Across the European Community the wholesale trade will experience several separate effects:

1. There will be a reduction in administrative barriers and frontier delays and a liberalisation of transport regulations which will reduce costs and raise potential profitability.

2. There will be an increase in cross-border competition by wholesalers in neighbouring countries, the extent of which will depend on the degree of tax harmonisation and the mechanism adopted for the collection of indirect taxes. Unless the Irish wholesale sector is not to be too seriously affected, indirect taxes must be brought more closely into line with those in other EC countries. Assuming that tax rates are harmonised, the direct competitive effects on the Republic of Ireland, other things being equal, may not be dramatic, because the strength of retail multiples in the UK has resulted in a weakened wholesale sector there. Hence the Irish wholesale sector may not be as adversely affected as might otherwise be expected. In fact, there may even be opportunities in Northern Ireland for wholesalers from the Republic.

3. To the extent that the macro effect of the Single Market is positive for Ireland and raises incomes, then household and other spending will be higher than otherwise and this will also be positive for the wholesale sector.

4. Finally, the changes in the retail trade (discussed below) that will result from the Single Market programme will weaken the wholesale sector. There are likely to be major changes at the retail level and these indirect effects will have a larger influence than the direct effects on the wholesale sector.

The retail sector in Ireland has undergone a major rationalisation over the past quarter century and is now heavily concentrated. Unfortunately, the 1977 Census of Distribution is too dated to be of much practical use in determining the economics of the retail sector. However concentrated the sector now appears, it must be borne in mind that it is minute when compared with the major multiples in the United Kingdom. The retail sector will be affected indirectly and directly by the Single Market. The indirect effects are likely to prove the most important.

UK multiples are likely to see the Single Market as providing a further stimulus to expansion throughout the European Community, particularly if retail performance in the United Kingdom is weak. At present non-tariff barriers (frontier, technical and fiscal) are not a major constraint; what has been lacking is detailed knowledge of markets and this has been stimulated by the single market programme. The continental market offers large UK multiples opportunities to realise further economies of scale from marketing, centralised purchasing and distribution networks. The continental market is an ideal one to enter because the structure is highly fragmented and incomes are generally high. Finally, any intention to look for markets in Europe must have been strengthened by developments in Eastern Europe, where reconstruction and the development of more market-oriented policies will lead to increased incomes and output. It is inevitable that some multiples will see an expansion into the Irish market as a natural element of this outward-looking strategy.

Over the past decade UK firms have gained some experience in the Irish retail market, and while not all were successful, the principal lesson may very well have been that it is very difficult to succeed in an economy that is undergoing an extended recession. In 1990 the domestic recovery was in its third year. Medium-term forecasts suggest continued output and income growth at least to the mid-1990s, with no major fiscal or balance of payments problems. Quite apart from the Single Market programme, this is the type of market environment that one could expect UK multiples to penetrate.

It is to be expected that retail companies from other member states would seek to enter the UK market. Entry to the Irish market may seem a natural extension of this strategy. Consequently, one might expect some penetration of the Irish retail market by non-UK companies.

The above analysis is highly speculative because developments in Eastern Europe may well pull both UK and Western European multiples towards Eastern European markets.

While the analysis suggests that existing retailers may be affected adversely by increased and new competition, consumers will benefit from lower prices and a wider range of products. Ultimately, new retail outlets will replace those that have been adversely affected.

If VAT rates and excise duties are harmonised across the member states, there will be a shift in cross-border retailing. This will be particularly noticeable between the Republic of

Ireland and Northern Ireland, where the effect of the differences in indirect taxes are suppressed by frontier controls. The differences in tax rates potentially distort trade, but this distortion is limited by frontier controls and by the suspension of duty-free facilities for travellers by means of the "48-hour rule". It is widely believed that since the differing tax rates are still distortionary, consumers in border counties of the Republic continue to purchase goods in Northern Ireland despite customs restrictions. The harmonisation of indirect taxes will limit trade-distortionary effects, while the removal of customs formalities will allow consumers to arbitrage and to experience a wider choice of goods and retail environments.

However, it cannot be assumed that because tax rates are harmonised and consumers are free to shop without restriction that this will benefit the retail trade in the border areas of the Republic. Both Derry and Belfast are large cities with good shopping facilities. In an unrestricted environment, these would act as the natural shopping centres for many border areas; Dublin, Cork and Limerick perform the same function in the East, South and Midlands. Thus the Single Market will have two contrary effects: first, the harmonisation of taxes will reduce trade distortionary effects at the retail level and, second, the removal of border restrictions will divert trade from border towns to the major shopping centres in Northern Ireland.

The largest single direct effect on the retail trade of the Single Market programme, however, is likely to be in the mail-order business across national frontiers. At present mail order is relatively undeveloped in the Republic of Ireland. By contrast, the UK mail-order business is very highly developed and accounts for a significant proportion of consumer spending. There are also strong mail-order companies in France and Germany. While some foreign companies do trade in the Republic, there are perceived barriers, in the form of customs delays/VAT issues, responsibility for delivery, consumers' rights and financial arrangements, which have limited the spread of foreign mail-order companies. However, mail order is now likely to become more international, and must be expected to make a significant impact on the retail trade. Consumers will have a wider range of products from which to choose, available in highly competitive foreign markets, where centralisation of facilities will result in lower costs and prices. Initially, mail-order growth may be limited to low bulk items, but as this market grows, direct delivery from the UK and other member states could develop. These developments will benefit consumers, but existing retail trade across a wide range of products will be affected adversely. It is not likely that any existing mail-order companies will extend their business outside the island, because many are subsidiaries of UK companies, and the existing level of activity is limited and expensive relative to companies overseas.

Financial services

The international financial services sector has been undergoing significant changes as a result of deregulation, the globalisation of markets, and the introduction of new products. Underpinning these developments has been a rapid change in technology. A continuation of these developments would result in the marginalisation of financial institutions in fragmented markets because American, Japanese and, to a lesser extent, British players increasingly would dominate the corporate market. International aspects of financial services have been examined by Price Waterhouse (1988). This section, however, will concentrate on the Single Market as it affects the Irish financial services sector. The single market programme, by reducing the fragmentation of markets caused by differing regulatory authorities, provides an opportunity for increasing competition, the achievement of economies of scale so that companies can rival their US and Japanese competitors, and a wider range of products and services to customers at lower prices. This will lead to significant benefits for the Community as a whole. The EC Commission (1988) estimated that the liberalisation of financial services would add 1.5% to the Community's GDP, would result in the general price level being 1.4% lower than otherwise, and would improve the public finances of EC governments by the equivalent of 1% of GDP as a result of a reduction in the debt burden.

Nevertheless, although it is one thing to estimate aggregate benefits, it is quite another to see how those benefits are distributed between countries. The output gains and the achievement of economies of scale will be concentrated on those with lowest costs for any given service, and to a lesser extent on those in niche markets.

The regulatory environment in all the member states imposes varying degrees of cost. A priori, one would expect the financial sectors that are least regulated to do better within the single market. Realistically, almost irrespective of how favourable the regulatory environment, the Irish financial sector is not going to dominate in Europe, but it should not be placed at a competitive disadvantage.

At present, the Irish financial sector is both heavily regulated and subject to a variety of supervisory bodies. The degree of regulation has resulted in the application of different rules by a single regulator to essentially similar institutions (e.g., the distinction between associated and non-associated banks, and between domestic and foreign by the Central Bank). Similarly, the diversity of regulators has resulted in different rules between institutions that effectively are competing with one another. Furthermore, there are differences in the treatment of tax returns from different institutions and this prejudices the direction of new and existing savings. These regulatory and tax differences have market implications for different types of institution.

In recent years some tax distortions have been reduced, and the regulatory environment has been simplified. The Central Bank Act 1989 has centralised a number of regulatory functions. In addition, the act has widened the powers of the Central Bank to deal with the potential problems caused by new financial instruments, has imposed new charges to finance a deposit insurance scheme, and has widened its powers to cover firms in the International Financial Services Centre and certain other financial sector activities.

Irish banks already face significant competition in lending from overseas banks. This has resulted in a declining share of new business going to Irish banks. While the position has stabilised in recent years, the greater freedom of establishment and the cross-border provision of services will widen the choices available to bank customers. In this situation, outside bodies must be expected to win a bigger share of this business, particularly in the corporate market. Furthermore, the Irish market is too small for some specialist services to be offered by Irish banks, whereas foreign institutions can service their Irish customers' needs without incurring extra costs.

Banks will experience greater competition for large deposits once exchange controls have been dismantled fully. Customers can pick and choose where to deposit their funds, and differences in tax treatment (e.g., the withholding tax) will be important. The creation of the Single Market will create opportunities for banking institutions if the regulatory environment is relatively favourable. Finally, while it is easy to see Irish banks and banks in other small countries facing difficulties *vis-à-vis* their larger competitors, foreign banks lack both a distribution and a customer base and these are not readily acquired. Finally, as a means of withstanding competition, domestic banks can decide to strengthen their own base by acquisition and by growth abroad; the major banks have done this to a certain extent.

Building societies will be affected directly by the provision of the directive (draft) on mortgage credit that will allow them to raise funds and to grant mortgages throughout the EC and subject them to competition from other countries' mortgage credit institutions. Although this will increase competition in the mortgate market in Ireland, building societies possibly are more interested, in the long run, in widening the scope of their activities away from mortgages. In recent years they have experienced serious competition in their traditional market from commercial banks as the banks sought to provide more complete financial services to their customers. Irish building societies are relatively small by European standards, so there seems little prospect of their being successful abroad.

The Irish insurance industry has also experienced significant competition from overseas and many foreign companies have established offices in Dublin. Existing Community law allows companies with a head office in one member state to establish branches in other member states or to carry out insurance on a service basis without the need for branches. The freedom of companies to do the latter is governed by a recent directive — the Non-Life Directive — which has the effect of protecting the existing non-life market in Ireland on a phased basis up to the end of 1998. It is widely believed that, in addition to increased choice, there will be a reduction in premium payments once competition has been established since there are wide differences in rates across Europe, with those in Ireland being particularly high. However, the source of these differences needs to be established, i.e. whether it is due to institutional factors, such as the methodology of settling claims, high costs or monopoly prices, or inefficiencies in insurance firms. Prices can be narrowed through competition only if inefficiencies exist in Irish insurance companies. If, however, the price difference is due to institutional factors, a price reduction would not be expected. By contrast with non-life insurance, life assurance companies are believed to be in a relatively strong position *vis-à-vis* continental EC companies as a result of innovative life policies, and large price differentials, with continental EC life policies being more expensive.

Software and other market services

Much of the rest of the market services sector consists of specialist subsectors, none of which directly are major employers, e.g. the legal profession, the appliance services sector and consultancy services. For some of these sectors the opportunities and threats of the Single Market are remote — they will benefit to the extent that the sectors they serve benefit.

Advertising agencies are an exception to this because there could easily be more centralisation of advertising functions built around European-wide products and made possible by developments in communications (e.g. satellite television). Thus agencies in Ireland serving the products of multinationals could suffer a loss of revenue to centralised marketing, but find increased outlets for their expertise in the domestic market as that market expands because of other aspects of the Single Market.

In spite of recent liberalisation, the airline market remains highly regulated. However, the effects of liberalisation to date are, in all probability, not fully reflected in consumer behaviour, traffic volumes and air traffic-handling facilities. Thus, this market will develop to a greater extent, further liberalisation will cause a continued increase in traffic, while the income effects of the Single Market will raise demand again. It is clear that the air passenger transport services sector will increase its output. Indigenous companies command a certain brand loyalty and, in the case of Aer Lingus, this will be copper-fastened by planned purchases of new aircraft. Since aircraft shortages are projected to be a feature of the 1990s, aircraft availability will prove an important characteristic of the success of indigenous companies. These developments are somewhat independent of the Single Market because airline deregulation is an international trend. The Single Market does provide a focus and a framework within which this deregulation can proceed. To the extent that deregulation does occur, ancillary services of airlines, such as aircraft maintenance and catering, will continue to grow.

Similarly, many consultancy services, such as engineering and general consultancy, will develop depending on the growth in the sectors they serve. During the 1980s, when Ireland's economy performed very badly, many firms in the consultancy sector were obliged to seek business abroad, either by subcontracting work or by establishing operations overseas. The Single Market will not materially affect companies' ability to do this to any extent. Such firms have already proven their ability and, to the extent that the single market does lead to an expansion of demand, they will benefit even further.

The situation confronting these companies, and indeed many others in the services sector, can be well illustrated by the Irish software industry. There is a strong and growing Irish software industry, currently employing about 3,000 people. Selected data on the software industry are presented in Table 12.3.

Table 12.3: **Selected data on the Irish software industry, 1989**

Software companies — number	200
of which: independent (non-subsidiary) companies	150
subsidiary companies	50
Employment	3000
Turnover	$150 million
Exports as share of total sales — per cent	50

Source: Irish Computer and Software Association

The industry effectively is divided into two segments — one predominantly serving the domestic market, though seeking expansion via foreign sales, the other essentially using Ireland as a base for the development of software for world markets, though also seeking sales domestically.

As indicated in Table 12.4, the product mix of the Irish software industry is similar to that of the industry worldwide, though the Irish industry is small by world standards. Packaged software is the largest part of the software industry in Ireland. Packaged software in Ireland is almost entirely concentrated in applications software for end-users, rather than in computer systems software. Applications software in Ireland is heavily geared towards particular sectors, such as banking, or particular types of service, such as payroll administration.

Table 12.4: **Turnover by product/service, 1985 (percentage)**

	Ireland	World
Packaged software	43	39
Processing services	23	33
Custom software and consultation	27	19
Training and other activities	7	9
	100	100
Output value $ million	100	50,000

Source: European Computer and Software Association

Software demand increased worldwide by 12.5–15 per cent in real terms in the 1980s. Forecasts for future demand suggest a growth of about 10 per cent for the 1990s from a base level of demand of $100bn in 1990. The industry has been characterised by a high degree of technological change in hardware, the need to develop software to deal with this change, and changes in software technology itself. These have resulted in the software industry worldwide being 'supply constrained'. In spite of this, many apparently well-managed and hitherto profitable firms are experiencing financial difficulty, because of overexpansion, adherence to outmoded technology (either hardware or software), or being overtaken by lower-cost competitors. This has affected companies domestically and abroad.

There are few technical barriers to trade in the software industry, though public procurement barriers do exist. Within the EC there are no restrictions, though the portability of software has created problems where VAT rates differ between countries. VAT harmonisation will reduce these problems. The most obvious opportunity arises with public procurement policies. In several of the member states, public procurement policies in respect of software have deliberately favoured national companies. These policies have been illegal for some time and the Commission has stated its intention actively to pursue open competitive tendering. Where the industry has been protected by public procurement policies, the likelihood is that the absence of competitive pressure will have increased costs and reduced innovation. Thus, non-protected software companies are likely to find their performance improving, though it must be recognised that software companies in major markets always will enjoy an advantage in their own country.

The Irish public sector has not given favourable treatment in public procurement to local software companies. Instead, they were obliged to seek out markets internationally, while the industry supplying the domestic market was obliged to compete with a range of off-the-shelf software from a wide variety of sources. The industry thus has operated in a very competitive environment.

Underlying the success of Irish software companies has been (i) the application of business insight and technique to what is still a technology-driven industry, (ii) a steady stream of well-qualified software graduates. One consequence of the restriction on entry to third-level education has been a general improvement in the average quality of student intake and in the quality of graduates.

Ireland has a comparative advantage in the development of software because of the high quality labour input relative to other countries. However, companies find it difficult to retain staff at competitive wage rates given the Irish tax system, where the problem is not so much the highest rate of income tax but the fact that one reaches it at relatively low income levels. As a consequence, the domestic industry is supply-constrained also, and is not developing as rapidly as might be expected. Some firms have developed imaginative methods for dealing with this, e.g., setting up in the UK and retaining staff, who wish to migrate, as employees in the UK. This strengthens the position of the firm, but, of course, is not directly reflected in output or employment in Ireland.

The Single Market creates opportunities for the sector, but there were many opportunities in any event. Many of the constraints on the sector will not be affected by the Single Market.

The solution of some of the problems facing the software sector lies within the context of Irish economic policy.

Summary

This chapter has examined the factors likely to affect indigenous services in the context of the Single Market. The largest indigenous service sector is the distribution sector. While retail and wholesale distribution are not purely tradeable internationally, the Single Market will encourage centralisation of wholesale and retail activities within the European Community. Firms now operating in the domestic Irish market will be subject to increased competition from new market entrants. The harmonisation of indirect taxes and the removal of customs and frontier restrictions simultaneously will reduce trade-distortions at the retail level arising from tax differences — which should be positive for the domestic retail trade — but there will be some trade redistributed to major urban centres in Northern Ireland. The chapter also examined the impact of liberalisation on the financial services sector.

Other market services that reflect only domestic demand will be affected because the sectors they serve are affected. Internationally traded services will be affected to the extent that demand in the European Community grows. For these latter services, the 1980's recession in the Republic of Ireland was the main spur to seeking overseas markets. Finally, the impact of the Single Market was considered in the specific case of the software industry.

13

Building and Construction

OWEN KEEGAN and GEORGE HENNESSY

This article is based on a report entitled *1992 and the Construction Sector* prepared by DKM Economic Consultants and published by the Europen Bureau of the Department of the Taoiseach in November 1989.

The construction sector here covers the activities of enterprises and individuals engaged in the building and civil engineering industries, in the construction professions, and in the manufacture and distribution of building products and materials. In addition, other sectors of the economy and a range of agencies, from local authorities to mortgage lending institutions, play an important role in the construction sector. Because of the special nature of the industry's output and its role in the provision of social and economic infrastructure, its activities impinge on ordinary individuals to a greater extent than perhaps is the case with other branches of industry. The importance of the industry's output is reflected also in the high degree of state support it enjoys and in the detailed regulations to which it is subjected.

Given the size and importance of the construction sector and the high degree of state intervention to which it is subjected in every member state, it is not surprising that the programme for completion of the internal market contains a number of important measures targeted primarily at the construction sector. The European Commission is convinced that a diminution in the barriers to trade and the creation of a single market for construction products and services, with an end to discrimination in public procurement, will increase competition, will reduce costs and prices, and will generate additional output in the sector.

The creation of a single market for construction products via the construction products directive, and the opening up of public procurement to increased outside competition via the public procurement directives, are two important measures that primarily affect the construction sector. In addition, other developments that will contribute to the completion of the internal market, and which have important implications for building and construction, include an increase in structural fund expenditure, the harmonisation of indirect taxes, and the mutual recognition of higher education diplomas in respect of architects, engineers and other related professions. The purpose of this chapter is to present a brief outline of these measures and to consider their likely impact in Ireland.

Measures affecting building and construction

Construction products directive

The White Paper, *Completion of the Internal Market* (European Commission, 1985), proposed a new approach to overcoming the protracted delays associated with securing agreement on the technical specifications for construction products before the use of a particular product could be made mandatory in all member states. The Commission proposed that future directives would include only statements of 'essential requirements', conformity with which would qualify products for free movement, marketing and use across all member states. The task of preparing detailed technical specifications would be handed over to European standards bodies headed by CEN (European Committee for Standardisation). While European standards were being developed, the mutual acceptance of national standards, with agreed procedures, would be the norm.

The construction products directive was enacted in December 1988. Laws, regulations and administrative procedures in member states must comply with the provisions of the directive by June 1991. It requires member states to ensure that construction products offered for sale in their territory shall be 'fit' for their intended use. Products must be such that the finished structures in which they are used can satisfy, if properly designed and constructed, six 'essential requirements':

- mechanical resistance and safety
- safety in case of fire
- hygiene, health and environmental protection
- safety in use
- protection against noise
- energy economy and heat retention.

A manufacturer will be able to demonstrate conformity with the 'essential requirements' by several means, including conformity with a harmonised European standard, holding a European technical approval (e.g. European 'Agrément' certificate), compliance with an EC-approved national standard where a European standard does not exist, and compliance with all the 'essential requirements', independent of whether a standard exists that has been certified by an approved testing body.

Only products that comply with one of the above are entitled to bear the 'CE' mark or symbol of conformity, and member states are required to ensure their free movement, marketing and use. The Commission will draw up a list of construction products that play only a minor part with respect to health and safety. These products will have to be manufactured in accordance with 'the acknowledged rule of technology'. Where a manufacturer makes a declaration of conformity in this regard, the product may be freely marketed, but may not carry the 'CE' mark.

The directive clearly specifies that members states will allow construction products to be marketed only if they fall into one of the categories specified above. These categories cover all situations, including the marketing of construction products on the domestic market as well as in other member states.

Public procurement directives

The Commission has accorded a high priority to the opening up of competition in the public procurement of goods, services, and works throughout the member states. These developments are particularly relevant for the construction sector, given the important role of central, regional and local authorities and other public sector agencies in financing construction output. The original directives of public procurement placed severe limitations on the scope and coverage of these public bodies. In addition, the public contracting authorities failed to advertise in the EC official journal, the restricted and negotiated forms of tendering were abused, and restrictive requirements were adopted in tender documents. Other violations perpetrated were: the insistence on compliance with national standards, in violation of EC law; the use of discriminatory selection criteria; the circumvention of monetary thresholds for the application of the directives by splitting contracts; and the failure to allow sufficient time for the preparation of tenders.

The Commission is now proposing a four-pronged approach to opening up public purchasing, which is intended to tackle the deficiencies in the original directives. First, to ensure that tender award procedures are more transparent, the original legislation for public works and supply procurement has been overhauled and the definition of public bodies covered by its provisions has been widened. Second, matters excluded from earlier directives will now be specifically covered, albeit by separate directives. Third, public procurement in services will be covered by a separate directive. The public services directive will cover a range of service activities, including architectural, civil and other engineering services, among many others not specifically connected with the construction sector. Finally, the Commission is proposing a major tightening up of its enforcement powers to ensure that contracting authorities comply with the directives.

A new public supplies directive was adopted in March 1988 and came into effect in January 1989. A new public works directive was adopted in July 1989 and operates from July 1990, except in Greece, Portugal and Spain, where the effective date is March 1992. These directives will encourage competition for public works and supply contracts by:

- requiring improved notification and early warning of contracting authorities' requirements, with additional time for advertising, for the preparation of applications to bid and for the preparation and submission of bids

- limiting the use of single tendering or negotiated procedures, and ensuring a strong presumption in favour of open tendering in the case of supplies contracts
- requiring the specification of national standards which will implement European standards where such standards exist. If a European standard does not exist, a national standard may be used, but the principles of equivalence and mutual recognition must be observed
- providing for public notification about the contracts that have been awarded
- enabling excluded candidates or tenderers to find out why their applications and tenders were rejected.

A new draft directive is being prepared, to cover public procurement in the water, energy, transport and telecommunications sectors. This draft directive will introduce greater transparency into the procurement procedures of public and private sector enterprises operating in these sectors and will provide for increased competition. However, the draft directive differs from the supplies and works directives by providing greater flexibility to the contracting authorities in relation to the tendering procedures they can adopt and to the selection and qualification of contractors and suppliers. Furthermore, the Commission is preparing a draft directive to cover the public procurement of services. The directives on services procurement will fill the remaining gap in public procurement. The Commission has identified a number of priority sectors for the application of the proposed services directive. One of these includes construction-related services covering architecture, civil engineering and some applied specialist services like quantity surveying.

In December 1989 the Council of Ministers adopted a compliance directive that will come into effect on 1 January 1992. The directive, which will apply to public works and supplies contracts, requires member states to introduce procedures that will allow suppliers and contractors effective and rapid remedies through national administrative and/or judicial bodies at all stages of the procedures for the award of public contracts against infringements of Community law or national rules implementing Community law on public procurement.

Harmonisation/Approximation of VAT

We now examine other aspects of the Single Market proposals which have a less direct but nonetheless important impact on building and construction.

The proposed removal of fiscal barriers to trade by the harmonisation or approximation of expenditure taxes throughout the Community has implications for the construction sector, the precise nature of which will depend on the final form of the indirect tax harmonisation measures. In fiscal year 1990, VAT was charged at 10 per cent on construction output in Ireland and there is wide variation in the VAT treatment of construction in different member states. Under the Commission's revised proposals of May 1989, construction is not included in the list of products/services to be taxed at the reduced rate (i.e. between 4 per cent and 9 per cent). Consequently, construction output may be taxed at the proposed standard rate (i.e. above 14 per cent). However, the final decision on the specific products and services to be taxed at the low rate, and indeed on the tax rates, will be the subject of negotiation and agreement between member states. There is a possibility that at least some aspects of construction, especially housebuilding, may be included at the low rate, which would reflect the current practice in a number of member states.

Structural fund expenditure

The need for a revitalised Community regional policy was seen from the beginning as an integral component of the completion of the internal market if the benefits of the process are to spread to the peripheral regions and if the political cohesion that lies at the heart of the concept of the European Community is to be maintained. It was agreed that the completion of the Single Market by 1992 would be accompanied by an expanded regional policy. The goal of strengthening economic and social cohesion is written into the Single European Act. The act pledges the Community to reduce disparities between the various regions and in particular to improve the position of the least-favoured regions. Ireland is in the latter category, and the Community is commited to increase the level of available resources to remedy economic and social structural deficiencies in Ireland as part of the process leading up to 1992. This commitment to tackling structural problems in Ireland embraces all three structural funds: the Regional Fund, the Social Fund, and the Guidance Section of the Agricultural Fund, together with the European Investment Bank.

The structural funds arrangements contain a commitment that total aid from them will be doubled for the less developed regions in real terms by 1992, and doubled overall by 1993. Provision was also made for an increase in the rates of contribution from the structural funds up to a maximum of 75 per cent.

The *National Development Plan* set forth the structural measures that Ireland proposes to implement over the period 1989 to 1993 to be financed by the state, by the EC and by the private sector. A significant proportion of the planned expenditure involves the provision of new physical infrastructure and the upgrading of existing infrastructure. The Commission's response to the plan was given in November 1989 when the *Community Support Framework for Ireland* was published. While the assistance levels are lower than was anticipated in the *National Development Plan*, the construction industry will be a major direct beneficiary of the proposed structural fund expenditure over the four-year period.

Mutual recognition of construction professions

Since 1985, the Commission has been pursuing a general approach to the mutual regulation of professional qualifications, instead of the sectoral approach that was adopted previously. A general directive on the recognition of higher education diplomas, awarded on completion of professional training of at least three years' duration, was adopted in January 1989. This directive differs from earlier sectoral directives in several important respects. It is general in character and applies to all regulated professions for which a higher education training of at least three years is required and which have not been the subject of a specific directive. Recognition is based on mutual confidence, and there is no need for prior coordination of the education and training systems for the different professions in question. As a basic principle, a member state may not refuse access to a regulated profession to a national of another member state who holds the required certificate for the exercise of such profession in the member state of origin. Recognition is accorded to the 'finished product', i.e. a fully qualified professional having completed any professional training that may be required in addition to a higher education qualification. Finally, in the case of important differences in education and training, or in professional structure, the directive lays down compensatory mechanisms, in the form of an adaptation period or an aptitude test.

The directive applies to professions that are regulated in a member state. If a profession is not regulated in any member state, it is not covered there. If someone comes to a member state where the profession is not regulated, whether they come from a state that regulates the profession or not, then the directive does not apply. However, if a person goes to a member state that regulates the profession, even if the profession is not regulated in the member state of origin, then the migrant's qualifications must be recognised under the terms of the directive.

The general directive covers engineers, surveyors and planners and possibly other building professions that may be regulated in a member state. Provided that it is regulated in a host member state, then freedom of movement is guaranteed under the directive, subject to the individual possessing higher education and training qualifications of at least three years' duration. Architects are already covered by a separate architects directive.

The implications

Before considering the likely implications for the construction sector in Ireland of the various measures being implemented as part of completion of the internal market, it is important to review the extent of trade in building materials in Ireland and in other member states. Trends in Irish construction output, in construction materials production, and in the import and export of construction materials since 1981 are set out below.

The data suggest that production of construction materials in Ireland in 1987 was just below its level in 1981 in value terms. Allowing for price inflation in building materials over the period, the volume of production is estimated to have declined by 28 per cent between 1981 and 1987, compared with a 38 per cent decline in the volume of total construction output over the same period. Greatly improved export performance has alleviated the full impact of the decline in construction demand on the building materials sector in Ireland. However, there is evidence that import penetration actually increased during the 1980s. Imported materials accounted for 42 per cent of total building materials used in 1981 and for 50 per cent in 1987. When considering the high level of import penetration in the building materials sector in Ireland, a distinction should be made between 'competing' and 'non-competing' imports. Approximately half of Ireland's building material/product imports are estimated to be in the 'non-competing' category.

Table 13.1: **Trends in construction output, trade and production of construction materials in Ireland 1981–87**

Year	Construction output £m	Material consumption* £m	Imports £m	Exports £m	Production £m
1981	2186.6	918	383	135	670
1982	2270.5	954	357	162	759
1983	2034.4	854	349	185	690
1984	1948.2	818	395	208	631
1985	1916.3	805	381	238	662
1986	1931.5	811	366	225	670
1987	1861.6	782	392	254	644

*Assumes value of material consumption equivalent to 42 per cent of output

A study commissioned by the European Commission — 'BIPE — Bureau d'Informations et de Prévisions Économiques (1988)' — gives information on production, consumption and trade in construction materials in 1985 in each member state. Using the information in the study, we have estimated the extent of import penetration in building materials in each member state in 1985 (i.e. imports of building materials as a proportion of total consumption of building materials). The relevant data, which are based on a very narrow definition of what constitutes building materials, are given in Table 13.2. In general, we expect imports to account for a smaller proportion of materials consumption in larger countries.

The data show that in Ireland in 1985, imports accounted for 56 per cent of total consumption of building materials (as defined by BIPE) in value. They suggest further that the building materials sector in Ireland is among the most open of all the member states. The data also suggest that this sector is relatively open in the UK, with 53 per cent import penetration level in 1985. In contrast, building materials markets in most mainland countries are less open, despite the existence of long land frontiers in some cases. Import penetration levels are lower than the UK in France (33 per cent), Denmark (30 per cent), West Germany (23 per cent), Italy (17 per cent), Portugal and Greece (both 11 per cent) and Spain (8 per cent). In part, these variations can be attributed to the differences in the size of the economies and in the extent of the various land frontiers. Nevertheless, at the aggregate level, the data appear to confirm the relative openness of the building materials sector in Ireland.

Table 13.2: **Construction materials†: production, consumption and trade in EC countries 1985 (billions of ECU)**

	Production	Imports	Exports	Consumption	Imports as % of consumption
W. Germany	36.5	7.6	11.1	33.0	23
Italy	22.4	3.4	6.2	19.6	17
France	16.7	5.4	5.6	16.5	33
Spain	12.2	0.8	2.9	10.1	8
UK	11.8	7.0	5.6	13.2	53
Benelux	5.7	5.4	7.1	4.0	*
Netherlands	4.1	3.3	2.8	4.6	72
Denmark	3.4	1.1	0.8	3.7	30
Portugal	3.0	0.3	0.6	2.7	11
Greece	2.8	0.3	0.4	2.7	11
Ireland	0.8	0.5	0.4	0.9	56

†Includes non-metallic minerals, metals and metal products, timber and wood products, chemical products, textiles, paper and packaging, rubber and plastics, and electrical materials.
*Cannot be calculated.

The UK accounted for 49 per cent of Irish construction material imports and 63 per cent of exports in 1986. A study that examined trade flows in a wide range of construction materials in 1988 (Chaldecott, 1989) showed that 66 per cent of Irish exports of all material products examined were destined for the UK. The next European economy in terms of dependence on another member state for a high proportion of its exports of building materials was Denmark, where 39.5 per cent of exports went to West Germany.

The structure and operation of the construction process in Ireland are very similar to the system in the UK. The similarities with regard to work practices, language and the regulatory environment have allowed Irish contracting and professional service firms to establish and operate in the UK with relative ease. Given the degree to which a single market already exists between Ireland and the UK, it is doubtful if any of the measures to be implemented as part of the process of creating the Single European Market will create many more opportunities. Given the similarity between the Irish and the UK construction systems, and the countries' geographical proximity, it is not surprising that the UK accounts for a very high proportion of Ireland's construction imports, and its exports of contracting and professional services and of building materials.

It is clear that while the structure and operation of the construction sectors in Ireland and in the UK are broadly similar, distinctive systems operate in other European countries. Construction is by no means a homogeneous activity across all member states. Differences in organisational structure and operation, together with the role of the state in regulating and in financing construction output and the nature of the output itself result in the industry being subjected to a range of influences that do not arise to the same extent in other sectors. The fact that the final output is fixed in a specific location, and therefore is relatively dependent on local factors of production, renders the industry subject to widespread regional variations throughout the Community. Moreover, there are substantial variations in taste affecting design and quality factors. All those factors that impede trade in contracting and professional services and in construction products will persist long after 1992. The exploitation of opportunities on mainland Europe will continue to be hampered by language differences and (more importantly) by differences in construction systems long after other barriers are removed. For these reasons, the creation of new opportunities is likely to be the preserve of a few larger or specialist firms with a strong home/UK base, given the range of obstacles that will remain to be overcome.

In this regard, Ireland is relatively poorly equipped because of the small number of large firms in the construction sector to avail of the export opportunities that will arise because of the Single Market.

The volume of construction output in Ireland is estimated to have fallen by 42 per cent between 1981 and 1988, while direct employment in the industry declined by 30.6 per cent, or 31,000, in the same period. The downward adjustment in construction output in Ireland during the 1980s followed a period of unsustainable growth in the sector during the late 1970s and the very early 1980s. The simultaneous expansion of both private and public investment that fueled the boom in output between 1977 and 1981 has been mirrored in their simultaneous decline since 1981.

The poor performance of the Irish economy during the 1980s until 1987 — a significant reduction in employment, rising unemployment and emigration, declining real disposable incomes and very sluggish consumer demand growth — contributed to reduced demand for construction output across a number of sectors, including private housing and industrial, office and retail developments. In addition, high levels of industrial and semi-state construction during the late 1970s and early 1980s reflected major investment projects in fields as diverse as electricity generation, telecommunications, gas distribution and urban transport; these are now largely completed. In recent years the emphasis in industrial policy has shifted away from the construction of advance factories and, consequently, industrial building has declined. In the education, local authority housing, health and sanitary services sectors, high levels of investment were maintained up to the mid-1980s and the backlog of accumulated needs declined. However, investment levels have since fallen considerably, reflecting both more modest needs and the state's reduced capacity to finance capital projects.

The Irish economy appears to have entered a period of strong economic recovery and of rapid employment and consumer demand growth, in stark contrast with the experience between 1981 and 1987. A recovery of this scale will have a very significant impact on construction demand and should ensure strong growth over the next few years. In particular, it will underpin further growth in the private residential sector — both new and repair and maintenance activity — and will boost demand in the industrial, retail and office-building sectors. Finally, the expenditure proposals in the *National Development Plan*, if implemented, will contribute an estimated 9 percentage points to total construction industry output growth over the period 1990 to 1993 and 4 percentage points to output growth in 1990 alone.

The above analysis suggests that the industry has entered a period of sustained output growth after a prolonged period of decline. In these circumstances, the domestic growth opportunities available to contractors, material producers and to the building professions, at least into the early 1990s, are likely to be significant, and the industry may be less inclined to pursue the limited opportunities that will arise from the completion of the internal market in construction in the Europe Community.

Increased competition will be the inevitable consequence of the removal of national technical barriers to trade and the opening up of public procurement to outside firms. However, the extent of the additional competition will vary across sectors and products, and indeed between member states, as barriers based on different construction systems will continue to be significant. The cost structure of Irish manufacturers and the achievement of economies of scale will be central to their ability to compete on the home and on export markets. The construction products and public procurement directives will reduce costs and facilitate firms that wish to compete in other member states. However, with the reduction in technical barriers to trade, it will become even more important to ensure that Irish firms are not unduly penalised by higher relative costs as a result of national policies to do with company and individual taxation, and pricing policies in relation to energy, telecommunications, postal and transport services. The implementation of the directives should ensure a phased impact on competition. A number of factors suggest that building and construction in Ireland has room for optimism in the domestic market from the completion of the 1992 programme. These include the recent success of Irish manufacturers, contractors, and building professional firms in expanding their UK operations, albeit in a very buoyant market, the relative openness of the construction products market and of public procurement procedures in Ireland, and the fact that the anticipated recovery in the Irish construction market will provide a stronger home market base for exporting firms. However, as was noted above, the possibilities of substantially exploiting the opportunities throughout the Community are limited.

In theory, the public procurement directives are designed to provide a basis for Community-wide competition. Whether in practice they will provide a platform for increased exports is a different matter. A fundamental requirement for successfully competing for contracting work abroad is a good knowledge of the local market. A wide range of factors is involved here, such as language, foreign forms of contract, differing insurance and bonding requirements, differences in taxation, labour costs and availability and sourcing of materials. All these factors are outside the scope of the public procurement directives. It is unlikely that the Commission will propose harmonisation in any of these matters, preferring instead to allow national peculiarities to continue, providing that they are non-discriminatory towards firms from other member states.

A further consideration for contractors is the fact that contracting authorities in member states can use the restricted tendering procedure with an open call for candidates under the provisions of the works directive. In such circumstances, the choice of contractors invited to tender is at the sole discretion of the contracting authority. It is generally accepted that national contractors, with an established record, will continue to be favoured over new foreign contractors. Given the extent to which this form of restricted procedure is used in preference to open competition, the opportunities for Irish contractors to tender for public works contracts abroad will continue to be severely limited.

The extent to which foreign firms will be attracted to compete for public procurement contracts in Ireland is essentially a mirror image of the opportunities for Irish exporters considered above. The size of the threshold for the application of the public works directive (i.e. £3.9m. net of VAT), and the scope for the use of restrictive tendering procedures, will limit the opportunity for foreign firms to secure public works contracts.

Apart from any impact on competition, the procurement and construction product directives have important implications for the tendering and contract award procedures of a wide range of public and private organisations. New procedures will have to be put in place, particularly with regard to standard times, before the closing dates for receipt of tenders, and rules in relation to technical specifications and specific tendering formats (i.e. open, restricted and negotiated procedures). Firms will have to become familiar with the new procedures because they will apply to all contracts above the stated thresholds, irrespective of whether there is a likelihood of foreign competition.

A reduction in the rate of VAT on residential construction from 10 per cent to, say, 9 per cent would have a modest impact on demand. On the other hand, any increase in VAT on other construction output would have an adverse impact on demand, the extent of which will depend on the size of the increase. The main losers would be final consumers, as in the case of individuals engaging contractors for housing repair and maintenance work, or organisations, such as local authorities, health boards and financial institutions, who cannot reclaim VAT. The supply of construction services to local authorities, government departments, some semi-state bodies (including Telecom Eireann and An Post), financial institutions and a large number of services, welfare, educational, religious and sporting organisations, would be adversely affected by any increase in the rate of Value Added Tax.

14

Ireland as a Location for Multinational Investment

DAVID JACOBSON and BERNADETTE ANDREOSSO

This chapter examines the impact of the Single Market on Ireland as a location for multinational investment. First, the theoretical framework for analysing multinational enterprises is outlined, and briefly applied to Ireland. Section 2 presents an empirical examination of past foreign direct investment in Ireland and assesses future prospects. Conclusions are presented in Section 3.

The 'eclectic' approach (Dunning, 1981, 1988) emphasises three main factors in a firm's internationalisation: ownership advantages, location advantages and internalisation. Ownership or 'firm-specific' advantages include superior technology, information, management, organisation and marketing. Location or 'country-specific' advantages include markets and resource endowments, both tangible — raw materials — and intangible — skills. Internalisation refers to the allocation of resources by a firm itself, rather than through the market. Vertical and horizontal corporate integration are examples of internalisation. Firm-specific advantages and internalisation together explain why a firm undertakes foreign direct investment rather than exporting goods or services; country-specific advantages explain the choice of location for foreign direct investment.

The motivation for economic integration between countries is related to the motivation of firms to invest abroad. A major objective of the integration of countries, for example, is to "overcome structural market distortions e.g. tariff barriers, subsidies etc. and to encourage competition" (Dunning and Robson, 1987, p. 105). The competition to be encouraged is that among intra-regional firms, although this is not always explicit. This should result in increasing efficiency and, as a result, increasing competitiveness *vis à vis* non-member countries. From the point of view of an extra-regional firm, however, economic integration such as that undertaken by the European Community has the effect of increasing the region-specific advantages, though it may well diminish some of the country-specific advantages. Thus the removal of tariff barriers from imports into Germany may have reduced the need to set up a plant there, but the free movement of goods among the original six member states, together with the common external tariff, increased the attraction of manufacturing within that region in order to avoid the common external tariff and so service the larger market (Balassa, 1977).

Furthermore, integration between countries aims to "facilitate the possibility of product and process specialization of firms within the region, and promote trade in intermediate products" (Dunning and Robson, 1987, p. 105). If extra-regional firms are more advanced, their entry may prevent this.

The main impact of the Single Market for multinational enterprises in Ireland — leaving aside for the moment how much of a change this actually is — is on its country-specific advantages, i.e. its relative attractiveness as a location for foreign direct investment. If a subsidiary was established in Ireland in order for the multinational enterprise to gain access to the EC market, then, at first sight, the completion of the Single Market will improve that particular country-specific advantage of Ireland. Moreover, very few, if any, manufacturing subsidiaries of multinational enterprises were set up in Ireland specifically to exploit the domestic market, so from this perspective it appears that manufacturing subsidiaries already in the country are unlikely to leave as a result of further integration. This also applies to subsidiaries of multinational enterprises in the service sector, other than those involved exclusively in distribution.

In terms of future foreign investment flows, it must be remembered that the other eleven member states also will have their country-specific advantages enhanced by the more complete access of their exporters to the Single Market. The Single Market may even make the core countries more attractive than the peripheral ones. The possibility of industries concentrating at the core must be offset by regional and other policies at the European level (Jacobson and Andreosso, 1988; NESC, 1989).

The operation of multinational enterprises is one of the major elements affecting the divergence that accompanies integration. Being mobile, they will tend, if the eclectic model applies, to locate where the advantages are greatest. Infrastructure, skills and proximity to final consumers will attract multinational enterprises to particular locations, which, as a result, will experience higher growth rates.

The main reasons for choosing to locate in Ireland include the following:

- Tariff-jumping: firms that intend to market products in the Community, set up there to avoid having to pay the common external tariff.
- Fiscal advantages: this applies to both Community and non-Community firms attracted to Ireland by the low corporate tax rate.
- Special government assistance, particularly that which is cost-reducing.

These three reasons are all 'artificial' or 'man made'. They do not relate to the natural comparative advantages that the Irish economy has over other economies. Tariff-jumping suggests why non-European (for example, US and Japanese) multinational enterprises wish to set up in the Community. The second and third points explain why, having decided to establish in Europe, multinational enterprises (irrespective of origin) might choose Ireland rather than any other location. All three reasons are the result of governmental decisions, which could be changed in the short term.

There are other reasons why multinational enterprises choose Ireland as the country in which to locate their subsidiaries, and these are related to more fundamental aspects of the Irish economy: the general macroeconomic performance of the economy; the availability of an educated and skilled labour force, and the fact that this labour force is English-speaking. Some of these country-specific advantages are amenable to development by government action, others are not. Irish authorities can contribute to the raising of skill levels but clearly cannot ensure that oil deposits exist off the Irish coast. Where country-specific advantages can be enhanced by government action, this usually can be achieved only over the medium-to-long term. Obvious exceptions to this are the capital and other grants offered to multinational enterprises.

Removal of Ireland's artificial country-specific advantages in a complete harmonisation of tax and grant regimes in the EC would have a dramatic and negative effect on Ireland's locational attractiveness. The EC Commission, however, has decided to allow such state incentives to industrialisation in the less developed member states. Ireland easily satisfies this condition, and, as a result, 'a more stringent application of the policy [expected after 1992] is likely to have little direct impact on the economy of the Republic' (NIEC and NESC, 1988, see also Simpson, 1989, p. 105). It is important that this continues to be so.

Four possible cases can be identified of foreign direct investment into Ireland being affected by the Single Market. First, extra-EC multinational enterprises may be encouraged by European integration to set up production facilities (or expand existing facilities) in Europe by virtue of the increased size of the protected market. Second, as a pre-emptive strategy, extra-European multinational enterprises that do not already have them, are likely to set up subsidiaries in order to protect market share in the face of expected European industrial rationalisation (Knickerbocker, 1973; Kojima, 1978). Third, for intra-EC multinational enterprises, regional integration encourages foreign direct investment because it reduces the barriers to the international organisation of production, leading to product and process specialisation in separate European plants. This is more likely to be vertical than horizontal integration. Finally, and this applies to both intra- and extra-EC multinational enterprises, there is an opposing, discouraging effect of regional integration on corporate internationalisation. This is where the reduced barriers to trade reduce the incentive to have production plants in the target EC country. In this case, firms may resite production closer to the home country if they are intra-EC multinational enterprises, or towards a single production location within the Community if they are extra-EC multinational enterprises.

These four cases will inform the empirical analysis that follows.

Empirical examination of foreign direct investment into Ireland and future prospects

A review of foreign direct investment following Ireland's entry into the EC in 1973 provides a background to the analysis of the impact of further integration. Ireland's membership certainly influenced both the origins and the volumes of investment.

By 1973 the United Kingdom was still — as it had always been — the most important source of foreign capital in Ireland. The US had increased in significance but still accounted for only 25.3 percent of foreign firm employment, as compared to a UK share of 45.7 percent of the total (Boylan and Cuddy, 1988, p. 77). The US continued to increase in significance as a source of foreign direct investment in Ireland, and in 1986, it accounted for 48.1 percent of foreign manufacturing employment in Ireland, compared to 17.1 percent for the UK (CSO, 1989, Table 5). Other countries that have grown in both absolute and relative terms as origins for foreign investment in Ireland are Germany, the Netherlands and, more recently, Japan.

A sharp increase was both expected and realised in the volume of foreign investment into Ireland during the first nine years of the country's entry into the Community, 1973 to 1981 (see NESC, 1989, pp. 99). Indeed, it has been argued that, by the beginning of the 1980s, Ireland was "the most attractive location for foreign investors in Europe" (Ruane, 1984, p. 343). According to the same source, however, the increase in non-EC investment into Ireland during the 1970s was "unlikely to be sustained in the 1980s" because of the January 1981 removal of export profit tax relief. This relief meant zero taxation on profits on export sales and had attracted foreign investors. Its removal had been imposed on Ireland by the country's membership of the Community (Ruane, 1984, p. 338). Even though export profit tax relief was replaced by a relatively low tax rate of 10 percent on manufacturing profits, Ireland became less attractive after 1980.

Foreign direct investment indeed did decline during the early 1980s, both in foreign investment inflows (FitzPatrick, 1988, p. 71) and in employment (CSO, various years). To some extent this may reflect a decline in Ireland's attractiveness to foreign investment, but the world recession must also account for part of the decline. Foreign direct investment to Spain was increasing despite the recession (see Fig. 14.1). This may be indicative of a growth in multinational enterprise interest before Spain's entry into the EC in 1986, comparable to the increase in foreign direct investment to Ireland around 1973. Whatever the reason, there was a decline in Ireland's country-specific advantages relative to Spain's during this period.

Figure 14.1: **Foreign direct investment in Spain and Ireland**

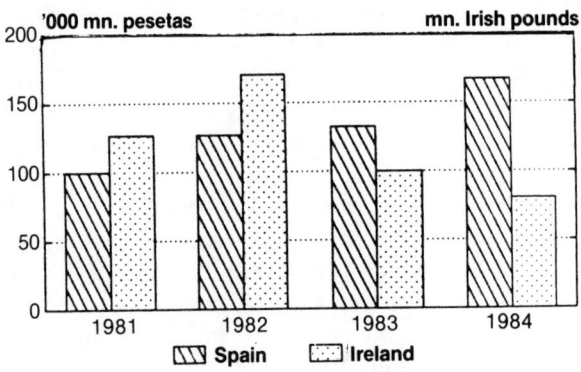

Source: Euromonitor, 1987; OECD, 1985

US companies in Ireland

The United States accounts for one-third of the total of 1,000 multinational enterprise subsidiaries in Ireland (IDA, 1988a). Moreover, the US firms in Ireland are larger, on average, than any other foreign companies. Of the five categories — Irish, UK, Other EC, US and Other non-EC — the US accounted for more industrial employment growth between 1979 and 1985 than any of the others. It was one of only two categories — other non-EC grew only very slightly — that experienced growth at all (see Fig. 14.2). Thus even during the first half of the 1980s, when Ireland apparently became less attractive to multinational enterprises as a location for subsidiaries, US foreign direct investment continued. Most of the growth in employment in US subsidiaries in Ireland during this period was accounted for not by the expansion of existing establishments, but by the setting up of new establishments. Indeed, 44 percent of all employment generated by new establishments between 1979 and 1985 was accounted for by US foreign direct investment (Keating and Keane, 1989, Appendix 15); and, 'of total new fixed asset investment by foreign firms in 1986, the USA accounted for over , 40 per cent' (FitzPatrick, 1988, p. 67).

Figure 14.2: **Employment in foreign firms**
   (change by country of ownership)

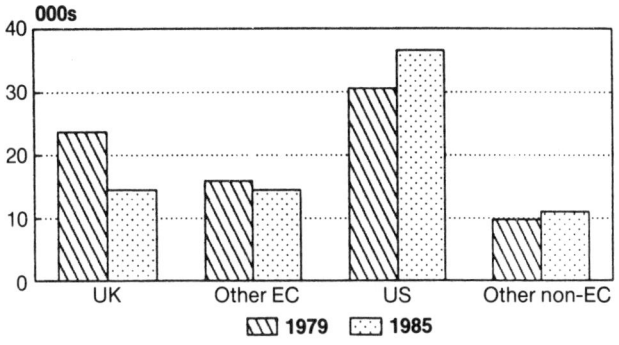

Source: Keating and Keane, 1989, p. 44

US manufacturing foreign direct investment into the EC was stagnant during the early 1980s. It had reached $10,752 million in 1980, but had slowed to only $9,520 million in 1987. In 1988 there was a sharp upturn to $11,371 million and a further growth to $13,216 million was expected in 1989 (US Department of Commerce, 1981 and 1989). According to the US Department of Commerce, it is the preparations for the Single Market that have led to this upsurge in US investment in Europe: first, "in order to compete with domestically owned European companies to expand or maintain market shares"; second, because of concern that "lower barriers within the EC-12 may lead to increased protectionism against non-EC countries" (Quijano, 1989).

Table 14.1: **Capital expenditure by US manufacturing firms in Ireland (current prices)**

	1983	1984	1985	1986	1987	1988	1989 (forecast)
Ireland ($ mn.)	124	170	193	201	195	232	349
Share of EC 12 (%)	1.6	2.3	2.5	2.3	2.1	2.0	2.6

Source: US Department of Commerce, *Survey of Current Business*, various issues

Table 14.1 shows that Ireland's share of US foreign direct investment in the EC has been stable since 1983. There was a relative decline between 1985 and 1988, but the forecast for 1989 was for a significant increase in Ireland's share of US foreign direct investment in the Community. This expected growth over the period 1988 to 1989 is important. If Ireland can increase its share of US foreign direct investment in a period during which that investment into the twelve member states is also increasing, it suggests that American plans for the Single Market include a substantial role for Ireland. Recent information provided by the IDA also suggests that there has been a sharp improvement in Ireland's attractiveness to American investors, with 17 of the 32 American-backed greenfield investment projects in Europe as a whole during 1988 coming to Ireland (Ahlstrom, 1989).

This rather positive check for US foreign direct investment in Ireland is substantiated by another source, a survey undertaken by the Bank of Boston (Economics Department, Bank of Boston, 1989). In the survey, carried out in January and published in February 1989, 1,234 chief executives were polled on their attitudes to the Single European Market. These executives were from firms with sales averaging $35 million, mainly in the high-technology industries. The UK was clearly the most important path (both past and future) for these companies into Europe. Greece and Portugal were not mentioned at all, and Denmark and Spain were consistently regarded as a likely location by the same or fewer firms than Ireland. Of those surveyed whose firms did not have a European location, 7 percent of those planning to establish a branch or subsidiary in Europe were planning to do so in Ireland, well above the 3 percent for Spain and 0 percent for Denmark (Economics Department, Bank of Boston, 1989, Chart 11).

A somewhat different picture emerges from a survey undertaken by Ernst and Whinney, for *Fortune* magazine, in March and April 1989. In this survey, 694 responses were received to a detailed questionnaire on various firms' preparations for the Single Market. The sample was chosen from four main groups of companies: US *Fortune* 500, US medium-sized, Japanese and EC. Details of the methodology and results were reported in the French edition of *Fortune* in the July/August 1989 issue.

In this study, Ireland consistently performed below Spain (as did Italy), as a country in which firms were likely to concentrate their preparations for the Single European Market. Ireland was preferred only to Denmark, Greece and Luxembourg, and even then not in all cases. The manufacturing *Fortune* 500 firms ranked West Germany first, followed closely by Spain and France. In descending order, the UK, Italy, Belgium and Portugal were next, followed by the Netherlands and Ireland, and then Denmark, Greece and Luxembourg.

The most detailed study of this kind is that of Business International (June 1989), in which the findings were very similar to those of the *Fortune* study. 'Over 400' companies assessed Spain and the UK as the best production sites for domestic and export sales in the Community, Ireland ranking at the bottom, below Greece and equal to Denmark.

It is interesting to note that while the Bank of Boston study was reported in the main newspapers in Ireland, few, if any, have given details of the *Fortune* and Business International studies. The significant difference between the Bank of Boston study and the other two is Ireland's far better, and Spain's far worse, relative performance, in terms of preference by multinational enterprises. US and European data, on foreign direct investment to Spain and Ireland suggest that the *Fortune* and Business International studies are more accurate than the Bank of Boston one (see Figs. 14.1 and 14.3).

Figure 14.3 shows that Ireland's share of US foreign direct investment to the EC was declining slightly between 1985 and 1988, while Spain's was increasing. Ireland's expected increase in 1989 reverses this trend, however, and if the estimate proves correct, Ireland's share will be fairly stable through the period.

If such stability is maintained, then the single market will have a positive effect on US foreign direct investment to Ireland.

Figure 14.3: **Capital expenditure by US manufacturing firms in Ireland and Spain**

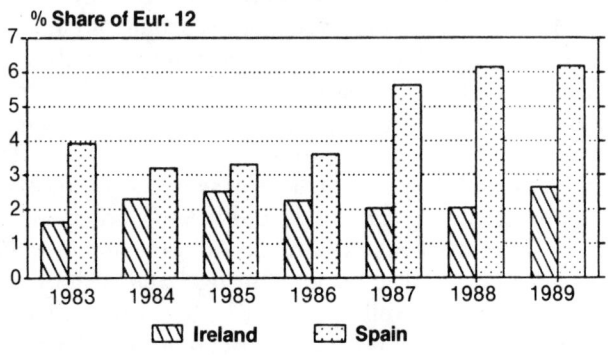

Source: US Department of Commerce, various years

One industry in which Ireland has been highly favoured by US MNEs is the electronics industry. The most recent success in attracting major firms in this industry (such as Intel) is, according to the IDA, much more dependent on the abundance of educated labour than it used to be. The establishment of so-called 'screwdriver plants' among new FDI in this industry will, if this is true, be much less prevalent than it used to be (Ahlstrom, 1989). Screwdriver plants are set up to gain access to markets and add very little value to the product in the host country. Another reason why more significant value added is likely in the future, according to O'Donnell (1989, p. 25) is that 'the Community is strengthening its anti-dumping measures by imposing mandatory local content rules'. This may attract investment into Europe, but not necessarily to Ireland. A factor in the success of attracting firms in this industry (in addition to educated and skilled labour) may be that its products have a high value-to-weight ratio, and therefore the relative disadvantage of Ireland as a peripheral location is minimised.

Another industry in which US firms have dominated is the pharmaceutical industry. The US, with 17 firms, accounts for 58 per cent of total employment and 69 per cent of foreign employment. There is evidence of a slowdown in new FDI to Ireland in this industry (Simango, 1989), at least in part accounted for by the fact that the major American MNEs already have set up subsidiaries in Ireland. The impact of the SEM on this industry is difficult to assess because it it is not clear, particularly due to the high degree of state intervention in pharmaceuticals, to what extent the measures to complete the internal market will be implemented (see O'Donnell, 1989, pp. 34–35).

One set of measures concerning environmental protection may be implemented vigorously and may have an important impact on the industry in Ireland. The manufacture of active ingredients is the part of the pharmaceutical production process that tends to be located in Ireland and in a few other centres in Europe. This has a more deleterious environmental impact than the final stages of pill production and other dosage conversions, and packaging, which are more decentralised. A recent study has suggested that the country-specific advantage that attracted this industry to Ireland was the state's less than rigorous implementation of environmental legislation — the result of the absence of appropriate monitoring systems (Keohane, 1989). If this is true, a standardisation of environmental impact monitoring and control in Europe will reduce or remove this country-specific advantage, and further reduce the flow of US pharmaceutical foreign direct investment into Ireland. The decision of Merrill Dow not to go ahead with plans for a plant in County Cork may reflect the decline of this country-specific advantage in the face of an increasingly 'green' Irish and European population. The IDA's subsequent decision to change its marketing strategy for Ringaskiddy, from exclusively chemical/pharmaceutical to a mix of industries, may be an acknowledgement of this decline.

Harmonisation of other rules affecting the pharmaceutical industry may have an opposite effect. The present patent period affecting ethical drugs is 16 years in Ireland, compared to 20 years in most of the rest of the Community. A change to the EC norm may encourage some firms to come to Ireland that might not otherwise have done so. It may also prevent some from leaving. Smith Kline French, for example, has threatened to pull its Tagamet production out of Ireland if the patent is not extended for a further four years.

The net result of the Single European Market for the pharmaceutical industry is likely to be negative. Given that the

Irish market is too small to encourage the final stages of the production to be carried out in Ireland, and given that bulk production is unlikely to grow at the same rates as in the past, a decline, or at least a static situation, is likely. Moreover, any growth in a marketing presence to offset the decline (or lack of growth) in manufacturing is unlikely, since most of these companies already have distribution networks in Ireland.

Each industry would have to be analysed in order to enable us to generalise about the effects of the Single Market on US multinational enterprises in Ireland. Space does not allow this industry-by-industry analysis, but what we have done substantiates the hypothesis with which we began: that where the completion of the internal market eliminates or reduces country-specific advantages that have been significant to an industry, and does not introduce additional country-specific advantages, then that industry is likely to experience a diminution in foreign direct investments. Where Ireland's country-specific advantages are not directly affected by the Single Market, then, paradoxically, growth is likely. An increase in the inflow of US electronics firms into Europe, for example, is likely to increase foreign direct investment into Ireland if Ireland's country-specific advantages for this industry was and remains its educated labour force.

There is some evidence that an important country-specific advantage for US multinational enterprises is Ireland's low (or effectively zero) tax rate on manufacturing firms (Stewart, 1987, Chapter 4). This facilitates profit-switching transfer pricing, which increases global, after-tax profits. Stewart (1989) has convincingly argued that such profit-switching transfer pricing is actually practiced by US multinational enterprises, particularly in the apparently high value-added electronics and pharmaceutical industries, and soft drink concentrate manufacturers.

One significant way in which profits are switched is through underpayment for technology. Proposals made by the US Treasury in October 1988 to enforce payment of royalties at market rates would, if implemented, reduce this country-specific advantage. This could affect both the flow and stock of US multinational enterprises in Ireland, and, independent of the Single Market, act to offset some of the positive implications of the Single Market for these multinational enterprises in Ireland.

Japanese companies in Ireland

There are about 25 Japanese companies in Ireland. Nineteen of
these are manufacturing companies (Maruya and Jacobson, 1989).
This accounts for only a very small proportion (around 2 per
cent) of the total number of subsidiaries of multinational
enterprises in Ireland. The Netherlands, for example, accounts
for 40 of the subsidiaries of multinational enterprises in Ireland
(IDA, 1988a). The fact that there are relatively few subsidiaries
of Japanese companies in Ireland is more indicative of special
factors in their own economic development than of a lack of
Irish country-specific advantages. Japanese foreign direct
investment to all countries was, until recently, disproportionately
low.

Data for Japanese companies have been listed separately by
the Central Statistics Office (CSO) since the 1983 Census of
Industrial Production. Although they are the most reliable data
available, there are some reservations about them, relating, for
example, to differences in the number of Japanese companies
reported by different sources (Maruya and Jacobson, 1989).

Even with these reservations about the Census, it is clear
that, in general, the importance of Japanese foreign direct
investment in Ireland was declining during the first half of the
1980s (CSO, 1987-89). On the basis of what we know about
employment, in 1987 the trend was reversed from decrease to
increase and in 1988 Japanese investment in Ireland rose sharply.
Japan's Ministry of Finance's statistics on Japanese foreign direct
investment show that, while there was additional foreign direct
investment of only $3 million between March 1983 and March
1985, between March 1985 and March 1987 it grew by $153 million
(including non-manufacturing) (Ministry of Finance, Japan, 1983,
1985, and 1987).

Why was Japanese foreign direct investment into Ireland low
and declining during the early 1980s? First, we can compare
Japanese foreign direct investment into Ireland during this period
with its trend in the rest of the EC and, second, we can compare
Japanese with other foreign direct investment into Ireland. With
respect to the first comparison, Japanese foreign direct investment
to all destinations did not grow significantly between 1978 and
1985; it was not until the revaluation of the yen in 1985 that

sharp increases became evident. Despite this, an upward, albeit
erratic, trend of Japanese foreign direct investment into the UK
was evident between 1980 and 1984 when its trend into Ireland
was downward (Maruya and Jacobson, 1989). (In this context,
it is important to note that, in a survey of foreign companies
in Ireland, the UK was identified as the alternative location most
frequently considered — FitzPatrick, 1984.)

It appears, then, that Ireland became relatively less attractive
as a place for Japanese investment during the early 1980s. While
not directly comparable to (and in some respects contradicting)
the financial data, JETRO (Japan External Trade Organisation)
figures on numbers of Japanese manufacturing enterprises in
Europe — see Figure 14.4 — tend to substantiate this decline
in Ireland's country-specific advantages for Japanese foreign direct
investment. The trend in Ireland's share is down, while that of
the UK is up, particularly between 1984 and 1987.

The second comparison is between Japanese and other foreign
direct investment into Ireland during the first half of the 1980s.
While Ireland's share of US foreign direct investment grew
between 1983 and 1985 (Fig. 14.3), its share of Japanese foreign
direct investment was declining (Maruya and Jacobson, 1989).

Figure 14.4: **Japanese manufacturing enterprises in the EC**

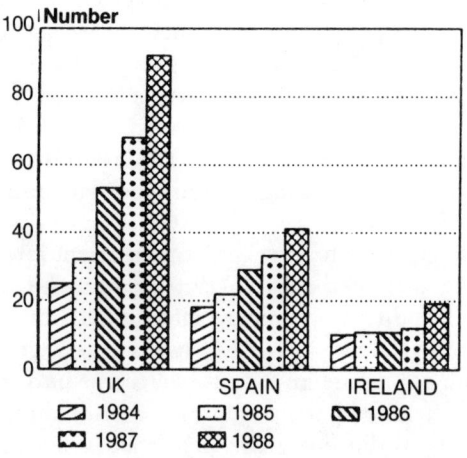

Source: JETRO, London (1989)

Thus, Ireland's country-specific advantages for Japanese as compared to US (but probably not UK) companies declined during the early 1980s. Ireland's attractiveness to Japanese companies also declined relative to other countries, particularly the UK.

Some possible explanations are provided by the results of a survey (see Maruya and Jacobson, 1989). More than half the Japanese companies experienced unexpected set-up problems. Moreover, during this period, Japanese companies' growth in the UK was remarkable, and for Japanese companies seeking an English-speaking location in Europe, Ireland and the UK are in direct competition. The relatively poor performance of Ireland's public finances also would have been taken into consideration.

On the other hand, in the interviews with the local chief executives — all Japanese — the explanation generally given for the performance of the company was the prevailing market situation in relation to its industry, and not the fact that it had set up in Ireland. The leading companies in the early 1980s belonged to the more traditional industries, textiles for instance, which were more susceptible to the recession.

Whatever the reason, it is clear that, in general, employment and new foreign direct investment by Japanese companies in Ireland declined during the early 1980s. Since 1985, global Japanese foreign direct investment has risen sharply. It rose by 83 percent to fiscal year 1986 and by 49 percent in fiscal year 1987, and has continued to rise at only slightly lower rates since then (*Fuji Economic Review*, July-August 1989). One key change in 1985 explains this upswing: the revaluation of the yen. This resulted in a decline in the profitability of exports and a reduction in the cost in yen of foreign acquisitions and other forms of foreign direct investment. In addition, it must be be pointed out that Japanese investment in Europe has grown from less than 9 percent of total Japanese foreign direct investment in 1981, to 20 percent in 1988, and it is expected to continue to grow as we approach 1992 (Jones, 1989). Thus, if Ireland merely maintains its existing share of Japanese investment in Europe, the prospects for the medium term of an increase in Japanese foreign direct investment into Ireland are good. Moreover, the improvement in Ireland's public finances may enhance the country's position in the eyes of some potential Japanese companies considering foreign direct investment in Europe, particularly if the principal alternative location is the UK.

Recent technological developments in the organisation of production by Japanese (and other) firms must also be considered. A closer relationship between manufacturers and the suppliers of components is a concomitant of the 'just in time' system of production (which aims to cut costs through the organisation of smoother production flows, for example by reducing the amount of stock held) (see, for instance, Cusumano, 1985). Japanese firms that are considering setting up major subsidiaries in Ireland will also take into consideration that some of their most important suppliers might follow them. As a result, increasing attention will be paid to the possibility of competition for skilled labour in specific locations, which may limit the size and type of companies that are interested in Ireland.

On the other hand, where the required skills are not in short supply, then the effect of the 'just in time' system, is likely to be positive for employment in Ireland. A Japanese precision metal manufacturing company, Oshima Kogyo, has announced that it is setting up a manufacturing operation in Dublin that will employ 75 people within two years. A critical factor in the decision to establish in Dublin, according to a company statement, was the wish to locate near its principal customer, Fujitsi Isotec, which opened a plant in Blanchardstown, Co. Dublin in 1989 (*The Irish Times*, 11 October 1989).

The strong yen and the Single Market may encourage some Japanese firms to set up in Ireland, and where they do, others (generally their suppliers in Japan) are likely to follow. However, this gives rise to two problems. First, the potential that the Japanese original equipment manufacturers provides as a market for components will be realised by Japanese rather than by Irish firms. Second, as in the past, the major Japanese investments are likely to go to the UK and the European mainland, where market size can justify the investments necessary for the production of most consumer durables. Now, however, component production in these industries will also be undertaken to a large extent by associated Japanese supplier firms, which will locate themselves near to their customers, and again a potential market for Irish components' manufacturers will not be realisable. The proximity issue is important, for, as Cusumano

(1985, pp. 299 ff.) has argued, American car manufacturers have found it difficult to introduce the 'just in time' system because of the geographical distance between plants. Even where assembly plants receive components from other states within the USA, this diminishes the applicability of the 'just in time' system. Thus an assembly plant in the UK, organised on this system, is likely to have a supplier firm nearby and is unlikely to import components from Ireland.

European companies in Ireland

After the USA, the UK is the second most important source of foreign direct investment into Ireland. Together, the rest of the member states account for around 40 per cent of the subsidiaries of multinational enterprises in Ireland, far more in number (though less in employment) than the USA. Figure 14.5 shows the number of firms and employment classified by origin, i.e. UK, total EC, US and total non-EC.

The average number of persons employed in EC firms (77) is less than that of non-EC firms (120). The gap in size would be greater if we compared European (i.e. EC and other European) firms with non-European firms.

The smaller size is suggestive of a number of other differences between the EC and non-EC firms in Ireland, and underlines the fact that the motivations for being in Ireland are different. As we have explained above, an important reason for non-EC multinational enterprises coming to Ireland is to have a production plant within the Community. Many of them will be producing for the entire region. On the other hand, the EC firms are already in the Community and do not gain any tariff or other trade-restriction advantage by being in Ireland. Their reasons for being in Ireland are either the artificial country-specific advantages of tax, grant and other policy attractions, or natural country-specific advantages, including proximity to raw materials (particularly in the food industry) and the availability of skilled labour.

At first UK firms were in Ireland in order to manufacture behind the Irish protectionist barriers for the Irish market. Few of the medium to large UK or other EC firms remain that still produce primarily for the Irish market. Unlike the older, smaller

Figure 14.5: **Manufacturing multinational enterprises in Ireland, 1986**
Establishments and Employment

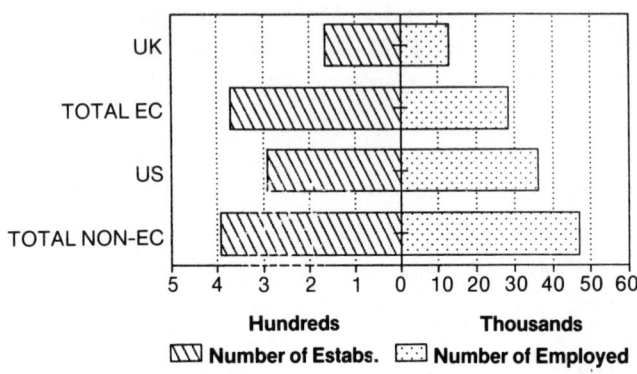

Source: CSO (1989)

firms, they manufacture mainly for export, locating a small, relatively straightforward part of their production process in Ireland. Thus a car company like Leyland, which had been an assembler in Ireland, became a manufacturer of relatively simple components (seat frames). Other automotive component manufacturers, such as Kromberg and Schubert, were attracted to Ireland mainly by the artificial country-specific advantages of tax and grant policies. These firms are strongly export-oriented, mainly to the European market, and it remains to be seen whether the attractions will continue to be significant enough in the more competitive post-1992 situation.

The fact that the EC firms in Ireland are smaller than non-EC firms is not necessarily indicative of lack of sophistication in the production process. However, figures on output (both gross and net) per person engaged differ sharply between UK and EC on the one hand and US and non-EC on the other. Figure 14.6 shows that output per person is nearly twice as high for non-EC firms as for EC firms in Ireland.

These differences are evident both within and between industries. In relation to the pharmaceutical industry, for example, there are fewer EC firms. They are smaller, too, and those that have a manufacturing presence in Ireland tend to be more involved

Figure 14.6: **Manufacturing multinational enterprises in Ireland, 1986**
Gross and Net Output per person

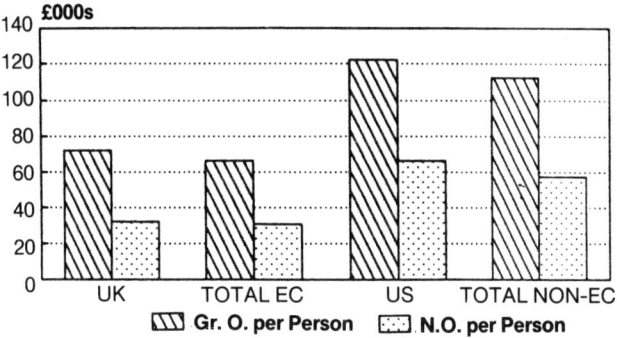

Source: CSO (1989)

in the final stages of production than US firms, but the European firms are far more likely to be involved exclusively in sales and distribution (Simango, 1989). As its European presence (for this particular stage of the production process), the US firm's subsidiary in Ireland is bound to be far more important than that of the EC firm, which may have many other plants throughout Europe. The US firm's investment in manufacturing in Ireland is thus more likely to be vertical, and the EC firm's is more likely to be horizontal. (Emerson et al., 1988, p. 66, point out that the European pharmaceutical industry, among others, is 'not so strongly positioned and rationalized with respect to the European market itself' as US multinational enterprises.)

The differences between industries can be shown in two ways. First, among the twelve largest (by turnover) foreign-owned firms, the US are engaged mainly in electronics and the UK in food and drinks (FitzPatrick, 1988, p. 68). Second, in each of the mainly traditional industries — non-metallic mineral products (including glass and ceramics), food, textiles, clothing, and footwear and leather — there are more firms and less employment in the EC than in the non-EC category. In only one industry at the 3-digit NACE code level* is it clear that

*The NACE (Nomenclature générale des activités economiques dans les Communautés Europennes) is a general industrial classification of economic activities within the European Community.

there are both more firms and more employment by EC than by non-EC multinational enterprises, and this is rubber products (including tyre retreading), an industry to a large extent based on the local market. Even in this industry the largest firms are non-EC, and these are the ones producing tyres for export (CSO, 1989). It is likely in many of these cases that the foreign direct investment is horizontal; in other words, the European firms produce the same goods in Ireland as they do in the source country.

Firms such as those in the tyre retreading business must be close to the market they are serving. This is also true for some firms in each of the traditional industries. There will continue to be a role for such firms after 1992.

Where EC firms have invested in Ireland because of remaining non-tariff barriers, the impact of the Single Market is likely to be negative. Buckley and Artisien (1987, p. 225) have argued in the case of EC multinational enterprises in Spain, Greece and Portugal that we 'can expect many more firms to rationalize production across Europe as tariff barriers fall and the market becomes more homogeneous'. This would apply also if non-tariff barriers are included. Buckley and Artisien differentiate between horizontal and vertical investment in terms of the expected impact of further European integration:

> [Horizontal] investment will decline in importance as harmonization takes place in the EC and will be replaced by investment in vertically linked activities. The consequent rationalization may well cause reductions in employment in host countries (1987, p. 228).

Some of the switch from horizontal to vertical investment has already taken place in Ireland, of course, and is represented, for example, by the US-dominated electronics and pharmaceutical industries discussed above. There is no obvious reason why Ireland would be chosen by an EC firm for such vertical investment, other than artificial country-specific advantages. Spain would be preferred as a peripheral location that is also part of the continental road and rail network. In addition, because of Ireland's small market size, such factors as local taste differences, which ameliorate the effects of intra-EC rationalisation, will be minimal in comparison, say, to Spain.

There is indeed evidence of intense horizontal rationalisation activity among European companies, both through mergers (Jacquemin, Buigues and Ilzkovitz, 1989) and through internal company restructuring (*Ciba-Geigy Journal*, 1989). This will lead to a reduction in the number of locations of production, and unless the Irish authorities provide strong location-specific advantages for siting part of the production process in Ireland (vertical investment), and even stronger attractions for European than for non-EC firms, then the prospects for EC multinational enterprise investment in manufacturing in Ireland are probably not as good as they have been up to now. The *Fortune* study referred to earlier ranks Ireland, with Denmark, on zero, at the very bottom of the list of countries in which EC multinational enterprises might set up subsidiaries in preparation for the Single Market.

Multinational enterprises in the services sector in Ireland

The services sector may be divided into various economic activities, of which two are characterised by the presence of foreign interests. These are distribution (wholesale and retail) and insurance, finance and business services. These two sub-sectors together make up 35 percent of service employment in Ireland (wholesale 8%, retail 20%, and insurance, finance and business 7%) (1985 figure) (O'Rourke, 1987, p. 423).

Although there are a number of multinational enterprises with subsidiaries in services in Ireland (and five of the top eight are distribution subsidiaries of the oil majors), their contribution is far smaller than that of multinational enterprises in manufacturing. This underlines the traditionally marginal contribution of foreign-tradeable services in the Irish economy. Part of the explanation for this is the existence of barriers to trade. The protection of domestic suppliers of services from foreign competition is a common characteristic of developed economies, and the removal of the barriers to trade began to be discussed in the framework of the General Agreement on Tariffs and Trade only relatively recently (Uruguay Round of negotiations, to be completed by 1990: see Blankart, 1989).

The Single Market and a new Irish strategy together will have a major impact on the attractiveness of Ireland as a location for service multinational enterprises. These will be discussed for each of the sub-sectors mentioned above — distribution and insurance, finance and banking.

Distribution: The impact of 1992 on the distribution sub-sector has been discussed in detail by FitzGerald (1989). It is necessary here only to reiterate his conclusions. FitzGerald argues that the major loss of employment will be among importers/wholesalers. Among the factors leading to this result are:

> [more] centralised distribution; the increased tendency for retailers to deal directly with producers; a tendency for Ireland and the UK to be treated as a single unit for distribution purposes and serviced from the UK (FitzGerald, 1989, p. 67).

Where after-sales service is required, there will be less decline. Multinational enterprises may continue to provide such service through subsidiaries in Ireland because of the high transport costs of providing it directly from Britain. Some expansion in employment arising from firms treating Ireland North and South as one economic area will offset only partly the above declines (FitzGerald, 1989, p. 67).

In retailing, FitzGerald foresees an increasing rationalisation and concentration, growing size of firms, and an increased presence of multinational enterprises, particularly from the UK, in the Irish market. However, 'overall, the effects of 1992 on the Irish retail trade will be felt more on its organisation than on total employment' (1989, p. 66).

Insurance, Finance and Banking: Despite the increasing internationalisation of banking (Pecchioli, 1983), of the top eight non-manufacturing multinational enterprises subsidiaries in Ireland, only one, American Express, is in this sub-sector. This, at least in part, is due to the protection that the major Irish banks, with government acquiescence, were able to maintain, through a partial cartel, until the mid-1980s (Walsh, 1985). Long before this, foreign banks had already entered Ireland, but never captured more than 10 percent of the banking market (McGowan, 1986, p. 28). This small foreign share is a further indication of the high levels of concentration in the Irish banking industry. 'Apart from Greece, Ireland has a more concentrated banking industry than any other EEC country' (McGowan, 1986, p. 31). One result of this is the difference between foreign investors' perceptions of the economy as a whole and their perceptions of the financial sector in Ireland. Ireland is in the top ten in terms of business confidence, but ranks just twentieth in terms of financial dynamism, followed only by Portugal and Greece (CII, 1989).

Ireland was thus faced with a paradox: it was perceived as being a sound manufacturing base, but the complementary financial activities were inhibited by non-competitive natural country-specific advantages, and by the lack of artificial or government-generated incentives. Certainly in 1986 one knowledgeable observer felt that the push towards increasing European integration would 'encourage banks in Member States to do business across country boundaries', not necessarily through a local presence (McGowan, 1986, p. 38). The existence of a financial centre in Dublin, it was thought, would be likely to work as an additional incentive for attracting foreign direct investment to the non-manufacturing sector. This consideration led to the creation of the International Financial Services Centre in the Custom House Docks Area in Dublin in 1987.

The incentives to be offered to the potential occupiers of the site were discussed with representatives of the European Commission, to ensure that they would comply with Commuity law on state aids. These incentives are based primarily on a 10 per cent corporate tax rate offered to any financial operation setting up on the site. (For the criteria of eligibility, see Doyle, 1988.) The incentive package includes: absence of local taxes, of capital gains tax on traded income, of exchange control for dealings in overseas currencies to overseas clients, and of VAT on output; a 100 per cent capital allowance; and a double deduction of rent.

The operators targeted are primarily US, Japanese and UK financial institutions, but also domestic companies. The aim of the former two is to build up a presence in the EC unified financial market. By 1989, over 40 certificates had been granted by the Minister for Finance to financial services companies intending to set up in the Custom House Docks Area (Benson, 1989), bringing more than 1,000 jobs. The number of projects is expected to reach 100 by 1990 (Larkin, 1988).

Among the companies that have committed themselves to setting up in the International Financial Services Centre, a large group (ten at the end of September 1989) are captive insurance firms. These are firms such as the Sedgwick James Group, managers of the worldwide insurances of BMW, the German automotive company. The attraction of Ireland for these firms, according to the IDA, is

> a chance to come 'on-shore' and avail of a low, but legitimate tax rate agreed by the EC with full access to the emerging single market in Europe. (Cronin, 1989)

Other firms that are going to operate in the Centre include Chase Manhattan and Wang International Leasing from the USA, and the British and Commonwealth Bank and Kredietbank from Europe (FitzPatrick, 1988). A number of Japanese financial institutions have also expressed interest and in November 1989 the Minister for Industry and Commerce announced that 'one of the largest Japanese banks' was to set up in the centre, initially employing sixteen people (McGill, 1989).

The two main pillars of the European Financial Area are the directive adopted by the Council in 1988 on the liberalisation of capital movements by July 1990, and the Second Banking Directive on the freedom of establishment, which at time of writing had not been finalised. This directive gives the right to any financial institution to establish itself or provide cross-border services in any other member state without the need to obtain prior authorisation. It corresponds to the provision of a 'single licence' that is valid throughout the EC. The host country authorities will be responsible for the regulation of that institution's activity, but within a regulatory framework that has to conform to the EC requirements stipulated by this directive (Dassesse, 1989).

The parallel creations of the Financial Services Centre in Dublin on the one hand, and of a unified European capital market on the other seem to be a priori contradictory, since the former enhances intervention in the financial regulatory framework of the EC, and the latter aims to remove such state intervention.

In fact, these two actions are reconciled by special transitional arrangements introduced by the Commission to help member states with a less developed financial systems 'to adapt to the requirements of financial integration in the Community'. Special derogations are allowed to Ireland; for example, the country was given until 31 December 1992 to achieve the liberalisation of capital movements.

These derogations are temporary. The Commission's

programme encompasses their gradual dismantling. However, it should be emphasised that, although Ireland suffers comparative disadvantage with respect to most manufactured products because of its peripheral location, the infinite value-to-weight ratio of information removes this disadvantage for any 'product' that can be delivered (transmitted) electronically. Thus such country-specific advantages as good telecommunications networks and a young, well-educated and computer-literate workforce may continue to attract financial multinational enterprises even after the eventual removal of the artificial country-specific advantages.

Activity by financial multinational enterprises outside the International Financial Services Centre may be indicative of some of these attractions (although it must be pointed out that these, too, are subject to the relatively low 10 percent corporate tax rate). The takeover by the National Australia Bank of the Northern Bank, though admittedly part of a much larger deal, is one way in which a foreign financial institution has gained a presence in Ireland (O'Shaughnessy, 1987, p. 35). (It could have sold the Northern Bank had it not wanted this presence.) A second example is the decision of New York Life Insurance to locate its 100-job data-processing facility in Listowel, Co. Kerry (IDA, 1989). A number of other, similar firms have since expressed interest in this type of operation in Ireland.

Conclusions

This chapter has shown, in general, that there are few reasons for anyone concerned with the future economic development of Ireland to be complacent about the impact of the Single Market on multinational enterprises. In each case examined — US, Japanese, EC manufacturing firms, and service sector multinational enterprises — there were significant indications of possible negative effects of the Single Market. In each case, also, although to varying extents, there appears to be a continuing dependence on artificial country-specific advantages.

US multinational enterprises

The US has been shown to be the most important source of multinational enterprises in Ireland. The Single Market will result in a surge of US foreign direct investment into the EC, and there are some indications that Ireland will hold or even increase its present share of this investment.

Some industries will perform better than others: the electronics industry is likely to see more US foreign direct investment than the pharmaceutical industry. Other factors, such as US tax legislation, may offset some of the positive effects of the Single Market. However, Intel and other companies that recently announced plans in Ireland have not been put off by the possibility of changes in this legislation. The change is, of course, independent of the Single Market, and the two may be acting in opposite directions, but if the change further reduces the attractiveness of Ireland as a location for screwdriver plants, then those (perhaps fewer) plants that are set up in Ireland are likely to have, on average, higher real levels of domestic value added than heretofore.

Japanese multinational enterprises

Following a decline during the early 1980s, there has been a growth in Japanese foreign direct investment to Ireland in recent years. As for the US foreign direct investment, the Single Market has been an important factor in the upward trend of Japanese foreign direct investment to the EC in general, though the revaluation of the yen in 1985 was even more significant, at least in the year or two following the change in exchange rates.

In terms of share of Japanese investment in Europe, there are indications that Ireland's trend is downward while the UK's is upward.

Changing technology, and in particular 'just in time' as a system of organising the relationship between firms and original equipment manufacturers, will also affect Japanese foreign direct investment to Europe.

It is not clear what the net results of the above factors will be. There are clearly positive implications for Japanese foreign direct investment into the Single Market. To the extent that this foreign direct investment is to Ireland, it will be further enhanced by the implications of the 'just in time' system. However, to the extent that it is to other EC members, the impact on foreign direct investment into Ireland, and, more particularly, on the stock of all, not just Japanese, foreign direct investment in the component manufacturing industry in Ireland, may be negative.

EC multinational enterprises

Subsidiaries of European multinational enterprises in Ireland are smaller and less complete than those from the non-EC countries. They are more likely to be horizontal investments than non-EC subsidiaries, which are more likely to be vertical.

Where rationalisation takes place in preparation for the Single Market, Ireland is likely to lose both from its stock of EC foreign direct investment and its share of new EC foreign direct investment. European firms are likely to see Spain as a more attractive location, since Spain has a larger home market and therefore will be able to attract some horizontal investment. Moreover, it is on the European road and rail network and therefore will be more attractive for vertical investment too.

To the extent that Ireland is able to hold its share of European foreign direct investment, it is likely to be through the attractions of its artificial country-specific advantages.

Service sector multinational enterprises

In distribution, foreign direct investment, particularly from the UK, is likely to increase. However, while this may mean an increase in employment by multinational enterprises in Ireland, it will probably be at the cost of employment in indigenous firms.

In relation to insurance-finance-and-banking, while the International Financial Services Centre will mean an increase in foreign direct investment, from US, EC and Japan, some of the jobs located in the Custom House Docks by indigenous firms may well have been created elsewhere in preparation for the Single Market, even in the absence of the International Financial Services Centre.

The artificial country-specific advantages appear to be important in attracting insurance-finance-and-banking firms, though, in the longer term, firms in this type of industry — in which the product has an extremely high value-to-weight ratio, the skill content is high, and a telecommunications infrastructure is essential — should be those most likely to be attracted by these natural country-specific advantages. Other examples of such industries are software development and information databases.

It remains to be seen whether this potential is realised by multinational enterprises or indigenous firms. In the absence of this or other industries based on natural country-specific advantages, the end of the Single Market surge, and the erosion of artificial country-specific advantages through competition from other member states (Krugman, 1987, p. 130), will have adverse economic consequences for Ireland.

15

The Labour Market Implications of the Completion of the Internal Market

JERRY SEXTON

Ultimately, the success or otherwise of the post-1992 developments will be measured in terms of their impact on people, and this outcome, in turn, will depend crucially on the pattern of change that emerges in the labour market. This chapter analyses the possible employment and other labour market effects on Ireland of completing the Single Market. These are issues that are subject to even more uncertainty than other changes that are anticipated to arise because of the Single Market. They are discussed under three headings:

- the employment changes that are likely to emerge as a consequence of the output changes brought about by deregulation
- specific social and labour market measures that the EC Commission is seeking to introduce as part of and in parallel with the basic 1992 changes
- European demographic structure and Irish emigration.

Likely employment changes consequent on deregulation

The completion of the internal market will give rise to fundamental shifts in almost all the principal economic factors, such as the level of demand, productivity and prices, all of which will impinge in turn on the behaviour of the principal actors in the labour market and in particular on employers. Without covering ground dealt with in other chapters, a brief description of the principal changes that the completion of the internal market will bring about will be helpful, before trying to identify the nature of the consequential impact on employment. The principal changes in question are:

i) deregulatory provisions (the abolition of customs barriers, the opening up of public procurement, and financial market integration)
ii) supply side effects (increased competition, exploitation of scale economies)
iii) tax harmonisation.

When viewed piecemeal, it is a daunting prospect to begin to assess the employment outcomes that will follow from the above-mentioned changes. In so far as labour demand is concerned, for example, conflicting and interrelated influences will make it very difficult to assess the net effect. It is inevitable, therefore, that any conclusions must be largely judgemental. However, among the aspects included in the ESRI *Medium Term Review 1989-1994* (Bradley and Fitzgerald, 1989) is a description of an application of the HERMES macro-economic model, designed to estimate the effects of the post-1992 provisions. This simulation is concerned solely with estimating the net effects of the completion of the internal market, apart from the influence of other developments, including those that derive from the National Development Plan.

However, one must have regard to the necessary qualifications in interpreting the results of this simulation. The main advantage in using a macro-economic model is that it makes it possible to consider simultaneously a range of interacting influences; it also imposes a logical coherence on the application of these effects. However, any such model is crucially dependent on the assumptions made and on the range of specified model mechanisms. Once they have been decided on and put in place, these impose a discipline on the system which to a large extent predetermines the outcome. Clearly in the context of this discussion, the 'external' assumptions used (i.e. those relating to events outside the country) are decisive. The adjustments[1] made to such factors (e.g., assumed rates of growth and price levels in a world and European context) are based on estimates made in the Cecchini Report (Cecchini, 1988), which contains estimates of the changes that are expected to occur at the European level for a range of economic entities consequent on the completion of the internal market. The macro-economic model was rerun with those adjustments incorporated, in order to assess the consequential impacts on changes on items such as Irish GDP growth and employment. In summary, because of the inevitable uncertainties surrounding the exercise, it is necessary to echo the words of the authors of the model, that the results of the simulation should be regarded as 'indicative rather than precise measures of what the impact of 1992 is likely to be'.

The process is perhaps best understood by referring to a specific instance; for example, the integration of financial services. A basic premise of the Cecchini Report, in this context, is that capital market integration will force interest rate equalisation since capital will be free to locate within the Community wherever the rate of return is highest (see Chapter 6). This effect, however, will be relative rather than absolute because there is already a substantial degree of capital movement within Europe. The Cecchini Report estimated that, as a result of the further liberalisation of financial and capital markets, long-term interest rates will fall to about 0.5 per cent below the levels that otherwise obtain. Cecchini also estimated that, as a result of this and other related effects, there will be a medium-term (over a period of seven years) increase of 4.5 per cent, on average, in GDP across the Community. In order to capture the effects of interest rate changes on the real economy, specific adjustments were made to the macro model involving alterations imposed on the commercial sector through capacity output, and on the personal sector through a reduction in the savings ratio. An exogenous boost was applied to world demand in order to reflect the incremental rise in Community GDP attributable to financial market integration.

The reduction in the savings ratio results in a stimulus to consumer demand over and above benchmark levels. Consumer demand is further boosted by the increase in real disposable income arising from a reduction in prices. This effect originates in lower import prices as cost reductions feed into international suppliers' prices. Even though the effect of lower interest rates will encourage some substitution of capital for labour, it is anticipated — on the basis of the model simulation — that the increased output induced by greater demand will give rise to a net increase in industrial employment of some 2,500 by 1994. However, any employment gains in other sectors are likely to be marginal because of the offsetting effects of rationalisation in financial services activities, where it is anticipated there will be net job losses amounting to about 1,000. This out-turn in many ways typifies the nature of the effects of the completion of the Single Market, in so far as any costs are borne by the sheltered sector, with the benefits accruing to the exposed sectors of the economy, whose performance in the new environment in turn boosts the sheltered sector.

The results of the ESRI macro-economic simulation for all sectors, taken together, suggest that the introduction of the 1992 deregulation provisions would result in a growth increment of some 8,000 to total employment over the period from 1989 to 1994. However, as we have already illustrated, this global figure conceals some significant variations; it is anticipated that during this period there will be a fall of about 5,000 in the numbers at work in market services (mainly because of job losses arising from the removal of customs barriers and the integration of financial markets) but that this will be more than offset by a rise of some 13,000 in other sectors, mainly in industry. It should also be mentioned that *total* employment is predicted to fall during the early years of the deregulation process, but this is expected to be a temporary phenomenon because subsequently employment is predicted to grow as the economy begins to reap the benefits of higher levels of demand (particularly external demand) brought about when the effects of deregulation begin to take hold across the Community.

It must be borne in mind that the results of the above-mentioned macro-economic simulation essentially reflect current or past behavioural patterns. This is unavoidable because the model mechanisms are based on a framework of economic relationships estimated from data for a recent period (in the case of the ESRI model, the period 1966–1986). The model can be regarded as 'neutral' in that it does not embrace a new or different view as to how these behavioural aspects will evolve in the years ahead. However, it can be regarded as providing a valuable benchmark, or point of departure, for assessing different possible scenarios.

Much of the current debate about the benefits or otherwise that will materialise after 1992 revolves around arguments as to how the Irish economy will perform in the context of the changed ground rules that will apply in a completely deregulated market. The Cecchini Report holds that the peripheral regions of the Community will benefit more from the introduction of an integrated market since they stand to gain most from the deregulatory process (in particular, the abolition of customs barriers and the introduction of more efficient transport arrangements). On this basis, one could perhaps argue that the perceived benefits would be greater than those indicated by the ESRI macro-economic model simulation. However, the recently published NESC Report, *Ireland and the European Community: Its Performance, Prospects and Strategy*, and Chapters 17 and 18 of this book, take a very different stance. They broadly argue that the long-run benefits of market completion will tend to be unevenly distributed, with the greatest benefits accruing to those regions that can take advantage of economies of scale and that are more innovative. Obviously Ireland does not fall in this category. This in effect means that there would be an increased concentration of economic activity, and therefore of employment opportunities, in the more economically advanced regions of the Community. The NESC report concluded that 'the completion of the internal market should not be expected to narrow disparities between regions in the EC, let alone bring about convergence' (NESC, No. 88, p. 343).

If the situation envisaged in the NESC report and in Chapters 17 and 18 below comes to pass, then the employment consequences could be serious. The macro-economic simulations referred to earlier indicate that most of the modest post-1992 employment gains will derive from the industrial sector, either in direct form or in the manner of induced market services employment. If, for the reasons stated in the NESC report, the levels of industrial activity are likely to be lower than anticipated, then these gains probably will be more than offset and the long-run effects of the completion of the Single Market are likely to contribute to a reduction in the level of total employment. The possible impact on the industrial sector is dealt with in Chapters 10, 11, 13 and 14 of this book.

Some further aspects of the likely structural changes that will result from deregulation tend to reinforce this view. Essentially, deregulation involves the dismantling of barriers and the elimination of the need for intermediaries. It cannot be overlooked that European countries (and Ireland is no exception) have heretofore been characterised by the existence of multi-stage procedures (in regard to wholesaling for example) and relatively high levels of regulation. Therefore, the reduction in services employment, which it is acknowledged will follow deregulation, may be more substantial than is currently anticipated. When this is considered with further possible losses in the services sector, arising from a more disadvantageous disposition of industrial investment, the employment consequences for Ireland of completing the internal market do not seem to be optimistic.

The above-mentioned disadvantageous scenario, however, may be mitigated to the extent that the degree of concentration may depend on the rate of economic growth (see Kennedy, 1988). When growth rates are high (particularly for a sustained period), the developed centres begin to experience congestion in capacity, labour and skill shortages, which tends to increase the attractiveness of the peripheral regions as locations for new investment. Conversely, during a downturn, as the developed centres also begin to feel the pinch, they also begin to engage in activities designed to attract investment, to the detriment of the peripheral regions. Kennedy therefore asserts that an important plank in Ireland's strategy *vis-à-vis* the Community should be the formation of alliances with other less developed member states in pressing for the attainment of higher levels of growth.

Any benefits or disadvantages arising from deregulation may be seen as relative (in relation to other regions or countries) rather than absolute. It is argued that the very fact of deregulation will induce higher growth, which will convey additional benefits on all regions, even if the distribution of this growth is not entirely even. In other words, while Ireland may experience growth, the more developed centres may expand even faster under deregulation, thus widening regional disparities.

1992 social and labour market provisions

While the deregulatory processes discussed in the preceding section are expected to convey benefits *in a broad Community sense* when viewed in purely economic or commercial terms, there is also a genuinely held fear that there may be consequential social disadvantages. The supply side effects that are likely to emerge in the process of completing the internal market will compel enterprises to be more efficient if they are to survive in the new, more competitive environment. In the circumstances of a fixed exchange rate regime and other restrictions on government's freedom to introduce alleviating measures, there may well be a tendency to depress wages and/or social costs in the quest for efficiency. This could cause disruption in the labour market, which then could offset some of the economic gains of the Single Market. In the interest of promoting social cohesion, therefore, the EC Commission has been pressing to introduce a range of social provisions in parallel with the 1992 economic initiatives.

The introduction of social legislation at Community level is not of course new. The first such measures date back to the late 1960s (freedom of movement and employment rights for all EC nationals in every member state) and over the years the Commission has secured the agreement of the EC Council for legislative provisions covering such aspects as equality in the workplace and in social security schemes, the employment of disabled people, and the protection of workers against certain health hazards. Many of these provisions derive from the Programme of Social Action submitted to the Council of Ministers in 1974.

The Commission's approach to the problem of securing a consensus on a range of social measures related to 1992 is essentially a middle-of-the-road one. Consideration was given to pursuing what might be described as a normative approach which would have involved attempting to introduce a comprehensive range of social regulations. However, this was never a serious possibility given the opposition of some large member states (such as the United Kingdom and, to a lesser extent, West Germany) who are unsympathetic, if not openly hostile, to the notion of any Commission-inspired social legislation, let alone a whole range of such measures.

The possibility of pursuing a completely decentralised approach to social issues has also been aired. This is based on the premise that there is no general model in this sphere with which member states gradually could become aligned. Community action should be restricted, on the one hand, to the fight against unemployment and to the search for stronger growth, and on the other to areas where national policies have 'external effects' (the Community having good reason to act in cases where a policy followed by a member state has major cross-frontier implications). Proponents of this view acknowledge the need for common basic rules in the fields of health and safety but wish to seek competition between social systems and a minimisation of social legislation.

The Commission rejects the latter view on the grounds that it takes no account of the need for social cohesion. It is argued that the rejection of all forms of standardisation could have serious consequences since basic social standards may contribute positively to development by helping to create a more balanced industrial relations climate in which innovation and change would be realised more readily. There is also a need to prevent abuses and distortions of competition; realistic labour standards help to protect the least privileged and weakest members of society, who would be most at risk in the process of social adjustment that will occur during the completion of the Single Market.

Essentially what the Commission appears to have achieved is the adoption (with the UK dissenting) of a Community Charter of the Fundamental Social Rights of Workers — in other words, a sort of quasi-constitutional social framework that purports to convey certain rights on workers and that places a moral obligation on member states to respect those rights. The Charter embraces the principle of subsidiarity in the sense that it is not necessarily seen as a basis for Community action if the required initiatives can be carried out by the member states. Thus, while states are expected to respect the principles enshrined in the Charter, they are free to develop their domestic legislation as they see fit.

The Charter as currently consititued (it used to be much longer) involves the following elements in so far as workers are concerned:

1. The right to enjoy a decent wage.
2. The right to freedom of association, to be covered by collective agreements, and the right to strike.

3. The rights to social security, access to state employment services, annual paid leave and health protection at the workplace.
4. The rights to information, consultation and participation within firms at both national and international levels.
5. The promotion of women's equality in regard to training and employment opportunities.
6. The introduction of standards ensuring total freedom of mobility of European citizens, with special reference to migrant workers.
7. Mutual recognition of professional qualifications and diplomas.
8. The rights to have access to training and to the necessary leave for this purpose throughout one's working life.

Elements 6, 8 and, to a lesser extent, 3 will facilitate the mobility of labour, while the other elements broadly constitute the social dimension.

In parallel with the above-mentioned developments, the Commission wishes to promote the organisation of industrial relations at a European level in order to facilitate the implementation of the Social Charter and to provide a Community-wide forum within which the social partners can discuss mutual problems. What is envisaged here is not at all clear, but it appears that some sort of new Community institution or body involving the social partners is contemplated, which would: facilitate further harmonisation of social legislation where this is possible (in matters where it would be mutually beneficial to both workers and employers); encourage the two sides of industry to organise more effectively at European level; and provide a forum for holding detailed discussions on social issues related to the completion of the Single Market. This notion is given impetus by the expectation that, in a deregulated market, there will be greater uniformity, or even integration, in the activities of firms (particularly multinational) and the feeling is that this should be balanced by similar developments on the workers' side.

The above-mentioned proposals met with a hostile reception from a number of member states with conservative administrations, particularly the United Kingdom. They consider the approach to be outdated in that it is attempting to impose structures that are more appropriate to the 1960s or 1970s on what is now a flexible, market-oriented society. The provision relating to workers' rights to information about their firm's activities is especially resented since the UK in particular thinks that such institutional change would create a serious imbalance in employer/worker relationships, in favour of the latter (see, for example, Roberts, 1989).

It is unfortunate that much of the debate concerning initiatives in the labour market has been influenced by ideological stances. The arguments tend to be dominated, on the one hand, by proponents of the pure labour market approach, who wish to deregulate everything and depress the social costs borne by employers, and on the other hand by those who advocate a heavy-handed interventionist approach which would encumber the labour market with a plethora of legislative provisions. It is difficult to pursue a central path, not necessarily because one wishes to stay in the middle of the road in order to try and please all, but to be in a position to select the most appropriate features from the different approaches. The first approach may create commercial or economic efficiencies in the short term, but, it would create significant long-term social problems. The second would give rise to serious inefficiencies in the labour market, would have a detrimental effect on the creation of employment and would enlarge the size of the black economy.

The notion of 'deriving the best' from each approach can be exemplified by considering jointly the questions of labour market flexibility and the need to have adequate social insurance cover. While a basic framework of labour law is necessary to prevent the exploitation of employees, the evolving labour market conditions point to the need for greater flexibility, particularly in regard to aspects such as the elimination of labour market restrictive practices, a more enlightened attitude to the introduction of new technology and work methods, and the ability to alter employment levels. Indeed, the environment that is likely to emerge from an integrated European market may well force this trend of increased flexibility and mobility, whether we like it or not. However, in these circumstances of greater job mobility and change, it is all the more necessary to have an adequate safety net in the form of a comprehensive manpower support system which will sustain persons financially and facilitate their readaptation in the event of job loss or change. For this, society, and employers in particular, must be prepared to pay.

If the process of European integration is to give rise to a highly deregulated labour market without an adequate fall-back system, the result will be an ever-increasing incidence of marginalisation in society with all the social and perhaps destabilising consequences that this would entail. It must be remembered that the movement towards greater flexibility in the labour market is of fairly recent origin and most of those affected by it are still relatively young. Although one may be prepared to accept volatile and uncertain employment experiences early in one's career without worrying unduly about the need to make provision for the future, at a later stage in the life cycle when financial and other responsibilities tend to be greater, the consequences of inadequate skills and/or insufficient social insurance cover can be severe. In other words, the full impact of the social disadvantages of untrammelled deregulation could take some time to surface, but there is no reason why these could not be mitigated, or even avoided, if the parties can agree on alleviating measures, while at the same time leaving sufficient space for the more beneficial effects of greater flexibility to operate.

On balance, I consider that the EC Commission's approach to labour market social issues in the context of 1992 is broadly correct, even though doubting the effectiveness of a purely voluntary arrangement. Clearly some initiatives are needed to counter the possible harsh effects that could emerge in a highly competitive market, particularly in circumstances where member states are precluded by the process of integration from mitigating these effects. Progress by dialogue on the basis of an agreed Charter also seems to offer the best prospect for advancing the position, even if it may be difficult to reach agreement on some of the aspects involved. Perhaps a better balance could be struck if some of the more contentious issues (such as worker participation) were afforded less priority, and a greater degree of compliance was insisted on with regard to more fundamental rights, such as adequate earnings levels and working conditions, and manpower support.

European demographic structure and Irish emigration

This part of the chapter is concerned with a brief discussion of changes in European demographic patterns and the effect that these are likely to have on Irish emigration. Clearly, the closer integration of EC economies will encourage greater intra-Community migration because of the removal of any residual barriers related to residence rights and access to employment, the movement towards mutual recognition of qualifications, greater proficiency in foreign languages, and because of the probable greater concentration of economic activities.

There is likely to be a further impetus to migrate from Ireland because of the particular population structure that pertains *vis-à-vis* those evolving in other European countries. In Ireland the potential for strong labour force growth will continue for many years. The influence of past high birth cohorts (the number of births peaked in 1980) will continue to give rise to sizeable labour force growth throughout the 1990s, to the extent that the net annual potential labour force increase between now and the turn of the century is likely to exceed 20,000 (Sexton, 1990). On the other hand, in other European countries youth labour forces will undergo a rapid decline as the cohorts reaching labour market entry stage will become progressively smaller because of the rapid decline in birth rates that occurred in many western countries from the early 1970s. The general European situation is explicitly illustrated in Table 15.1 which shows that, over the period from 1988 to 2000, even though the total Community population will show a modest rise (from 324 million to 332 million), the population aged 15 to 24 years will fall by nearly 25 per cent, from 52 million to just over 40 million. Most of this decrease will occur in the 'developed core' of the Community (Germany, the United Kingdom, the Netherlands, France and Belgium) where the attractions for would-be Irish emigrants are likely to be the greatest.

In summary, throughout the 1990s the Irish youth labour market will continue to be characterised by oversupply, while conditions in corresponding labour markets in the major member states will become extremely tight. In effect, this represents a confluence of 'push' and 'pull' factors that is likely to open up wide gaps in relation to employment opportunities and to conditions of work and rates of pay. These developments, when considered with the overall effects of deregulation, will provide a strong incentive for many young people to emigrate. Domestic policy initiatives, however intensive, may not be able to counter this.

Table 15.1: **Aggregate EC population (twelve countries) in 1988, classified by age, along with projections for 1995 and 2000**

Age	1988	1995	2000
		000s	
0–14	60,639	58,968	59,015
15–24	51,971	43,930	40,131
25–44	91,822	98,953	99,716
45–64	73,891	77,094	80,096
65+	45,638	50,380	53,057
Total	323,961	329,326	332,015

Source: EUROSTAT, Demographic Statistics 1989. The figures are aggregates of projections for individual EC countries.

The European 'pull' factors will not only tend to increase the size of the migratory outflow; they will also alter its composition — to Ireland's disadvantage. Many of the opportunities arising abroad during the coming decade will be in skilled/qualified jobs, and the attractions primarily will be income-related. This may cause more of Ireland's qualified and innovative young persons to leave — a feature that appears to have already emerged in the form of high levels of emigration among those who have recently acquired third-level qualifications. Table 15.2 shows that, of the third-level award recipients graduating from full-time education in 1988, nearly 30 per cent had emigrated by the spring of 1989; this compares with a corresponding proportion of less than 10 per cent in the early 1980s. For individual disciplines the incidence of emigration is much higher; for example, among graduate engineers it was nearly 50 per cent in 1988.

Table 15.2: **Post-graduation status of third-level award recipients who left full-time education, 1980–88**

Status	1980	1981	1982	1983	1984	1985	1986	1987	1988
					%				
At work in Ireland	80.0	77.6	71.9	69.3	69.3	67.4	65.7	60.4	62.5
Unemployed	11.6	14.5	19.9	22.3	17.5	16.9	15.0	11.1	8.1
Emigrated	8.4	7.9	8.2	8.4	13.1	15.7	19.3	28.6	29.4
Total	100.0	100.0	100.0	100.0	100.0	100.0	100.0	100.0	100.0
Domestic Unemployment Rate	12.7	15.7	21.7	24.3	20.2	20.0	18.6	15.5	11.5

Sources: These figures have been derived from the annual Higher Education Authority publication, *First Destination of Award Recipients in Higher Education* (Dublin, various years).

Notes: 1. The years indicated are the years in which the award recipients actually graduated.
2. Post-graduation status relates to the position in the spring of the year following graduation.
3. The coverage of third-level institutions was not complete during the earlier years of the period indicated.
4. The figures are based on details of award recipients for whom information was obtained from the annual HEA surveys. The response rate was 82.1 per cent in 1988; it was higher in earlier years.
5. The 'unemployed' category includes those accommodated on manpower schemes.

Apart from again emphasising the need for policies designed to promote employment, this scenario raises serious questions about higher level educational provision. Since Ireland is likely to suffer substantial human capital losses because of the increased outflows of qualified young people during the coming decade, this may give rise to a need to reassess the relative allocations to different educational sub-sectors. It should also create interest in policy initiatives based on student loan schemes and should emphasise the issue of funding for third-level education.

Summary

This chapter has attempted to summarise the likely labour market implications of the completion of the Single Market and its associated developments. While a broad macro-economic simulation suggests that the post-1992 deregulation could have a modest beneficial effect on employment, much will depend on how different economic and social actors respond to the new environment. These matters are discussed throughout the book.

In a comparatively deregulated market, with its associated competitive cost pressures, workers could be put at a disadvantage in terms of pay and conditions. Therefore, a social dimension is necessary in the context of the 1992 provisions. The response in this regard — the Community Charter of the Fundamental Social Rights of Workers — is less than satisfactory. It embodies the principle of subsidiarity, which effectively allows member states to sidestep or ignore aspects they do not like. However, the initial approach by the EC Commission was much too broad and could be construed as an attempt to impose a political philosophy rather than a coordinated series of measures designed to protect the position of workers. It would have been better if the initiative was confined from the outset to more fundamental needs (such as manpower support activities), backed up by measures that could be implemented effectively.

The most significant labour market changes that are likely to occur in Ireland during the 1990s will be caused by demographic influences, even though the parallel completion of the internal market probably will accentuate those effects. The combination of continuous labour force oversupply, coupled with a sharply declining youth labour force in the rest of Europe, will create a strong incentive for young people to emigrate, and this will be difficult to counter. Mutual recognition of qualifications and other labour mobility measures will facilitate this to a greater extent than heretofore. The main concern here will be not only the size, but also the nature of the outflow because the attractions abroad will be greater for the more highly qualified.

There are formidable challenges ahead, not only in the matter of job creation, but also in regard to the allocation of resources and the methods of funding education.

Note

1. The adjustments referred to here represent variations on those that apply to what is termed 'The Central Forecast' in the *Medium-Term Review 1989–1994*. For example, there is a further set of adjustments designed to capture the effects of the National Development Plan.

16

The EC Social Charter and the Labour Market in Ireland

JOHN BLACKWELL

This analysis of the EC Social Charter complements the preceding chapter. It examines the Social Charter and its implications for Ireland. This is done by setting out the labour market background, outlining some of the main ways in which the completion of the internal market is likely to affect employment, detailing the Social Charter's provisions and assessing their implications.

The labour market

The outcomes in the labour market, whether in terms of employment, hours of work, conditions of work or earnings, are a result of the working of a complex set of elements, which in turn are influenced by both market forces and government intervention. The market forces are, on the one hand, the demand for labour by employers and, on the other, the supply of labour in the form of the number of people who are seeking work. Government actions take the form of minimum wage-setting (through Joint Labour Committees), regulation of working conditions, employment protection legislation (on such things as minimum notice), actions on centralised pay bargaining and the setting of pay for its own employees. Government actions in the field of social welfare (social security) are also relevant here.

The rules about social security, the rates of payment of benefit and social insurance tax rates can all influence the extent to which people seek work at certain wage rates and can also influence employers' demand for labour.

Changes in the labour market in the 1980s

Three aspects of the changes in the labour market that have occurred since the early 1980s are particularly relevant to any analysis of the Social Charter. These are the broad changes in employment, sectoral trends and the rise of 'atypical' forms of work. They shall be examined in turn.

Table 16.1 shows the change in employment in the main branches of economic activity between 1980 and 1988. In the period since 1980, total employment fell from 1,156 thousand to 1,091 thousand in 1988. The unemployment rate rose from 6.9 per cent of the labour force in April 1979 (the closest date to 1980 for which data are available) to 16.7 per cent in April 1988 (Labour Force Survey data).

Table 16.1: **Estimated employment in the main branches of economic activity 1980, 1988**

Sector	Thousands 1980	1988
Agriculture, forestry and fishing	209	166
Mining, quarrying and turf production	11	7
Manufacturing	243	209
Building and construction	103	70
Electricity, gas and water	14	14
Commerce, insurance and finance	202	222
Transport, communication and storage	70	64
Public administration and defence	71	70
Other non-agricultural economic activity	233	269
Overview		
Agriculture	209	166
Industry	371	300
Services	576	625
Total at work	1,156	1,091

Source: Department of Finance, *Economic Review and Outlook*, 1981 and 1989

Even at the broad aggregate level, this tells only part of the story of the changing labour market in Ireland, for a number of reasons:

i) There has been an increase in the rate of net emigration from Ireland since the late 1970s

ii) A rise has occurred in the proportion of those defined as long-term unemployed

iii) Some workers have left the labour force because of discouragement at the prospects of finding jobs.

These aspects are now taken up, successively. First, the rate of net emigration from Ireland has tended to reflect the extent of job opportunities in Ireland compared with those elsewhere. The presence of a common labour market with Britain, dating back many years, has meant that employment prospects and net wage levels in Ireland have influenced Irish emigration. Since the early 1980s when net emigration was close to zero, it has increased markedly to 14,400 a year on average in 1981–86 and to 35,000 a year on average in the three-year period 1986–89. This means that the rise in unemployment in Ireland has understated the extent to which employment in Ireland has fallen further and further short of the potential labour force. Taken together, unemployment and net emigration indicate that a marked deterioration has occurred in the labour market since the end of the 1970s. Emigration is concentrated in the younger age-groups. The highest emigration propensity is in the 20–24 age-group and the third highest is in the 15–19 age-group.

Second, the proportion of unemployment of long duration (a year or more) has increased markedly, from 35 per cent in April 1980 to 45 per cent in April 1988 (Live Register data). This means that much of the increase in measured unemployment has affected older workers, many of whom find it difficult to find new employment.

Third, some people, especially older workers and women, are in the 'hidden' labour force. That is, they have stopped actively seeking work because of discouragement at the prospects of finding jobs. Again, this means that the potential labour force is higher than the actual one. Despite the rise over time in labour force participation rates (the proportion of the population in the labour force) in Ireland, these rates are still much lower than in the rest of the EC. For instance, for married women aged 25–49 in 1987, the rate was 35.1 per cent, compared with

56.1 per cent for the EC as a whole (Statistical Office of the European Communities, 1989).

With regard to sectoral trends, between 1980 and 1988 there was a decline in agricultural employment (from 209 to 166 thousand), a decline in employment in industry, i.e. manufacturing, mining, electricity and building, (371 to 300 thousand), and a rise in employment in services (576 thousand to 625 thousand). While manufacturing employment as a whole fell by 6 per cent between 1979 (the closest date to 1980 for which data are available) and 1988, employment in textiles, clothing, footwear and leather fell by 41 per cent. The latter broad sector was particularly hard hit by job losses, some due to sluggish domestic demand and some due to difficulties in adapting to increased competition in both domestic and foreign markets.

The growth in 'atypical' forms of work is now considered. By these forms of work is meant part-time work, temporary (including casual) work and work done on a contract basis. Undoubtedly, not all these forms involve workers who are in a disadvantaged position. There can be marked differences in levels of well-being across individual workers who are classed as 'atypical'. Nevertheless, these workers as a group can be regarded as being on the fringe of the labour market. Often, they are not entitled to the same occupational benefits (e.g., holidays and pensions) as are permanent full-time employees; they can have less access to training, limited opportunities for promotion and are not on incremental scales. They can find themselves only partially (if at all) covered for social security benefits and not covered under employment protection legislation.

Table 16.2 puts the change in part-time work since 1977 in context by showing the number of full-time jobs and part-time jobs in 1977 and in 1988. Over time, there has been a rise in the amount of part-time work. Between 1977 and 1988, the number of full-time regular jobs declined from 1,044 thousand to 1,019 thousand. The number of part-time regular jobs increased from 39 thousand to 72 thousand.

The growth of part-time work for women has been particularly notable. The number of part-time regular jobs held by women almost doubled from 1977 to 1988. The proportion of all employment that is accounted for by regular part-time jobs increased from 3.6 per cent in 1977 to 6.6 per cent in 1988.

In the same period, the proportion of women's employment that was in regular part-time jobs increased from 9.0 per cent to 14.3 per cent.

Table 16.2: **The employed by type of job and by sex 1977, 1988**

	Year	Men	Women	Thousands Total
With a regular job	1977	784.5	298.8	1,083.3
	1988	738.3	352.9	1,091.2
of which: full-time	1977	772.1	271.8	1,043.9
	1988	716.4	302.8	1,019.2
part-time	1977	12.4	27.0	39.4
	1988	21.9	50.1	72.0
With an occasional job	1977	10.1	32.9	43.0
	1988	8.7	11.9	20.6
of which: full-time	1977	2.1	2.1	4.2
	1988	3.5	1.8	5.3
part-time	1977	8.0	30.8	38.8
	1988	5.1	10.0	15.1

Note: Totals may not sum exactly because of rounding.
Sources: Central Statistics Office, *Labour Force Survey 1988*, Table 34; special tabulation from 1977 Labour Force Survey.

There has also been a rise over time in the amount of temporary work. In 1987, temporary employees amounted to 8.5 per cent of all employees, in comparison with 6.0 per cent of all employees in 1983 (Dineen, 1989). Between 1983 and 1987 the number of employees in temporary jobs increased by over 38 per cent, in contrast with a decline in 2 per cent in the number of total employees. Some of the increase in temporary employment reflects the growth of government employment schemes for young people. Nevertheless, some of the increase in this form of employment has reflected the preferences of employers: by hiring temporary workers, they can handle uncertainty about the future growth in demand and can deal with seasonal or temporary fluctuations in demand.

One form of 'atypical' work about which little is known is sub-contracting: where some of the work of a firm is put out to firms or people who do not have an employment contract.

This can take a number of different forms, including the hiring of temporary staff and the use of self-employed workers. While these forms have always existed, they are now used systematically by firms in order to reduce their risks in the face of uncertainty about demand and in the face of fluctuations in demand. The growth of non-agricultural self-employment from 63,400 to 71,900 between 1979 and 1988 may be indicative of this phenomenon, but it is quite a crude indicator.

Impacts of the single market on the labour market

As the preceding chapter showed, there is a certain disagreement between estimates that have been made of the employment impacts of the completion of the internal market. If there was to be a rise in aggregate unemployment due to the completion of the Single Market, say in the short run, this would have a bearing on the Social Charter since it can be argued that the Community as a whole, which is supposed to benefit from the Single Market, should compensate those who lose their jobs — for instance, by means of unemployment compensation, training opportunities and mobility allowances. The same points apply even if there is no change in aggregate employment due to the Single Market, since undoubtedly there will be gainers and losers, with employment rising in some sectors and falling in others. Throughout this analysis, of course, one is asking what is the impact of the Single Market in a world where there are many other influences on employment in particular sectors, such as competitiveness, technological change and underlying domestic and foreign demand. Over and above these influences there are likely to be sectoral impacts, to which we now turn.

A priori, it is possible to identify certain sectors where there could well be job losses and a need for adjustment to increased competition, as a result of the completion of the Single Market. This is evident both from work done at EC level and work done on the likely effects on specific Irish sectors (for instance, Commission of the European Communities, 1988, 1989; Baker and Scott, 1989; Fitzpatrick and Associates, 1989; O'Malley, 1990, and various chapters in this book). The 'sensitive' industrial sectors across the EC in which there could be job losses include tightly regulated sectors with a dependence on public procurement (e.g., pharmaceuticals); high-technology sectors that rely on public procurement (e.g., office equipment and telecommunications); industries facing rationalisation (e.g., drinks); labour intensive sectors that involve relatively unskilled activities; distribution channels, and cases where there could be increased competition from newly industrialising countries. Some of the most marked impacts are likely in parts of the service sector such as distribution, insurance and other financial services.

Some indication of the likely employment effects of the Single Market in Ireland can be had from the studies of three sectors — electronic, electrical and instrument engineering; metals and mechanical engineering; and textiles, clothing and footwear. It is evident that some of these effects will depend on the performance of foreign investment in the EC. The general conclusions of the studies are that the Single Market presents a number of opportunities for firms to increase output in these sectors; that these sectors do not seem to be especially vulnerable to the removal of non-tariff barriers; and that the impact of the Single Market is unlikely to be greater than that of the technical and other economic changes of recent years. However, the smaller firms in textiles, clothing and footwear are likely to face new difficulties.

Aside from the sectoral impacts, the question arises about the likely impact of the Single Market on 'atypical' forms of working. Here, the main driving forces seem to be associated with economic change, which is not essentially linked to the Single Market. That is, it seems likely that the new forms of working are likely to persist, for reasons that include the following:

  i) A shift towards service sector or tertiary employment, which has a relatively high proportion of part-time and temporary forms of working.
 ii) Competitive pressures on firms, which lead them to hire part-time workers, temporary workers and workers who are employed on contract terms, are likely to continue.
iii) The use of more flexible forms of working by firms as a response to the greater degree of business uncertainty in recent years.
 iv) The use of 'atypical' forms of working as a means of reducing social security contributions. This is in the context of a rise in the social security contributions paid by firms as a ratio of total payroll costs.

Background to the EC social charter

The Treaty of Rome has always contained social provisions, although not all are binding. In only a few cases can such provisions be adopted by qualified majority, and the Treaty relies to an extent on market forces in order to achieve harmonisation. Nevertheless, there has been scope for social provision, depending on the interpretation of the spirit of the Treaty. For instance, some EC policies have been concerned with the social impacts of the reductions in trade barriers — for example, in cases of aid for textile and clothing workers and training expenditure under the EC Social Fund. Moreover, the successive enlargements of the Community resulted in increased disparities in living standards and social conditions between member states: this was bound to lead to a renewed focus on social issues. An indication of current disparities in living standards across EC countries can be got from data on private consumption per head of population in ECUs: in Ireland, this is 60 per cent of the EC-wide average. Private consumption per head of population is lowest in Greece at 40.5 per cent of the EC average, and highest in West Germany, at 26.0 per cent higher than the EC average (Commission, 1989a, forecasts for 1990).

With the Single Market in prospect, there was concern in some member states about the 'structural adjustment' that would occur with the rise and fall of individual sectors. Related to this, many people felt it desirable to achieve a harmonised labour market in which workers could relocate without compromising their working conditions and their rights to social security. There was a wish, at least in certain quarters, that greater mobility of labour, expected as a result of the Single Market, should not be at the expense of a reduction in the degree of social protection that workers enjoyed. Various drafts of a Social Charter were completed in 1989, emphasising both the freedom of movement of workers and matters related to the social changes that are likely to occur with the completion of the Single Market.

It is notable that the moves towards a Social Charter to some extent go against current thinking on deregulation and withdrawal of government intervention in labour markets. Certain member states, the UK being the most enthusiastic, have tried to encourage more flexible working patterns in recent years.

Bluntly, this means reducing the degree of government regulation in labour markets and letting market forces operate more freely in the belief that this is more efficient and leads to higher employment. Ireland has been less enthusiastic than certain other EC states about such deregulation.

Although it is difficult to make cross-country comparisons of the degree of regulation, we can note that the level of labour market regulation in Ireland has been less than in some other EC countries — examples are given below in relation to International Labour Office conventions. Furthermore, there have been no moves to increase regulation of the labour market in Ireland, with the exception of the case of part-time workers, where (at time of writing) draft legislation on their rights is in prospect.

EC social charter

The 'Community Charter of the Fundamental Rights of Workers' was adopted at the Strasbourg European Council on 9 December 1989. Its main provisions are as follows:

Freedom of movement
Workers in the EC shall have the right to freedom of movement throughout the Community.

Employment and pay
All employment shall be fairly remunerated; to this end, workers shall be assured of a wage sufficient to enable them to have a decent standard of living.

Improvement of living and working conditions
The Single Market must lead to an improvement in the living and working conditions of workers in the Community.

Social protection
Every worker in the EC shall have a right to adequate social protection and shall enjoy an adequate level of social security benefits.

Collective bargaining
Employers and workers shall have the right of association and people shall have the freedom to join or not to join such

organisations. There shall be rights to conclude collective agreements.

Vocational training
The public authorities, and the two sides of industry, should set up continuing training systems, enabling every person to undergo retraining, especially through leave for training purposes.

Equal treatment for men and women
Action should be intensified to ensure the implementation of the principle of equality between men and women, particularly with regard to access to employment, pay, working conditions, social protection, education, vocational training and career development. Measures should be developed to enable men and women to reconcile their occupational and family obligations.

Information, consultation and participation for workers
Information, consultation and participation for workers must be developed, especially in such cases where the introduction of technological changes have major implications for the workforce, where mergers or restructuring have an impact on employment, and where there are instances of collective redundancy.

Health protection and safety at the workplace
Every worker must enjoy satisfactory health and safety conditions in the working environment. Appropriate measures must be taken to achieve further harmonisation of these conditions.

Protection of children and adolescents
Children and adolescents must be protected in such matters as minimum employment age, equitable remuneration, vocational training and duration of work.

Elderly persons
Every worker at the time of retirement must be able to enjoy resources that afford him or her a decent standard of living.

Disabled persons
All disabled persons must be entitled to the additional measures that will help to improve their social and professional integration.

The foregoing sketch of the Charter provisions gives rise to a number of immediate comments. The section on improvement of living and working conditions refers to 'the duration and organisation of working time and forms of employment other than open-ended contracts, such as fixed-term contracts, part-time working, temporary work and seasonal work', in such an obscure manner that it is unclear what force it could have, although it obviously relates to the growth of 'atypical' forms of working discussed above.

The Charter contains a section on information, consultation and participation for workers. This is quite a weak provision, referring to 'appropriate lines' of development being desirable, 'taking account of the priorities in force in the various Member States'. This weakness will be particularly regretted in Ireland by those who have campaigned for more disclosure and more information about private and public decision-making.

By contrast with an earlier draft of the Charter, dated early October 1989, the provisions in the Charter adopted in December 1989 have been weakened, and more emphasis is now placed on the responsibility of the individual member states and the two sides of industry, rather than on the Community. For instance, a passage which said 'a decent wage shall be established, particularly at the level of the basic wage' has been deleted; proposed improvements to maximum duration of working time and weekend working, night work, shift work and systematic overtime have been deleted. Draft rights to 'adequate levels of social security benefits proportional, where appropriate, to length of service and pay and to their financial contribution to the appropriate social protection system' have been changed to 'shall . . . enjoy an adequate level of social security benefits'.

The implementation of the Social Charter also invites comment. The balance between the policies of individual countries and the policies of the Community is of particular concern. The Community relies on the principle of subsidiarity; that is, that the desired level of administration of a function is the lowest level at which it can be formed effectively. It is possible that the Community will develop legal instruments. For the moment, though, monitoring of changes is all that is in prospect.

Some proposed actions of the Commission have a bearing on the Social Charter, but have developed independently of it. The Commission proposes to reinforce its activities in the field of supervision of health and safety at work on the basis of Article

118A of the EC Treaty (Commission of the European
Communities, 1989b); and the Commission proposed the inclusion
in the 'Supplies' directive (77/62) of a provision enabling
authorities that award public contracts to exclude applicants who
do not comply with their obligations with respect to labour law
and equal opportunities for women, handicapped persons and
minority groups (Commission, 1988).

In summary, the Social Charter is couched in very general
terms. These terms, together with the basic reliance on the
measures that are currently in force in member states, mean
that there is likely to be little impact by the Charter on the
labour markets of member countries, at least in the short term.
However, it is worth asking whether the completion of the Single
Market is likely to bring pressures that could promote the use
of the Social Charter or that could lead to pressure for more
explicit clauses in the Charter. The possibility of such pressure,
and the likely relevance of the Social Charter, are now taken
up under the successive headings of labour mobility, wage levels,
minimum wage rates, equal treatment for men and women,
working conditions and social security. At the same time, the
particular implications for Ireland are discussed.

Labour mobility

The provision about a common labour market are likely to affect
other EC countries more than Ireland. The reason for this is
that Ireland has already enjoyed a common labour market with
Britain, as mentioned above. There has been a high degree of
labour mobility for younger workers between Ireland, on the
one hand, and Britain and the United States on the other, at
times when economic trends diverged markedly between these
countries. The prospects for the 1990s are for declines in the
indigenous labour supply in the younger age-groups in continental
Europe. This is likely to lead to some increase in net emigration
between Ireland and continental Europe. However, it is likely
that aggregate rates of net emigration from Ireland will decline
because of (a) some increase in unemployment in Britain, and
(b) the relative tightening in the Irish labour market, attributable
to the levels of net emigration of recent years.

Wage levels

Currently, there are marked differences in average wage levels across the EC countries. For instance, hourly labour costs for workers in ECUs in 1984 in some sectors were twice as high in West Germany as in Ireland; in turn, hourly costs were twice or more than twice as high in some sectors in Ireland as in Portugal or in Greece (Commission of the European Communities, 1988, Annex 3).

Such comparisons say little about competitiveness, for a number of reasons. First, from the point of view of competitiveness in a narrow sense, what matters is not so much labour costs as labour costs per unit of output — that is, wage costs adjusted for productivity levels. Thus, West Germany may have high wage costs in absolute terms, but when allowance is made for productivity, West German firms can compete effectively with those of other EC countries.

Second, labour costs depend not just on wage costs — such as are covered in the above comparisons — but on the non-wage costs (mainly fringe benefits and public and private social security contributions) of employing workers. Some of these costs are fixed, others (such as employers' social insurance taxes) are related to wage levels. There are marked differences across EC countries in the proportion of labour costs that are accounted for by non-wage labour costs, with the proportion in Ireland being about a half of that in some other EC countries (OECD, 1986). In Ireland, the statutory social security costs of employers (13 per cent) as a proportion of total labour costs are about midway between the relatively low proportions of Denmark and the United Kingdom (4 and 7 per cent respectively) and the highest proportions (22 per cent in Belgium and 31 per cent in Italy) (Statistical Office of the European Communities, 1987).

Third, competitiveness depends not just on labour costs adjusted for productivity, but on other elements, such as the quantity and quality of capital employed and the organisation of production.

The foregoing means that, although wages costs are significant, one cannot conclude from a comparison of wage costs alone that there are differences in competitiveness across countries. It is possible to say, though, that in relatively labour-intensive sectors such as clothing and footwear, large differences in wage levels across countries can put the relatively high-wage countries under pressure. In turn, this can lead the firms in these high-wage countries to try to increase productivity by increases in the capital stock and reductions in the workforce and to move 'up-market' to higher quality lines of production.

Bearing in mind these qualifications, Table 16.3 shows the change over time in unit labour costs in Ireland in a common currency relative to nineteen industrial countries. This shows that, while there has been a good deal of year-to-year fluctuation, unit labour costs in 1988 were lower than in 1980. Moreover, there were differences ranging from a decline of 18.6 per cent over the period in Belgium/Luxembourg to an increase of 16.7 per cent in Italy (Commission, 1989a).

Table 16.3: **Nominal unit labour costs in Ireland relative to 19 industrial countries (in US dollars, 1980 = 100)**

Year	
1980	100
1981	94.8
1982	97.9
1983	100.1
1984	97.1
1985	98.0
1986	103.6
1987	100.1
1988	95.5

Source: Commission of the European Communities (1989a)

Finally, on wage rates, there is the question of whether, without any Social Charter, there would be inexorable pressures towards convergence of wage levels in EC countries. The textbook models of the labour market suggest that this would tend to happen, as workers moved from areas of labour surplus towards areas of labour shortage. However, this is an idealised model and there are reasons why one would not expect market forces to accomplish such a convergence. This is in part because rates of mobility differ between different workers (being higher for young workers than for older workers), partly because of the reluctance of workers to move for reasons such as the attachments that people have to particular localities and their 'sunk costs' in housing. What tends to happen when there are differences in the balance of labour supply and demand is that unemployment, rather than wages, takes the brunt. This can be seen in the EC in so far as there remain sharp differences in unemployment rates across the different countries. At the end of 1989, unemployment rates ranged from 1.5 per cent in Luxembourg, and 5.9 per cent in the UK, to 17.8 per cent in Ireland (Statistical Office of the European Communities, 1990).

On balance (though leaving aside questions of minimum wage rates and equal treatment, taken up below), the Social Charter is not likely to lead to much change in relative earnings in the EC. The underlying changes in the demand for and the supply of labour, together with domestic government policies concerning the labour market, are likely to be much more influential than the Charter.

Minimum wage rates

Statutory minimum pay has been one of the most contentious issues in the debate about the Social Charter. On this subject, one has to begin with the existing provisions in the different member states. Of the twelve member states of the EC, five (France, Luxembourg, the Netherlands, Portugal and Spain), have statutory national minimum wages varying in their application by age of worker from the ages of 18 to 23; two, Belgium and Greece, have a general minimum wage set by collective agreement at national level. In the remaining five countries, minimum rates of pay are set either by collective agreement at industry level (Denmark, West Germany and Italy) or only for certain industries through special bodies. The latter is the case in Ireland and the UK, where Joint Labour Committees and Wages Council respectively operate.

The subject of minimum pay is of particular interest because there already exists a 'social charter', operated by the Council of Europe, which includes minimum pay in its provisions. Under the European Social Charter of the Council of Europe, the signatory governments — which include Ireland — commit themselves to securing rights 'by all appropriate means'. This Charter is discussed below. In 1977 the Committee of Independent Experts of the Charter (which reports on the application of the Charter by different countries) proposed taking a level of 68 per cent or two-thirds of the national average wage as a 'decency threshold'. Workers who received less than this would not be regarded as receiving a fair or decent remuneration (Committee of Independent Experts, 1977).

The task of the Committee of Independent Experts is to assess whether member states are fulfilling the obligation to ensure 'fair remuneration'. However, in its report of 1988 the Committee was not able to reach a conclusion on whether or not Ireland was adequately fulfilling its responsibility. Statistics were available 'covering less than half of the Irish population'. The position is in fact worse than this. The reference is to statistics on average earnings only; what is needed is information on the distribution of earnings across workers so that the incidence of low pay can be observed. Moreover, the data cover only about a quarter of employees. The Committee noted that minimum pay rates set through Joint Labour Committees were only around 40 per cent of the average wage. Earlier, in 1986, the Committee had concluded unfavourably both on the position of the lowest paid women workers and on the Irish response with regard to information (Committee of Independent Experts, 1986).

The state of Irish earnings statistics is indeed a lamentable one. For instance, it is over twenty years since there was a regular series on the distribution of earnings in Irish industry. It is notable that Ireland has persistently failed to abide by at least the spirit of the Council of Europe charter by not monitoring the distribution of earnings and the extent of low pay.

If one takes 68 per cent of the average earnings of men and women on adult rates of pay in 1987 (weighting the respective pay data by the number of male and female employees from the Labour Force Survey of that year), the 'decency threshold' is £132 a week. This in fact coincides with the low pay threshold which would be established in another way — by taking the cut-off point which marks out the bottom 10 per cent of *male* workers on the pay distribution (taking usual earnings) (Blackwell and Nolan, 1990). Table 16.4 shows that 28 per cent of employees fall below this threshold. Taking a much lower threshold of £100 a week, 17 per cent of employees fall below that level.

Table 16.4: **Employees with usual gross pay below various thresholds**

Low pay threshold £ per week	Percentage of employees with gross pay below threshold
80	12.7
90	15.5
100	17.3
110	20.9
120	23.5
130	27.6
140	31.9

Source: Blackwell and Nolan (1990)

Of the low paid who fall below £130 a week, some 39 per cent are part-time workers. Of all part-time employees, 65 per cent fall below the low-pay threshold, while of all full-time workers, 23 per cent fall below the threshold. A large proportion of women are in low pay, and 62 per cent of those who fall below the threshold are women. Of the full-time workers who fall below the threshold, 54 per cent are women; of the part-time workers who fall below the threshold, 85 per cent are women.

One of the most striking features of the 1987 findings on low pay is the consistency in pattern over time — between 1979/1980 and 1987. The industrial and occupational composition of the low paid is broadly similar, despite the many changes in the labour market over this period. The relative stability of the wage structure over time — going back to the early 1960s — is notable. Since 1960, the pay structure has, if anything, become more unequal, with those at the bottom of the distribution faring worse than those on average earnings. This *relative* stability has occurred despite a number of things: the rise and fall of centralised pay bargaining over the period; attempts to change the wage structure by introducing a certain flat-rate element into wage increases; and changes in the social welfare code such as the introduction of Family Income Supplement. It has also occurred in the face of many changes in the labour market, including the changes in employment across sectors, the entry of more qualified cohorts of young workers onto the labour market, and the rise in the 'atypical' forms of work.

It seems that labour market measures designed to improve the lot of those at the bottom end of the labour market — those in insecure, low-skilled jobs with little or no prospect of career enhancement — have had little or no impact on the pay distribution to date. The operation of the Joint Labour Committees has not prevented the persistence of low pay, in roughly similar form, over time. The evidence suggests that past efforts at flat-rate increases in pay have seen the restoration of previous pay differentials. Furthermore, the concentration of women in low-skilled and low status jobs, with little increase in real earnings with age, by comparison with men, over their life cycle does not seem to have changed much during the past decade. It is here that some of the biggest problems with regard to tackling low pay still exist.

One lesson in particular bears on the likely impact of the EC Social Charter on pay. The Council of Europe Charter is 'tougher' in a number of respects, in as much as it sets a defined target and requires regular monitoring. Yet it has had such little impact in Ireland that a set of earnings statistics persists which makes regular monitoring impossible.

The debate on minimum pay, which was sparked off by the Social Charter, has reflected a long-standing discussion about the effects on employment of the imposition of minimum wages, or the raising of existing minimum rates. This discussion has raised a number of important questions. Would the result be an increase in unemployment, especially for those with little bargaining power (including young workers, unskilled workers and many women) and those in export industries? Or would an imbalance in bargaining power between employers and certain workers be redressed? And would the effects of minimum wage increases result in increases in productivity (output per worker)?

The impact of a rise in minimum wage rates on employment will depend on the level at which the minimum is set and also on whether wage differentials across the economy are affected by the setting of the minimum wage. On balance, the results from other countries suggest that there is some reduction in employment (that is demand for labour) resulting from rises in minimum wage rates, with relatively little increase in labour supply and a relatively small net increase in unemployment.

Equal treatment for men and women

The likely impact of the EC Social Charter provisions on equal treatment for men and women can be assessed only in the light of the existing national provisions and their impacts. After the passing of the Anti-Discrimination (Pay) Act of 1974 and the employment equality legislation of the mid-1970s, both under the influence of the EC, the ratio of women's earnings to those of men increased over a number of years, but since the early 1980s essentially there has been no change in the ratio (Table 16.5). It is notable also that women currently comprise the majority of the low paid (see above), just as they did in the late 1970s.

Table 16.6 shows the variation that exists in the male-female earnings ratio in manufacturing across the EC countries, with the ratio in Ireland being among the lowest. Of course, these data are very aggregative in nature. Ideally, one needs data on women's pay relative to men in particular industries and occupations and for particular skill levels and levels of responsibility.

Regrettably, the data that would enable the effective monitoring of equal treatment legislation to take place are not collected, which itself suggests that equal treatment has hardly been made a priority. It is clear, though, that equal treatment cannot be guaranteed by equality legislation alone.

Two critical reasons why many women in the labour force have been relatively marginalised are now set forth (Blackwell, 1986a, 1989). First, they have not had equal access to higher paying and higher-status jobs, by comparison with men; the underlying reasons for this range from attitudes in society (about what are 'appropriate' jobs for women) to education and training opportunities. Second, many women drop out of full participation in work for a period in their lives because of child-rearing responsibilities. This means that they can miss out on opportunities for training and promotion as well as encounter age discrimination when they try to return to the labour force. This means that national policies (and national attitudes) on women's roles, on training and education, on child care and the policies of individual firms, are likely to be more influential for the position of women at work from now on, than are current EC provisions, including the Charter.

Table 16.5: **Ratio of average gross earnings of women to average earnings of men (on adult rates of pay) in industry 1977–88**

	Hourly earnings	Weekly earnings	Hourly earnings	Weekly earnings
	Manufacturing		Transportable goods industries	
1977	61.3	53.1	61.7	52.9
1978	63.9	55.4	63.9	55.3
1979	65.8	57.0	65.8	56.9
1980	68.4	59.0	68.4	58.8
1981	68.0	59.1	68.0	59.0
1982	68.4	60.1	68.0	59.6
1983	68.5	59.9	68.1	59.4
1984	67.9	59.7	67.6	59.3
1985	68.0	60.0	67.7	59.7
New series	*Manufacturing*		*All industries*	
1985	67.2	59.2	66.5	58.4
1986	67.6	59.8	67.0	58.9
1987	67.6	60.4	66.9	59.7
1988	68.4	61.2	67.4	60.1
1989(a)	68.4	60.5	67.5	59.4

Note: (a) Refers to first quarter of the year
Sources: Blackwell (1989); *Statistical Bulletin*

There remains the question of the likely impacts of the Single Market on the employment of women. Because of the Single Market, there will be both job opportunities and threats to jobs in services. These could have particular implications for women because a high proportion of the women at work are in services. There is likely to be a further growth in 'atypical' jobs, including part-time jobs, given that many women are in these jobs, but this would happen irrespective of the Single Market. It is curious that an EC Commission report (Commission, 1989b) should cite the likely growth (or at worst, constancy) in demand for women in services linked to social development (e.g., domestic service, child care) without drawing attention to the fact that these women are among the most marginalised groups in the workforce and have remained so over several decades.

Table 16.6: **Average gross hourly earnings of manual workers in manufacturing industry, female/male ratio, EC countries, 1986–87**

	Percentage	*Date*
Belgium	73.4	October 1986
Denmark	85.9	October 1986
France	78.8	April 1986
Germany	73.0	April 1987
Greece	77.5	October 1986
Ireland(a)	68.7	October 1986
Italy	84.4	October 1985
Luxembourg	60.8	October 1986
Netherlands	74.2	October 1985
United Kingdom	67.7	October 1986

Note: (a) Adults only
Source: Blackwell (1989)

Working conditions

Over the past decade or two, EC governments have strengthened their laws and regulations with regard to occupational safety and health. Across many of the member states, health and safety provisions are bedevilled by problems of data comparability between countries, the inadequacies of the data and the difficulties that arise because of this. In Ireland, there have been significant developments in the Safety, Health and Welfare at Work Act, 1989, under which the National Authority for Occupational Safety and Health has been set up. Among other things, the Act provides for the making of regulations and for the obtaining and disclosure of information. The overall objective of the Authority is to ensure a safe and healthy working environment for workers, especially by influencing employers and workers. The Authority has set out a programme of work for 1990–92 which includes monitoring, the carrying out of safety campaigns, the production of guidelines on safety statements and safety consultations, education and training.

The Social Charter of the Council of Europe covers health and safety; Article 3 deals with the right to safe and healthy working conditions and the contracting parties undertake to enforce safety and health regulations. In a 1989 report, a Committee of this Charter (Government Committee of the European Social Charter, 1987) concluded unfavourably about Ireland's compliance with these regulations. In reaching its conclusions, the Committee observed in particular that certain categories of self-employed workers were not sufficiently protected for health and safety at work, despite earlier recommendations of the Commission of Inquiry on Safety, Health and Welfare at Work (Ireland, 1983).

For the future, the likely changes in employment structure will mean some shift away from high risk fields (such as agriculture) but are likely to see new dangers in new technology and automation.

In summary, depending on how the Social Charter is monitored, there is an opportunity to learn from the experience of other countries in occupational health and safety. For instance, it is unclear what is the best mixture of government policies between information to firms, exhortation, punitive measures and government leadership through the public employment sector.

There is also the issue of the costs that may fall on employers as a result of employment protection legislation. In particular, it has been argued that, under the Unfair Dismissals Act and the Protection of Employment Act, costs fall on firms in cases where they wish to reduce their workforces; and because of this, firms may be more reluctant to hire workers than would otherwise be the case. It may be the case that employment protection legislation has an above-average impact on small firms, especially in the early years when the firms may be uncertain about the nature of demand. Nevertheless, a survey of employers' attitudes to employment protection legislation (Department of Labour, 1986) shows that, while employment protection legislation has been a certain irritant for firms, it has hardly had any marked impact on their hiring practices.

Social security

The current arrangements for social security in the member states of the EC have two different lineages. The continental European system (owing its origins to the time of Bismarck) is based on coverage for social protection through social insurance, with benefits tending to be related to income. The British system, on the other hand, whose structure was set for more than forty years by the Beveridge Report of 1944, depends more on flat-rate benefits and is a mixture of social insurance-based benefits and a floor established by social assistance rates. The Irish system of social welfare at EC entry in 1973 had a structure more akin to that of the UK than to the continental system. While the levels of payment were lower than in the UK, the Beveridge structure of flat-rate payments for flat-rate contributions was essentially the one in place, together with a system of social assistance of last resort. The latter system was replaced in 1975 by the Supplementary Welfare Allowance, with a basic rate payable as of right and a standard means test. However, both in Ireland and in the UK, the system of income support for those with little or no other form of income in the 1970s and the 1980s began to adopt a role that was never envisaged in the original Beveridge model. This change was a reflection of a social security system that increasingly was coming under strain as a result of the rise in unemployment and in particular in long-term unemployment.

One interesting question that is relevant to the Social Charter is whether EC entry of itself led to any greater degree of harmonisation in social security between Ireland and other EC countries. The answer is that there have been some changes in the structure of social security in Ireland since 1973, which have moved the system somewhat closer to that in continental Europe. However, the structure remains more 'Beveridge' than 'Bismarck'. The structural changes have been:

- the introduction of pay-related benefit in 1974, the first time that an Irish social insurance scheme related a payment to the income of the recipient
- the change in social insurance contributions from a flat-rate basis to a wholly pay-related basis in 1979

- the introduction of Family Income Supplement in 1984, designed to maintain incentives to work

- the coming into effect in 1986 of the legislative provisions on equality of treatment of women and men in social security required under an EC directive

- moves towards increased reliance on government regulation, in particular with the setting up of the National Pensions Board in 1983.

It is likely that EC entry has had an effect on Irish social security provision over and above the structural changes that have been instituted. The increases in real levels of benefit which have occurred since 1973 — admittedly, from low levels in relation to earnings in many instances — probably have been influenced to some degree by a desire for a convergence in living standards towards those of the Community as a whole.

While real levels of benefit increased over time, there was concern at government level at the possibility that the level of social security benefits relative to net income from work (called the replacement ratio) acted as a disincentive to work. Reflecting this concern, the Family Income Supplement was introduced (as we saw above) and reforms were made to pay-related benefit. This led to a lowering of the replacement ratio (Table 16.7). A consequence of this was that the average real level of transfer payments for recipients of unemployment benefit in Ireland, which had increased by 24.2 per cent between 1976 and 1982, declined by 18.3 per cent between 1982 and 1988 and in the latter year was only 1.5 per cent higher than its level of 1976 (OECD, 1989). This picture of decline is scarcely altered by the improvements in unemployment benefits in the 1989 and 1990 Irish national budgets.

It should be said that the effect of the replacement ratio on work incentives has been exaggerated in much of the commentary on these matters (with some examples of the latter given in Blackwell, 1986b). Comparing replacement ratios in Ireland in the early 1980s with those for a selection of OECD countries in 1981 (Klau and Mittelstädt, 1985), it is probably correct to say that the Irish ratios were higher than in a number of the OECD countries.

However, one cannot argue that high replacement ratios are a major cause of unemployment. The highest replacement ratios apply to low-paid workers with large families, yet these workers are a minority of those on the Live Register of the unemployed (Blackwell, 1988). Moreover, a marked relative rise in unemployment has occurred among the long-term unemployed, who will no longer be entitled to pay-related benefit.

Certain developments affect social security and would operate irrespective of EC measures. For instance, many of those who are engaged in 'atypical' forms of work are women, many of whom in turn are on relatively low pay. In the case of men engaged in these kinds of work, they may be among the low paid in any event.

Table 16.7: **Replacement ratio for unemployment benefits: married employee with two children**

	Short-term(a)	Annual(b)
1980	81.4	73.9
1981	83.2	78.5
1982	86.7	83.1
1983	81.8	78.1
1984	80.1	76.8
1985	79.5	76.3
1986	77.4	74.6
1987	66.3	75.9
1988	65.5	65.5

Notes: (a) Unemployment benefit plus pay-related benefits at the initial maximum rate of male worker on average industrial earnings (excluding income tax rebates).
(b) Annual entitlement to unemployment benefit plus pay-related benefits for the prototype worker as at (a), at assumed maximum rates.
Source: OECD (1989)

Second, social security systems in general have reflected an economy where the 'typical' job was a full-time and tenured one. While the treatment of 'atypical' workers under social security varies across the EC states, in general, the rights that these workers have under social security are less favourable than for other workers, or at worst, completely absent. For instance, benefits are often calculated on the basis of previous earnings or on the basis of contributions built up over a certain period, or only if remuneration reaches a certain minimum level during the reference year. Temporary workers are not entitled to social security.

The EC Social Charter of itself is unlikely to do much either to change the structures of social security in member states or to push the systems in individual countries towards a greater degree of harmony. When one considers the structures of invalidity benefits, family benefits and unemployment benefits across the member states, not only is there the 'Bismarck–Beveridge' divide, but even among continental European countries there is considerable diversity in benefit structures. Arguably, these diversities in structure have become greater over the past decade, due to efforts by member governments to reduce public expenditure and to attempts to grapple with the problems presented by ageing populations and intractable long-term unemployment. For example, some countries have tried to reduce the public commitment to pensions and sick pay and to use private systems instead. Yet another aspect of diversity is the marked difference across member states in the way in which benefits are financed, with continental EC countries relying more than Ireland on social security contributions (essentially payroll taxes) to finance benefits.

The harsh judgment would be that in its current form the Social Charter is rather irrelevant to the social security concerns of the 1990s and beyond. In the 1990s, the debate about the structure of social security is likely to centre on four broad topics (not in any order of priority):

   i) how to cope with an ageing population (a matter of less immediate concern for Ireland)

  ii) how systems of social insurance, where contribution conditions and benefit entitlements have been linked to labour force status, can cope with an increasingly fragmented labour force. The concern here is with the best way of achieving coverage for people in 'atypical' jobs and with the appropriate minimum standards of social protection for people in these jobs.

 iii) whether there should be a move toward 'targeting' benefit more on those who are regarded as being in the greatest need

iv) whether to move towards a basic income guarantee for all, which essentially would aim to weaken, if not sever, the connection between income and labour force status.

Even without a Social Charter, it is likely that there would be some convergence in social security benefits across EC countries. This is partly because the standards and expectations of those EC members that have the least developed welfare states would be influenced by those countries with the most developed welfare states. It is partly also because, to some extent, people may migrate from states with low levels of benefit to states with higher levels.

The work of Walsh (1978), though tentative, suggests that one way in which increases in unemployment compensation had an impact on the Irish level of unemployment in the past was through reduced net emigration from Ireland.

'Social dumping'

Related to the questions of wages, working conditions and of social security is the issue of 'social dumping'. The fears that have been expressed about this take two forms:

i) the possibility that countries with low labour costs, low levels of employment protection, and of health and safety and other working conditions, will take a larger share of markets and obtain a larger share of company investment

ii) the possibility that levels of social protection, at least in those countries with relatively more advanced welfare states, will come under pressure and that there could be a certain 'downward levelling' of social protection as a result.

One would not expect 'social dumping', if it occurs, to apply with equal force across all sectors of the economy. It would affect in particular the relatively labour-intensive sectors.

The issue of social dumping can be analysed under the headings:

i) wage levels and labour costs
ii) health, and safety and other working conditions
iii) the informal economy
iv) social security.

The issues concerning wage levels, health and safety and working conditions, and social security have already been discussed; the informal economy is discussed below. Meanwhile, it can be observed that as long as an adequate system of collective bargaining and channels for the redress of grievances exist in member states, the dangers of social dumping are correspondingly reduced.

The informal economy

An inherent feature of the informal economy is that workers do not pay income taxes or social security contributions; indeed, it seems that, in some cases, employers and employees may collude to avoid income tax and social security contributions. From time to time, fears have been expressed that firms in those countries with a relatively large black economy would have an unfair advantage over firms in other countries.

The fears about 'social dumping' with regard to the black economy have probably been exaggerated, for the following reasons. First, the informal economy has been most prevalent in non-traded services and in building, construction and crafts. Second, the trend towards deregulation, which has been in evidence in a number of EC labour markets, has meant that activities that formerly would have been outside the 'formal' economy are now within that economy. Third, 'informal labour' in the EC does not tend to move over large distances. Fourth, while it is true to say that 'underground' firms in the south of Europe produce labour-intensive goods and offer stern competition to northern European firms, it is likely that many of these southern firms have a comparative advantage in these products in any event, whether out of or in the formal economy.

There remains an inherent tension in the concerns of governments about the informal economy. On the one hand, governments wish to maintain social cohesion and to respond to taxpayers and workers who pay income taxes and social insurance taxes. On the other hand, governments may not wish to inhibit entirely 'those who may be too enthusiastically enjoying the enterprise culture' (Pahl, 1988) on the grounds that economic activity is being generated.

The black economy in Ireland is almost certainly smaller than in many other EC countries. With all due qualifictions, a study (Pahl with Blackwell, 1988) concluded that the black economy in Ireland was dominated by the self-employed and by PAYE workers doing second jobs, and said 'it is perfectly plausible that the size of the black economy in Ireland is amongst the lowest in the EC.'

Other social conventions

The Social Charter cannot be assessed in isolation from other social conventions. Those of the Council of Europe and of the International Labour Office (ILO) are of particular interest. The European Social Charter of the Council of Europe was drawn up in 1961. It has been ratified by sixteen member states of the Council, including Ireland. The Charter guarantees the enjoyment, without discrimination, of a large number of fundamental rights, including the right to safe and healthy working conditions, the right to a fair remuneration, the right to vocational training, the right to protection of health and the right to social security. This protocol is of particular relevance to the Social Charter. The protocol guarantees four rights: to equal opportunities and treatment in occupational and employment matters without discrimination on grounds of sex; to information and consultation within the firm for workers; for workers to take part in the determination and improvement of working conditions and the working environment; and to social protection for the elderly. The protocol has been signed by nine member states and ratified by Sweden. To date, Ireland has not signed the protocol.

The Council of Europe monitors compliance with the provisions of the Charter through a system of international supervision. This requires each contracting state to submit a report every two years to an independent committee of experts. The conclusions of this committee are then submitted for examination to a governmental committee with observers from European federations of employers and trade unions. An example, drawing on the published ninth report of the governmental committee, has been given above under health and safety.

Ireland has ratified some International Labour Office conventions that relate to the provision of a 'minimum' set of social provisions: the right to collective bargaining, annual holidays with pay and the minimum age for admission to employment. However, twenty other ILO conventions have been listed as likely to be relevant to minimum social provisions in the EC (Interdepartmental Working Party, 1988) and have not been ratified by Ireland. These include conventions on discrimination in respect of employment and of occupation, minimum wage fixing, paid educational leave, and the safety and health of workers.

Conclusion

The likely impacts of the Social Charter have to be assessed in the light of the twofold influences on the labour market that arise from market forces and from government regulation. Ideally, one should use the 'with–without' test by questioning whether, in the light of the probable outcomes in the labour market, the Social Charter is likely to make any difference, compared with a world in which it did not exist. At least in the short term, the impact of the Social Charter is likely to be muted, especially in comparison with changes in the other elements that influence the outcomes in the labour market, such as the nature of demand, the state of technology, the structure of industry, and competitiveness in the widest sense. The completion of the Single Market will influence the outcomes in the labour market, but in ways that in part will reinforce existing trends, such as by the liberalisation of trade and the deregulation of services.

One lesson from recent years is that a good deal still depends on the measures that member governments put in place. There remains in Ireland a marked divide between 'good jobs' and 'bad jobs', and there are still notable differences in employment opportunities for women and men. In tackling these problems, domestic policies in education, social security and direct taxes, and direct intervention by governments in labour markets by setting regulations, e.g., on minimum standards, are likely to be more apposite than resorting to the Charter. One field where the Charter could make some difference, depending on the spirit in which it is interpreted, is training and retraining. The nature of training and retraining, and lifetime opportunities for training and education, will have an important influence on both the labour market and on poverty and inequality. Here is where hard questions need to be asked about the appropriateness and success of Irish policies, and where careful evaluations of policies are required.

Currently, the Irish labour market does not seem to be as regulated as other EC labour markets. There is little evidence of a will to regulate the market further, with the exception of the case of part-time workers. Hence, greater harmonisation of working conditions and of health and safety conditions will not happen automatically, either through the completion of the Single Market or through the Charter. There is a slight contrast in the field of social security: here, EC entry has led to some slight convergence in provision between Ireland and other EC countries, whether through 'demonstration' effects or (less likely) through migration in response to differences in social security provision across states. There remain both large structural differences between the Irish social security system and that in continental Europe, as well as differences in real levels of benefit. Comparisons between relative levels of benefit in Ireland and in continental Europe are almost impossible to make, given that Irish benefits are flat rate while the continental system is based more on relating benefit to income and has a different and more generous method of family income support. The Social Charter is unlikely to lead to any marked convergence in social security across member states, especially bearing in mind the differences in structure between the social security systems in the various member states.

It would be unfortunate if one looked at the Social Charter and its evolution as merely a set of measures concerning employment, social security and other matters, each in isolation. The changes in the labour market and in the nature of poverty have shown that labour market policies and social security policies are increasingly interrelated. If the evolution of the Charter and the spirit of its interpretation are to help those who have gained least or nothing from EC entry and the moves to the Single Market, this point needs to be recognised.

17

Ireland: A Peripheral Region

MICHAEL P. CUDDY and MICHAEL J. KEANE

An eclectic analysis of the Irish economy's performance within the Single Market would draw principally on theories of development, international trade, and regional economics. However, as its title underlines, this chapter emphasises the spatial dimension. It is laid out as follows: section two examines the concept 'peripheral' as against 'core' and argues that there are inherent economic disadvantages associated with the periphery — a contention supported by the literature on regional economics; section three draws on the work of Keeble et al ('distance from markets' index) and other attributes, which shows that Ireland is clearly a peripheral region; section four examines the impact of the creation of a Single Market on peripheral regions and challenges the thesis that they will be better off; section five evaluates the proposed expenditure of the structural funds as set out in the *National Development Plan 1989-1993* (1989) and their likely ameliorative effect on Ireland's peripheral disadvantage in the context of the Single Market; section six draws some conclusions.

Peripheral region: some issues

Core and periphery are key concepts in the spatial analysis of economic activity. The core refers to areas where the important economic activities — the dynamic sectors of production, the key economic decision-making units and the entities that wield market power — are concentrated, while the periphery refers to those areas that are remote from, but yet very much affected, by the core. This core–periphery apparatus can be adopted to cover a range of theoretical possibilities involving the two regions: to investigate a set of structural relationships in which the core region is dominant, to analyse dualism, or to study the effects of proximity or remoteness (Seers, 1979). The notion of periphery typically is associated with geographical remoteness from a single core area. The key issue for firms in peripheral regions is access to markets at the core. Distance from markets implies additional costs to suppliers. The most obvious are transport costs, which were analysed in Chapter 9. However, other factors impose extra costs on peripherally located firms and therefore leave them at a relative market disadvantage *vis-à-vis* their counterparts at the core.

Transport costs traditionally have received the greatest consideration at the theoretical, empirical and policy levels. These costs relate not just to the movement of goods, but also to the movement of personnel and to the general cost of keeping in touch with the market on both the input and the output side. The greater the distance to markets, the greater the costs involved and, therefore, the greater the disadvantage. Costs are not linearly related to distance. They depend on the type and quality of the transport network, as well as on the various attributes of the products being transported. For example, the higher the value added per unit weight/volume, the less important is the transport cost. If inputs must be transported into a region and the finished product transported out, this adds doubly to transport costs and increases the competitive disadvantage of the firm and the region. Telecommunication, postal and information-gathering costs are also related to distance from markets. Information-gathering is becoming increasingly important because the information content of production has increased rapidly in recent years. However, the costs involved tend to be offset by the development of information and telecommunications technology.

Another direct cost associated with peripherality is the cost of storage. Because the plant is far from the market, a higher average stock must be held than would be the case if it was nearer. This applies both to the input and output sides. In particular, the ability of firms to implement a 'just-in-time' regime decreases as distance from the market and suppliers increases. There is also a strong likelihood of encountering monopoly or monopolistic suppliers in regions of dispersed economic activity and limited demand, particularly in service industries; this can raise input costs above what they would be at the centre.

An indirect effect of a limited local market is that the growth of the firm is constrained, even where monopolistic structures exist. This makes it difficult to realise the benefits associated with scale economies and, as a result, economic efficiency is impaired. Some of this loss in efficiency may be offset by lower labour costs, of course, or by a particular local advantage. Firms in peripheral regions in general tend to lag behind in technological dynamism and innovation. They tend to concentrate on production at the end, rather than at the beginning, of the product cycle. This arises from their role in the international division of labour, wherein the greater concentration of skilled personnel, of research, of development, of interaction functions, and of innovation functions are to be found at the core. The mature 'end of product cycle' production activity locates at the periphery.

The factors that bestow economic advantage on core regions and disadvantage on peripheral regions have been empirically documented in various studies. Kilby (1980) demonstrates the importance of transport costs and states that 'Freedom of investment choice and the need to minimise transport costs has of course favoured the Golden Triangle countries in the EEC and operated to the disadvantage of the peripheral industrial countries'. Peida (1984) confirms this but, in addition, identifies other costs associated with distance from the markets: 'These revolve around the difficulties of maintaining market contact and ensuring input supply at a distance'. Goddard et al. (1983) highlight considerable differences between core and peripheral countries in the Community with respect to both the cost and quality of telecommunications. A number of studies confirm that firms at the periphery generally rely more on local markets and are smaller in size than those at the core (Commission of the European Communities, 1981; Aydalot, 1986; Chisholm, 1985). Goddard et al. (1986) established that there is greater technological dynamism and innovation at the core than at the periphery, and that this difference in the use of technology and in the adoption of innovations has been increasing.

The net result of the various factors that contribute to the relative disadvantage of peripheral regions is that there is a differential growth rate which favours the core. Furthermore, the core is privileged over the periphery on a number of key socio-economic indicators, and the gap between the former and the latter, at least in absolute terms, continues to grow (Keeble, Owens and Thompson, 1981; Keeble, Offord and Walker, 1988; Commission of the European Communities, 1984, 1987). This cumulative process of unevenness is an important dimension in the workings of industrial capitalism (Scott and Storper, 1986). However, as capitalism undergoes restructuring, the locus of economic advantage may shift somewhat. Recent structural changes — a decline in traditional, manufacturing employment, a resurgence of small new firms (often in less industrialised regions), rapid growth in high technology industries, a surge of new inward multinational investment into Europe (see Chapter 14), and an absolute and relative shift from manufacturing to service activities — have brought certain benefits to the peripheral regions. Keeble (1989) shows how, at least for the nine-member Community (excluding Greece, Spain and Portugal), there has been some diminution of certain core-periphery disparities. The relevant data in Table 17.1 show that central and peripheral regions recorded the worst and best manufacturing employment performances, respectively, in the early 1980s. Even more encouraging is the trend of convergence of manufacturing structures between central and peripheral areas, the latter revealing an increasing, the former a decreasing, ratio of 'modern' to 'traditional' manufacturing industries. Finally, the perhiperal regions have recorded the best performance in recent service industry employment creation in the pre-1986, nine-member European Community, with inner central regions faring the worst of all. Unfortunately, as Table 17.2 shows, the gains for remote regions like Ireland and, within Ireland, the west region (Galway and Mayo) have been very modest. The 1980s have witnessed a significant reduction in manufacturing jobs. There has been some small increase in service employment, but little of this growth has taken place in the so-called producer services. The improvement shown in manufacturing structures has been largely due to new inward multinational investment, primarily from the USA and Japan.

Table 17.1: **Centre-periphery disparities in the nine-member EC: trends in the 1980s**

Regions	Manufacturing employment change 1979-83	Manufacturing structure indices 1979-83			Service industry employment change 1979-83
	Mean %	Mean 1979	Mean 1983	Trend + or −	Mean %
Inner central	− 11.1	1.323	1.216	−	+ 7.7
Outer central	− 10.6	1.243	1.137	−	+ 11.1
Intermediate	− 6.6	1.069	1.051	−	+ 10.1
Inner Periphery	− 7.2	0.528	0.580	+	+ 11.2
Outer Periphery	+ 6.2	0.289	0.354	+	+ 15.3
Total (EUR9)	− 7.4	1.031	1.004	−	+ 10.2

Source: Keeble (1989). The manufacturing structure index is the ratio of employment in 'modern' (electronics, vehicles, aerospace) NACE 3 industries to that in 'traditional' (clothing, footwear, food and drink) NACE 4 industries.

Table 17.2: **Changes in manufacturing employment, in manufacturing structure and in service employment in Ireland and the west region in the 1980s**

Regions	Manufacturing employment change 1981-85	Manufacturing structure indices 1981-85			Service industry employment change 1981-85
	% change	1981	1985	Trend + or −	% change
Ireland	− 16.3	.469	.547	+	+ 2.8
West region	− 3.4	.440	.469	+	+ 5.2

Source: Census of Industrial Production, Labour Force Surveys. The manufacturing structure index is as defined in Table 17.1, but here the ratio is establishments in NACE 3 to establishments in NACE 4.

From time to time peripheral regions obviously can experience modest improvements in their relative economic position. However, these regions are unlikely to experience any long-term fundamental improvements within the normal processes of change and restructuring that take place under the influence of market forces. The fundamental factors that cause disadvantage are powerful and difficult to overcome.

Is Ireland a peripheral region?

Recent work by Keeble et al. (1988) clearly establishes Ireland as a peripheral region within the Community. Using an index of accessibility to Community markets, Ireland is classified as an 'outer perhiperal' region, the lowest in a five-category spatial classification used by Keeble. Its accessibility score is only 55% of the average of all the regions of the Community and only 21% and 17%, respectively, of Rheinhessen-Pfalz and Greater London, which belong to the central or core group. It is important to note that two aspects of the Irish situation have led to an overestimation of the accessibility index for Ireland. First, Irish exports as a percentage of Gross Domestic Product are 51.4%, compared with 22.9% for the Community as a whole. Second, the additional costs of sea crossings have not been taken sufficiently into account. By not allowing for these facts, the calculation is misleading and tends to underemphasise Ireland's remoteness. Another important point to note is that there are likely to be considerable intra-regional differences in the index. This is well illustrated in the Scottish case, where the Edinburgh region has a market accessibility score that is 73% of the Community average, but the Highlands and Islands region has a score of only 46% of the Community average. Clearly this pattern also applies to Ireland since there are significant differences between regions.

The 'outer periphery', which includes Ireland, accounts for 40% of the land area of the Community, 20.3% of the population, but only 12.9% of Gross Domestic Product (see Figure 17.1 for the definition of 'outer periphery'). It accounts for 44.6% of agricultural employment, but only 12.9% of manufacturing and 14.1% of service employment. This 'outer periphery' has 23.3% of the unemployment in the Community. Thus it has significantly less than average shares of GDP, of manufacturing and services employment and higher than average shares of agricultural employment and unemployment.

Ireland is clearly in the outer periphery category on the basis of GDP per capita (see Table 17.3). On the basis of agricultural and manufacturing specialisation, it is close to, although somewhat better than, the 'outer periphery' region. It is also significantly better as regards changes in GDP and GDP per capita between 1977 and 1983. If, however, one looks at GNP rather than GDP, the margin is considerably narrower. This is due primarily to

Table 17.3: **Socio-economic indicators for the EC, Ireland and inner central and outer peripheral regions in the EC**

	GDP per capita 1983* (Purchasing Power Parity)	GDP per capita growth 1977-1983* (% change)	GDP Growth 1977-1983* (% change)	Unemployment (%)	Agricultural specialisation (%)	Manufacturing specialisation (%)
EC (12)	10.320	8.1	10.3	9.5	12.9	23.8
Inner central	13.183	7.9	9.6	8.9	3.0	26.1
Outer peripheral	6.910	8.0	10.74	12.6	27.0	17.5
Ireland	7.094	11.7	19.6	14.06	16.8	19.5

	Manufacturing structure indices	Change in manufacturing employment 1979-1983 (%)	Service specialisation (%)	Service structure indices	Change in services employment 1979-1983†	Total employment change 1979-1983 (%)
EC (12)	.875	– 11.1	52.8	.25	+10.2	+ 2.2
Inner central	1.218	– 13.0	61.2	.32	+11.1	+ 1.6
Outer peripheral	.433	– 1.4	44.3	.22	+15.3	+12.5
Ireland	.531	– 10.1	53.8	.25	+ 8.2	+ 1.8

Source: Keeble et al (1988) (various tables), Eurostat (1987), Government (1984), Central Statistics Office (1979, 1983) and Industrial Development Authority (unpublished).
*The Keeble et al data were updated to be consistent with Eurostat (1987).
†Europe (10).

the fairly heavy reliance in Ireland on foreign investment through the 1960s and the 1970s and the corresponding outflow of expatriated profits. The servicing of the foreign component of the national debt has also contributed. Service specialisation and service structure in Ireland are considerably better than in the 'outer periphery' and are similar to the Community average. The most disappointing aspect of the Irish situation is in relation to all levels of the labour market: level of unemployment and changes in manufacturing, services and total employment. All these indicators are worse for Ireland than the corresponding figures for the 'outer periphery'. By using the Keeble index and other key economic statistics, it is plain that Ireland falls into the category of peripheral region and more particularly into the category of 'outer periphery' within the European Community.

Figure 17.1:

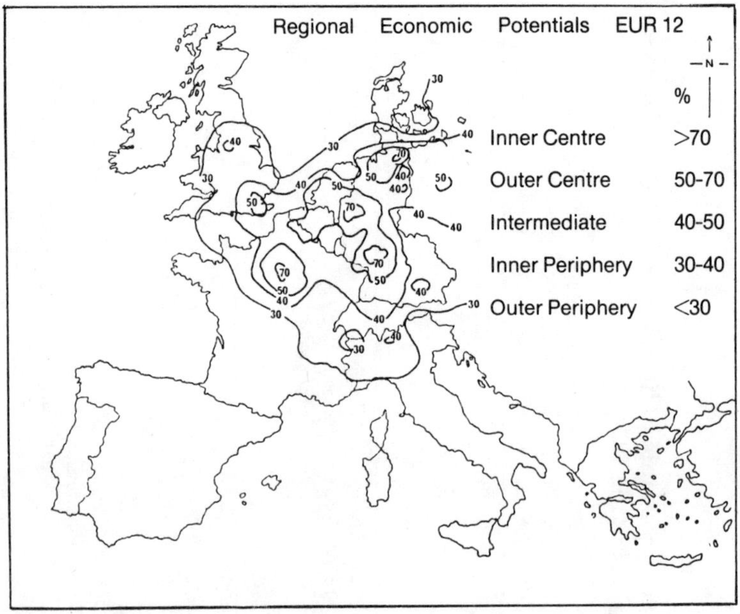

The impact of completion of the internal market:
a core-periphery perspective

It is clear that the completion of the internal market will generate technical, organisational and spatial changes in economic activity.

A large body of literature analyses these changes and they are discussed throughout this volume. Removal of trade barriers will reduce costs directly, while greater market access will enhance competition, thus adding to cost and price reductions. This process will remove non-competitive or inefficient firms and bring about a restructuring of industries through amalgamations, mergers and buyouts. Economies of scale will be realised in research, innovation and development, production, marketing and distribution. Greater concentration of economic activity will generate agglomeration economies. This cumulative process will lead to a more efficient use of resources and a corresponding growth in the economy. The expected concentration of economic activity through the enlargement of firm size runs counter to the current international trend of reduction in firm size (Carlsson, 1988). However, this response will take place within the Community at the existing level of technology, and is simply a structural shift in response to market forces unleashed by an enlargement of the market. The longer term trend in structures is likely to re-emerge as a new equilibrium is established and evolving technology reimposes its requirements.

Although there are few serious reservations within the 1992 literature about the economic benefits of market integration (see Chapter 2 for details of these), there is uncertainty about how the benefits will be distributed geographically. For peripheral regions remote from the core of the Community's markets, this concern may be a well-founded one. The prospective spatial or regional consequences have received only brief and passing mention to date, as the following passage illustrates:

> Difficult as it is to estimate the aggregate gains from market integration, this task is relatively manageable compared to that of forecasting its distribution by country or region. While the latter task has not been attempted, it is worth noting that neither economic theory nor relevant economic history can point to any clear-cut pattern of likely distributional advantage or disadvantage. Theories of vicious circles of divergence of regional fortunes resulting from market integration exist, but so do alternative theses that point to more balanced or indeterminate outcomes, the latter theses including important recent developments in the analysis of trade between industrialised countries. Smaller countries, in

particular those having recently joined the Community, with relatively protected economic structures, have proportionately the biggest opportunities for gain from market integration. In any case, policy instruments exist to provide an insurance policy to help losers recover. (Commission, 1988)

As Begg (1989) rightly states, the only inference that can be drawn from this statement is that little attention has been paid to the issue of how the gains from the Single Market are likely to be distributed throughout the regions of the Community. The attitude, and indeed almost all the analysis on the impact of the Single Market, seems to be that, provided the macroeconomic gains for the Community as a whole are realised, questions about the spatial impact of the Single Market are of secondary importance. The Commission has recently (Commission, 1989) referred again to how difficult it is to evaluate *a priori* the specific regional distribution of the effects of 1992. Currently the Commission is undertaking extensive research into the issue, including the potential effects of Community support from the structural funds and through the Community's borrowing and lending instruments.

The Commission's statement (quoted above) is interesting in that it recognises the fact that the particular assumptions and theories that might be used to evaluate outcomes in fact can lead to quite different conclusions about what is likely to happen. The assumptions and models typically used by the Commission to estimate the potential benefits of fully integrating the market are those of a competitive neoclassical equilibrium variety. A good example is the analysis of the gains accruing from the capital market. Here it is argued that

The completion of the internal market, and in particular the abolition of the remaining exchange controls, will also result in net gains, by ensuring that investment will take place for those projects which have the highest returns, irrespective of the country (region) in which they are located. The capital flows generated by this pursuit of the highest returns should generate forces tending to equalise real interest rates, real rates of return, and so the marginal efficiency of capital throughout the Community. These movements will also increase the output and income of the Community as a whole.

This outcome is illustrated in a simple two-country (region) case in Figure 17.2.

Marginal efficiency of capital schedules are shown for two regions, A and B. Real rates of interest in the two regions before integration, r_A and r_B, are also shown. In region A (the left-hand axis) investment will proceed until the marginal efficiency of capital (mec_A) equals the real rate of interest r_A at point D. For region B (right-hand axis) equilibrium is at point E.

Figure 17.2: **Impact of capital market integration on the level of production and income**

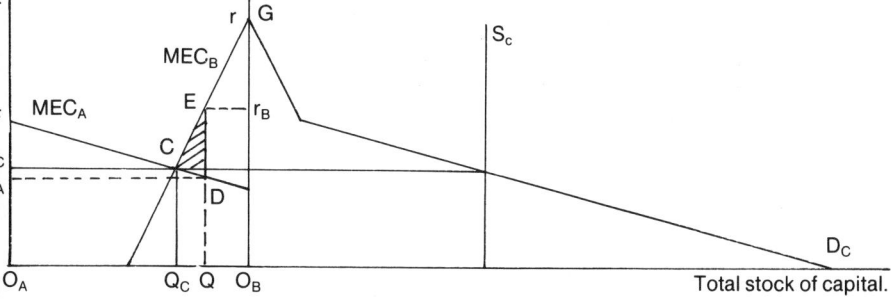

Source: European Commission (1988)

Before the movement of capital takes place, the regional product in A is given by O_AFDQ: the return on capital by O_Ar_ADQ and the total of income from employment by the triangle r_AFD. For region B the relevant regions are O_BGEQ, O_Br_BEQ and the triangle r_BGE. After the movement of capital, an equilibrium interest rate r_C is established and region A exports Q-Q_C of capital to region B, where the returns are higher. The total product of the two regions increases by the area CDE.

The model and analysis of Figure 17.2 are based on the frictionless neoclassical view of the world. However, the model can be modified to accommodate some different perspectives. One simple modification is to recognise the economic effects of distance between the two regions. If region B happens to be a geographically remote region, this could impose extra costs to lending in B and it may justify higher interest rates there. Straightforward distance effects can be fitted easily within the neoclassical model (Greenhut, 1988). The model is sufficiently general that it can accommodate some non-neoclassical views, like that of core-periphery (Bradfield, 1988). Suppose the two regions are described as being unequal in terms of location and market power. Region B is the peripheral region, while A is the central or core region. B suffers because of remoteness, both directly, in the form of higher costs or difficulty of access, and indirectly through various psychological barriers that are associated with remoteness. The central region A is wealthier. It is where the main financial market is located and also is where economic power is concentrated. The two regions are in an uneven relationship with each other and this may change significantly the outcome in Figure 17.2. Financial institutions may now seek to discriminate between borrowers in the two regions. The assessment of loan applications generates for the financial institutions ideal conditions for discriminatory behaviour. These conditions are created by a likely lower demand elasticity among borrowers in region B, because of less competition amongst financial institutions, and by the bank's assessment of differences in risk between the two regions.

Figure 17.3 shows the same supply and demand conditions as Figure 17.2. The right-hand diagram shows the total demand and supply of funds. It is now assumed that financial capital is being lent by a price discriminator, who acts to set different interest rates in the two regions according to the elasticity of demand in them. With a total stock of capital of S_C and total demand of D_C in Figure 17.3, the lender who practices third-degree price discrimination will allocate funds to the two regions to have marginal revenue (mr) equal, rather than setting a single market clearing rate of interest r_C. Capital funds are allocated in the two regions so that they earn the same marginal revenue in both regions on the last pound lent. Because of the different slopes of the regional demand curves (i.e. mec_A and mec_B) and of the corresponding marginal revenue curves (i.e. mr_A and mr_B), the amount $O_A Q_1$ of funds are allocated to region A and $O_B Q_1$ to region B. The rates of interest charged will be r_A * and r_B * respectively, with region B paying a higher rate of interest than A. Lenders of capital receive a higher return than was the case in the competitive model. The total output of the two regions is also increased, but the gain is now less than in the competitive model i.e. FHLK in Figure 17.3 is less than CDE in Figure 17.2. The relative gains in region B are distributed much more in favour of capital in Figure 17.3.

The significance of this example is to show how it is possible to derive quite different scenarios about the way and the efficiency with which financial institutions can allocate funds between regions. In each scenario the relevant variables are the same. The difference between the two is that Figure 17.3 recognises some underlying differences and imperfections that may exist between regions, whereas Figure 17.2 ignores such differences. This latter approach is favoured in most of the theoretical discussions that the Commission puts forward as a way of estimating gains from market integration. At the same time the Commission does recognise that, in its attempt to create a European financial area which will mean a more efficient capital market, 'there are inevitable differences in market conditions in terms of risk and custom by country or even region, as well as the likelihood of some remaining degree of imperfect competition' (Commission, 1987, p. 90). The Commission goes on to acknowledge that 'In practice it is impossible to estimate the margin by which the fully integrated Community financial market of the future will fall short of the conditions that would establish the law of one price'. The Commission's empirical estimates on potential falls in financial product prices as a result of completing the internal market (Commission, 1988, Table 5.1.4) are consistent with the above analysis.

Figure 17.3: **Price discrimination in capital markets**

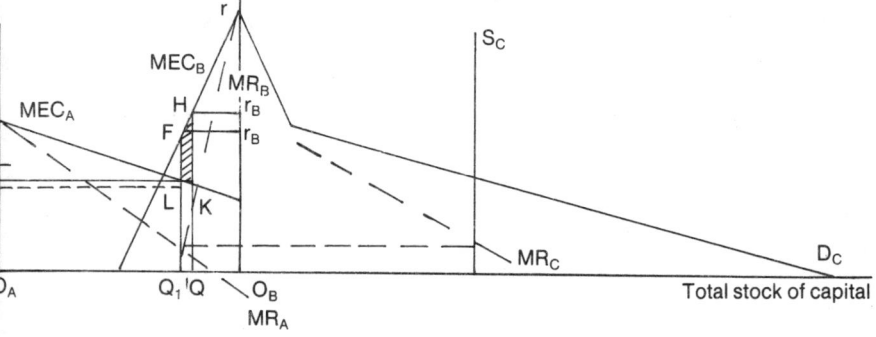

The data in question are measures of current product prices for a total of sixteen banking, insurance and securities products in eight EC countries (Ireland unfortunately is not included in this comparison). For each of these products, current prices were estimated on the basis of surveying a sample of market participants, which, when converted into ECU, enabled inter-country comparisons to be made. The average of the four lowest prices was taken to represent a low, competitive price standards for the countries studied, and prices were compared with this average. Both theoretical potential price reductions and indicative price reductions were calculated. The purpose of calculating the indicative price reductions was to try to gauge the extent to which the perfectly competitive and integrated conditions, of the kind assumed in Figure 17.2, would not be attained. A general hypothesis from the analysis of Figure 17.3 is that, whereas the theoretical prices for the different products should approximate closely the law of one price, the estimates of indicative prices should show greater variation across the different regions/ countries. A simple coefficient of variation test (Table 17.4) on the current and computed prices of banking products supports the hypothesis. The smaller the value of the coefficient of variation, the less the relative dispersion amongst a given set of prices. The estimates of theoretical prices, as expected, display small variations relative to the average, while the variation among indicative prices is considerably greater. The data and the various estimates of both theoretical and indicative prices are obviously crude. Nonetheless, the test is indicative and helps to highlight how various regional differences and imperfections within the financial market can prevent inter-regional equality from taking place. These same factors reduce the size of the efficiency gains expected from integration and also affect the geographical distribution of these gains.

Table 17.4: **Coefficient of variation for banking prices**

Current prices	14.35%
Theoretical prices	6.97%
Indicative prices	9.89%

The imperfections analysed were attributed to the effects of space and especially to differences in market power. It is not difficult to construct similar formalisations of other markets and arrive at similar kinds of conclusions about the likely persistence of regional inequalities in long-run equilibrium. A further difficulty with these inequalities is that, once they get established, they tend to be self-generating and cumulative. For example, the differences in capital costs between regions, highlighted in the previous section, will imply differences in capital/labour ratios and long-term equilibrium wage differences. These differences will affect the industry mix in a region and the region's competitiveness. The cumulative effect will be to widen the disparities between regions as capital, labour and enterprise are attracted away from the less well-off regions and towards the most prosperous ones.

The push to realise economies of scale will bring about increased concentration and relocation of economic activity. This relocation is also likely to be towards the centre and away from the periphery because of the attraction of agglomeration economies. These agglomeration economies are further enhanced by the recent trends for the independent growth of producer services which are concentrating in core locations (Keeble, 1989). Innovation, a key factor in competitiveness and survival, will also be more abundant at the centre than at the periphery (Keeble, 1989). It is also most likely to take place in the high demand and high technology industries which are more concentrated at the centre. The low technology, low demand, local demand resource-based industries and products at the later stages of the product cycle are more likely to be located and to dominate industry mixes in the periphery. These latter industries are more valuable and more vulnerable to swings in the fortunes of the market.

A key question is what the periphery has to offer to offset the advantages held by the core. Core firms will have many different advantages which, although individually small, collectively are important. Peripheral firms will therefore require substantially lower wage costs to offset these advantages and permit a return to capital comparable to that obtained at the core. If firms are to stay at or be attracted to the periphery, this wage differential must be established. There is then the question of whether the (lower) local wages and social infrastructure are sufficient to prevent the migration of labour to the centre. If labour moves before the necessary wage differential is established, then, because of the migration, local wages in fact will increase and the peripheral region will become even more unattractive to external investment, as well as more unprofitable for existing firms. The process will be a cumulative downward spiral of economic activity in the periphery.

One of the critical issues in Ireland is the tax wedge — the difference between the labour cost that the employer has to pay and the net return that the worker receives. It is of the order of 37% (on average; this figure is of course considerably higher on the margin) of total labour cost as a result of income tax, PRSI and other levies, and about 60% when indirect taxes are taken into account. This tax wedge is so high because of the very narrow tax base (comprised mainly of employed labour), the high dependency and unemployment rates, and the relatively high level of social services that Ireland wishes to provide. Thus, it is extremely difficult to have a labour cost low enough to the employer that will compensate for the region's lack of advantages and at the same time provide a sufficiently attractive net wage to the worker.

So far, this argument about the disadvantages of the periphery, and the wage differential necessary to offset the advantages of the core region, has assumed that there is only one type of production technique available. Obviously if we are thinking of a capital intensive method of production, it will be difficult for the peripheral region to compete. It will require a very high wage differential to compensate for the region's lack of other advantages. Ironically, if firms are using capital intensive techniques, the savings generated by the cheaper labour costs are reduced correspondingly and, in order to compensate for the lack of other cost advantages, labour costs in the periphery must be even cheaper. However, if in the first instance the periphery offers some labour cost advantage, then by encouraging the use of labour intensive techniques, some of these difficulties can be avoided. The more labour intensive the production method, the greater the savings accruing to firms as a result of locating in the low-wage region; this can help firms to offset the other disadvantages found in the periphery.

If the sectors that are likely to benefit and grow most from the completion of the Single Market are the capital intensive ones, then this growth will be concentrated in the centre since that is where the capital intensive sectors will be located. The mobility of capital within the Single Market guarantees that capital will go only where it will make the highest return. As long as the underlying advantages of the centre persist and continue to attract capital, then the benefits of the Single Market are unlikely to stimulate the peripheral regions very much. Unless the periphery can offer other compensations to offset its disadvantages, or can find growth opportunities in more labour intensive techniques, the prediction must be that it will gain little from the Single Market. There is a possibility, of course, that growth itself may alter some of the underlying conditions at the centre and thereby give opportunities to the periphery. The telecommunications revolution, for example, may encourage individuals and businesses to escape the pressures and the deteriorating environmental quality of the industrial heartlands and to relocate in the cleaner and more attractive peripheral regions. On a less wholesome note, it may be the desire of industry to escape the constrictions of environmental pollution that it has caused in Europe's industrial centre, and to move to 'green field' sites. These latter locations, it has been argued (Johnson and Convery, 1988), are more conducive to employees' health and enjoyment and meet the more exacting requirements of environmental purity demanded by 'high-tech' industry, while, at the same time, being less encumbered by tough and stringent environmental regulations.

These forces are not, of course, new to the Irish economy. Ireland has made tremendous strides in industrial development since it became an open international economy instead of a sheltered, relatively closed, economy. This development has been led mainly by international investment, primarily American. The international success of indigenous companies has been very limited (see Chapter 10). The international companies' operations have concentrated on manufacturing products that have reached the mature end of the product cycle. Research and development and product innovation have been rather limited in the Irish branches of these international companies. The Irish firms that have made the most important impacts in the international arena have been those whose products are based mainly on domestic raw materials. The strategy used in this internationalisation process has been a classical development policy: direct and indirect subsidisation of production factors and tax concessions to firms that participated, at the expense of those that did not participate. The latter were producing mainly for the relatively closed domestic market, which was dominated by 'sheltered' activities, with low price elasticities and high income demand elasticities. The costs of this development policy were borne mainly by labour and, to a lesser extent, by the domestic saver.

It is not clear that these policies will continue to be successful now that the 'playing field' is being 'levelled'. Two factors are critical here. First, all barriers to trade, and capital and labour mobility are being removed. Thus, the captive domestic market, which remained to a large extent closed and which therefore could be relied on to cross-subsidise the open sector, can no longer be counted upon. The domestic savings, which were mainly invested in the Irish market and subsidised domestic investment, now will have access to the large capital markets of Europe. Labour is now assured of equal access to the European job market, with reciprocal acceptance of professions and skills, as well as all the social services (see Chapters 15 and 16). So labour can no longer be forced to carry the main burden of the transfer/ cross-subsidisation process. Second, there may be pressure for harmonisation of subsidisation of international companies across the Community. Consequently, Ireland may not be able to rely on the old methods to forge ahead of other peripheral regions in the Community.

Addressing the peripheral disadvantage: Community structural funds

In anticipation of the new pressures facing peripheral regions and by way of renewing the often-stated aspiration in Community documents for cohesion and convergence, the Community has set about doubling the structural funds in the period up to 1993, with 60% of funds going to objective (1) regions, that is regions where development is significantly lagging behind the Community as a whole. Ireland is an objective (1) region.

The Irish government prepared a *National Development Plan* (1989) in part preparation for the Community Support Framework, which gives the outline structures and references within which the structural funds and matching national finances are expanded. The Cecchini projection — that the Single Market will lead to intensification of competition, economies of scale and the efficient use of resources, which will lead to economic growth — is accepted (p. 35). However, it is recognised that the benefits theoretically could gravitate towards the centre (p. 11). The Cecchini Report also recognises Ireland as a peripheral region with low productivity, high dependency (implying the need for relatively high taxes) and a low level of investment per capita (p. 15). More specifically, the peripheral characteristics are explicitly identified as cost disadvantages associated with transport and the smallness of the Irish market, indirect costs of distance like customer contact, infrastructure deficiencies and a traditional indigenous sector, dominated by small firms that are deficient in essential business functions (pp. 13-14). However, the plan still aspires to 'convergence' in terms of both employment and incomes (p. 26) and sees this as possible within a Single Market through 'the development and intensification of competitive advantage' (p. 25) by efficient production and product development across all sectors (pp. 16-19). This goal of convergence is seen as a two-tier process: macroeconomic policies to provide the stable economic environment, which will be conducive to enterprise, and microeconomic sectoral policies to 'facilitate and encourage exploitation of the economy's comparative advantages' (p. 26). The structural funds are seen, primarily, as supporting the implementation of the microeconomic and sectoral policies. Clearly then, the problems associated with peripherality and the Single Market challenge, which have been identified in the *National Plan*, are along the general lines that one would expect. However, they are not stated as explicitly or as systematically as might be anticipated. Indeed, they are often implicit rather than explicit. In particular, the clear role that innovation must play, according to theory and logic, in even holding onto existing market share is not clearly identified.

In the *Plan*, development measures were drawn up, in broad terms, to help to overcome the deficiencies of the economy's underdeveloped state, its peripherality and the increased competitive pressures of the Single Market. Demands were then made on the three European Funds corresponding to the measures proposed, with 48.4% of the total Community contribution to come through the European Regional Development Fund (ERDF),

31.7% from the European Social Fund (ESF) and 19.9% from the European Agricultural Guidance and Guarantee Fund (EAGGF) (Table 17.5). These Funds are normally associated, respectively, with improving economic development structures, with training and unemployment and with agricultural development.

The major share of ERDF funds is devoted to transport, with 75% of these going to roads and almost all the remainder going to sea and air transport. Clearly, the emphasis is on minimising export and import transport costs to industry. Despite stating that there was a 'substantial shift in the industrial budget to the support of measures to upgrade capability in key areas of business competence', two-thirds of the ERDF funds allocated to industry are earmarked for capital projects. Only 17% is allocated to enhance technology for R & D facilities in industry and their links with third-level institutions, 14% to marketing and less than 3% to enhance the other 'key areas of business competence'. Tourism is allocated a significant share (9.9%) both for product development and capital investment, while the remaining portion of the ERDF is earmarked for sanitary and other infrastructure development, including energy, telecommunications and postal services.

ESF funding is allocated primarily to training linked to industry and development. However, almost two-thirds of what is earmarked for training for entry into the workforce will be administered by the Department of Education. What is not allocated to training is to be spent, about equally, on recruitment into the workforce and for temporary employment.

The two largest components of the EAGGF go to farm investment, including product diversification, and compensatory payments. The food-processing sector will take a little over one-fifth of EAGGF, which will be applied to 'total support' for the industry, but in particular capital and marketing. Forestry is being allocated a very significant share, while support for the fishing industry is being sought under other Community regulations. Rural Development, which emphasises alternative non-farm enterprises and local community development, is allocated less than 4% of EAGGF funding.

It is not possible here to assess the various levels of priority accorded to the different sectors of the economy and the levels

Table 17.5: **Breakdown of structural funds allocation (%)**

ERDF	48.4	Transport	45.5	Roads	75.0
				Rail & Bus	2.7
				Sea & Air	22.3
					100.0
		Industry	31.5	Capital	66.2
				Technical facilities	17.0
				Marketing	13.9
				Advisory/support	2.9
					100.0
		Tourism	9.9		
		Sanitary & other local services	7.8		
		Other infra-structure	5.4		
			100.0		
ESF	3.17	Training	71.3	Dept. of Education	64.7
				FAS	25.3
				Other	10.0
					100.0
		Recruitment	13.7		
		Temporary employment	15.0		
			100.0		
EAGGF	19.9	On farm investment	28.9		
		Compensatory payments	28.9		
		Marketing and processing	20.5		
		Forestry	16.3		
		Set aside, production conversion	1.7		
		Rural development	3.7		
	100.0		100.0		

Source: Government Ireland: *National Development Plan 1989-93*
Due to rounding, totals may not always sum to 100.

of structural funds allocated to them. There is little to suggest a fundamental departure from previous planning approaches about this *Plan* and the application of funds therein. It is basically an extension of existing programmes within various central government departments. There has been a very strong emphasis on the physical aspects of development, with over 50% of total funds going directly into physical structures. Transport stands out as receiving considerably in excess of what *a priori* considerations would suggest: transport is only one aspect of cost associated with distance from the market, and distance is only one of several disadvantages associated with peripherality. The heavy emphasis on support for capital intensive investment to industry is also surprising in view of the findings of the Telesis Report and *A Stategy for Development 1986-90* (NESC, 1986) which argued that 'excessive reliance on these instruments [tax-based incentives and grants for fixed asset investment] has contributed to the failure to develop a sufficient number of indigenous firms capable of competing in international markets.' This 'hardware' emphasis also runs somewhat counter to the more recent thinking on regional development and indeed to some of the ideas on development strategies emanating from within the Commission itself (Martinos, 1989).

A significant stimulus has been directed in the *Plan* to the natural resource-based industries, in order to capitalise on Ireland's advantage here. This is consistent with the recommendations of economic theory. Tourism, food processing and forestry, in particular, have been privileged. Technology and research and development have been neglected. Since product innovation will be vital to Ireland's competitiveness, the support of only 2.6% of total structural funds for it appears totally inadequate. Another surprising neglect is the small allocation to the non-agricultural aspect of rural development, in contrast to the very significant level of resources given to agriculture. This is contrary to current Commission thinking as expressed in *The Future of Rural Society* (Commission, 1988), which emphasised the non-agricultural sector's role in rural society. It is also inconsistent with trends in rural Ireland. The share of agricultural employment in rural areas has dropped from approximately 75% in 1971 to about 35% in 1987. Obviously, the non-agricultural sectors are now significantly more important to the well-being of Irish rural society than agriculture. Finally, a very significant share of ESF funding (46.1%) is being administered by the Department of Education. This raises the question of whether ESF funding will be substituted for national funds in the provision of education, rather than being added as required by the 'additionality' clause. Indeed, it is not possible to discern whether additional monies are to be spent by the Irish government, whether the only additional funding being put into the system is the Community money, and even here whether there is a substitution of Community money for Irish government expenditure.

One cannot seriously question the priorities and sectoral allocations of funds without carrying out a full cost-benefit analysis of each sector. It is doubtful whether such analyses were conducted and, therefore, the fund allocation could be optimal only by sheer chance. Transport is identified in the plan as a major sector for investment. There is no (at least published and widely known) evidence on the detailed role of transport costs in Irish industry, on what the transport cost savings to industry from increased transport investment might be and, most importantly, what the likelihood is that any transport savings can be reflected in, say, trade growth and hence national growth (Mansergh, 1985, provides a good discussion on the issues as they relate to roads investment). Thus, while transport is of major importance, there are significant questions in relation to it and, unless we have a fair idea about the answers, there will be little coherence in the manner in which transport investment priorities are established. Both NESC (1989) and Chapter 9 of this volume warn of the dangers of pursuing improvements in transport infrastructure in isolation from other considerations. For example, while geographical distance has obvious economic consequences in terms of the costs that it imposes, there are other 'distances' — cultural and social distances — that are significant and costly to overcome. Measures to eliminate or reduce these barriers can also improve accessibility. Similar unevennesses in policy emphasis and focus can no doubt be identified in other sectors where major increases in expenditure are planned. On the other hand, all aspects of structural and human resource development in Ireland lag so far behind the Community that it will take considerable expenditure to bring up the general level.

Conclusion

Ireland is clearly a peripheral region and thus is disadvantaged relative to the core of the EC. Consequently, its economic performance across a range of criteria lags behind the European norm and, in particular, that of the centre. All the economic forces released by the creation of the Single Market will accentuate the differences between the 'core' and 'periphery' by reinforcing the tendency for concentration towards the centre. The Community's structural funds certainly will help to ameliorate the relative deterioration of Ireland's position. However, it is questionable whether the proposed expenditure is based on any cost-benefit analysis of alternative expenditure structures. Improvements of all aspects of infrastructure — in particular transport — and the general raising of production efficiency have been emphasised. Perhaps a more effective approach would have been to concentrate expenditure on those areas where Ireland has, or could create, comparative advantage based on innovation, human capital, a clean environment and other natural resources.

The success of the Community in promoting convergence amongst the regions of the EC has been equivocal (even allowing for enlargements). This lack of success could be taken as evidence of how difficult it is for disadvantaged regions to make gains against market forces that tend to favour the centre. The Single Market proposals are aimed at extending the scope for market processes and enhancing competition. There must be a serious concern about the ability of remoter regions to participate in the opportunities that are expected to follow from the completion of the internal market. The most effective and immediate response for a peripheral region seeking to prepare for these new forces must be to improve its competitiveness. It can do this best by identifying its own particular resource advantage and by playing on its own particular strengths. While the National Plan emphasises important matters such as tourism, more attention must be given to identifying the appropriate areas for Ireland's economic development. The proposals for the use of the structural funds appear to be caught between two stools: they attempt to get some balance between, on the one hand, the very legitimate need for measures that will promote long-term economic development and the more immediate task of improving the economy's competitiveness. The *Plan*'s proposals appear to give too much emphasis to the former at the expense of the latter. It may be politically difficult and financially awkward to break with old structures and long-established priorities. But unless there is an effort made to determine the relative importance of different factors that currently retard the development of Ireland's manufacturing and service sectors and identify how best to deal with them in order to improve the country's competitiveness, Ireland may still find itself unable to benefit fully from the new developments in Europe.

18

Northern Ireland and the Republic of Ireland in the Single Market

RICHARD T. HARRISON

Northern Ireland and the Republic of Ireland share the common features of a peripheral European location, with living conditions and standards significantly below those of the core regions. This position must be viewed in the context of considerable disparities in income levels, unemployment and levels of economic development in Europe (Boltho, 1989), with income per head measured in purchasing power parities in the enlarged Community being almost five times as high in the two richest Community regions as in the two poorest (Commission of the European Communities, 1987). Further, since 1973, regional disparities have widened: although growth in lower income regions has been slightly above the Community average, this has been offset by a faster rate of population growth and by reduced rates of outmigration from weaker regions as the general rise in European unemployment has reduced the opportunities available (Begg, 1989a). These demographic pressures have been compounded by a decline in the number of firms prepared to move to or open new factories in the peripheral and less-developed European regions (Wadley, 1986). This has led to increased and, in the case of the Republic in particular (Chapter 14 above, and Hart and Harrison, 1990), often successful competition for the reduced volume of internationally mobile investment available. This decline, has been offset only in part by an increase in American and Japanese investment in particular to gain a foothold in the perceived post-1992 'fortress Europe'.

However, the influence of 'fortress Europe' on decisions by multinational enterprises about location should not be overemphasised (Panic, 1989). The mechanism by which the completion of the Single European Market will affect economic growth is a straightforward derivative of neoclassical trade theory: the abolition of barriers to trade removes obstacles to entry by foreign producers into national markets, and competitive pressures force domestic firms to improve efficiency and so reduce costs and prices. The outcome, according to the European Commission studies (Cecchini, 1988; Emerson et al., 1988), is the stimulation of demand through lower prices, and leading to greater specialisation, output and employment and to higher incomes. As Begg (1989a, 1989b) has recently pointed out, many of the gains anticipated from completion of the internal market depend not on the static reallocative effects of the removal of barriers, but on the dynamic changes that this will enable to take place. However, many of the underlying tenets of this dynamic macroeconomic approach to integration and customs union are disputed in recent trade theory (Helpman and Krugman, 1985). In addition, regional imbalances of the sort characteristic of the Community are assumed away (Begg, 1989b) and the economists' long run, over which dynamic effects are held to arise, 'can be very long and indeed does not refer to calendar time at all, and in the meantime the short run costs are real' (Desai, 1989).

In the remainder of this chapter, the impact of the completion of the internal market on economic relations between Northern Ireland and the Republic of Ireland will be assessed with respect to, first, the general implications for regional development and policy in the two economies in the wider context of a changing European economy, and second, some specific aspects of relations between the two economies, particularly external trade and cross-border shopping flows.

Regional disparities in Europe

Much of the available data on regional economic disparities in Europe have been summarised with respect to the Irish situation

in a joint report from the Northern Ireland Economic Council
and the National Economic and Social Council (NIEC/NESC,
1988). Using the synthetic index of regional disparity,* devised
by the European Commission to give a multidimensional view
of regional problems, both Northern Ireland and the Republic
of Ireland are ranked near the bottom of the European league.
The top and bottom ten regions in this index are shown in Table
18.1, with the addition of Northern Ireland. The less favoured
regions are, without exception, in the periphery of Europe and
are heavily dependent on agriculture; in contrast, the most
prosperous regions are characterised either by high concentrations
of modern industry or are important administrative and services
centres. Overall, the Republic of Ireland is the sixth weakest
region in Europe, and Northern Ireland is the thirty-third weakest,
elevated in the league table by the significant contribution to
regional GDP made by public sector transfer payments from
the national exchequer in London. Thirty-six regions lie more
than one standard deviation away from the Community average:
these include all of Greece, Portugal, Spain and the Mezzogiorno
of Italy (excluding the Abruzzi), together with Ireland North
and South, emphasising the significant impact of the enlargement
of the Community on the scale and pattern of regional disparities
(Kowalski, 1989).

If, as in the European Commission's view (Cecchini, 1988;
Emerson et al., 1989), the benefits of integration and the
completion of the internal market stem from the improved
allocation of resources, the potential for enhanced, rather than
reduced, regional disparities is clear:

> The Commission is firmly convinced that the completion of
> the Internal Market will provide an indispensable base for
> increasing the prosperity of the Community as a whole. The
> Commission is, however, conscious that there may be risks
> that, by increasing the possibilities for human, material, and
> financial services to move without obstacle to areas of greatest

*The measures used to construct the synthetic index (and their respective weights) are:
GDP per person employed (0.25), as a productivity measure; GDP per head of population
(0.25); unemployment rate adjusted for underemployment (0.40); and prospective labour
force change until 1990 (0.10), as a dynamic element in the index. See Commission
of the European Communities (1987) for further details.

economic advantage, existing discrepancies between regions could be exacerbated and therefore the objective of convergence jeopardized. (Commission of the European Communities, 1985)

Table 18.1: **Regional disparities in the European Community, synthetic index (EC12 = 100)***

Rank	Region	Country	Score
		Bottom Ten	
1	Basilicata	Italy	36.9
2	Calabria	Italy	38.0
3	Andalusia	Spain	38.8
4	Extremadura	Spain	39.2
5	Canaries	Spain	46.1
6	Ireland	Ireland	47.6
7	Sardegna	Italy	49.4
8	Castilla Mancha	Spain	50.0
9	Thrakis	Greece	50.4
10	Molise	Italy	50.6
33	Northern Ireland	UK	64.4
		Top Ten	
1	Darmstadt	Germany	171.8
2	Oberbayern	Germany	165.7
3	Stuttgart	Germany	160.5
4	Hamburg	Germany	158.7
5	Ile de France	France	151.5
6	Karlsruhe	Germany	151.3
7	Luxembourg	Luxembourg	144.2
8	Rheinhessen	Germany	143.4
9	Valle d'Aosta	Italy	142.4
10	West Berlin	Germany	141.7
15	Greater London	UK	135.0

*Bottom ten and top ten regions as measured by the synthetic index, showing the top and bottom ranked regions in the UK for comparison. There are 160 regions defined by the Commission for this analysis.
Source: Commission of the European Communities (1987)

As Begg (1989a) suggests, the Commission's view is that the gains from integration are generated endogenously and come about because of a once-off shift in resource allocation, rather than being the result of an exogenous change such as technological progress. For any region, therefore, the benefits of integration will come from two mechanisms. First, on the assumption that the forecasts of improved performance for the European economy (Emerson et al, 1988) are correct, and there are reasons for supposing that the gains will not be as significant as the Commission's studies suggest (Desai, 1989), at least some of this additional growth will 'trickle down' to all regions, though not evenly. However, the process of regional development since 1973, has led to a widening of inter-regional disparities in the Community. This suggests that these 'trickle down' effects cannot be relied on to remove regional disparities and set currently disadvantaged regions on the periphery of the Community on a growth path significantly above the European average, and above that of those regions currently comprising the core of the 'Golden Triangle' (Vanhove and Klaassen, 1987).

Second, in a dynamic context the process of reallocation and resource movement will lead to net inflows and outflows of factors of production. In the neoclassical world that is assumed in much of the Commission's analysis, the consequent factor cost adjustments, the changes in regional specialisation, and regional patterns of comparative advantage would not be expected to give rise to regional problems. However, experience of the regional development process (Armstrong and Taylor, 1985) suggests that adjustment does not occur in this way. Instead, plant closures (caused by changes in relative factor costs and by the pursuit of economies of scale in an enlarged market), losses of skilled labour (in response to the removal of barriers to mobility), and outflows of capital as exchange controls are lifted, are cumulative in their effects and lead to worsening regional economic problems. It has been argued, therefore, that 'for uncompetitive regions ... the rationalisation of production on which the success of the [Single Market] is predicated could cause severe difficulties' (Begg, 1989a).

There is evidence to suggest that both the Irish and the Northern Irish economies are relatively uncompetitive in a European context. This is a clear conclusion of recent comparative research on the manufacturing sector in Northern Ireland, which suggests that labour productivity levels may be up to 20 per cent below the British average, and in some sectors may be up to 50 per cent below the national figure (Hitchens and Birnie, 1989). In the Republic of Ireland, a long-standing concern of industrial policy has been the lack of competitiveness of much of the indigenous industrial sector, and the general failure of a great deal of foreign direct investment to maximise its contribution to the local economy through local sourcing, technology transfer and management development (Chapter 10 above; Telesis Report, 1982; Kennedy et al., 1989). The past performance, and current position in the European prosperity league table (see Table 18.1), identifies the two Irish economies as relatively uncompetitive, and hence likely to suffer in an integrated Europe.

To offset this potential stimulus to divergence, the 1985 White Paper called for an expansion of the structural funds. These have since doubled in size, with major reallocations to favour Objective 1 regions on the European periphery. Given the considerable debate surrounding the structural fund allocations in 1989, it is important to maintain a perspective on the magnitude and significance of the EC budget in relation to major beneficiaries such as the two Irish economies. The existing scale of EC grants and loans to Northern Ireland and the Republic of Ireland between 1973 and 1986 is summarised in Table 18.2. For Northern Ireland, the European Regional Development Fund (ERDF) represented almost 11 per cent of EC receipts, compared with 7 per cent in the Republic of Ireland. Over the period 1975–84 Ireland received about 6 per cent of total ERDF assistance granted, compared with an estimated 2.6 per cent for Northern Ireland (Table 18.3). These data refer to EC10, i.e. excluding Spain and Portugal. In both economies over the same period, ERDF grants were used primarily to fund infrastructure projects (65.6 per cent in Northern Ireland, 71.3 per cent in the Republic of Ireland) with almost the entire remainder going on industrial projects.

Overall, however, the EC budget represents a small proportion of Community GDP. Between 1972 and 1986 expenditure on the structural funds rose from 4.1 per cent to 16.3 per cent of the Community budget, representing a rise from 0.02 per cent to 0.16 per cent of Community GDP over the

Table 18.2: **EC financial assistance to Northern Ireland and the Republic of Ireland 1973–86**

	Northern Ireland £m	%	Republic of Ireland IR£m	%
EAGGF	652.4	44.8	5568.7	79.1
ERDF	150.1	10.8	499.0	7.1
ESF	273.6	19.6	676.5	9.6
EMS interest subsidies	—	—	229.7	3.2
Special measures for the UK	294.6	21.1	—	—
Urban renewal	52.4	3.8	—	—
Other	—	—	107.7	0.7
Total grant receipt	1396.1	100	7081.7	100

Source: NIEC/NESC (1988)

Table 18.3: **ERDF assistance granted 1975–84**

	Million ECU	% Total ERDF
Belgium	114.41	1.0
Denmark	131.88	1.1
France	1683.51	14.5
Germany	544.79	4.7
Greece	1091.70	9.4
Republic of Ireland	713.44	6.2
Italy	4368.74	37.7
Luxembourg	11.97	0.1
Netherlands	156.18	1.3
United Kingdom	2782.01	24.0
of which: Northern Ireland	299.34	2.6
Total	11598.63	100

Source: Commission of the European Communities (1985) *The European Community and its Regions*

same period (NIEC/NESC, 1988). By 1986, the total Community budget still represented less than one per cent of Community GDP. Given the large share of public expenditure in most European countries, it follows that EC expenditure is dwarfed by the budgets of member states. This is true in the Irish case (Table 18.4). Total EC receipts in 1986 represented 3.2 per cent of total public expenditure in Northern Ireland, having reached a peak of around 7 per cent in 1981–83 because of the grant of almost £300m. for the special programme for Northern Ireland within the framework of the Supplementary Measures for the UK (SMUK). In the Republic of Ireland, although the available data are more restricted in coverage, ERDF expenditure represents about 4.5 per cent of the public capital programme, a percentage that has risen in recent years as the public capital programme has fallen, against a minor increase in ERDF receipts (Table 18.4).

Table 18.4: **EC receipts and public expenditure in Northern Ireland and Republic of Ireland**

| | Northern Ireland | | | Republic of Ireland | | |
	Public Expenditure £m	EC Receipts £m	%	Public Capital Programme IR£m	ERDF Receipts IR£m	%
1973	728	7.5	1.02	—	—	—
1974	907	15.1	1.66	—	—	—
1975	1191	21.5	1.81	470.3	1.8	0.37
1976	1412	33.0	2.33	547.5	8.5	1.55
1977	1594	32.0	2.01	662.7	8.5	1.28
1978	1855	41.5	2.24	815.8	11.1	1.36
1979	2163	61.7	2.85	1022	25.5	2.5
1980	2491	81.2	3.26	1305	46.4	3.5
1981	2831	182.6	6.45	1766	54.6	3.09
1982	3128	230.7	7.37	1898	64.0	3.37
1983	3381	235.4	6.95	1748	56.0	3.2
1984	3621	154.3	4.26	1734	65.3	3.76
1985	3849	169.0	4.39	1695	76.0	4.48
1986 (est)	4114	131.1	3.19	1647	77.1	4.68

Source: NIEC/NESC (1988)

The implication of these figures is clear. Even allowing for the benefits to the two economies, and in particular to that of the Irish Republic, arising from the doubling in size of the structural funds as part of the internal market process, their small-scale relative to total GDP suggests that EC funds will continue to have a primarily ameliorative rather than a transformational effect. The volume of income transfers to these less favoured regions is therefore unlikely significantly to improve the prospects of inter-regional convergence in the Community, a concept that itself is open to multiple interpretations (Sutherland, 1986). As Begg (1989b) has commented, under the 1992 proposals the enhanced structural funds have been cast in the role of an insurance policy for 'losers', rather than as an integral mechanism for furthering aggregate economic growth through balanced regional economic development. Despite the attention given to both the theoretical (Jacquemin and Sapir, 1989a) and empirical (Emerson et al., 1988) implications of the European internal market, the distributional effects between countries have been almost overlooked (Chapter 17 above; Emerson et al., 1988 p. 9).

One framework for analysing some of the regional implications of the internal market proposals has been put forward by Begg (1989b). He distinguishes between three types of impact. First, sector-specific effects on regions arise from the incidence of measures furthering integration in sectors such as food processing, public procurement, road haulage or financial services, where current barriers are a strong deterrent to exporting. Second, national influences on regions will depend in part on the balances of advantage accruing to members of the customs union from the reallocation of production, and more particularly on the dynamic macroeconomic effects of integration. Third, the regional impact of the internal market will be influenced by a range of 'region-specific' attributes and factors, including factor costs and availability, sectoral composition and the policy assistance that is available.

The remainder of this chapter will comment on two issues of particular relevance to understanding economic flows between Northern Ireland and the Republic of Ireland in the context of the internal market. First, among national level influences on the regions, monetary policy, and in particular the choice of exchange rate regime and its influence on trade and competition, is a very important influence on the dynamic macroeconomic impact of the internal market. Second, the harmonisation of national fiscal policy, particularly in respect of indirect taxation, will have a major influence on the likely pattern of cross-border shopping. Two further sets of influences are also relevant. First, among the regionally specific factors influencing the regional and inter-regional impact of the internal market is the location of a region relative to the core of the Community's markets, and in particular the likely effects of the opening of the Channel Tunnel in 1993 on the pattern of peripherality for non-contiguous regions in the Community. Second, among the sector-specific influences identified by Begg (1989b) are the possible expansion of small firms into new markets either directly or through appropriate forms of cross-border cooperation, such as acquisition and joint ventures, and also the impact of rationalisation as opportunities to exploit economies of scale are pursued in economies in which branch plants account for a significant part of economic activity.

Monetary policy and external trade

In its economic performance during the 1980s, the Republic of Ireland compares poorly with the United Kingdom in a number of respects. UK tax rates have fallen, whereas the tax burden in the Republic of Ireland has increased (direct and indirect taxes as a percentage of GDP rose from 35 per cent in 1980 to 46 per cent in 1988). Economic growth in the UK accelerated after 1980, but showed signs of slowing down towards the end of the decade. In contrast, the Republic's economy recovered strongly towards the end of the decade, having stagnated throughout most of the 1980s. Unemployment in the UK fell rapidly in the 1980s, partly due to a series of administrative and definitional changes, whereas unemployment rose in the Republic of Ireland: between 1983 and 1988 the average differential was about seven percentage points.

However, on the monetary front the Republic of Ireland compares more favourably with the UK. As a result of the Republic's full membership of the European Monetary System (EMS), the economy experienced a considerable degree of exchange rate stability in the latter part of the 1983–89 period, compared with the high degree of volatility in sterling over the last six or seven years. This is most clearly indicated from a comparison of effective exchange rates for the UK and the Republic of Ireland (Figure 18.1). The volatility of sterling of

Figure 18.1: **United Kingdom and Republic of Ireland effective exchange rates (1985 = 100)**

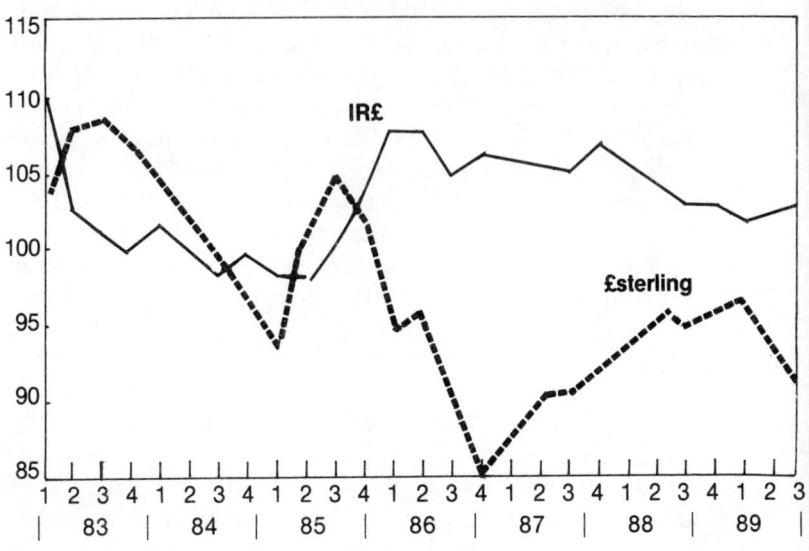

Figure 18.2: **United Kingdom and Republic of Ireland exchange rate (£ sterling per IR£)**

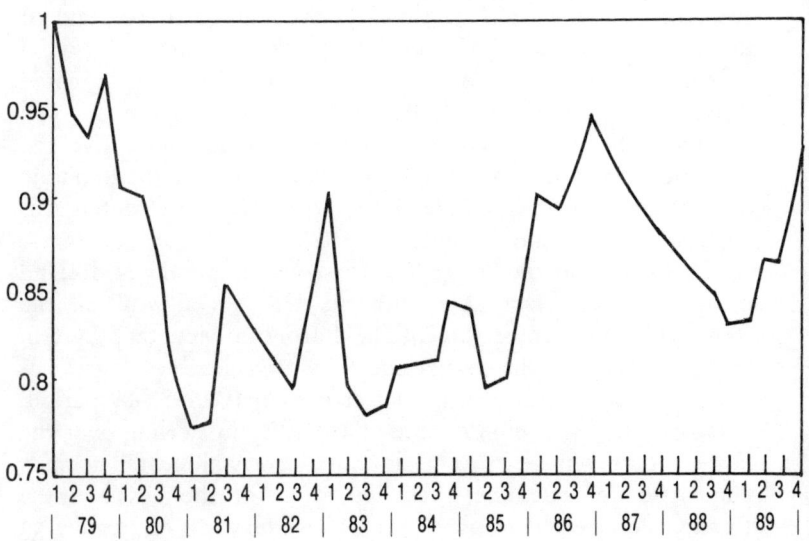

course is reflected in particular in the direct £ sterling/IR£ exchange rate which has fluctuated substantially (Figure 18.2). Partly as a result of EMS membership, the Republic had lower interest rates and lower inflation than the UK at the end of the decade. Furthermore, in contrast to record UK balance of payments deficits, the Republic's balance of payments was in surplus in the latter years of the 1980s. There has been a significant turnaround in the Republic's public finances as the Exchequer borrowing requirement as a percentage of GDP has declined. Moreover, the visible trade surplus has increased significantly, largely because of considerable export growth and the slower import growth that is attributable to sluggish domestic demand (Table 18.5). As the ESRI medium-term assessment makes clear (on the basis, *inter alia*, of an assumption that the tax harmonisation proposals of the Single European Act will be neutral in impact, with higher expenditure taxes offsetting lost excise and tax revenues, and the fact that there will be full implementation of the National Development Plan proposals), this positive picture was predicted to continue, and to result in significant GNP growth and reduced unemployment, as is indicated in Table 18.6 (ESRI, 1989).

Table 18.5: **Irish balance of payments 1984–88**

	1984	1985	1986	1987	1988
Visible trade (IR£m)	–197	+137	+435	+1310	+2025
Current balance of payments (IR£m)	–945	–650	–509	+239	+437

Source: Central Statistics Office, Ireland

The external trade statistics for the Republic of Ireland are summarised in greater detail in Table 18.7. During the 1980s an initial trade deficit was converted to a significant surplus, largely as the result of the rapid expansion of exports to North America and to European Community countries apart from the UK. From the data, a number of particular features stand out. First, Ireland's trading pattern has been moving away progressively from its once heavy dependence on Britain, which accounted for only 38 per cent of imports and 29 per cent of Irish exports in 1988, having been 47 per cent and 36 per cent respectively in 1980. Second, Irish trading patterns have become more strongly orientated towards the rest of the European Community and to the United States and Canada. Imports from North America increased threefold and exports quadrupled (in nominal price terms) between 1980 and 1988, although the Irish economy continued to run a heavy deficit with North America. Of greater significance is the fact that between 1980 and 1988 the percentage of Irish exports destined for other member states increased from 32 per cent to almost 39 per cent. As a result, Britain has been overtaken by the rest of the EC as the single most important trading partner for the Irish economy, a situation first recorded in 1982, since when the gap has grown constantly. Third, Irish trade with countries other than the EC and North America has not expanded as rapidly as the overall volume of trade, and accordingly the share of Irish trade attributed to these residual categories fell slightly in the 1980s. Fourth, the relative significance of recorded North-South trade fell during the 1980s, although not quite as substantially as was the case with trade with Britain. Although the value of imports from and exports to Northern Ireland has expanded significantly in nominal terms (Table 18.7), this has been at a slower rate than the rate of increase in the value of Irish external trade. As a result, Northern Ireland accounts for only 3.8 per cent of Irish imports and 6.2

Table 18.6: **ESRI medium-term forecast**

	1988	1989	1990	1991	1992	1993	1994
GNP growth (%, real terms)	1.6	4.0	7.1	5.6	4.6	4.8	3.2
Balance of payments (% GNP)	+2.3	+3.0	+2.6	+2.4	+2.8	+2.4	+3.1
Exchequer borrowing requirement (% GNP)	−3.3	−4.0	−1.3	+1.2	+2.3	+2.9	+3.9
Unemployment rate (%)	16.6	16.0	14.6	13.4	13.0	12.8	12.7
Inflation (%, consumer prices)	2.0	3.3	4.2	4.2	3.5	3.0	3.5

Source: Economic and Social Research Institute, *Medium-Term Review 1989–1994.*

Table 18.7: **Ireland: imports and exports classified by area of origin/destination**

	Imports (£m)			Exports (£m)		
	1980	1988	% Change	1980	1988	% Change
Northern Ireland	223.5	391.6	75.2	300.4	757.0	152.0
	(4.1)	(3.8)		(7.4)	(6.2)	
Britain	2531.2	3910.2	54.5	1463.4	3592.1	145.5
	(46.7)	(38.2)		(35.8)	(29.2)	
Other EC	1087.1	2450.2	125.4	1310.1	4752.3	262.7
	(20.1)	(24.0)		(32.1)	(38.6)	
Other Europe	356.0	561.5	57.7	267.0	785.6	194.2
	(6.6)	(5.5)		(6.5)	(6.4)	
US and Canada	547.8	1717.5	213.5	269.4	1070.8	297.5
	(10.1)	(16.8)		(6.6)	(8.7)	
Other countries	675.1	1182.2	75.1	472.3	1342.9	184.3
	(12.5)	(11.6)		(11.6)	(10.9)	
Total	5420.7	10213.1	88.4	4082.5	123007	201.3
	(100)	(100)		(100)	(100)	

Note: Percentage distribution in parenthesis
Source: Central Statistics Office, *Trade Statistics of Ireland.*

per cent of exports, compared with 4.1 per cent and 7.4 per cent respectively in 1980.

One element in the strong visible trade performance, and in particular the export performance, of the Republic's economy during the 1980s was the exchange rate stability consequent upon EMS membership. As De Grauwe (1987) has recently pointed out, the success of the EMS in stabilising exchange rates has had a positive impact on intra-EMS trade, and it is reasonable to suggest that Ireland has benefited from this. Certainly, the evidence from Table 18.7 that the external trade of the Republic has been reorientated away from the UK to other member states, which now constitute Ireland's largest export market, has been facilitated by the relative stability of exchange rates. By contrast, a recent econometric analysis of intra-EC trade for the 'Big Four' (France, West Germany, Italy and UK) suggests that the

UK has had a systematically inferior trade account with the Community since 1973, although the difference between the UK and the other three countries narrowed between 1973 and 1983 (Jacquemin and Sapir, 1989b).

The strong external trade performance of the Irish economy recorded in Table 18.7 also reflects the influence of a number of other factors, including the role of intra-corporate trade (which in part accounts for the sharp relative increase in imports from North America) and patterns of multinational market access (where Ireland has been chosen as a production base for entry to the EC market, thus contributing to the strong recorded export performance in other EC markets). This success also reflects an improving competitive position of the Irish economy with respect to the European Community and the United Kingdom.

Table 18.8: **Variations in industrial labour costs (Measured in ECUs)**

Monthly labour costs: EC12 = 100	1978	1981	1984	Average
West Germany	131.3	113.5	114.6	119.8
France	103.6	106.0	99.0	102.8
Italy	75.8	77.9	88.2	80.6
Netherlands	131.7	109.9	107.9	116.5
Belgium	133.1	118.5	98.1	116.6
Luxembourg	127.4	102.6	89.8	106.6
UK	65.0	87.2	80.9	77.7
Northern Ireland	56.4	75.8	69.4	67.2
Republic of Ireland	64.1	72.4	81.2	72.6
Denmark	121.2	101.2	98.9	107.1
Greece	na	48.8	35.6	na
Spain	49.6	54.7	50.4	51.6
Portugal	24.0	24.7	22.0	23.6
EUR-12	100.0	100.0	100.0	100.0

Source: Begg (1989a, p. 92)

There are considerable disparities in industrial labour costs in Europe (Table 18.8) which tend to be fairly stable over time (the main exception being the UK, where labour costs appear to have risen sharply to 1981 and then fallen back again, due largely to exchange rate fluctuations). Although industrial labour costs in the Republic of Ireland are slightly higher than in Northern Ireland, both are about 12–15 per cent below UK levels, around 30 per cent below average EC levels, and less than half the level in the highest cost regions of the Community. Furthermore, the competitiveness of the Republic of Ireland with respect to its EMS partners has improved further since the 1986 IR£ devaluation. This favourable industrial labour cost position in Ireland has been reinforced by an encouraging productivity performance in the Irish economy relative to those in Britain and Northern Ireland (Figure 18.3). Despite the lower levels of labour productivity in Northern Ireland relative to Britain (Hitchins and Birnie, 1989), productivity growth in the two economies has been similar since 1983, with a relative slowdown in Northern Ireland since 1987. In the Republic of Ireland, by contrast, productivity growth has been much more rapid than in the UK, and this will enhance the competitive position of the Irish economy in European markets relative to the economy of Northern Ireland.

Figure 18.3:   **Productivity growth: United Kingdom, Northern Ireland and Republic of Ireland: manufacturing (1985 = 100)**

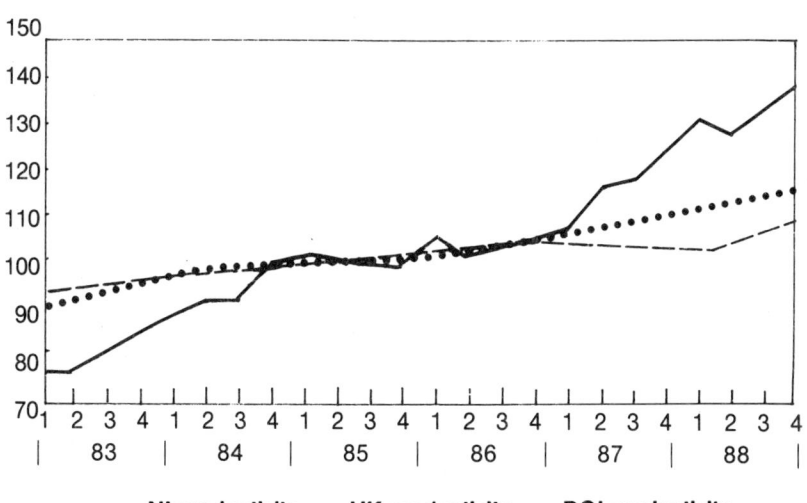

-— NI productivity ••• UK productivity ——ROI productivity

Figure 18.4: **Percentage of manufacturing sales by region (Third Quarter 1989)**

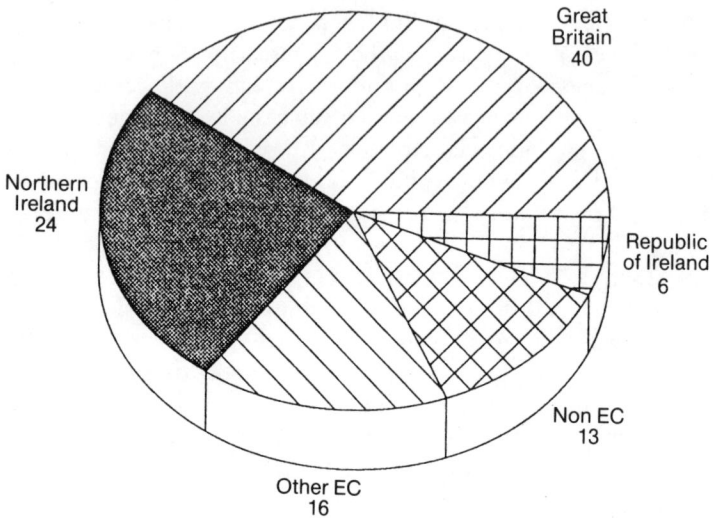

As Table 18.7 has indicated, the volume and relative significance of recorded cross-border trade is minor, and fell as a percentage of total Irish external trade in the 1980s. Although comprehensive data are not available for Northern Ireland, it is estimated that the Republic of Ireland accounts for about 6 per cent of manufacturing sales by Northern Ireland firms, equivalent to around 8 per cent of sales outside Northern Ireland (Figure 18.4). The changing sectoral composition of trade between Northern Ireland and the Republic of Ireland is shown in Table 18.9, using the section and division breakdown of the Standard International Trade Classification (SITC). A number of features of the inter-sectoral pattern of trade stand out. First, recorded cross-border trade is dominated by food and live animals (Section 0), which account for around one-third of imports from the North and 40 per cent of exports to the North. In both cases the figures for the 1980s are rather lower than the 1972 position (Section 0 represented 45 per cent of imports from and 48 per cent of exports to Northern Ireland). Within Section 0, the most important division has been the trade in live animals, although this is also the least reliable set of figures in the trade statistics because of distortions in the pattern of movement resulting from the operation of the Common Agricultural Policy (CAP). However, although live animals still represent 18 per cent of total exports to Northern Ireland (reflecting the economics of the CAP and the meat-processing industry), live animals are now an insignificant element in imports by the Republic of Ireland from Northern Ireland, down to under 3 per cent of the total in 1988, compared with 13 per cent in 1980 and 39 per cent in 1972. As Matthews (1989) has recently argued, the development of the agriculture and food-processing sectors in the Republic of Ireland is likely to be affected by a wide range of factors other than the Single Market process, and it is here that the

Table 18.9: **Republic of Ireland: exports to and imports from Northern Ireland (percent)**

SITC	Imports			Exports		
	1972	1980	1988	1972	1980	1988
Section 0 Food and Live Animals	44.5	34.0	31.7	47.9	39.6	41.9
of which: Division 00 Live Animals	39.1	13.4	2.8	27.5	13.8	18.1
Section 1 Beverages and tobacco	1.9	1.6	6.4	7.4	4.5	4.1
Section 2 Crude materials, except fuels	5.4	4.5	3.7	2.8	3.7	4.2
Section 3 Minerals, fuels	0.7	0.9	0.5	1.6	0.7	1.0
Section 4 Animal and vegetable oils	1.0	0.5	0.5	0.4	0.9	0.4
Section 5 Chemicals	3.2	10.7	14.6	2.4	5.1	5.9
Section 6 Manufactured goods	26.7	27.0	19.8	19.9	19.5	15.8
Section 7 Machinery and transport equipment	4.0	6.5	10.0	2.5	14.9	13.2
Section 8 Other manufactured articles	8.2	9.9	10.8	8.8	10.8	12.6
Section 9 Other	4.0	1.3	2.0	6.4	0.4	1.0
Total	100	100	100	100	100	100

Source: Central Statistics Office

future implications for this most important aspect of cross-border trade lie.

Secondly, between 1972 and 1980, both imports and exports of manufactured goods (i.e. sections 5–8 of the SITC) grew, with most of the increased share, particularly in exports, coming from the machinery and transport equipment sector. Exports of manufactured goods from the Republic of Ireland to Northern Ireland as a share of total exports declined slightly, while imports of manufactured products as a percentage of total imports remained substantially the same. By 1988, however, trade in manufactured goods had fallen to about 40 per cent of cross-border trade in Sections 6–8 combined, with the sharpest falls recorded in Section 6, and in specific sectors such as textiles and non-metallic minerals. In other sectors, the most notable features were a sharp progressive rise in imports of chemicals and allied goods, almost entirely accounted for by fertiliser imports, which represented over 11 per cent of Irish imports from Northern Ireland in 1988, and a similar rise in imports of beverages and tobacco, almost exclusively accounted for by beverages (6.3 per cent of Irish imports from the North in 1988).

Yet in value terms, exports from the Republic of Ireland to Northern Ireland in the 1980s rose twice as rapidly as imports and, as a result, the surplus on visible trade with the North had risen from IR£77m. in 1980 to IR£365m. by 1988. Given recent trends in competitiveness between the two economies, and the exchange rate stability consequent on the Republic of Ireland's membership of the EMS, this North-South trade gap is likely to widen further, even allowing for a further progressive reorientation of the Republic's export trade to other EC countries. The implications for Northern Ireland and its trading position vis-à-vis the Republic of eventual full UK membership of the EMS will depend critically on the exchange rate parities determined on entry, and the width of the band established for £ sterling fluctuations within the exchange rate mechanism. However, even if this does provide a necessary stimulus to UK export performance in general (Davies, 1989), the continued existence of supply constraints and competitiveness problems in major sections of the Northern Ireland economy will reduce the extent to which these UK-wide benefits will affect significantly the existing pattern of cross-border trade.

Fiscal policy and cross-border shopping

There is little doubt that the Commission's fiscal proposals have become one of the most politically contentious aspects of the internal market programme, with the result that implementation as originally proposed is highly unlikely (Kay and Smith, 1989). Although, under the assumption of full capital mobility, it is technically feasible for the member states to maintain fixed exchange rates through coordinated monetary policy in a single market while maintaining independent fiscal policies, existing levels of European interdependence make it "hard to avoid the conclusion that this [fiscal harmonisation] is the systematic change most needed in the near future" (Krugman, 1989). Furthermore, fiscal harmonisation will have a major impact on consumer welfare (Borooah, 1980) and on the pattern of cross-border shopping in particular (Fitzgerald et al., 1988).

The Commission's proposals for fiscal harmonisation have been discussed in detail elsewhere (Kay and Smith, 1989). In essence, the Commission originally proposed a partial harmonisation of VAT rates, with member states free to choose a higher rate in the range 14–20 per cent and a lower rate in the range 4–9 per cent. This compares with the present UK rate of 15 per cent standard, with a zero rate on selected goods (including food, books and newspapers), and with a standard rate of 23 per cent in the Republic of Ireland, with reduced rates of zero and 10 per cent in 1990. It is likely that exemptions, such as the UK's zero-rating of food and children's clothing, will remain after harmonisation (Borooah, 1990). Excise duties for 1986 in the UK and the Republic of Ireland, along with the Commission's proposals, are shown in Table 18.10. The major difference between the Republic of Ireland and the UK is in the scale of excise duties imposed on alcoholic drinks, with smaller differences in excise duties on hydrocarbon oils. For both economies, however, there will be substantial reductions in the taxation levels for alcoholic drinks, which are of such a magnitude to make it impossible to predict their effects through conventional forecasting methods (Kay and Smith, 1989). The Commission's proposals represent a major change for both the UK and the Republic of Ireland in the structure of tobacco excise duties, which will have very little impact on the relative prices between the two economies. Finally, although excise duties on hydrocarbon oils are higher in Ireland than in the UK, as Table 18.10 shows, both economies will face the same shift in the structure of recommended duties to significantly favour diesel, with possible consequences for new car-purchasing behaviour in both economies. On the assumption that spending patterns will remain unchanged, the revenue consequences of fiscal approximation, including both VAT and excise duty changes, are as follows (Kay and Smith, 1989):

	percentage of indirect tax receipts	percentage of total tax receipts
UK	+2	+0.6
Ireland	−10	−4.4

Table 18.10: **Excise duties in the United Kingdom and Republic of Ireland (in ECUs, April 1986)**

	UK	Republic of Ireland	Commission Proposal
Alcoholic Drinks			
Spirits (per 0.75 litre bottle)	7.45	8.17	3.81
Wine (per litre)	1.54	2.79	0.71
Beer (per litre)	0.68	1.13	0.17
Cigarettes			
Specific tax	0.96	1.00	0.39
Ad valorem tax (%, incl VAT)	34	35	52–54
Hydrocarbon Oils (per litre)			
Petrol	0.31	0.38	0.34
Derv	0.26	0.29	0.18
Gas oil (domestic heating)	0.17	0.24	0.50

Source: Kay and Smith (1989)

As Fitzgerald et al. (1988) noted, VAT plus excise duties in the Republic of Ireland represent 15.6 per cent of GDP, only marginally below the figure for Denmark (15.7 per cent) and significantly higher than for the UK (10.7 per cent) or Italy (at 7.1 per cent, the lowest figure in the Community, EC-9). Based on a detailed analysis of the relative prices of key commodities affected by excise duties (spirits, beer, petrol and colour televisions), Fitzgerald et al. (1988) demonstrated a widening gap between prices, in Northern Ireland and in the Republic of Ireland, which is substantially due to rising excise duties in the Republic, often exacerbated by exchange rate movements, and to a much lesser extent due to changes in relative tax-exclusive prices. With respect to the latter, the most significant change occurred in the period 1985–87 since tax exclusive prices in the Republic did not adjust downwards in response to the devaluation of sterling. As a result of these price differences, the removal of border controls as part of the deregulation of the internal market would lead to a significant redistribution of trade to Northern Ireland, intensifying existing trends. Even in the absence of the Commission's fiscal harmonisation proposals, the scale of cross-border shopping and the consequent loss of revenue and trade (particularly for traders in the border counties) makes a realignment of VAT and excise duties between the Republic of Ireland and the UK a necessity.

From the Economic and Social Research Institute's analysis of cross-border shopping (Fitzgerald et al., 1988) a number of conclusions can be drawn. First, the cross-border trade in consumer goods in 1986 was ·about IR£200 million, equivalent to 2 per cent of personal consumers' expenditure. At its peak, cross-border shopping is estimated to have represented up to 6 per cent of total consumer spending in Northern Ireland (TSB, 1987). This includes both the expenditure of households on shopping trips from the Republic to Northern Ireland and an estimate of IR£60 million for commercially smuggled spirits and television sets. However, the estimates exclude the legal importation of goods by retailers who bypass domestic distribution channels because of higher tax exclusive prices in the Republic of Ireland. If the tax exclusive price differential in favour of the North continues in the Single Market, the scale of this trade may be expected to increase, with negative implications for employment in the distribution sector in the Republic. Emphasising the predominant South-North flow in cross-border shopping, the ESRI study estimated that only IR£7 million was spent in the Republic by shoppers from the North, mainly on clothing, the tax on which was lower in the Republic. From survey evidence, it appears that households in the Republic have an exaggerated perception of price differentials between the two jurisdictions, which has stimulated the volume of cross-border shopping to levels above those expected on the basis of tax-inclusive price differentials only.

Second, the introduction in March 1987 of the "48-hour rule" restricting shopping in Northern Ireland (and in the rest of the EC) is likely to have had its most marked effect on the shopping patterns of those furthest from the border, particularly those who have organised coach trips to the North, and to have had less impact on private motorists and those living close to the border. Fitzgerald et al. have commented that "the change in regulations did bring about a significant reduction in cross-border shopping, especially by those living far from the border, but . . . the volume of such shopping by border households still remains substantial. Clearly the change in regulations will have had little effect on commercial smuggling" (Fitzgerald et al., 1988).

Third, cross-border shopping has particularly serious implications for border areas. Part of the recorded trade, of course, will reflect convenience factors and would occur in the absence of price differentials. Survey evidence for 1986 suggests that for households living in border counties, two-thirds of petrol, almost all alcohol bought for consumption at home, and two-thirds of certain consumer items were bought in Northern Ireland. Cross-border shopping represented about 10 per cent of the total expenditure of households in border areas. Based on an analysis of the sensitivity of purchases to the magnitude of the North-South price differential, Fitzgerald et al. (1988) conclude that much of the cross-border trade in petrol, food and groceries would disappear if existing price differentials were reduced by half, but that the reduction that would be required to affect trade in alcohol and consumer goods (particularly commercial smuggling) may have to be much greater. There is a high degree of substitution between purchases of spirits in Northern Ireland and in the Republic. Changes in the price differential, if excise duties are equalised following completion of the internal market, may be expected to lead a reduction in cross-border purchases.

Fourth, on the assumptions that all cross-border shopping were to be contained within the Republic and that spending patterns were to remain unchanged, exchequer revenues would have been up to IR£100 million higher in 1986. However, the actual receipts from a complete reorientation of shopping patterns would be less than this because spending patterns do change in line with relative price changes. More generally, Fitzgerald et al. (1988) suggested that, for commodities at least, fiscal harmonisation may not have negative consequences for budgetary policy. In particular, reductions in tax-inclusive prices in the Republic to levels closer to those obtaining in Northern Ireland will tend, in the case of goods such as spirits and television sets where commercial smuggling is significant, to leave total tax revenues unchanged as consumers' shift spending from smuggled (non-taxed) to legitimate (taxed, but at lower rates than at present) purchases. Yet this situation will not apply for other commodities. Outside the border counties, the ESRI study suggested that quite significant cross-border price differentials can remain for everyday items and foods that are difficult to transport or store, without seriously distorting private individuals' shopping patterns. However, in border counties this does not apply, and the negative impact of North-South price differentials on turnover, profits, wages and employment in the retail trades will continue in the absence of substantial price harmonisation. Furthermore, fiscal harmonisation will deal only with part of the problem, because for many of the commodities affected by cross-border shopping, tax exclusive prices are lower in Northern Ireland than in the Republic. As a result there is an incentive, already reflected in the illegal cross-border trade in spirits, for retailers and wholesalers in the Republic to source their supplies north of the border. Although the processes involved are complex, and the outcomes only partially understood, a convergence of cross-border tax-inclusive and tax-exclusive prices arising from fiscal harmonisation on the one hand and from the elimination of high margins accruing to either importers or foreign producers on the other will have a negative impact on the level of activity in the Republic's distribution sector (Fitzgerald, 1989). However: "if there is not a rapid approximation of tax exclusive wholesale prices on the completion of the internal market this would have very serious implications for the distribution trade in Ireland" (Fitzgerald et al. 1988).

Conclusion

According to the EC Commission's analysis, the creation of an internal market of 320 million people will lead to a substantial gain in economic welfare as costs and prices fall and, after some time lag, the greater dynamism of the competitive process will stimulate trade, promote new investment, lead to the restructuring and internationalisation of firms, stimulate location changes and foster technological change. As a result, increased growth and employment will ensue (Commission of the European Communities, 1988).

As part of the process of harmonisation for the Single Market, there is scope to eliminate major distortions in economic relations. Notable among these is the significant volume of cross-border shopping in Ireland, which at its peak represented about 2 per cent of consumer spending in the Republic (and 10 per cent of the spending of households in border counties), equivalent to around 6 per cent of consumer spending in Northern Ireland. On the assumption that VAT and excise duty rates will be approximately harmonised, and that tax-exclusive prices in Northern Ireland and in the Republic also converge as the internal market process advances, much of this cross-border shopping will disappear. In part, the exchequer loss in the Republic arising from lower VAT and excise duties will be offset by increased legal and recorded consumption, as legitimate purchases replace the consumption of smuggled goods, notably spirits and television sets. In part also, the removal of the cross-border distortion, as prices in the Republic fall following fiscal approximation, if not full harmonisation, will provide a minor stimulus to exchequer revenues because purchases in the Republic will be substituted for those in Northern Ireland. However, this will not be sufficient to make an impact on the net revenue loss arising from fiscal harmonisation (Kay and Smith, 1989).

The impact of monetary integration on the other aspect of North-South economic flows discussed in this chapter — visible trade — is rather less easy to predict. The Irish economy increasingly has orientated itself away from an overdependence on the UK market, and in export terms in particular has developed strong ties with other EC economies and with North America. Given its competitive and wage cost advantage over the UK economy, the Irish economy may be better placed than the Northern economy to take advantage of any increased trade, within and outside the Community, that results from completion of the internal market. However, the precise nature of this advantage will depend crucially on when and at what rate the UK becomes a full member of the EMS. If the Irish government takes the opportunity of eventual UK entry to return to parity, a great deal of the administrative obstruction to trade with the UK, and with Northern Ireland in particular, would be removed. This may well act as a stimulus to greater cross-border trade, particularly among small companies making their first move outside the local market, for whom barriers such as exchange rate differences, even if contained within the exchange-rate-mechanism of the EMS, are significant impediments to trade. If, on the other hand, full entry to the EMS occurred at a punt/sterling exchange rate of, for example, between 85 and 90 pence, this would provide Irish exporters with a competitive edge and would reinforce the fiscal deterrent to cross-border shopping.

However, as was argued in the first section of this chapter, the major determinant of the reaction of the two Irish economies to the completion of the internal market will be their position as less-developed peripheral regions. Although the Commission's analysis of the economics of the Single Market paid almost no attention to the differential regional impact of the Single European Act proposals, the expansion of the structural funds is a tacit recognition than in the Single Market there will be losers as well as winners. The description of both Northern Ireland and the Republic as Objective 1 regions is a recognition both of the scale of the economic development problem and of the need to concentrate EC resources in such regions to facilitate the Single Market adjustment process. However, relative to the scale of domestic public expenditure in the two jurisdictions, the scale of EC structural fund expenditure is minor. It is difficult to escape the conclusion that the level of funding is ameliorative rather than transformational. If regions such as Northern Ireland and the Republic of Ireland are not to experience a major deterioration of their position relative to the core economies of the Community, consideration needs to be given, on distributional grounds, to a major strengthening of regional policy in the Community (Begg, 1989a). In particular, regional policy would have to become a truly European policy, rather than just a collection of national policies, and thus mirror the Europeanisation of fiscal, monetary and external trade policies. Without such a strengthening of the role of regional policy, much of the prospective benefit of the completion of the internal market will leave the two Irish economies, not only geographically but also economically, on the fringe of Europe.

19

Conclusions

MICHAEL MULREANY and ANTHONY FOLEY

The Single Market programme is essentially an exercise in removing fiscal, technical and administrative barriers to trade. Most of its proposals were part of earlier aspirations for the European Community. Indeed, the initial response was muted, as was evidenced by Margaret Thatcher, the British Prime Minister's assessment of the Single European Act as a 'modest decision' (Bressand, 1990). However, the Single Market programme gained credibility and momentum and outgrew the EC Commission's 279 measures on market integration by giving an increased impetus to monetary union, institutional reform, social cohesion and political union. The attitudes of European businesses towards EC markets also have become more positive.

By early 1990, every one of the White Paper measures had been drawn up and put to the European Council; indeed, roughly 60 per cent of them had been passed. As the Single Market programme has evolved, fresh proposals have arisen in such fields as public procurement and financial services. Considerable progress has been made in proposals to remove technical barriers. However, particular problems have been encountered with tax measures, many of which give rise to national sensitivities in some member states about revenue losses, or the effects of the measures on producers and consumers. Tax decisions by the European Council require unanimity, and extended debate seems likely to lead to a breach of the December 1992 deadline. However, this need not be fatal to the Single Market programme:

there are other ways, such as more limited harmonisation, to deal with the problems raised by variations in indirect tax and its administration (Kay 1988, Pinder 1989). Even if indirect taxation is not harmonised, market forces could be expected to narrow differentials as people shift purchases over borders to low tax countries — unless administrative barriers prevent them from doing so.

Chapter 7 presents an estimate, based on the EC Commission's original proposals, of the loss of indirect tax revenue to the Irish exchequer. Although by mid-1990 agreement on indirect tax measures had not been reached it seems inevitable that for Ireland there will be a loss of indirect tax revenue. On the expenditure side of the budget the Irish exchequer may gain from cheaper tenders for public procurement contracts from firms in other member states. However, there already is a significant degree of competition in public procurement in Ireland and where gains can be made they are likely to be limited.

Leaving aside these sensitive issues, the great majority of the Single Market measures will be passed before 1993. However, their enforcement could give rise to problems. Member states are permitted one-and-a-half years to comply with EC directives by altering national laws or amending administrative rules. By January 1990 only 14 Single Market measures out of a possible 88 had been implemented in the national laws of all member states (*The Economist*, 20 January 1990). Of course, this disguises the fact that some member states had implemented over 50 of the measures, but it illustrates the time-lag in achieving universal implementation. Moreover, implementation is quite different from observance. In 1989 the EC Commission examined almost 1,400 complaints about unfair barriers to trade. Once again there are time-lags. More importantly, to the extent that governments, either intentionally or by accident, frustrate the operation of the Single Market measures, then the less will be the benefits. Indeed the programme to some extent may be a victim of its own success: the speed with which it has progressed may have rendered its institutions ill-equipped to referee national governments.

The EC's previous attempts to promote market access have not always been successful. In public procurement, for example, since 1971 there has been a requirement that construction contracts exceeding 1m ecu must be put out to tender throughout the Community. Since 1977 there has been a similar requirement for public purchasing orders exceeding 200,000 ecu. However, by 1988 only about 2 per cent of contracts were being awarded to other member states.

Competition policy is a major safeguard against the frustration of Single Market benefits by private business or by government. Monopolistic practices or government intervention to protect 'national champions' could prevent the anticipated price reductions. The EC Commission is alert to this danger (Emerson et al., 1988, pp. 178–80), but, without action, potential benefits may be lost.

Moreover, realistic appraisal of a more integrated EC market must discount illusory gains. The EC responded to the barriers imposed by customs delays and formalities by implementing a number of customs measures in 1988. Among these measures was the introduction of a Single Administrative Document; this replaced over 200 EC administrative documents. It has been argued that the Single Administrative Document is complex and that there has been little change in the workload borne by hauliers and agents (Campbell, Pepper and Barnes, 1989). This particular problem may be overcome by increased harmonisation of health safety and technical standards or by the replacement of the Single Administrative Document or removal of the need for cross-frontier documents. The general problem of illusory gains, however, could persist in certain areas.

Fortunately, the Single Market programme has coincided with a period of growth in both the EC economy and in the world economy. Previous EC initiatives, such as the 1970 Werner Report on monetary union, were undermined by international recession. It was made clear in Chapter 4 that the outlook for the world economy and the EC economy is reasonably favourable because inflation and fiscal imbalances have been reduced. The duration of the current cycle of growth indicates that there have been structural improvements in world economies. Forecasts are hazardous, but it seems likely that growth in the world economy will continue to accompany the Single Market programme and assist its implementation.

The Single Market is just one element in the EC economy. EC and, *a fortiori*, world economic growth would have occurred in the absence of the Single Market programme. A rudimentary 'with-without' test indicates that the globalisation of captial markets, the increasing internationalisation of business and the trend toward deregulation would have progressed independently. The Single Market programme, however, worked with the grain of these developments and contributed to them.

Without the Single Market, there would have been independent development, but the programme has given rise to the prospect of additional economic growth in the EC. The EC Commission assessed the following effects on economic activity: the removal of trade barriers, the exploitation of economies of scale, improvements in business efficiency due to increased competition, and reductions in border delays. The growth effect of the Single Market was forecast as between 4.3 per cent and 6.4 per cent over the medium term. However, the Commission's estimate omitted some 'dynamic' factors, such as increased innovation. Baldwin (1989) has argued that significant dynamic gains should be added to the EC Commission's estimate.

The growth effects of the Single Market programme are discussed more fully in Chapter 4. The potential benefits are predicated on factors such as the maintenance of competition. Moreover, the growth effects must be seen in the context of continuing economic problems in the EC, such as the relatively high rate of unemployment. Thus, although the Single Market is a welcome fillip to economic performance, it is not a solution to the EC's economic problems.

Growth in the EC economy also raises distributional questions. We have already adverted to one distributional issue in stressing the need for a competition policy. In the absence of such a policy, some of the potential for price reduction induced by the Single Market will not be realised by consumers, and income will be distributed in favour of producers. Income also can be distributed among factors of production. If, for example, trade liberalisation enables greater specialisation in a member state's exports, then the factor of production that is more intensively used as a result will experience a relative price rise. Relative factor prices might also be affected by the wage provisions of the Social Charter. However, as was argued in Chapter 16, the Social Charter may have a relatively negligible effect.

Distributional issues among member states give rise to the

greatest concern. There is much historical evidence that customs unions have detracted from economic development in some regions and have promoted it in others (Padoa-Schioppa, 1987, pp. 21–22). The Single Market programme, and particularly the process of monetary union, have given rise to fears that labour and capital will move from the peripheral regions of the EC to the core areas. This argument is developed in Chapters 2, 3, 17 and 18 and we shall return to it below. However, we note here the difficulty in making structural adjustments in peripheral nations and the inadequacy of the EC budget for this purpose. In 1989 the EC budget was equivalent to just 1.1 per cent of Community GDP, but it was a higher percentage of Community investment and public development funding. The magnitude of the task of tackling the EC's regional imbalance is illustrated by the fact that, even with the increased structural funds, the size of the EC budget in 1992 will be less than half of what was considered necessary by the MacDougall Report in 1977 to have a significant redistribution effect (Shackleton, 1989, p. 139).

The Single Market programme has raised questions about growth and distribution within the EC but has also caused some uncertainty about the Community's economic relations with other major trading blocs. Just as '1992' is the colloquial expression for the Single Market within the EC, 'Fortress Europe' is its counterpart in non-EC countries. Both are misnomers. The Single Market programme culminates at the end of 1992; it is not an event in 1992. The Single Market is in essence concerned with deregulation and improved market access; it is not primarily protectionist in intent, though admittedly, some member states responding to domestic pressures may propose protectionist measures. It is correct that a major motivation for the Single Market was the desire to improve the competitivness of EC industry *vis à vis* Japan and the USA. These countries were perceived to have integrated domestic markets that placed them at an advantage over the fragmented EC economy. This fragmentation obstructed the realisation of economies of scale and imposed cost burdens on firms in the form of technical and other barriers.

The Single Market measures will indeed confer benefits on EC industry that will improve competitiveness but, as was argued in Chapter 3, industries from other countries can benefit from the programe. For example, a non-EC exporter selling to several EC countries before the implementation of Single Market measures bore the initial cost imposed by the common external tariff barrier and the further costs associated with moving goods between member states and with satisfying different national standards. These latter costs will be reduced. On the other hand, EC firms will not benefit from reciprocal reductions in non-tariff barriers in other trading blocs. In such cases, of course, there may be trade diversion from non-EC producers to cheaper sources of supply within the EC which better fit the fortress analogy. However some of the anxiety among the EC's trading partners probably can be attributed to the fact that EC competitors will not longer be constrained by fragemented markets. On the other hand, the Single Market may entail either a movement of trade policy towards the practices of more liberal member states or a general desire by the EC to be seen, for example, at the GATT as anti-protectionist. In such circumstances, anti-dumping regulations, reciprocity clauses and local content rules may not emerge, as the EC's trading partners had feared.

The Single Market programme, and particularly the idea of mutual recognition, has given rise to some important international developments. The standards applied in one member state must be recognised as equivalent to those applied in another. Therefore, the conditions exist for 'competition between rules' (*The Economist,* 1988, p. 11). In other words, a member state with more 'competitive' industrial standards and tax provisions may attract industry capital and people and may lead to matching adjustments in other member states. For example, capital mobility would lead to a transfer of savings to member states with lower withholding taxes on interest and a consequent alignment of such taxes throughout the EC. Bressand (1990) emphasises that 'competition between rules' has not been accompanied by the growth of a governing institutional framework and is a new departure in international economic relations.

In passing we might note that if freedom of capital mobility leads to volatility in capital movements then the stability of the EMS might be threatened. In turn the benefits that Ireland has gained through exchange rate stability in the EMS could be undermined. However, problems of volatility are likely to arise in the event of shifts in economic policy in member states. The dangers posed by volatility in capital movements will diminish with movements towards monetary union.

Movements toward harmonisation in the EC should not obscure the existence of considerable diversity. The member states differ in their economic size, their openness to trade and their stage of economic development. In Chapter 2 Vanhove and Sanders distinguish between 'nominal' convergence in price stability and control of public finances, and 'real' convergence between member states living standards. In view of the diversity between member states, there seems little *a priori* reason to expect real convergence. Ireland has a relatively high proportion of employment in agriculture, a high labour force dependency rate and high population growth, all of which contribute to low income per head. Such factors make real convergence difficult. Indeed, given Ireland's demographic structure and labour force participation rate, an equalisation of output per worker with the EC average would still leave Irish income per head below the EC average.

Single Market-induced growth effects may trickle down to the peripheral regions, but there is no certainty that progress toward convergence will be made. Ireland's growth rate of GDP at constant prices in 1988 was effectively the same as the EC average. If we assume, purely for the purposes of illustration, that the Single Market measures were to add 1 per cent to Ireland's growth rate and 2 per cent to the EC average, there would be divergence. Ireland could experience at once an absolute improvement and a relative disimprovement.

Notwithstanding the obvious difficulties involved, there is a notable omission of forecasts of regional effects from the Commission's assessment of the benefits of the Single Market. This is at least consistent with shortcomings in quantified objectives, in long-term vision, in coordination with other policies and in evaluation, which have characterised EC regional policy. Moreover, within Ireland, assessment of the effects of the Single Market have not included detailed consideration of the impact on individual Irish regions.

Others have attempted to assess the regional effects. The arguments presented in Chapters 17 and 18 envisage little real benefit for the Irish economy. On a positive note, high levels of economic growth can lead to high wage costs, congestion and rising property prices in core areas. The periphery then becomes a more attractive location. However, when economic growth falters, these attractions wane. Leaving aside the ebbs and flows of economic growth, developments within peripheral member states are important. If wage levels are low, then investment may flow in, but skilled labour may emigrate. Perversely, if wage levels are high, then skilled labour may be less mobile, but there will be less inward investment.

Structural funds, though they represent a relatively high proportion of investment in Ireland, are comparatively limited in view of Ireland's regional disadvantages. Of course, limitations on resources place a premium on efficient allocation. However, even allowing for the highest levels of efficiency, the structural funds seem an insufficient means to regional improvement. Aside from the size of the funds, there is also a doubt about their reliability. The doubling of the structural funds covers the period to 1993. Thereafter there is little certainty about the level of funding. In such a situation, planning is obviously difficult, and medium-term prospects for the economy, and for particular beneficiaries like the construction sector, are difficult to predict. The fact that the structural funds were increased to deal with the impact of the Single Market on peripheral areas is a recognition of the expectation that peripheral regions will have difficulty maintaining their positions. This contrasts with arguments that peripheral countries may benefit most by means such as reduced transport costs.

Neven (1990) has argued that peripheral member states, particularly Greece, Portugal and Spain, may gain from the Single Market programme. His argument is that trade liberalisation will lead to the exploitation of comparative advantage and that the additional trade will disproportionately benefit the smaller economies as they exploit their comparative advantage in low labour costs. In addition, Neven has argued that the Single Market will enable the exploitation of economies of scale and that the peripheral member states will gain disproportionately because scale economies largely have been attained already in the more developed member states. However, Neven does not take account of external economies of scale, such as enhanced business opportunities in larger markets, which should disproportionately benefit the more developed member states. Furthermore, he does not deal with the possibility that the development of peripheral economies along existing comparative advantage lines may produce a quality of industrial structure below that of advanced countries.

Even allowing for this proviso, it still would be unwise to apply Neven's reasoning uncritically to Ireland. Irish indigenous manufacturing has been unsuccessful in significantly developing an export capacity, although there were some improvements at the end of the 1980s. Potential for gains from comparative advantage does not automatically transmit to realisation of these gains. Potential for development of the foodstuffs and tourism sectors in the Single Market needs to be actively developed. We must also take into account that the exploitation of economies of scale, and consequently lower costs in more developed member states, in the past have acted as barriers to Ireland's entry to their markets. Moreover, we must take account of the possibility of factor mobility out of peripheral member states. We have already adverted to the possibility of labour outflows. The freeing of capital movements could lead to capital outflows. The picture is further complicated by the fact that location decisions are affected by corporate taxes. Devereux and Pearson (1990) argue that, despite having higher costs of production, Ireland might attract German investment if rates of corporation tax were lower. Harmonisation of corporate tax rates would eliminate this distortion. On balance, any optimism about Ireland's relative performance *vis-à-vis* the core EC economies, in terms of the specific impact of the Single Market, must be qualified with extreme caution.

We have noted that distributional concerns arise in several ways. Apart from worries related to the distribution of gains among member states, there are distributional issues within member states. If competition is allowed to work, consumers will benefit; if not, then the benefits will flow to producers. To a large extent, Ireland must rely on the EC to apply competition policy in order to ensure the consumer gains. Many pricing decisions for goods on sale in the Irish economy are made externally by oligopolistic suppliers. However, within the Irish economy there may be areas where domestic policy and administration could ensure that consumers gain from the Single

Market. Domestic action would have an effect on the distribution of gains if, for example, price reductions on goods entering Ireland were not being passed on to consumers.

Distributional consequences within Ireland could also arise between sectors, within sectors and between factors of production. If, for example, the foodstuffs industry was to realise a potential comparative advantage, then it may attract resources from a declining sector. There may also be reallocation within sectors. For example, if high-technology industry prospers, it may attract resources from declining low-technology industry. The implications for distribution between factors of production would depend on the factor intensities in the old and new uses. These reallocations are part of the normal process of economic adjustment and are continuously operating in the economy. The Single Market programme however, will work through these channels.

An assessment of the effect of the Single Market on different sectors of the Irish economy is complicated by factors such as incomplete knowledge of the determinants of EC patterns of production and trade, differing effects in the short and medium term, concerns about ability to compete, and uncertainty about the public policy and business policy responses within Ireland. For example, there is a lack of knowledge about the scale of unexploited economies of scale in the member states. Still, we can make some definite observations. Chapter 10 showed that Ireland's indigenous industry has a limited presence in manufacturing industries with high technical barriers and, in general, a relatively low presence in industries significantly affected by the Single Market. For indigenous industry, therefore, both the threats and the opportunities of the Single Market are relatively limited.

The EC's stance on state aid also has implications for industrial policy. State aid takes several forms, including tax concessions, low interest loans and subsidies. Competition-distorting subsidies can increase exports or reduce imports. The EC Commission increasingly has intervened where it is suspected that inefficient industries were being protected. All the member states give state aid to a greater or lesser degree. Indeed, EC intervention in this area could prove a testing ground for the independence of national governments. Ireland's rationale for state aid, based on the need for reductions in regional disparities, should provide a strong case for retention.

Business policy is also important for the performance of the Irish economy and its sectors. The Single Market will make the markets of the various member states more accessible; it will not make them more similar. There will be greater integration on the supply side of the European economy, but, despite indirect tax harmonisation, the demand side will still be fragmented by differences in incomes, tastes and languages. There will also be national preferences. Irish business therefore will continue to face barriers to entry on the demand side. In order to overcome these, it is necessary for Irish business to become more fully informed about the characteristics of the different national markets.

Exports are an important component of Irish economic growth. It might be expected that the Single Market will facilitate Irish exports because of factors such as Ireland's dependence on trade, the relatively great distance from major EC markets, and the fact that Irish exporters cross many borders in order to get to major markets. However, such an interpretation must be treated cautiously. Many of the factors work in reverse and allow easier access to Ireland. Moreover, Ireland has a locational advantage with the UK, which is its single biggest market among EC states. If other member states benefit relatively more than Ireland in terms of access costs to the UK, then Ireland could suffer a competitive disadvantage in its major market. Moreover, it appears that in the past other member states encountered greater non-tariff barriers than Ireland in the UK market. To the extent that the Single Market removes this advantage, Irish exports to the UK will suffer.

In general, however, the Single Market makes access to export markets cheaper and easier and somewhat facilitates the task of developing an export capacity. If Irish firms are to maximise the gains from the Single Market, then, in addition to confronting the demand-side barriers, they must address competitiveness on the supply side. Gains in competitiveness are important not just for indigenous industry, but also as a signal to attract foreign direct investment.

There was considerable improvement in competitiveness and in other economic indicators in Ireland in the latter half of the

1980s. Contributory factors to the economic recovery were world growth, improvements in the public finances, and wage moderation, which led to competitiveness gains. The Irish economy is now in a better position to compete in a Single Market than at any time in the 1980s. In some respects, such as labour skills, management competence or potentially vulnerable industries, the Irish economy is in a better position to compete than when Ireland entered the European Community in 1973. However, the fiscal imbalance remains serious and the underlying growth in the labour force does present problems. In order to capitalise on Single Market opportunities, there is a need to direct policy at those areas under Irish control that help to maintain industrial competence and competitiveness.

The Single European Market:
A Review of Selected Published Sources

FERGAL LYNCH

This appendix provides a readily accessible introduction to the major documents that deal with both the concept of the Single Market and with its impact on Ireland.

The following section deals with selected official EC documents and the succeeding section with a variety of Irish documents. Space limitations do not permit consideration of other than official EC documents. Hence other literature that adopts a general European Community perspective, such as special issues of economic journals, has not been included. In considering Ireland, a wider range of documents has been examined. However, space limitations meant that individual articles were not considered.

A chronological order has been adopted, with the focus being on the general context of the major documents. An assessment of each document is not attempted; rather, the aim is to identify the main subject headings and the way in which they are presented, thereby providing a reference guide for those who are seeking detailed information on any specific topic.

European Publications

Completing the Internal Market, White Paper from the Commission to the European Council (June 1985)

The White Paper is a detailed study of the measures required to establish an internal market within the European Community. *Part One* deals with the removal of physical barriers, including those at customs posts and immigration controls. The control of goods is discussed under such headings as commercial and economic policy, health, and transport. The free movement of persons is also examined.

Part Two looks at the removal of technical barriers, including those affecting the free movement of goods (section I) and of labour (section III). Section II discusses public procurement policy. The need for a common market for services, including finance, transport and new technologies, is discussed in section IV, followed by the main aims behind liberalising capital movements (section V). The creation of conditions suitable for industrial cooperation (section VI) and the means of enforcing EC law for the purposes of achieving market completion (section VII) are then considered.

Part Three examines the removal of fiscal barriers and considers the tax barriers facing business and individuals. The case for the approximation of indirect taxes and the Commission's proposals for this matter (since revised) are then presented.

Finally, the White Paper contains a detailed annex, setting out several hundred wide-ranging measures that are required for the completion of the internal market by 1992, with a timetable for each. The measures are presented under the headings of physical, technical and fiscal barriers.

Single European Act, Office for Official Publications of the European Communities, Luxembourg (1986)

The Single European Act was signed in February 1986 by the twelve member states. It amends the Treaty of Rome in a number of ways and formalises some existing arrangements, such as European Political Cooperation (EPC) and the European Council of heads of state.

The Act's main provisions concerning the internal market are in Title II, Articles 12–19. It defines the internal market and commits the Community to achieving it by 31 December 1992 (Article 13), provides for temporary derogations (Article 15), changes the rules regarding unanimity in decision-making (Article 16) and enables the Council to adopt tax harmonisation measures (Article 17). Decision by qualified majority voting on various other harmonisation measures is provided for, but exception is made of some specific cases, such as fiscal provisions and the free movement of persons (Article 18).

The Act includes a number of declarations by individual countries regarding issues that have special implications for them. Ireland made a declaration regarding its insurance industry.

Tomasso Padoa-Schioppa, *Efficiency, Stability and Equity: A Strategy for the Evolution of the Economic System of the European Community,* Oxford University Press (1987)

This is the report of a group, chaired by Tomasso Padoa-Schioppa, which was asked by the European Commission to review the Community's strategy for further integration in the light of (a) adoption of the objective of completing the internal market by 1992, (b) the signing of the Single European Act, and (c) enlargement of the EC to include Spain and Portugal. The report concludes that these steps have important implications for the Community, with particular reference to the European Monetary System and the need for EC budgetary reform. The report puts forward a comprehensive model for the Community's economic system, drawing on modern trade theory, macroeconomics and the economics of multi-tier government.

After a general summary in *Part A*, *Part B* (The Schema of Ideas) identifies a number of theoretical propositions founded in economic theory, and these are applied throughout the report. They include (i) the economic benefits of international trade and (ii) the disaggregation of public policy into allocation, stabilisation and distribution functions.

Part C (Appraisal of the Community system to date) reviews the present operation of the Community system by reference to goods and services markets (chapter 5), labour markets (chapter 6) and capital markets (chapter 7). Macroeconomic policy, including the EMS and other issues relating to the coordination of economic policies, are examined briefly, followed by a short analysis of some problems of the Community budget.

Part D proposes approaches to the 'harmonious and efficient development' of the EC system. It first summarises the challenges posed by market completion and then sets out its recommendations based on three main elements of economic policy — resource allocation, macroeconomic stabilisation and redistribution. These three components are discussed, respectively, with reference to the internal market (chapter 11), capital mobility and the EMS (chapter 12) and the EC budget (chapter 13). Finally, the requirements for growth, an essential condition for the success of the proposed strategy, are examined (chapter 14).

Technical annexes deal with such matters as conceptual issues in integration, schemes for macroeconomic policy coordination, and distributive aspects of the Community budget.

Research on the 'Cost of Non-Europe' – *The Cecchini Project*, Office for Official Publications of the European Communities, Luxembourg (1988)

An extensive research programme was conducted under the chairmanship of Paolo Cecchini on behalf of the EC Commission. The research was published in 16 volumes. A full list of the volumes is given below.

Volume 1   Basic studies: Executive summaries
Volume 2   Studies on the economics of integration
Volume 3   The completion of the internal market: A survey of European industry's perception of the likely effects
Volume 4   The 'cost of non-Europe'
            — Border-related controls and administrative formalities
            — An illustration in the road haulage sector
Volume 5   The 'cost of non-Europe' in public sector procurement
Volume 6   Technical barriers in the EC: An illustration by six industries
            The 'cost of non-Europe': Some case studies on technical barriers
Volume 7   The 'cost of non-Europe': Obstacles to transborder business activity
Volume 8   The 'cost of non-Europe' for business services
Volume 9   The 'cost of non-Europe' in financial services
Volume 10   The benefits of completing the internal market for telecommunications equipment in the Community
Volume 11   The 'cost of non-Europe' in the EC automobile sector

Volume 12   The 'cost of non-Europe' in the foodstuffs industry
Volume 13   Le 'cout de la non-Europe' des produits de construction
Volume 14   The 'cost of non-Europe' in the textile-clothing industry
Volume 15   The 'cost of non-Europe' in the pharmaceutical industry
Volume 16   The internal markets of North America. Fragmentation and integration in the US and Canada

Paolo Cecchini, *The European Challenge 1992: The Benefits of a Single Market*, Wildhouse Ltd (1988)

This book is based on and summarises the research carried out for the Cecchini Project. It is intended for a general readership.

Part One describes Europe's currently fragmented markets and the costs associated with border controls, government protectionism in procurement, divergences in technical standards and cross-border business. The costs imposed on service and the manufacturing sectors are also considered.

Part Two analyses the potential gains of completion in terms of present market costs and future benefits. Micro- and macroeconomic perspectives are presented, with a discussion of the global impact on the EC economy of the whole market completion process.

The Economics of 1992: An Assessment of the Effects of Completing the Internal Market of the European Community, European Economy, No. 35 (March 1988)

This study is based on the Cecchini Project and was issued under the responsibility of the EC Directorate-General for Economic and Financial Affairs, with the aim of evaluating the potential economic impact of completing the Single Market by 1992. The study was also published by Oxford University Press in 1988 under the title *The Economics of 1992: The EC Commission's Assessment of the Economic Effects of Completing the Internal Market*. It identifies a number of contributors, of whom Michael Emerson was the leader.

Part A contains a summary of the report and its conclusions.

Part B describes the dimensions and structure of the potential internal market and analyses the weaknesses of the present lack of integration. It presents a typology of market barriers, analyses their economic impact and discusses a number of economic methods of evaluating them.

Part C presents a discussion of the principal types of barriers (such as customs procedures, technical regulations and fiscal frontiers). An important distinction is made between the impact of cost-increasing barriers and those that limit market entry; the latter are often found to be more drastic in their effect.

Case studies of the industrial and services sectors are then presented, all focusing on the main barriers experienced in each branch, the approximate potential savings that would accrue if the barriers were removed, and some strategic or wider considerations. The case studies for industry include food-processing, pharmaceuticals, automobiles, textiles and clothing, building products, and telecommunications equipment. The service case studies are financial services (including banking and insurance), business services, surface and air transport, and telecommunications services.

Part D examines in detail the effects of market integration that are expected to promote efficiency through market size (chapter 6) and increased competition (chapter 7). The effects of competition on costs and prices are analysed, together with non-price effects such as improved organisational structure, product range and innovation. Chapter 8 discusses the Single Market from the viewpoint of the business community, including firms' perceptions of the opportunities and constraints of market completion and the strategies adopted by European firms in response. The anticipated roles of EC competition policy, common external policy and redistributive policy are also considered. Chapter 9 uses a partial equilibrium model to illustrate the gains that will accrue from completing the internal market.

Part E provides a quantitative assessment of the benefits likely to accrue from market completion, using microeconomic models. The detail of the micro- and macroeconomic methodologies are set out in appendices.

Commission of the European Communities, *Delors Committee Report on Economic and Monetary Union* (1989)

In June 1988 the European Council decided to establish a committee to propose 'concrete stages' leading to the progressive realisation of economic and monetary union. It was chaired by Jacques Delors, President of the European Commission. The group reported early in 1989.

Part One of the report examines past and present developments in economic and monetary integration, with particular reference to the European Monetary System and the European Currency Unit. The Single European Act and the related Single Market programme are also considered.

Part Two examines in detail the meaning and practical implications of monetary and economic union, together with the institutional arrangements required to bring them about. Action in three areas — competition policy, regional and structural policy, and macroeconomic policy — is identified as necessary for economic and monetary integration. Each is considered in detail.

Part Three proposes three major steps towards economic and monetary union, to be viewed as a single process ('The decision to enter upon the first stage should be a decision to embark upon the entire process'). The three stages are: the closer coordination of economic and monetary policies; the adoption of macroeconomic policy guidelines; and the irrevocable locking of exchange rates. Each stage is described by reference to the economic and monetary fields, with details of developments required within them. The need for a new treaty to formalise economic and monetary union, which would have to be in force by the end of stage one, is explained. The options of a new treaty for each stage and a single comprehensive treaty are considered briefly, but no recommendation is made.

Commission of the European Communities, *Community Charter of the Fundamental Social Rights of Workers* (1989)

The EC Commission's Social Charter was adopted in December 1989. *Title 1* of the charter sets out a number of 'fundamental social rights of workers'. These rights are organised under twelve headings: freedom of movement; employment and remuneration; improvement of living and working conditions; social protection; freedom of association and collective bargaining; vocational training; equal treatment for men and women; information, consultation and participation for workers; health protection and safety at the workplace; protection of children and adolescents; elderly persons; and disabled persons.

Title 2 of the Charter deals with implementation and makes provision for an annual report on the application of the Charter.

The Social Charter is accompanied by an action programme containing 47 proposals to give effect to its provisions. The action programme broadly reflects the headings of the Social Charter, but includes some specific proposals on such matters as holiday and sickness pay and the mutual recognition of qualifications.

Irish Publications

J. Bradley et al., *The Economic Consequences of European Union*, ESRI Policy Research Series, Paper No. 6 (April 1986)

The papers were presented at a symposium held in May 1985 to discuss some policy aspects of European Union. In his introduction *Dermot Scott* outlines the background to the movement towards closer integration and the growing concern of member states to act as a more coherent economic unit in the face of American and Japanese competition.

John Bradley analyses the macroeconomic consequences of market completion, with particular reference to the issues raised in the 'Dooge Report' (Report to the European Council by the ad hoc Committee for Institutional Affairs), and the EC White Paper on completing the internal market. The main economic aspects of the Dooge Report are summarised, and the key concepts of convergence, coordination, harmonisation and interdependence as they affect Ireland are analysed. The meaning of economic and monetary union (EMU) and the effects of EMS membership are considered briefly.

John Fitzgerald considers the implications of tax harmonisation (a) for the Irish tax system, (b) for the Irish economy and (c) for Irish economic policy. The likely structure of any harmonised indirect tax system is examined, together with the implications of harmonisation for corporation tax.

Miceal Ross examines the issues of subsidiarity, regional development and nation-building in the context of market completion. The principle of subsidiarity (that 'responsibilities must be discharged at the most decentralised level in society consistent with their effective performance') is considered in relation to the European parliament's draft treaty and the concept of 'nation-building'. Weintraub's framework of nation-building, based on a core-periphery model, is used to examine the relative strengths and weaknesses of the EC core and its periphery. The need for an appropriate sharing of power between the core and the peripheral member states is emphasised.

Richard Kearney (ed.), *Across the Frontiers: Ireland in the 1990s*, Wolfhound Press (1988)

The book presents a series of essays on various cultural, political and economic issues facing Ireland in the 1990s. A number of the essays deal with aspects of market completion, including *Michael D. Higgins* ('Ireland in Europe in 1992: Problems and Prospects for a Mutual Independency'). *Eithne Murphy* ('Ireland's Economic Welfare in a Barrier-Free Europe') assesses, for Ireland, some of the likely economic implications of market completion. Issues examined include the distributional consequences arising from Ireland's peripheral location and economy. The harmon-isation of indirect taxation and the performance of traded and non-traded sectors are considered, with separate treatment of the services sector. Finally, the essay examines the role of industrial and social policy in the process of development.

Alan Matthews ('The Role of the European Community's Structural Funds in the 1990s') examines the likely impact of increased EC structural funds for Ireland and describes the major changes in the types of projects eligible for support and the rules governing them.

Economic and Social Review, *European Monetary System 10th Anniversary Issue*, Vol. 20, No. 2 (January 1989)

This issue of the *Economic and Social Review* examines the first decade of the EMS. The value of the lessons learned during the ten years are debated, the achievements of the system are considered and Ireland's experience in the EMS is analysed, with reference to real exchange rates and purchasing power parity. Other articles consider price determination in Ireland in the context of different exchange rate regimes and present a systems approach to modelling the EMS exchange rate mechanism.

Ireland: National Development Plan, 1989–1993, Stationery Office (1989)

The government submitted the *National Development Plan* to the

European Commission in March 1989 as part of its application for funding under the expanded and reformed EC structural funds. The Plan sets out the proposed structural measures to achieve greater economic and social cohesion in the context of the internal market. The document provides an economic and social analysis (chapter 1) at an overall level (such as demographic and labour factors, industrial structure) and at a sectoral level, including brief examinations of industry, agriculture, forestry, transport, energy and telecommunications. Chapter 2 sets out the objectives, commencing with a statement of economic strategy on fiscal and exchange rate policy, pay, taxation and sectoral development. The objectives are then outlined in macroeconomic and sectoral terms, with an emphasis on remedying structural weaknesses, and promoting productive investment.

Chapter 3 sets out the detailed development measures proposed for (a) industry, services and infrastructure, (b) education, training and employment, and (c) agriculture and rural development. In Chapter 4 the assistance Ireland sought from the European Regional Development Fund, together with associated state and private expenditure, is set out for each year of the Plan. Projected loan requirements from the European Investment Bank are also included.

Chapter 5 describes how the Plan will be implemented under operational programme headings such as industrial development, tourism, roads, transport and energy. Chapter 6 sets out the proposed expenditure for each of the seven sub-regions into which the country was divided for the purposes of the Plan. It contains a socio-economic analysis of each sub-region and details of its particular development proposals.

The EC Commission published its response to Ireland's proposals in October 1989, entitled *Community Support Framework for Ireland 1989–1993*. The CSF approves payments through the expanded structural funds of about £2.86 billion over the period to 1993. Assistance is set out under four priority headings: (i) agriculture, fisheries, forestry, tourism and rural development, (ii) industry and services, (iii) measures to offset the effects of peripherality, and (iv) human resource measures. The document reviews briefly the problems and priorities of the Irish economy and specifies the forms of assistance to be given. It also discusses the macroeconomic context, with particular reference to the labour market. Finally it sets out provisions regarding implementation of the Plan and the requirements regarding adherence to and the coordination of Community policies.

Seirbhís Phoiblí, *The Challenge of 1992*, Vol. 10, No. 1 (April 1989)

Seirbhís Phoblí, the journal of Ireland's public service, devoted its April 1989 issue to an examination of the meaning and implications of completing the internal market. The contributions include details and strategy regarding VAT approximation (*Don Thornhill*), the implications of removing customs and excise controls at EC frontiers (*Tom Duffy*), and an analysis of changes in public procurement after 1992 (*Aidan O'Boyle*). The implications of market completion for the Common Agricultural Policy (*Seamus Carroll*) and for industry (*David Croughan*) are also considered. There are also articles on the impact of 1992 on the political system and on the public service.

John Bradley et al., *The Economics of 1992: A Symposium on Sectoral Issues*, ESRI Policy Research Series, Paper No. 10 (June 1989)

This publication contains three papers presented at an ESRI symposium held in December 1988 to investigate some of the main effects on the Irish economy of completing the EC internal market.

John Bradley provides a brief introduction to the papers, the first of which, by *Rory O'Donnell*, is on manufacturing industry. He provides a framework for studying the costs and benefits to Irish industry of removing non-tariff barriers, followed by a detailed overview of how selected sub-sectors are likely to be affected by market completion, including metals and engineering, clothing, textiles, printing and publishing, and chemicals and pharmaceuticals. The paper concludes that in many sectors the main threats and opportunities will arise from technical and organisational changes, rather than the removal of non-tariff barriers.

John Fitzgerald examines the effects of the internal market on the distribution sector, particularly in relation to the pricing and sale of goods by manufacturers, importers, wholesalers and retailers. Tax harmonisation and competition policy are highlighted as prerequisites of a smooth transition to a completed

EC market. An examination of the distribution sector's structure and comparisons with other member states is followed by an analysis of the implications for the sector of the EC White Paper, *Completing the Internal Market* (1985). The reasons for price differences between Ireland and other member states are also examined and conclusions are offered.

Alan Matthews analyses the effects of completing the internal market on the agricultural and food sectors. Among the issues considered are restructuring and the removal of non-tariff barriers in the food industry, rural development and the use of EC structural funds, and the likely effects of market completion on the present system of monetary compensatory amounts payments and quotas.

NESC Report No. 88, *Ireland in the European Community: Performance, Prospects and Strategy* (August 1989)
This report is the result of a request by the Taoiseach, Charles Haughey, that the National Economic and Social Council should undertake a comprehensive study of (a) Ireland's comparative performance in the EC, including an assessment of the impact of EC membership, (b) the problems and opportunities presented by the Single Market, and (c) the policy options available to tackle the problems and so capitalise on the opportunities presented.

Part One summarises the position to date in the progress towards European integration, including a brief background to the development of the EC and an introduction to the concepts of the costs of 'non-Europe' and internal market completion. It also sets out the major theories of economic integration, which are drawn upon throughout the report.

Part Two analyses the impact of EC membership on Ireland's economic structure and performance since 1973. The various methods for measuring the effects of economic integration are assessed (chapter 3), followed by an examination of Ireland's performance with particular reference to manufacturing, agriculture and trade (chapter 4). Ireland's performance relative to other member states is then examined (chapter 5), followed by a discussion of intra-industry trade and industrial structure, using measures commonly regarded as important indicators of the effects of economic integration (chapter 6). A concluding chapter reviews Ireland's economic performance over two phases (1973–1980 and 1980–1986) and examines the lessons of the full period.

Part Three examines the likely effects of market completion in terms of threats and opportunities, beginning with an analytical framework for analysis (chapter 8) which is then applied to selected sectors — manufacturing (chapter 9) and services (chapter 10). The emphasis is on the effects of the Single Market, although chapter 10 also examines appropriate responses. Both the effects of the Single Market on regions and arguments concerning regional convergence and divergence are considered. The key conclusion is that the Single Market should not be expected to narrow regional disparities, let alone bring about convergence (chapter 11). The removal of frontiers and the approximation of indirect taxes are evaluated (chapter 12).

Part Four considers the major policy issues arising from the earlier analysis. Chapter 13 forms the core of the report, outlining the Council's recommended strategic approach to integration. It favours advanced economic and monetary union within the EC, as opposed to the less integrated models of a customs union and a common market. Chapter 14 examines and makes recommendations on appropriate corporate and public policy responses to the 'threats and opportunities' outlined earlier, focusing on manufacturing and agriculture. EC structural and regional policy is then examined, together with related issues, such as macroeconomic coordination and budgetary transfers (chapter 15). The social dimension of market completion is examined, with particular reference to economic integration (chapter 16), together with an appendix discussing the direct effects of the internal market on existing Irish social policy programmes (health, housing and social security). Chapter 17 summarises the report's conclusions on the impact of EC membership and its major recommendations.

Europe: What Kind of Solidarity? Studies (Autumn 1989)

Two articles deal specifically with the internal market. *Peter Sutherland* examines the Irish view of European integration, beginning with a historical perspective and followed by a consideration of the concerns of other member states. Two matters of particular concern are discussed: the power of veto and the need for a clearer Irish position on the goal of European union.

John Bradley and *Eithne Murphy* focus on some of the economic implications for Ireland of completing the internal market and, in particular, the issues of regional aid through the EC structural funds.

Dermot Keogh (ed.), *Ireland and the Challenge of European Integration*, Hibernian University Press (1989)

Some of the papers in this book consider economic issues relating to European integration. *Garret FitzGerald's* Robert Schumann inaugural lecture outlines the background to Ireland's entry to the EC and the gains that membership has brought. He examines the role played by Ireland in the EC and the country's approach to the Single European Act. The choice between EMU and national autonomy in economic and monetary policy is considered in detail, followed by a brief examination of the case for a common EC currency.

Kieran Kennedy provides an economic perspective to Ireland's participation in European integration. The country's long-term economic performance as a member of the EC is analysed, and reasons for its poor showing are suggested. The effects of membership on living standards and employment in Ireland are then considered, and the paper concludes with a discussion of appropriate economic strategies for the future.

John O'Dowd (ed.), *Ireland, Europe and 1992*, Tomar Publishing (1989).

This book, commissioned by the Civil and Public Services Staff Union, examines the implications for Ireland of market completion. It was researched and written by SUS Research Ltd. Chapter 1 details the origin and implications of the 1992 programme; chapter 2 examines the impact of the internal market on Ireland, with particular reference to the economic consequences, regional policy and the prospects of monetary union.

The third chapter considers the likely impact of market completion on manufacturing industry (both multinationals and indigenous), services (financial, transport and distribution), and the state sector (including public procurement and the future of state-sponsored bodies). The social dimension of market completion is also considered.

Confederation of Irish Industry, *Newsletters*
The CII publishes a weekly newsletter containing brief information on matters of interest to its members. Each month the newsletter contains a 'Euro Review' and other articles summarising developments relating to completion of the internal market. For example, the Newsletter has featured articles on the EC structural funds, mobile investment in Europe, and indirect tax harmonisation. The newsletter also provides a regularly updated checklist regarding progress on the measures identified by the 1985 EC White Paper as being necessary for market completion.

Córas Tráchtála, *Business Information Leaflets*
The Irish Export Board, Córas Tráchtála, has published a series of leaflets entitled '1992 and Your Markets'. They outline the scope of the changes arising from the internal market, the role of CTT in helping exporters meet the challenges, and the services available from CTT to achieve the necessary changes. There are leaflets on removing physical barriers, on liberalising transport and on public sector procurement. The implications for individual industries are considered in separate leaflets, including pharmaceuticals, construction and building materials, textiles and clothing, and food and drink. Leaflets on different export markets, including France, Germany and Italy, have also been prepared.

Europen Bureau, *'Europen' Reports*, Government Sales Publications Office, Dublin
The Irish government, through the Europen Bureau, has published a series of reports aimed at helping Irish industry plan for the internal market. The sectors covered are the food and drink industry; electronic, electrical and instrument engineering; metal and mechanical engineering; textiles, clothing and footwear; chemicals, pharmaceuticals and health care products; distribution; transport; tourism; financial services; and the construction industry.

Appendix B

Evolution of the European Community 1957–1989

FERGAL LYNCH

This appendix is a summary of the main landmarks in the evolution
of the European Community since the Treaties of Rome in 1957.
Material for the period up to 1987 is derived from *A Journey
through the EC* (Commission of the EC, 1987). Permission to use
this material is gratefully acknowledged.

	Development and organisation	Enlargement	Integration	External relations
1957	**25 March** Rome: Treaties establishing European Economic Community (EEC) and European Atomic Energy Community (Euratom) signed. Treaties ratified by the six national parliaments (Belgium, France, Italy, Luxembourg, Netherlands, West Germany) during the year.			
1958	**1 January** Treaties of Rome come into force.		**3-11 July** Foundations of Common Agricultural Policy laid at Stresa Conference.	
1959			**1 January** Gradual phasing out of customs duties and quotas within EEC begins with 10% reduction of duties.	**8 June** Greece requests association with EEC. **31 July** Turkey seeks association with EEC.
1960			**20 September** European Social Fund starts financing of retraining and resettlement measures for workers.	
1961		**31 July** Ireland applies for membership of European Communities. United Kingdom follows on 9 August and Denmark on 10 August. **8 November** Negotiations with United Kingdom begin in Brussels.	**10 February** Heads of State or Government of EEC States decide on closer political cooperation. **1 September** First regulation on free movement of workers within the Community comes into force.	**9 July** EEC–Greece Association Agreement signed in Athens. Enters into force on 1 November 1962 but is suspended between April 1967 and September 1974.
1962		**30 April** Norway applies for membership of the Community.	**14 January** Council agrees on first four agricultural market regulations, first financial regulation and the competition regulation. **17 April** Negotiations on political union	**9 February** Spain seeks negotiations for association with EEC. **18 May** Portugal applies for association with EEC.

1963	**14 January** General de Gaulle asserts that United Kingdom is not ready for membership of European Community. **28 February** Accession negotiation with United Kingdom broken off. As a result, negotiations also stopped with the other countries applying for membership or association.	**20 July** Yaoundé, Cameroon: first Association Convention signed with 17 African States and Madagascar. Enters into force on 1 June 1964. **12 September** EEC–Turkey Association Agreement signed. Comes into force on 1 December 1964. **14 October** Trade Agreement between EEC and Iran signed (first Agreement with a non-member country).
1964	**4 May** Kennedy Round of international tariff negotiations opens in Geneva — EEC takes part as single entity. **1 July** Regulation on European Agricultural Guidance and the Guarantee Fund enters into force. **15 December** Council agrees on common cereal prices.	
1965	**8 April** Treaty merging the executive organs of the European Coal and Steel Community, EEC and Euratom signed. **24 September** Victor Leemans becomes President of European Parliament.	**30 June** As Council President, French Foreign Minister breaks up Council meeting on Commission proposals for financing common agricultural prices, on Community own resources and on extension of rights of European Parliament. French Government pursues 'empty chair' policy.

Development and organisation	Enlargement	Integration	External relations
1966		**29 January** Special Council meeting in Luxembourg ends crisis begun on 30 June 1965 by abandoning majority decisions on matters where vital interests of one or more Member States are at stake ('Luxembourg compromise'). **11 May** Council adopts rest of agricultural market regulations, financial regulation and completion of customs union by 1 July 1968.	
1967 **1 July** Merger Treaty enters into force. **6 July** Commission of the European Communities starts work.	**May** New applications for membership from the Governments of Ireland and the United Kingdom (10 May) and Denmark (1 May). **25 July** New application for membership from Norway. **29 September** Favourable opinion from the Commission on accession of Ireland, the United Kingdom, Denmark and Norway. **19 December** Council fails to agree on resumption of negotiations with applicant countries.	**9 February** Council agrees on first medium-term economic policy programme and on introduction of a common VAT system.	
1968		**1 July** Customs union achieved. Duties between Member States eliminated. Common Customs Tariff instituted for trade with non-member countries. **8 November** Free movement for workers achieved (common labour market). **18 December** Commission submits Mansholt plan on reform of agriculture in the	**26 July** Arusha, Tanzania: Association Agreement signed between EEC and countries of East African Common Market (Kenya, Uganda, Tanzania). Comes into force on 1 January 1971.

Ireland, the United Kingdom, Denmark and Norway.

definitive financial arrangements for Common Agricultural Policy, transfer of own resources to the Community and strengthening of Parliament's budgetary powers. They also agree to enter into negotiations with the four applicant countries, to start to implement economic and monetary union and to introduce a system of cooperation in foreign policy.

31 December
End of the 12-year transitional period for implementing common market according to the EEC Treaty.

force on 1 September 1969.

29 July
Second Yaoundé Convention signed; enters into force on 1 January 1971.

24 September
Arusha Agreement renewed.

1970

30 June
Negotiations with the four applicant countries open in Luxembourg.

1 January
EEC countries embark on a Common Agricultural Policy.

21–22 April
Council agrees on changing budgetary provisions and extending Parliament's budgetary powers.

7–8 October
Werner Report on attainment by stages of economic and monetary union.

27 October
Member States approve Davignon report on political cooperation.

19 March
Trade Agreement between EEC and Yugoslavia signed.

29 June
Free Trade Agreement between EEC and Spain signed; enters into force on 1 October 1970.

5 December
Association Agreement with Malta signed; enters into force on 1 April 1971.

1971

22 March
Council determines beginning of first stage of Werner plan retroactively to 1 January 1971.

1 July
Community generalized preferences in favour of 91 developing countries.

8 November
EEC-Argentina Trade Agreement signed; comes into force on 1 January 1972.

Development and organisation	Enlargement	Integration	External relations
1972			
	22 January Act of Accession signed in Brussels.	**21 March** 'Currency snake' introduced: the Council and the Member States' Governments decide to let their currency exchange rates vary from one another by no more than 2.25%. Applicant countries also join the 'snake'.	**22 July** Free Trade Agreement with the non-applicant EFTA countries (Iceland, Austria, Portugal, Sweden and Switzerland) signed: comes into force on 1 January 1973 (Iceland — 1 April 1973).
	10 May Irish referendum approves EEC membership (83% vote 'yes').		**18 December** Preferential Agreement between EEC and Arab Republic of Egypt signed: enters into force on 1 November 1973.
	13 July The British House of Commons approves Community membership.	**19-22 October** Heads of State or Government, now nine, decide in Paris to develop the Community into European union and establish timetable for Community.	**19 December** Association Agreement with Cyprus signed; enters into force on 1 June 1973.
	25 September Referendum in Norway rejects Community membership (53.3% vote 'no').		
	2 October Danes vote in favour of Community membership.		
1973			
6 January Commission of the enlarged Community starts work.	**1 January** Treaty of Accession for United Kingdom, Ireland and Denmark enters into force.	**1 January** The Community receives full powers for common commercial policy of the Nine.	**2 April** Trade Agreement with Uruguay signed; enters into force on 1 August 1974.
		19 March Member States (except United Kingdom, Ireland and Italy) form a single currency block. The six countries jointly float their currencies against other currencies.	**14 May** Free Trade Agreement with Norway signed; enters into force on 1 July 1973.
		6 April European Monetary Cooperation Fund established in Luxembourg.	**26 June** EEC-Yugoslavia Trade Agreement signed; enters into force on 1 September 1973.
		22 November First Community action programme for the protection of the environment.	**5 October** Free Trade Agreement with Finland signed; enters into force on 1 January 1974.
			17 December Commercial Cooperation Agreement with India signed; enters into force on 1 April 1974.
			19 December Trade Agreement with Brazil signed.

11 October
United Nations General Assembly accords Community observer status.

21 January
Community social action programme approved.

10-11 December
Community Summit Conference of Heads of State or Government in Paris. Among the decisions:
(1) Heads of Government will meet three times a year as the European Council.
(2) More majority decisions in the Council of Ministers.
(3) Direct elections to the European Parliament from 1978; extended powers for the Parliament.
(4) Creation of a passport union.
(5) Creation of a Regional Fund.

1975

5 June
Two-thirds majority of voters in favour of keeping the UK in the Community.

12 June
Greece applies for membership of the Community.

18 March
Council formally decides to establish European Regional Development Fund.

14 April
First Community programme for a consumer protection and information policy approved.

10 July
French franc returns to the snake.

22 July
Brussels: Treaty strengthening Parliament's budgetary powers and establishing the Court of Auditors signed; enters into force on 1 June 1977.

29 December
Tindemans Report on European Union.

28 February
Lomé: Convention between Community and 46 developing countries in Africa, the Caribbean and the Pacific signed; enters into force on 1 April 1976.

11 May
First preferential Trade Agreement with Israel signed; enters into force on 1 July 1975.

15 July
Agreement on Trade Policy Co-operation between the EEC and Mexico signed; enters into force on 1 November 1975. Similar Agreement with Sri Lanka takes effect on 1 December 1975.

	Development and organisation	Enlargement	Integration	External relations
1976		**27 July** Accession negotiations with Greece open.	**14 March** French franc again withdraws from 'snake'. **12-13 July** Brussels: European Council determines number of seats for directly elected Parliament at 410. **20 September** Council adopts in Brussels the Act providing for direct election of members of European Parliament.	**25, 26, 27 April** Cooperation Agreements with Maghreb countries (Algeria, Tunisia and Morocco) signed. **1 June** Cooperation Agreement with Pakistan signed; enters into force on 1 July 1976. **6 July** EEC and Canada sign framework Agreement on economic and trade cooperation, the first cooperation agreement signed with an industrial country. **19 October** Commercial Cooperation Agreement with Bangladesh signed; comes into force on 1 December 1976.
1977	**6 January** New Commission takes office.	**28 March** Portugal aplies for membership of the Community. **28 July** Spain applies for membership of the Community.	**17 May** Council approves Sixth VAT Directive, which establishes uniform basis of assessment for collecting this tax. It also creates the possibility for complete introduction of system of Community 'own resources'. **1 July** Customs union achieved in enlarged Community. **31 December** End of transitional period for Ireland, Denmark and the United Kingdom.	**18 January** Agreements with Mashreq countries (Egypt, Jordan and Syria) signed. **3 May** Cooperation Agreement with Lebanon signed.

1978	**17 October** Accession negotiations open with Portugal. **22 November** First general meeting of Community Youth Forum. **3 April** Trade Agreement with China signed; comes into force on 1 June 1978.
1979	**17 July** First sitting of directly elected European Parliament in Strasbourg. **5 February** Accession negotiations with Spain officially opened. **28 May** Treaty of Accession signed with Greece in Athens. **13 March** European Monetary System enters into force. Nucleus of system is the ECU — the new European currency unit. **7-10 June** Community citizens elect members of European Parliament by direct universal suffrage for first time. **31 October** Second Lomé Convention signed. It governs relations between EEC and 61 African Carribean and Pacific (ACP) countries and takes effect on 1 January 1981.
1980	**30 May** Commission is given a mandate by Council to propose modifications to the structure of the budget and to Community policies. Commission presents its proposals on 24 June 1981. **7 March** Cooperation Agreement signed with ASEAN countries. Comes into force on 1 October 1980. **2 April** Cooperation Agreement signed with Yugoslavia; comes into force on 1 June 1980. **28 July** Trade Agreement with Romania signed. **18 September** Framework Agreement on economic and trade cooperation between Community and Brazil signed.
1981	**6 January** New Commission takes office. **1 January** Greece becomes 10th member of Community. **19 May** Community's second consumer protection and information programme approved by the Council. **19 November** Foreign Ministers Genscher and Colombo present to Parliament proposals for a 'European Act' and a draft statement on economic integration. **23 June** Agreement for commercial and economic cooperation between Community and India signed.

	Development and organisation	Enlargement	Integration	External relations
1982		**23 February** Referendum in Greenland on membership of the Community. Majority in favour of seeking new type of relationship. New arrangements come into force on 1 February 1985.	**27 May** Council adopts resolution on Community action to combat unemployment. **12 November** Commission sends Council a communication on revival of European internal market.	**4 October** Commission sends Council a memorandum on Community development policy.
1983			**24 January** European Parliament brings action before Court of Justice against Council for failure to act in the field of transport policy. **19 June** European Council issues Solemn Declaration on European Union.	**17 December** Economic cooperation agreement between Community and Andean Pact countries signed in Cartagena, Colombia.
1984	**14 and 17 June** Second direct elections to the European Parliament.		**14 February** Parliament passes resolution on draft Treaty establishing European Union. **25 and 26 June** European Council at Fontainebleau reaches agreement on principles relating to Community budget and on reform of agricultural policy and opens the door to new policies and Spanish and Portuguese accession. **13 July** Franco–German Agreement signed on gradual removal of border checks.	**26 September** Commercial and economic cooperation agreement initialled by China and Community. **9 October** Cooperation Agreement signed between Community and Yemen Arab Republic. **8 December** Third Lomé Convention signed between Community and 65 ACP States. Enters into force on 1 May 1986.

1985

6 January
New Commission takes office under Jacques Delors.

12 June
Treaty of Accession for Spain and Portugal signed in Madrid and Lisbon.

1 January
European passport introduced in all Member States except Germany, Greece and United Kingdom.

14 June
Commission publishes a White Paper on completing the internal market, giving details of measures for dismantling physical, technical and fiscal barriers by 1992.

28 and 29 June
European Council in Milan discusses the convening of an Intergovernmental Conference to work out a treaty on a common foreign and security policy and amendments to the EEC Treaty to improve the decision-making procedure and extend the spheres of Community activity.

2 and 3 December
European Council in Luxembourg reaches agreement on reform of the Community institutions and on the legal form for foreign policy cooperation.
The agreement is finalized as a single act by the Foreign Ministers meeting at an Intergovernmental Conference on 16 and 17 December.

30 April
Angola signs third Lomé Convention to become 66th ACP State.

21 May
Five-year Trade and Economic Co-operation Agreement between Community and China signed.

1986

1 January
Spain and Portugal become the 11th and 12th members of the Community.

17 and 28 February
Single European Act signed by Representatives of the Governments of the 12 Member States.

	Development and organisation	Enlargement	Integration	External relations
1987	**20 July** Council adopts amendments to its rules of procedure re putting matters to the vote in Council.	**14 April** Turkey applies for membership of the Community. **20 July** Morocco applies for membership of the Community.	**18 February** Conditions for achieving the aims of the Single Act presented by Commission President to Parliament. **13 May** Bank of Spain signs EMS Agreement of 13 March 1979. **26 May** Irish Constitutional referendum clears way for Government to deposit instruments of ratification of the Single European Act. **1 July** Single European Act enters into force. **10 November** Bank of Portugal signs EMS Agreement of 13 March 1979.	**22 October** Council adopts broad lines of Community position for negotiations on agriculture at Uruguay Round.
1988	**29 March** Cecchini Report on internal market published. **24 June** Council adopts legislation on own resources and budgetary discipline. **28 June** Jacques Delors reappointed President of the European Commission and appointed Chairman of a committee to propose the steps necessary for monetary union.		**24 June** Council adopts measures on reform of the EC structural funds and a directive on complete liberalisation of capital movements from 1 July 1990. **14 September** Commission adopts working paper on the social dimension of internal market.	**2 February** EC discusses internal market with the EFTA States. **26 April** Council adopts declaration on relations between the Community and Japan. **26 September** Community signs trade and economic cooperation agreement with Hungary.

1989			
15 and 18 June 3rd direct elections to the European Parliament.	**17 July** Austria applies for membership of the European Community.	**12 April** 'Delors Report' on economic and monetary union presented.	**19 September** Community signs trade and economic cooperation agreement with Poland.
28-29 November Council agrees in principle to establish a European Environment Agency and a European Environment Monitoring and Information Network.		**8-9 December** Eleven of the twelve member states adopt a Community Charter of Fundamental Social Rights of Workers ('Social Charter').	**19 December** Community and EFTA countries decide to start formal negotiations for a general agreement to strengthen cooperation.

Source: 1950–1986: Commission of the European Communities, *A Journey through the EC* (Third Edition, 1987).
1987–1989: *21st, 22nd and 23rd General Reports on the Activities of the European Community, 1987, 1988 and 1989.*

References

Chapter 1

Commission of the European Communities, *Research on 'The Cost of Non-Europe' Project* (Luxembourg: Office for Official Publications of the EC, 1988).

Delors, J., *Report on Economic and Monetary Union in the European Community*, Report to the European Council chaired by J. Delors (Brussels: Commission of the EC, 1989).

Emerson, M., *The Economics of 1992: The EC Commission's Assessment of the Economic Effects of Completing the Internal Market* (Oxford: Oxford University Press, 1988).

Foley, A., *The Role of the Foreign and Irish Sectors in Manufacturing: An Examination based on the Census of Industrial Production 1983–1985.* Dublin Business School Seminar Series No. 1. (Dublin: Dublin City University, December 1988).

Foley, A. and P. Walbridge, *The Socio-Economic Position of Ireland within the European Economic Community* NESC Report No. 58 (Dublin: Stationery Office, 1981).

National Economic and Social Council, *Ireland in the European Community: Performance, Prospects and Strategy*, Report No. 88 (Dublin: Stationery Office, 1989).

Nerb, G., *Research on 'The Cost of Non-Europe' Project*, Vol. 3: The Completion of the Internal Market: A Survey of European Industry's Perception of the Likely Effects (Luxembourg: Office for Official Publications of the EC, 1988).

O'Leary, J., 'Some Implications of the Revisions to the Balance of Payments and National Accounts', *Irish Banking Review* (September 1984), 13–34.

Chapter 2

Brealy, M., and C. Quigley, *Completing the Internal Market of the European Community, 1992 Handbook* (London: Graham and Trotman, 1989).

Clausse, J. G. and J. M. Rion, 'Evolution des Disparités Régionales dans la Communauté 1970–82: Analyse Statistique et Comparative', *EIB Papers* (September 1986).

Club de Bruxelles, *The Internal Market, European Economy* (Brussels: European News Agency, 2 June 1988).

Commission of the European Communities, *Report on the Regional Problems of the Enlarged Community* (Thomson Report) (Brussels: Commission of the EC, 1973).

Commission of the European Communities, *Research on 'The Cost of Non-Europe' Project*, Vol. 1: Basic Studies; Executive Summaries (Luxembourg: Office for Official Publications of the EC, 1988).

Commission of the European Communities, 'The Economics of 1992', *European Economy*, No. 35 (1988).

Commission of the European Communities, *The Regions of the Enlarged Community*, Third Periodic Report on the Social and Economic Situation and Development of the Regions of the Community (Brussels: Commission of the EC, 1987).

Coudert Brothers, *1992, A Working Guide* (Brussels: Coudert Brothers EEC Team, April 1989).

Dudley, J. W., *1992, Strategies for the Single Market* (London: Kogan Page, 1989).

Molle, W. and R. Capellir, *Regional Impact of Community Policies in Europe* (Aldershot: Gower, 1989).

van Ginderachter, J., 'La Réforme des Fonds Structurels', *Revue du Marché Commun* (May 1989).

Vanhove, N. and L. H. Klassen, *Regional Policy: A European Approach* (Aldershot: Avebury, 1987).

Chapter 3

Balassa, B., 'Trade Policies in Developing Countries', *American Economic Review* (May 1971), 178–87.

Balassa, B., *The Structure of Protection in Developing Countries* (Baltimore: Johns Hopkins Press, 1971).

Balassa, B. & Associates, *Development Strategies in Semi-industrial Economics* (Baltimore: Johns Hopkins Press, 1982).

Balassa, B., *The Importance of Trade For Developing Countries*. Report No DRD 248 (Washington: Development Research Department, World Bank, 1987).

Balassa, B. and H. Giersch, (eds), *Economic Incentives* (London: Macmillan, 1986).

Baldwin, R. E., *Structural Change and Patterns of International Trade*. Paper presented at the International Economics Study Group, 11th Annual Conference (September 1986).

Cawley, R. and M. Davenport, 'Partial Equilibrium Calculations of the Impact of Internal Market Barriers in the European Community', in *Research on 'The Cost of Non-Europe' Project*, Vol. 2: Studies on the Economics of Integration (Luxembourg: Office for Official Publications of the EC, 1988), 487–518.

CIO, *Final Report of Committee on Industrial Organisation* (Dublin: Stationery Office, 1965).

Devine, P. J. et al., *An Introduction to Industrial Economics* (London: George Allen & Unwin, 1985).

Dreze, J., 'The Standard Goods Hypothesis' in A. Jacquemin and A. Sapir (eds), *The European Internal Market: Trade and Competition* (Oxford: Oxford University Press, 1989), pp. 13–32.

Foley, A., 'Export Performance under Outward Looking Strategies — The Irish Experience', Paper presented at Development Studies Association Conference; The Queens University of Belfast (September 1989).

Helpman, E. and P. Krugman, *Market Structure and Foreign Trade* (Massachusetts: MIT Press, 1985).

Keesing, D., 'Outward-Looking Policies and Economic Development', *Economic Journal*, Vol. LXXVII, No. 306 (June 1967).

Keesing, D., *Trade Policy for Developing Countries*, World Bank Staff Working Paper, No. 353 (Washington: World Bank, 1979).

Keesing, D., *The Four Successful Exceptions: Official Export Promotion and Support for Export Marketing in Hong Kong, Singapore, Taiwan and the Republic of Korea* (Washington: Trade Policy Division, World Bank, 1988).

Kennedy, K. A. and B. R. Dowling, *Economic Growth in Ireland: The Experience since 1947* (Dublin: Gill and Macmillan, 1975).

Krueger, Anne O., 'Problems of Liberalization in A. M. Choksi and Demetris Papageorgiou (eds), *Economic Liberalization in Developing Countries* (Oxford: Blackwell, 1986).

Krugman, P. R., 'Introduction: New Thinking about Trade Policy' in Krugman *Strategic Trade Policy and the New International Economics* (Cambridge, Massachusetts: MIT Press, 1986).

Krugman, P. R., 'Economic Integration in Europe: Some Conceptual Issues' in T. Padoa-Schioppa (ed.), *Efficiency, Stability and Equity, A Strategy for the Evolution of the Economic System of the European Community* (Oxford: Oxford University Press, 1987).

Krugman, P. R., *Strategic Trade Policy and the New International Economics* (Cambridge, Massachussets: MIT Press, 1986).

Krugman, P. R., 'Import Protection as Export Promotion' in H. Kiersowski H. (ed), *Monopolistic Competition and International Trade* (Oxford: Oxford University Press, 1984).

Maizels, A., *Growth and Trade* (Cambridge: Cambridge University Press, 1970).

McAleese, D., 'Outward Looking Policies, Manufactured Exports and Economic Growth: The Irish Experience' in M. J. Artis and A. R. Noboy (eds), *Proceedings of the 1977 AUTE Conference* (London: Croom Helm, 1975).

Michaely, M., 'The Timing and Sequencing of a Trade Liberalization Policy', in A. M. Choksi and Demetris Papageorgiou (eds), *Economic Liberalization in Developing Countries* (Oxford: Blackwell, 1986).

Michalopoulos, C. and K. Jay, *Growth of Exports and Income in the Developing*

World: A neoclassical view. A.I.D. Discussion Paper, No. 28 (Washington: Bureau for Program & Policy Coordination).

National Economic and Social Community, *Ireland in the European Community: Performance, Prospects and Strategy*, Report No. 88 (Dublin: Stationery Office, 1989).

Neven, D., 'EEC integration towards 1992: some distributional aspects', *Economic Policy*, Vol. 10 (1990), 7–62.

O'Malley, E., 'Late Industrialization under Outward-Looking Policies: The Experience and Prospects of the Republic of Ireland', D.Phil thesis, University of Sussex (1982).

Pelkmans, J., 'The Assignment of Public Functions in Economic Integration', *Journal of Common Market Studies*, Vol. 21, Nos. 1 and 2 (September/December 1982), 97–121.

Pelkmans, J., *Market Integration in the European Community* (The Hague: Martinus Nijhoff, 1984).

Porter, M. E., *Competitive Strategy* (London: Free Press, Collier Macmillan, 1980).

Sodersten, B., *International Economics* (London: Macmillan, 1985).

Telesis Consulting Group, *A Review of Industrial Policy*, National Economic and Social Council Report No. 64 (Dublin: Stationery Office, 1982).

Ustunel, B., *Growth, Trade and Technology: from Trade Generated Growth to Growth Generated Trade and the Cases of Sweden, Japan, and Turkey.* IIES University of Stockholm Seminar Paper No. 18, Stockholm, (1972).

Venables, A. J. and A. Smith, 'Trade and industrial policy under imperfect competition', *Economic Policy*, (October 1986).

Viner, J., *The Customs Union Issue* (New York: Carnegie Endowment for International Peace, 1953).

Vollrath, T., *Development Consequences of Unrestricted Trade.* United States Department of Agricultural Economic Research Service, Foreign Agricultural Economic Report, No. 213 (1985).

Williamson, J., *The Open Economy and the World Economy: A Textbook in International Economics* (New York: Harper & Row, 1983).

World Bank, *World Development Report, 1987* (London: Oxford University Press, 1987).

Chapter 4

Albert, M. and R. J. Ball, *Towards European Recovery in the 1980s*, Report Presented to the European Parliament (Strasbourg: European Parliament, 1983).

Baldwin, R., 'The Growth Effects of 1992', *Economic Policy* (October 1989), 247–281.

Beenstock, M., *The World Economy in Transition* (London: George Allen and Unwin, 1983).

Boltho, A., 'Growth', in A. Boltho (ed.), *The European Economy: Growth and Crisis* (Oxford: Oxford University Press, 1983),, 9–37.

Catinat, M., 'The Large Internal Market under the Microscope: Problems and Challenges', in A. Jacquemin and A. Sapir (eds), *The European Internal Market: Trade and Competition* (Oxford: Oxford University Press, 1989), 334–356.

Catinat, M., E. Donn, and A. Italianer, *Research on 'The Cost of Non-Europe' Project*, Vol. 2: Studies on the Economics of Integration, Chapter 10: The Completion of the Internal Market: Results of Macroeconomic Model Simulations (Luxembourg: Office for Official Publications of the EC, 1988).

Cecchini, P., *The European Challenge 1992: The Benefits of a Single Market* (Aldershot: Wildwood House, 1988).

Commission of the European Communities, 'Facing the Challenges of the Early 1990s', *European Economy*, No. 42 (1989).

Dertouzos, M. L., R. K. Lester, and R. M. Solow, *Made in America: Regaining the Productive Edge*, (Cambridge, Massachusetts: MIT Press, 1989).

Emerson, M., *The Economics of 1992: The EC Commission's Assessment of the Economic Effects of Completing the Internal Market* (Oxford: OUP, 1988).

Ginsberg, R. H., 'US-EC Relations', in J. Lodge (ed.), *The European Community and the Challenge of the Future* (London: Pinter Publishers, 1989), 256–278.

Krugman, P. R., 'Economic Integration in Europe: Some Conceptual Issues' in T. Padoa-Schipppa (ed.), *Efficiency, Stability and Equity* (Oxford: Oxford University Press, 1987), pp. 117–40.

Lawrence, R. L. and C. L. Schultze, 'Barriers to European Growth: An Overview', in A. Jacquemin and A. Sapir (eds), *The European Internal Market: Trade and Competition* (Oxford: Oxford University Press, 1989), 251–297.

Maddison, A., 'Growth and Slowdown in Advanced Capitalist Economies: Techniques of Quantitative Assessment', *Journal of Economic Literature* (1987), 649–698.

Organisation for Economic Cooperation and Development, *Economic Outlook*, No. 46, 1989.

Organisation for Economic Cooperation and Development, *Japan*, OECD, 1989.

Olson, M., *The Rise and Decline of Nations: Economic Growth, Stagflation and Social Rigidities* (New Haven, Connecticut: Yale University Press, 1982).

Padoa-Schioppa, T. (ed.), *Efficiency, Stability and Equity: A Strategy for the Evolution of the Economic System of the European Community* (Oxford, Oxford University Press, 1987).

Solow, R. M., 'Technical Change and the Aggregate Production Function', *Review of Economics and Statistics* (1957), 312–320.

Chapter 5

Commission of the European Communities, *Research on 'The Cost of Non-Europe' Project* (Luxembourg: Office for Official Publications of the EC, 1988).

Delors, J., *Report on Economic and Monetary Union in the European Community*, Report to the European Council chaired by J. Delors (Brussels: Commission of the EC, 1989).

McAleese, D., 'What have we gained from the European Community?', *Seirbhis Phoibli*, Vol. 10, No. 1 (April 1989), 9–11.

Chapter 6

Artis, M. J., 'What has the EMS Achieved?', Paper delivered at the Irish Economic Association Conference, Dublin, 1989.

Bacon, P., 'The European Monetary System — Sterling and the Irish Pound', *Irish Banking Review* (Autumn 1988), 3–20.

Cecchini, P., *The European Challenge 1992: The Benefits of a Single Market* (Aldershot: Wildwood House, 1988).

Commission of the European Communities, 'The Economics of 1992', *European Economy*, No. 35 (1988).

Currie, D. and G. Dicks, 'The MTFS or the EMS: Which Way for Credible Monetary Policy?' *Economic Outlook 1987–1991*, Vol. 13, No. 9 (1989).

Delors, J., *Report on Economic and Monetary Union in the European Community*, Report to the European Council chaired by J. Delors (Brussels: Commission of the EC, 1989).

Doyle, M. F., 'A Decade of the European Monetary System: Achievements and Prospects', Paper delivered at the Irish Economic Association Conference, Dublin, 1989.

Gray, A., 'Impact of Completing the Internal Market in Financial Services', Paper presented at the Financial Services Industry Association, Dublin, 1988.

National Economic and Social Council, *Ireland in the European Community: Performance, Prospects and Strategy*, Report No. 88 (Dublin: Stationery Office, 1989).

Padoa-Schioppa, T. (ed.), *Efficiency, Stability and Equity: A Strategy for the Evolution of the Economic System of the European Community* (Oxford: Oxford University Press, 1987).

Pelkmans, J., 'The Assignment of Public Functions in Economic Integrations', *Journal of Common Market Studies*, Vol. 21, Nos. 1 and 2 (September/December 1982), 97–121.

Servais, D., *The Single Financial Market* (Brussels: Commission of the EC, 1988).

Chapter 7

National Economic and Social Council, *Ireland in the European Community: Performance, Prospects and Strategy*, Report No. 88 (Dublin: Stationery Office, 1989).

Thom, R., 'The Demand for Alcohol in Ireland', *The Economic and Social Review*, Vol. 15, No. 4 (July 1984), 325–36.
Thom, R., *The Revenue Implications of Tax Harmonisation* (Dublin: The European League for Economic Co-operation, 1988).

Chapter 8

Atkins Management Consultants, *Research on 'The Cost of Non-Europe' Project*, Vol. 5: 'The Cost of Non-Europe' in Public Sector Procurement (Luxembourg: Office for Official Publications of the EC, 1988).
Commission of the European Communities, *Completing the Internal Market*, White Paper from the Commission to the European Council, COM (85) 310 Final (Brussels: Commission of the EC, 1985).
Groupe MAC, *Technical Barriers in the EC: An Illustration by Six Industries* (Luxembourg: Office for Official Publications of the EC, 1988).
Groupe MAC, *Research on 'The Cost of Non-Europe' Project*, Vol. 6, Pt. 1: Technical Barriers in the EC: An Illustration by Six Industries (Luxembourg: Office for Official Publications of the EC, 1988).

Chapter 9

Abbati, C. degli, *Transport and European Integration* (Luxembourg: Office for Official Publications of the EC, 1987).
Central Statistics Office, *1987 Household Budget Survey: Initial Summary Results* (Dublin: CSO, 1989).
Chartered Institute of Transport in Ireland, *The Irish International Road Haulage Industry: A Study of its Competitiveness* (Dublin: CITI, April 1987).
Commission of the European Communities, *Completing the Internal Market*, White Paper from the Commission to the European Council, COM (85) 310 Final (Brussels: Commission of the EC, 1985).
Commission of the European Communities, *The Contribution of Infrastructure to Regional Development*, Infrastructure Study Group, Chairman: D. Biehl (Brussels: Commission of the EC, 1986).
Commission of the European Communities, 'The Economics of 1992', *European Economy*, No. 35 (1988).
Commission of the European Communities, *Fourth Progress Report of the Commission to the European Council and the European Parliament Concerning the Implementation of the Commission's White Paper on the Completion of the Internal Market* (Brussels: Commission of the EC, June 1989).
Commission of the European Communities, *Community Support Framework for Ireland* (Brussels: Commission of the EC, October 1989).
Confederation of Irish Industries, *Transport: Why It Is Critical to Ireland's Success*

(Dublin: CII, November 1989).

Corás Tráchtála, *1992 and Your Market: Liberalising Transport* (Dublin: CTT, 1988).

Dublin Port, *Five-Year Development Plan leading to 1993 and Beyond* (Dublin: Dublin Port, 1989).

Ferris, T., 'Implications of Channel Tunnel for Ireland', Paper presented to the 1992 Europen Conference on Tourism and Transport (Dublin: Department of Tourism and Transport, 2 November 1988).

Ferris, T., 'The Challenge of the Channel Tunnel for Ireland', Paper presented to the Second International Conference on 'Impact of Channel Tunnel on Freight Movement in Europe', City University, London (22 June 1989).

Fitzpatrick, J. & Associates, 'Travel and Tourism in the Single European Market' (London: EIU Special Report No. 2014, October 1989).

Kay, J., A. Manning, and S. Szymanski, 'The Channel Tunnel', *Economic Policy* (April 1989), 211–34.

National Economic and Social Council, *Transport Policy*, Report No. 48 (Dublin: Stationery Office, 1980).

National Economic and Social Council, *The Importance of Infrastructure to Industrial Development in Ireland – Roads, Telecommunications and Water Supply*, Report No. 54 (Dublin: Stationery Office, 1981).

National Economic and Social Council, *Ireland in the European Community: Performance, Prospects and Strategy*, Report No. 88 (Dublin: Stationery Office, 1989).

O'Mahony, D., 'Developments in Civil Aviation in Recent Years', *Seirbhis Phoibli*, Vol. 9, No. 3 (1988), 16–23.

O'Sullivan, L., 'Macroeconomic Effects of 1992' in J. Bradley and J. Fitzgerald (eds), *Medium-Term Review: 1989–1994* (Dublin: Economic and Social Research Institute, June 1989).

Pena, E., 'Creating a Single European Market: The Role of Competitive Transport', 1992 Europen Conference on Tourism and Transport (Dublin: Department of Tourism and Transport, 2 November 1988).

Quigley, D. B., 'Fiscal Dimensions of 1992', Paper Presented to the 1992 Europen Conference on Tourism and Transport (Dublin: Department of Tourism and Transport, 2 November 1988).

Stationery Office, *Ireland – Road Development 1989 to 1993* (Dublin: Stationery Office, Pl.6482, 1989).

Stationery Office, *National Development Plan 1989–1993* (Dublin: Stationery Office, Pl.6342, 1989).

Toomey, B., 'The Implications of the EC Single Market for the Transport and Tourism Sectors', *Seirbhis Phoibli*, Vol. 10, No. 1 (1989), 79–86.

Chapter 10

Buigues, P. and F. Ilzkovitz, *The Sectoral Impact of the Single Market* (Brussels: Commission of the EC, 1988).

Cecchini, P., *The European Challenge 1992: The Benefits of a Single Market* (Aldershot: Wildwood House, 1988).

Córas Tráchtála, *Annual Review and Outlook 1989/1990* (Dublin: CTT, 1990).

Emerson, M., *The Economics of 1992: The EC Commission's Assessment of the Economic Effects of Completing the Internal Market* (Oxford: Oxford University Press, 1988).

Ernst and Whinney, *Research on 'The Cost of Non-Europe' Project*, Vol. 4, Pt. 1: The Cost of Non-Europe: Border Related Controls and Administrative Formalities (Luxembourg: Office for Official Publications of the EC, 1988).

Europen Bureau, *1992 and the Textiles, Clothing and Footwear Sector* (Dublin: Stationery Office, 1989).

Europen Bureau, *1992 and the Food and Drink Industry* (Dublin: Stationery Office, 1989).

Europen Bureau, *1992 and the Metal and Mechanical Engineering Sector* (Dublin: Stationery Office, 1989).

Europen Bureau, *1992 and the Electronics, Electrical and Instrument Engineering Sectors* (Dublin: Stationery Office, 1990).

Industrial Development Authority, *End of Year Statement 1989* (Dublin: IDA, 1990).

Irish Goods Council, *Market Commentary* (Dublin: Irish Goods Council, 1988).

McAleese, D. and A. Matthews, 'The Single European Act and Ireland: Implications for a Small Member State', *Journal of Common Market Studies*, Vol. 26, No. 1 (September 1987), 39–60.

McHugh, D., *The Changing Face of Industrial Policy*. Paper delivered to the Annual Conference of the Development Studies Association, Queen's University, Belfast, September 1989.

National Economic and Social Council, *Ireland in the European Community: Performance, Prospects and Strategy*, Report No. 88 (Dublin: Stationery Office, 1989).

Nerb, G., *Research on 'The Cost of Non-Europe' Project*, Vol. 3: The Completion of the Internal Market: A Survey of European Industry's Perception of Likely Effects (Luxembourg: Office for Official Publications of the EC, 1988).

O'Malley, E., *Sectoral Implications of the Single European Market for Irish Manufacturing* (Dublin: Economic and Social Research Institute, 1989).

Ruane, F. and A. McGibney, 'The Role of Overseas Industry' in A. Foley and D. McAleese (eds), *Overseas Industry in Ireland 1990* (Dublin: Gill and Macmillan, 1990).

Stationery Office, *Programme for Industrial Development 1989–1993* (Dublin: Stationery Office, 1989).

Stationery Office, *National Development Plan 1989–1993* (Dublin: Stationery Office, 1989).

Telesis Consulting Group, *A Review of Industrial Policy*. National Economic and Social Council Report No. 64 (Dublin: Stationery Office, 1982).

Chapter 11

Commission of the European Communities, *Completion of the Internal Market: Community Legislation on Foodstuffs*, 1985, COM (85) 603 Final.

Dowling, M., 'Progress towards achievement of the 1992 deadlines from the perspectives of the Irish Administration'. Paper to Teagasc Conference, Dublin, September 1988.

Garvey, T., 'The EC Commission's Programme for achieving a Single European Market in the Food Industry', Paper to Teagasc Conference, Dublin, September 1988.

Groupe MAC, *The 'Cost of Non-Europe' in the Foodstuffs Industry*. Study for Commission of the European Communities (Luxembourg: European Communities, 1988).

Harris, S. et al., *The Food and Farm Policies of the European Community* (Chichester: John Wiley & Sons, 1983).

Josling, T., 'Implications for Non-EEC Countries'. Paper to Conference on the EEC's Food Industries, University of Reading, September 1989.

Keane, M., *Milk Seasonality, Pricing and Cheese Development*. Agribusiness Discussion Paper No. 6 (Department of Dairy & Food Economics, University College Cork, 1986).

Keane, M., *Producer Prices for Milk – Trends and Future Prospects*. Agribusiness Discussion Paper No. 9 (Department of Dairy & Food Economics, University College Cork, 1990).

Keane, M. and D. I. F. Lucey, *Positive MCAs and the EEC Dairy Budget*. Agribusiness Discussion Paper No. 1 (Cork: Department of Dairy and Food Economics, University College Cork, 1984).

Keane, M. and D. I. F. Lucey, *Irish Dairying – Modelling the Spatial Dimension*. Agribusiness Discussion Paper No. 10 (Department of Dairy & Food Economics, University College Cork, 1990).

Lucey, D. I. F., 'The Setting for Irish Cooperatives' in L. Garoyan (ed.), *Cooperative Growth – Potential and Strategies* (Cork: University College Cork, Centre for Co-operative Studies, 1984).

Matthews, A. 'Is "1992" Really Important for Irish Agriculture and Food'. Paper to Teagasc Conference, Dublin, September 1988.

Matthews, A. and R. O'Connor, 'The Food Processing Sector', in *Medium Term Review 1987–1992* (Dublin: Economic and Social Research Institute, 1987).

McCrea, C., 'The Strategy Options for Irish Food Companies'. Paper to Teagasc Conference, Dublin, September 1988.

National Economic and Social Council, *A Strategy for Economic Development 1986–1990*, Report No. 83 (Dublin: Stationery Office, November 1986).

National Economic and Social Council, *Ireland in the European Community: Performance, Prospects and Strategy*, Report No. 88 (Dublin: Stationery Office, 1989).

Pitts, E. and N. Simms, 'Detailed Implications of 1992 for Dairy Industry'. Paper to Teagasc Conference, Dublin, September 1988.

Sheehy, S., 'Irish Agriculture in the Nineties', *Irish Banking Review* (Autumn 1988), 21–32.

van Dijk G. and C. Mackel, 'Future Constraints to the Food Industries arising from Policy Developments in the Animal Production Sector in Europe'. Paper to OECD Symposium, January 1982, quoted in Simon Harris et al, *The Food and Farm Policies of the European Community* (Chichester: John Wiley & Sons, 1983).

Chapter 12

Commission of the European Communities, 'The Economics of 1992', *European Economy*, No. 35 (1988).

Price Waterhouse, *Research on 'The Cost of Non-Europe' Project*, Vol. 9: 'The Cost of Non-Europe' in Financial Services (Luxembourg: Office for Official Publications of the EC, 1988).

Chapter 13

BIPE — Bureau d'Information et des Prévisions Économiques, *Research on 'The Cost of Non-Europe' Project*, Vol. 13: 'Le Coût De La Non-Europe', Des Produits De Construction (Luxembourg: Office for Official Publications of the EC, 1988).

Chaldecott, N., *Building Materials Movements between EC Member States 1988* (London: National Council of Building Material Producers, 1989).

Commission of the European Communities, *Completing the Internal Market*, White Paper from the Commission to the European Council, COM (85) 310 Final (Brussels: Commission of the EC, 1985).

Chapter 14

Ahlstrom, D., 'The Economy's Electronics Manufacturing Powerhouse', *The Irish Times* (12 September 1989), 18.

Balassa, B., 'Effects of Commercial Policy on International Trade, the Location of Production and Factor Movements' in B. Ohlin et al (eds), *The International Allocation of Economic Activity* (London: Macmillan, 1977).

Bank of Boston, Economics Department, *US Manufacturing Firms' Attitudes Toward 1992* (Boston: Bank of Boston, February 1989).

Benson, F., 'The Financial Services Centre', *The Irish Institutional Investment Reference Journal* (1989), 151-56.

Blankart, F., 'Swiss Foreign Economic Policy: Worldwide and European Aspects', Address to Swiss-Irish Business Association (Dublin, 23 November 1989).

Boylan, T.A. and M. Cuddy, 'Multinational Companies and Economic Development: Aspects of the Irish Experience', *IBAR* Vol. 9 (1989), 76-86.

Buckley, P.J. and P. Artisien, 'Policy Issues of Intra-EC Direct Investment: British, German and French Multinationals in Greece, Portugal and Spain, With Special Reference to Employment Effects', *Journal of Common Market Studies*, Vol. 26, No. 2 (1987), 205-30.

Business International, *The 1993 Company Corporate Strategies for Europe's Single Market* (London: Business International, 1989).

Central Statistics Office, *Census of Industrial Production* (Dublin: Stationery Office, various years).

Ciba-Geigy Journal, 'Pharmaceutical Production to be Restructured for Europe 1992', Vol. 3 (1989), 5.

Commission of the European Communities, 'Creation of a European Financial Area', *European Economy* No. 36 (May 1988).

Cronin, C., 'Dublin Attracts Firms in Captive Insurance', *The Irish Times* (27 September 1989).

Cusumano, M., *The Japanese Automobile Industry: Technology and Management at Nissan and Toyota* (Cambridge: Harvard University Press, 1985).

Dassesse, M., 'Financial Services and 1992: Significance of Branching and Cross-Border Selling,' *European Trends,* EIU No. 2 (1988).

Doyle, P., 'Ireland in a Single Financial Area: A Case Study of How a Weaker EC Economy is Adjusting', *European Trends, EIU* No. 2 (1988).

Dunning, J. H., *International Production and the Multinational Enterprise* (London: Allen and Unwin, 1981).

Dunning, J. H., *Explaining International Production*, (London: Unwin Hyman, 1988).

Dunning, J.H. and P. Robson, 'Multinational Corporate Integration and Regional Economic Integration', *Journal of Common Market Studies*, Vol. 26, No. 2 (1987), 103-25.

Emerson, M., *The Economics of 1992: The EC Commission's Assessment of the Economic Effects of Completing the Internal Market* (Oxford: Oxford University Press, 1988).

FitzGerald, J.D., '1992: The Distribution Sector' in J. Bradley et al., *The Economics of 1992: A Symposium on Sectoral Issues* (Dublin: Economic and Social Research Institute, 1989).

FitzPatrick, J., *Ireland to 1992: Putting its House in Order* (London: EIU Special Report No. 1137, 1988).

FitzPatrick, J., *Republic of Ireland: Economic Prospects 1984-1988* (London: EIU, 1984).

Fortune, 'Vive Le Marche Unique!' No. 17 (Juillet-Aout 1989).

Fuji Economic Review, 'Japan's Surging Foreign Direct Investment' (July-August 1989), 14-16.

Industrial Development Authority, *Overseas Companies in Ireland* (Dublin: IDA,

March 1988).

Industrial Development Authority, *The Irish Economy Expenditures Survey: 1983-1987, Main Results* (Dublin: IDA, December 1988).

Industrial Development Authority, *Review of IDA's Three Business Areas, 1988* (Dublin: IDA, January 1989).

Jacobson, D. and B. Andreosso, 'Investment and Industrial Integration in Western Europe', *Administration* 36/2 (1988), 165–85.

Jacquemin, A., P. Buigues, and F. Ilzkovitz, 'Horizontal Mergers and Competition Policy in the European Community', *European Economy*, No. 40 (May 1989).

Jones, K., 'Why the Japanese Come Here' in *Japan: An International Report*, Supplement to *The Irish Times* (25 September 1989), vii.

Keating, W. and T. Keane, 'Irish Industrial Structures, 1979-1985: A Longitudinal Analysis', Paper Read Before the Statistical and Social Inquiry Society of Ireland (18 May 1989).

Keohane, K., 'Toxic Trade-Off: The Price Ireland Pays for Industrial Development' *The Ecologist*, Vol. 19, No. 2 (August 1989), 144-46.

Knickerbocker, F.T., *Oligopolistic Reaction and Multinational Enterprise* (Boston: Harvard Business School, 1973).

Kojima, K., *Direct Foreign Investment: A Japanese Model of Multinational Business Operations* (London: Croom Helm, 1978).

Krugman, P., 'Economic Integration: Some Conceptual Issues' in T. Padoa-Schioppa, *Efficiency, Stability and Equity: A Strategy for the Evolution of the Economic System of the European Community* (Oxford: Oxford University Press, 1987), 117-40.

Larkin, F.M., 'The Custom House Docks Development and its Impact on Financial Services', *Seirbhis Phoibli* Vol. 9, No. 3 (November 1988), 30–36.

McGill, P., 'Japanese Firms to Create 380 Jobs', *The Irish Times* (10 November 1989).

McGowan, P., 'Competition in Irish Banking' *Irish Banking Review* (Autumn 1986), 27-40.

Maruya, R. and D. Jacobson, 'Japanese Investment in Ireland'. Unpublished Typescript, Kobé University and Dublin City University (1989).

Monthly Journal of Financial Statistics, *Saisei Kinyu Tokei Geppou*, Vol. 380 (Dec. 1983), Vol. 404 (Dec. 1985), and Vol. 428 (Dec. 1987).

National Economic and Social Council, *Ireland in the European Community: Performance, Prospect and Strategy*, Report No. 88 (Dublin: Stationery Office, 1989).

NIEC (Northern Ireland Economic Council), *Economic Implications for Northern Ireland and the Republic of Ireland of Recent Developments in the European Community* (Belfast: NIEC, 1988 (Joint paper with NESC)).

O'Donnell, R., 'Manufacturing' in J. Bradley et al., *The Economics of 1992: A Symposium on Sectoral Issues* (Dublin: Economic and Social Research Institute, 1989).

O'Malley, E., *Sectoral Implications of the Single European Market for Irish Manufacturing* (Dublin: Economic and Social Research Institute, 1989).

O'Rourke, K., 'The Non-Traded Sector: Services and Building and Construction' in J.W. O'Hagan (ed.), *The Economy of Ireland: Policy and Performance* Fifth Edition (Dublin: Irish Management Institute, 1987), 408–32.

O'Shaughnessy, K., 'Changes in the Financial Services Market' *Irish Banking Review*, Winter (1987), 12–25.

Pecchioli, R. M., *The Internationalisation of Banking: The Policy Issues* (Paris: OECD, 1983).

Quijano, A. P., 'Capital Expenditure by Majority-Owned Foreign Affiliates of US Companies, 1989', *Survey of Current Business*, Vol. 69, No. 3 (1989).

Ruane, F., 'Manufacturing Industry' in J. W. O'Hagan (ed.), *The Economy of Ireland: Policy and Performance* Fourth Edition (Dublin: Irish Management Institute, 1984).

Simango, C. B., *MNEs in the Pharmaceutical Industry in Ireland* Typescript (Dublin: Dublin City University Business School, 1989).

Simpson, J., *Implications of 1992 for Northern Ireland*, mimeo (Belfast: QUB, 1989).

Stewart, J. C., *Corporate Finance and Fiscal Policy in Ireland* (London: Gower, 1987).

Stewart, J. C., 'Transfer Pricing: Some Empirical Evidence from Ireland', *Journal of Economic Issues*, Vol. 16, No. 3 (1989).

US Department of Commerce, *Survey of Current Business*, various years.

Walsh, M., 'The Control of Banking in the Republic of Ireland: A Review', *Irish Banking Review* (September 1985), 3–11.

Chapter 15

Bradley, J. and J. FitzGerald, *Medium Term Review 1989–1994* (Dublin: Economic and Social Research Institute, 1989).

Cecchini, P., *The European Challenge 1992: The Benefits of a Single Market* (Aldershot: Wildwood House, 1988).

Commission of the European Communities, 'The Social Dimension of the Internal Market', *Social Europe*, Special Edition (1988).

Kennedy, K. A., 'Ireland and European Integration — An Economic Perspective', in D. Keogh, (ed.), *Ireland and the Challenge of European Integration* (Cork: Hibernian Press, 1989).

National Economic and Social Council, *Ireland in the European Community: Performance, Prospects and Strategy*, Report No. 88 (Dublin: Stationery Office, 1989).

Roberts, B., 'The Social Dimension of European Labour Markets', in R. Gahdrendorf et al., *Whose Europe? Competing Visions for 1992* (London: Institute for Economic Affairs, 1989).

Sexton, J. J., *Labour Force Flows in an Overall Demographic Context: Projections of Potential Labour Supply*. Economic and Social Research Institute Seminar Paper, January 1990.

Chapter 16

Blackwell, J., *Women in the Labour Force: A Statistical Digest* (Dublin: Employment Equality Agency, 1986).

Blackwell, J., *Unemployment Compensation and Work Incentives*. Report of the Commission on Social Welfare, Background Paper No. 2 (Dublin: Department of Social Welfare, 1986).

Blackwell, J., 'Family Income Support: Policy Options', in B. Reynolds and S. J. Healy (eds), *Poverty and Family Income Policy* (Dublin, CMRS, 1988).

Blackwell, J., *Women in the Labour Force* Second Edition (Dublin: Employment Equality Agency, 1989).

Blackwell, J. and B. Nolan, 'Low Pay — The Irish Experience', in *Low Pay – The Irish Experience* (Dublin: Combat Poverty Agency and the Irish Congress of Trade Unions, 1990).

Commission of the European Communities, 'The Social Dimension of the Internal Market', *Social Europe*, Special Edition (1988).

Commission of the European Communities, *European Economy*, No. 42 (November 1989).

Commission of the European Communities, *Employment in Europe 1989* (Luxembourg: Office for Official Publications of the EC, 1989).

Committee of Independent Experts of the European Social Charter, *Conclusions V* (Strasbourg: Council of Europe, 1977).

Committee of Independent Experts of the European Social Charter, *Conclusions IX-2* (Strasbourg: Council of Europe, 1986).

Department of Labour, *Employers' Perceptions of the Effects of Labour Legislation* (Dublin: Stationery Office, 1986).

Dineen, D. A., 'Changing Employment Patterns in Ireland: Recent Trends and Future Prospects', Final Report, Prepared for the Irish National Pensions Board (1989).

Europen Bureau, *1992 and the Electronic, Electrical and Instrument Engineering Sectors* (Dublin: Stationery Office, 1990).

Europen Bureau, *1992 and the Metal and Mechanical Engineering Sector* (Dublin: Stationery Office, 1989).

Europen Bureau, *1992 and the Textiles, Clothing and Footwear Sector* (Dublin: Stationery Office, 1989).

Governmental Committee of the European Social Charter, *Ninth Report* (II) (Strasbourg: Council of Europe, 1987).

Klau, F. and A. Mittelstädt, 'Labour Market Flexibility and External Price Shocks', Working Paper No. 24, Economics and Statistics Department (Paris: OECD, 1985).

Organisation for Economic Cooperation and Development, *Employment Outlook* (Paris: OECD, September 1986).

Organisation for Economic Cooperation and Development, *Economic Survey: Ireland* (Paris: OECD, 1989).

Pahl, R. E., 'Conclusion: Whose Problem?', in *Underground Economy and Irregular Forms of Employment*, Final Synthesis Report (Brussels: Commission of the European Communities, 1989).

Pahl, R. E. and J. Blackwell, 'The Black Economy in Ireland', in *Programme of Research on the Black Economy in Europe*, Final Report (Brussels: Commission of the EC, 1988).

Stationery Office, *Report of the Committee of Inquiry on Safety, Health and Welfare at Work* (Dublin: Stationery Office, 1983).

Statistical Office of the European Communities, *Labour Costs 1984:* Vol 1 *Principal Results* (Luxembourg: Office for Official Publications of the EC, 1987).

Statistical Office of the European Communities, *Eurostatistics* No. 3 (Luxembourg: Office for Official Publications of the EC, 1990).

Walsh, B. M., 'Unemployment Compensation and the Rate of Unemployment', in H. G. Grubel and M. A. Walker (eds), *Unemployment Insurance: Global Evidence of its Effects on Unemployment* (Vancouver: Fraser Institute, 1978).

Chapter 17

Aydalot, P., 'The Location of New Firm Creation: The French Case', in D. Keeble and E. Wever (eds), *New Firms and Regional Development in Europe* (London: Croom Helm, 1986).

Begg, I., 'The Regional Dimension of the 1992 Proposals,' *Regional Studies*, Vol. 23, No. 4 (1989), 368-76.

Bradfield, M., *Regional Economics* (Toronto: McGraw-Hill, Ryerson, 1988).

Carlsson, B., 'The Evaluation of Manufacturing Technology and its Impact on Industrial Structure. An International Study.' A Paper Presented to the International Conference on Evolution of Technology and Market Structure in an International Context, Italy, 1988.

Central Statistics Office, *Labour Force Survey* (Dublin: CSO, 1979).

Central Statistics Office, *Labour Force Survey* (Dublin: CSO, 1983).

Chisholm, M., 'Accessibility and Regional Development in Britain: Some Questions Arising from Data on Freight Flows', *Environment and Planning A* Vol. 17 (1985), 963-980.

Commission of the European Communities, *The Regions of Europe:* First Periodic Report on the Social and Economic Situation of the Regions of the Community (Brussels: Commission of the EC, 1981).

Commission of the European Communities, *The Future of Rural Society* (Brussels: Commission of the EC, 1988).

Commission of the European Communities, 'The Economics of 1992', *European Economy*, No. 35 (1988).

Commission of the European Communities, *Employment in Europe*. (Luxembourg: Office for Official Publications of the EC, 1989).

Goddard, J.B., et al., *Study of the Effects of New Information Technology on the Less Favoured Regions of the Community* (Brussels: Commission of the EC, 1983).

Goddard, J. A. et al., 'The Regional Dimension to Technological Change in Great Britain, in A. Ansin and J. Goddard (eds), *Technological Change,*

Industrial Restructuring and Regional Development (London: Allen and Unwin, 1986), 140-56.

Greenhuit, M.L. et al., *The Economics of Imperfect Competition. A Spatial Approach* (Cambridge: Cambridge University Press, 1988).

Industrial Development Authority, 'Employment Data', Unpublished (Dublin: IDA).

Johnson, B. and F. J. Convery, *Environment and Development of the European Peripheral Regions: Realising the Potential.* Report of a Conference held at the European Foundation for the Improvement of Living and Working Conditions. Loughlinstown, Co. Dublin, 10-12 November 1988.

Keeble, D., 'Industrial Change in the United Kingdom', in W.F. Lever (ed.), *Industrial Change in the United Kingdom* (Harlow: Longmans, 1986).

Keeble, D., *Industrial Location and Planning in the United Kingdom* (London: Methuen, 1976).

Keeble, D., 'Recession and New Regional Dynamism in the European Community,' *Geography*, Vol. 74, No. 322 (1989), 1-11.

Keeble, D., R. Evans, and C. Thompson, *Updating of Centrality, Peripherality and EEC Regional Development Study* (Brussels: Commission of the EC, 1983).

Keeble, D. and T. Kelly, 'New Firms and High Technology Industry in the United Kingdom: The Case of Computer Electronics', in D. Keeble and E. Wever (eds), *New Firms and Regional Development in Europe* (London: Croom Helm, 1986), 75–104.

Keeble, D., J. Offord, and S. Walker, *Peripheral Regions in a Community of Twelve Member States* (Brussels: Commission of the EC, 1988).

Keeble, D., P. L. Owens, and C. Thompson, *The Influence of Peripheral and Central Locations on the Relative Development of Regions* (Brussels: Commission of the EC, 1981).

Keeble, D., P. L. Owens, and C. Thompson, 'The Urban-Rural Manufacturing Shift in the European Community', *Urban Studies*, Vol. 20, No. 4 (1983), 405–18.

Keeble, D. and E. Wever, 'Introduction' in D. Keeble and E. Wever (eds), *New Firms and Regional Development in Europe* (London: Croom Helm, 1986), 1–34.

Kilby, M.L., *Industrial Investment: Must Britain Always Lose Out?* (London Association of British Chambers of Commerce, 1980).

Mansergh, N., 'The Value of Cost Benefit Analysis of Road Projects', Economic and Social Research Institute. *Quarterly Economic Commentary* (April 1985), 36–47.

Martinos, H., *The Management of Local Employment Development Strategies. Local Employment Development Programme.* (Brussels: Commission of the EC, 1989).

National Economic and Social Council, *A Strategy for Economic Development 1986-1990* Report No. 83 (Dublin: Stationery Office, 1986).

O'Malley, E., *Industry and Economic Development: The Challenge for the Newcomer* (Dublin: Gill and Macmillan, 1989).

Peida Planning and Economic Consultants, *Transport Costs in Peripheral Areas.* Scottish Economic Planning Department. ESU Research Papers, No. 9, (1984).

Scott, A. and M. Storper, *Production Work and Territory* (Boston: Allen and Unwin, 1986).

Seers, D. et al. (eds), *Underdeveloped Europe: Studies in Core Periphery Relations* (Sussex: Institute of Development Studies, 1979).

Stationery Office, *Economic Review and Outlook* (Dublin: Stationery Office, 1984).

Stationery Office, *National Development Plan 1989–1993* (Dublin: Stationery Office, 1989).

Statistical Office of the European Communities, *Eurostat, Basic Statistics of the Community*, 1987 (Luxembourg: Office for Official Publications of the EC, 1987).

Chapter 18

Armstrong, H. and J. Taylor, *Regional Economics and Policy* (London: Philip Allen, 1985).

Begg, I., 'European Integration and Regional Policy', *Oxford Review of Economic Policy*, Vol. 5, No. 2 (1989), 90–104.

Begg, I., 'The Regional Dimension of the 1992 Proposals', *Regional Studies*, Vol. 23, (1989), 368–76.

Boltho, A., 'European and United States Regional Differentials: A Note,' *Oxford Review of Economic Policy*, Vol. 5, No. 2 (1989), 105–15.

Borooah, V. K., 'The Single European Market and Consumer Welfare in Northern Ireland', in: *1992: The Consumer View* (Belfast: General Consumer Council for Northern Ireland, 1990), 48–52.

Bradley, J. and J. Fitzgerald, (eds), *Medium-Term Review 1989–1994* (Dublin: Economic and Social Research Institute, June 1989).

Cecchini, P., *The European Challenge 1992: The Benefits of a Single Market* (Aldershot: Wildwood House, 1988).

Commission of the European Communities, *Completing the Internal Market*, White Paper from the Commission to the European Council, COM(85)310 Final (Brussels: Commission of the EC, 1985).

Commission of the European Communities, *The Regions of the Enlarged Community*, Third Periodic Report on the Social and Economic Situation and Development of the Regions (Brussels: Commission of the EC, 1987).

Commission of the European Communities, 'The Economics of 1992', *European Economy*, No. 35 (1988).

Davies, G., *Britain and the European Monetary Question*. Economic Study No. 1 (London: Institute for Public Policy Research, 1989).

De Grauwe, P., 'International Trade and Economic Growth in the European Monetary System', *European Economic Review* (Feb/March 1987).

Desai, M., '1992 — A Market Europe or a Social Europe?' *Irish Business and Administrative Research* Vol. 10 (1989), 9–18.

Emerson, M., *The Economics of 1992: The EC Commission's Assessment of the Economic Effects of Completing the Internal Market* (Oxford: Oxford University Press, 1988).

Fitzgerald, J. D., '1992: The Distribution Sector', in *The Economics of 1992: A Symposium on Sectoral Issues* (Dublin: Economic and Research Institute, 1989), pp. 43–69.

Fitzgerald, J. D. et al., *An Analysis of Cross Border Shopping*, Paper 37 (Dublin: Economic and Social Research Institute, 1988).

Hart, M. and R. T. Harrison, 'Inward Investment and Economic Change: The Future Role of Regional Development Agencies.' Paper to the Institute of British Geographers Annual Conference, University of Glasgow, January 1990.

Helpman, E. and P. R. Krugman, *Market Structure and Foreign Trade* (Brighton: Wheatsheaf, 1985).

Hitchins, D. and J. E. Birnie, 'Productivity Levels in Northern Ireland Manufacturing Industry: A Comparison with Great Britain', *Regional Studies* Vol. 23 (1989), 447–54.

Jacquemin, A. and A. Sapir, (eds), *The European Internal Market: Trade and Competition* (Oxford: Oxford University Press, 1989).

Jacquemin, A. and Sapir, A., 'International Trade and Integration of the European Community: An Econometric Analysis, in: A. Jacquemin and A. Sapir (eds), *The European Internal Market: Trade and Competition*, (Oxford: Oxford University Press, 1989).

Kay, J. A. and S. R. Smith, 'The Business Implications of Fiscal Harmonisation', in *1992: Myths and Realities* (London: London Business School, Centre for Business Strategy, 1989), 46–74.

Kennedy, K. A., T. Giblin, and D. McHugh, *The Economic Development of Ireland in the Twentieth Century* (London: Routledge, 1988).

Kowalski, L., 'Major Current and Future Regional Issues in the Enlarged Community', in L. Albrechts et al. (eds), *Regional Policy at the Crossroads: European Perspectives* (London: Jessica Kingsley, 1989), 90–106.

Krugman, P. R., 'Economic Integration in Europe: Some Conceptual Issues', in A. Jacquemin and A. Sapir (eds.) *The European Internal Market: Trade and Competition* (Oxford: Oxford University Press, 1989).

Matthews, A., 'The Economics of 1992: Agriculture and Food', in *The Economics of 1992: A Symposium on Sectoral Issues* (Dublin: Economic and Social Research Institute, 1989), 71–86.

National and Economic Social Council, *Economic Implications for Northern Ireland and the Republic of Ireland of Recent Developments in the European Community.* Joint paper by the Northern Ireland Economic Council and the National Economic and Social Council (Dublin: Stationery Office, 1988).

Panic, M. (1989), *The Impact of Multi-nationals on National Economic Policies*, Department of Applied Economics Working Paper No. 8905 (Cambridge: University of Cambridge, 1989).

Sutherland, P. D., 'Europe and the Principle of Convergence', *Regional Studies*, Vol. 20 (1986), 371–377.

Telesis Consulting Group, *A Review of Industrial Policy*. National Economic and Social Council Report No. 64 (Dublin: Stationery Office, 1982).

Trustee Savings Bank, 'Review and Outlook for the Northern Ireland Economy',
    TSB Business Outlook and Economic Review, Vol. 2, No. 1 (April 1987).
Vanhove, N. and L. H. Klaassen, *Regional Policy: A European Approach* (Aldershot:
    Avebury, 1987).
Wadley, D., *Restructuring the Regions: Analysis, Policy Model and Prognosis* (Paris:
    OECD, 1986).

Chapter 19

Baldwin, R., 'The Growth Effects of 1992', *Economic Policy*, Vol. 9 (1989) pp.
    247–81.
Bradley, J. and J. Fitzgerald, *Medium-Term Review: 1989-1994* (Dublin: Economic
    and Social Research Institute, 1989).
Bressand, A., 'Beyond Interdependence: 1992 as a Global Challenge', *International
    Affairs*, Vol. 66, No. 1 (1990), 47–65.
Campbell, J., C. Pepper, and I. Barnes, '1992: The Illusion of Change', *Public
    Administration*, Vol. 67 (1989), 319–28.
Devereux, M. and M. Pearson, 'Harmonising Corporate Taxes in Europe',
    Fiscal Studies, Vol. 11, No. 1 (1990), 21–35.
The Economist, 'A Survey of Europe's Internal Market', 9 July 1988, 1–52.
Emerson, M., *The Economics of 1992: The EC Commission's Assessment of the Economic
    Effects of Completing the Internal Market* (Oxford: Oxford University Press,
    1988).
Kay, J., 'The Single Market: Myths and Realities', *Accountancy*, November 1988.
Neven, D. J., 'EEC Integration towards 1992: Some Distributional Aspects',
    Economic Policy, Vol. 10 (1990), 13–62.
Padao-Schioppa, T., *Efficiency, Stability and Equity: A Strategy for the Economic
    System of the European Community* (Oxford: Oxford University Press, 1987).
Pinder, J., 'The Single Market: A Step Towards European Union', in J. Lodge
    (ed.), *The European Community and the Challenge of the Future* (London: Pinter,
    1989).
O'Sullivan, L., 'Macroeconomic Effects of 1992', in J. Bradley and J. Fitzgerald
    (eds.), *Medium-Term Review 1989-1994* (Dublin: Economic and Social
    Research Institute, 1989).
Shackleton, M., 'The Budget of the European Community', in J. Lodge (ed.),
    The European Community and the Challenge of the Future (London: Pinter,
    1989).

Index